Kirk MacGregor has written a game-changer. He demonstrates that Molina's understanding of the nature of grace was much more evangelical than what is commonly perceived. MacGregor shows that Molina didn't develop the notion of middle knowledge simply for the sake of philosophical speculation, but because of his deep concern for pastoral ministry. This book will become an invaluable resource in Molinism studies.

Ken Keathley, Professor of Theology, Southeastern
Baptist Theological Seminary

If you haven't discovered Kirk R. MacGregor, *Luis de Molina* provides a rewarding introduction to his work. Dr. MacGregor combines that rare ability to maintain scholarly rigor while making a seemingly remote historical figure come alive for the reader. His clear, concise prose combined with compassionate resonance with the characters in his account make for a surprisingly enjoyable reading experience. *Luis de Molina* is crafted with thoughtfulness, detailed research, and engaging narrative. Religion scholars with interests in Molinism and the doctrine of middle knowledge will acquire fresh insight into issues of God's sovereignty, grace, providence and predestination, and their relation to human free will and social justice. For the theologically minded, Dr. MacGregor's book becomes an indispensable guide through the often complex and controversial doctrinal debates that preoccupied the best minds in sixteenth-century Spain. Luis de Molina, one of the great philosophical theologians and ethicists of his time, made important contributions to Christianity, contributions that before Dr. MacGregor's exhaustive biography, have been misunderstood, misinterpreted, or largely ignored. The general reader will embark on a fascinating journey into the turbulent life and times of Molina, a world in which passionate theological debate could lead to torture or death—or threaten to unhinge the religious and political establishment. Once again, Dr. MacGregor has produced a volume that is both a fruitful resource and an inspiring and captivating reading experience.

John K. Simmons, Professor of Religious Studies,
emeritus, Western Illinois University

T0308391

While others have brought clarity to the discussion of middle knowledge, MacGregor has given us the most comprehensive treatment to date of Molina and his formulation of middle knowledge. Masterfully woven into the story of the life and times of Molina, he judicially places the development of middle knowledge within the larger theological and philosophical context of the day. Impeccably researched and skillfully written. More than a history, it is theologically informative, intellectually refreshing, and spiritually encouraging as MacGregor details the theological explanatory power of middle knowledge. An absolute must-read for the serious student of theology.

Bruce A. Little, PhD, Southeastern Baptist Theological Seminary, Wake Forest, North Carolina

As Kirk MacGregor notes in the introduction, his theological biography of Luis de Molina fills a void that has existed in the literature for some time, at least since the revival of interest in Molinism in the last thirty years or so. While some of MacGregor's claims will prove controversial, there can be no doubt that his work will promote further scholarly investigation and provoke not a little debate. There can be no doubt that MacGregor has made a significant contribution to the growing corpus of literature on Molina by evangelical scholars. It is a must-read for anyone interested in the debates over divine providence and human freedom, both past and present, and especially those with concern to Molina's part in those debates.

John D. Laing, Associate Professor of Systematic Theology and Philosophy, Southwestern Baptist Theological Seminary, Houston

At long last we have a tour de force on the life, theology, and legacy of an oft overlooked theological giant. In this work Kirk MacGregor masterfully weaves together Luis de Molina's life, spiritual pilgrimage, theological genius, and the heritage of Molinism he left to posterity. Anyone interested in divine sovereignty and human choice should read this book. Besides the theological reward that will be reaped from doing so, you will also be drawn into the fascinating life and times of a remarkable human being.

Chad Meister, Professor of Philosophy and Theology, Bethel College

LUIS DE MOLINA ✠ 1535 – 1600

LUIS de MOLINA

THE
LIFE and THEOLOGY
OF THE FOUNDER OF MIDDLE KNOWLEDGE

KIRK R. MacGREGOR

ZONDERVAN

Luis de Molina
Copyright © 2015 by Kirk R. MacGregor

This title is also available as a Zondervan ebook. Visit www.zondervan.com/ebooks.

Requests for information should be addressed to:
Zondervan, 3900 *Sparks Dr. SE, Grand Rapids, Michigan 49546*

This edition: ISBN 978-0-310-10209-0

The Library of Congress has cataloged the hardcover edition as follows:

MacGregor, Kirk R.
    Luis de Molina : the life and theology of the founder of middle knowledge / Kirk R.
MacGregor.
        pages   cm
    Includes bibliographical references.
    ISBN 978-0-310-51697-2 (hardcover)
    1. Molina, Luis de, 1535-1600. 2. Molinism. 3. God (Christianity)—Omniscience. I. Title.
BX4705.M598M33   2015
230'.2092—dc23   2015018760

Cover design: Tammy Johnson
Cover/frontispiece illustration: © Tristan Elwell / Shannon Associates
Interior design: Kait Lamphere

Printed in the United States of America

HB 02.22.2024

Contents

To my son, Dwiane

Acknowledgments

I WOULD LIKE TO THANK William Lane Craig and his Reasonable Faith ministry. When I was a master's student at Biola University (2000–2001), I received my first introduction to Molinism through Craig's writings and lectures in the Robert L. Saucy Lecture Series. Craig's scholarship sparked my abiding interest in Luis de Molina, which has grown from that point onward. Since 2013 I have been privileged to direct a chapter of Reasonable Faith on the south side of Chicago.

I owe a debt of gratitude to Ralph Keen and Raymond Mentzer, who were my doctoral coadvisers at the University of Iowa (2001–05). From them I received a stellar education in Reformation studies and learned the skills necessary for critically analyzing early modern primary sources. Without their investment in my academic career, the research completed in this book could not have been carried out. For their guidance, support, and friendship, I am extremely grateful.

Thanks also to my colleagues on the Middle Knowledge/Molinism Consultation of the Evangelical Theological Society for their engagement with my work and their stimulating conversations. In particular I am especially grateful to fellow Steering Committee members John Laing, Kenneth Keathley, Greg Welty, James Anderson, and Paul Copan, who have given me the opportunity to present my research on Molina and various applications of middle knowledge at the society's annual meetings.

I would also like to thank Madison Trammel, my editor at Zondervan, for his encouragement and assistance from the start of this project and for his outstanding suggestions regarding the content of the book. I appreciate the hard work of Jesse Hillman and Sarah Gombis at Zondervan. I wish to extend a special note of appreciation to Daniel Marrs and Kenneth Keathley for reviewing the manuscript in its entirety and providing extremely valuable feedback. Accordingly, I bear sole responsibility for interpretations of all doubtful points and decisions on what material to include and exclude. Any defects that remain in the book are therefore entirely my own.

Last but certainly not least, I would like to thank my wife, Lara, for her unwavering support and encouragement and for our numerous theological and philosophical discussions, which have greatly enhanced my scholarship.

Introduction

A THEOLOGICAL REFORMER FOR
THE UNIVERSAL CHURCH

Luis de Molina (1535–1600) has become well-known in evangelical circles and among philosophers of religion for his doctrine of middle knowledge (Lat., *scientia media*). Middle knowledge is God's knowledge of all things that would happen in every possible set of circumstances, both things that are determined to occur by those circumstances and things that are not determined to occur by those circumstances.[1] This knowledge was possessed by God logically or explanatorily prior to his decision to create the world or his making of any choices about what kind of world, if any, he would create. Significantly, middle knowledge includes God's awareness of what every possible individual would freely do in any set of circumstances in which he or she finds himself or herself as well as how utterly random, chance events would turn out in every possible set of circumstances. Armed with this knowledge, God can create a world providentially planned to the last detail where his purposes are achieved through free creaturely decisions and random events.

Molina's doctrine of middle knowledge is, in the judgment of many, one of the most fruitful theological concepts ever formulated. For, as we shall see in chapters 4 and 5, it appears to solve immediately the perennial dilemma between divine predestination and human freedom and to give a meticulous account of divine providence fully harmonious with human free choices. And as we shall see in chapter 10, its ability to solve other difficult problems is

---

1. In philosophical terminology, middle knowledge is God's knowledge of all counterfactuals. Counterfactuals refer to conditional propositions in the subjunctive mood and assume the following form: if something *were* the case (when in fact it may or may not be the case), then something else *would be* the case. I follow the accepted philosophical custom, established by David Lewis (*Counterfactuals* [Cambridge: Harvard University Press, 1973], 3, 26–30), of defining the term *counterfactual* to encompass not only statements that are contrary to fact, but also true conditionals in the subjunctive mood.

almost inexhaustible. Since the 1970s, philosophers of religion have success-fully applied middle knowledge to such diverse topics as biblical inerrancy, creation and evolution, the relationship between Christianity and other world religions, the problem of evil, and quantum indeterminacy.[2]

While Molina, like Desiderius Erasmus (1466–1536), chose to work for reform from within the ranks of the Roman Catholic Church, the issues with which he dealt — God's sovereignty, grace, providence, and predestination and their relation to human free will and social justice — are ecumenical in character and stand at the forefront of contemporary evangelicalism. It should be emphasized that little in Molina's thought is specifically Roman Catholic in its orientation; indeed, much of Molina's thought stood in direct opposition to the Catholicism of his day (though not to modern Catholicism). For his defiance of the doctrines of grace and salvation articulated by the Council of Trent (1545–63), Catholic authorities unleashed the Spanish Inquisition upon Molina in 1591, from which he was forced to escape. In addition, a special papal commission levied against Molina in 1598 nearly resulted in his being declared a heretic and burned at the stake. Because of its universal orientation, Molina's thought is quite relevant to Christians of all theological stripes, whether Protestant, Catholic, or Orthodox.

Today Molina's theological system, denominated Molinism, occupies a significant place at the table of evangelicalism. From the late 1980s to the present, scores of articles on middle knowledge and/or Molinism have appeared in such prominent evangelical forums as the *Journal of the Evangelical Theological Society*, *Philosophia Christi*, the *Westminster Theological Journal*, and *Faith and Philosophy*, and several evangelicals have authored books devoted wholly or partially to Molinism.[3] Papers on middle knowledge and/or Molinism have

---

2. See William Lane Craig, "'Men Moved by the Holy Spirit Spoke from God' (2 Peter 1:21): A Middle Knowledge Perspective on Divine Inspiration," *Philosophia Christi*, new ser. 1 (1999): 45–82; Del Ratzsch, "Design, Chance and Theistic Evolution," in *Mere Creation*, ed. William Dembski (Downers Grove, IL: InterVarsity, 1998), 289–312; William Lane Craig, "'No Other Name': A Middle Knowledge Perspective on the Exclusivity of Salvation through Christ," *Faith and Philosophy* 6 (1989): 172–88; Kirk R. MacGregor, "The Existence and Irrelevance of Gratuitous Evil," *Philosophia Christi* 14, no. 1 (2012): 165–80; John Jefferson Davis, *Frontiers of Science and Faith: Examining Questions from the Big Bang to the End of the Universe* (Downers Grove, IL: InterVarsity, 2002), 37–56.

3. A survey of the four aforementioned journals shows at least fifty articles related to middle knowledge and/or Molinism. Books by evangelicals devoted to middle knowledge and/or Molinism include William Lane Craig, *The Only Wise God: The Compatibility of Divine Foreknowledge and Human Freedom* (Grand Rapids: Baker, 1987); William Lane Craig, *Divine Foreknowledge and Human Freedom: The Coherence of Theism: Omniscience*, Studies in Intellectual History 19 (Leiden: Brill, 1990);

proven a staple in recent years at the annual meetings of the Evangelical Theological Society and the Evangelical Philosophical Society, leading to the organization of the Middle Knowledge/Molinism Consultation of the Evangelical Theological Society in 2012. Among evangelicals, Molinism is now considered one of the four principal views on divine providence and omniscience, alongside Calvinism, open theism, and simple foreknowledge.[4] Even for proponents of other theological persuasions who do not accept the system of Molinism as a whole, several have embraced God's possession of middle knowledge. Hailing the genius of Molina's doctrine of middle knowledge, not a few prominent Calvinists and open theists have attempted to incorporate middle knowledge into their own theological systems.[5] Indeed, the current literature demonstrates the compatibility of middle knowledge with Baptist, Anabaptist, Lutheran, Reformed, Wesleyan, Pentecostal, and Catholic theological traditions.[6]

Eef Dekker, *Middle Knowledge* (Peeters: Leuven, 2000); William Hasker, David Basinger, and Eef Dekker, eds., *Middle Knowledge: Theory and Applications*, Contributions to Philosophical Theology 4 (Frankfurt am Main: Peter Lang, 2000); Kirk R. MacGregor, *A Molinist-Anabaptist Systematic Theology* (Lanham, MD: University Press of America, 2007); Kenneth Keathley, *Salvation and Sovereignty: A Molinist Approach* (Nashville: Broadman & Holman Academic, 2010).

4. As evidenced in James K. Beilby and Paul R. Eddy, *Divine Foreknowledge: Four Views* (Downers Grove, IL: InterVarsity, 2001).

5. Among the Calvinists who have incorporated middle knowledge into their thought are Alvin Plantinga, Terrence Tiessen, Bruce Ware, John Feinberg, and Luke Van Horn. Among the open theists who have done the same are Gregory Boyd and Jason Nicholls. See Alvin Plantinga, *God, Freedom, and Evil* (New York: Harper & Row, 1974); Alvin Plantinga, "Reply to Robert Adams," in *Alvin Plantinga*, ed. James Tomberlin and Peter van Inwagen, Profiles 5 (Dordrecht: Reidel, 1985): 372–82; Terrence Tiessen, *Providence and Prayer: How Does God Work in the World?* (Downers Grove, IL: InterVarsity, 2000), 289–362; Terrence Tiessen, "Why Calvinists Should Believe in Divine Middle Knowledge, Although They Reject Molinism," *Westminster Theological Journal* 69, no. 2 (2007): 345–66; Bruce A. Ware, *God's Greater Glory: The Exalted God of Scripture and the Christian Faith* (Wheaton, IL: Crossway, 2006), 110–30; John S. Feinberg, *No One Like Him: The Doctrine of God* (Wheaton, IL: Crossway, 2001), 242, 282, 735–75; Luke Van Horn, "On Incorporating Middle Knowledge into Calvinism: A Theological/Metaphysical Muddle?" *Journal of the Evangelical Theological Society* 55, no. 4 (2012): 807–27; Gregory A. Boyd, "Neo-Molinism and the Infinite Intelligence of God," *Philosophia Christi* 5, no. 1 (2003): 187–204; Jason A. Nicholls, "Openness and Inerrancy: Can They Be Compatible?" *Journal of the Evangelical Theological Society* 45, no. 4 (2002): 629–49.

6. Regarding the Baptist tradition, see Keathley, *Salvation and Sovereignty*, and Millard J. Erickson, *God the Father Almighty: A Contemporary Exploration of the Divine Attributes* (Grand Rapids: Baker, 1998), 199–207. Regarding the Anabaptist tradition, see MacGregor, *Molinist-Anabaptist Systematic Theology*. Regarding the Lutheran tradition, see Michael Coors, *Scriptura efficax* (Göttingen: Vandenhoeck & Ruprecht, 2009), 314–17. Regarding the Reformed tradition, see Plantinga, "Reply to Robert Adams," 372–82; and Tiessen, *Providence and Prayer*, 289–362. Regarding the Wesleyan tradition, see David Basinger, "Divine Omniscience and Human Freedom: A 'Middle Knowledge' Perspective," *Faith and Philosophy* 1, no. 3 (1984): 291–302. Regarding the Pentecostal tradition, see J. Rodman Williams, *Renewal Theology: Systematic Theology from a Charismatic Perspective*, 3 vols. in 1

Yet little is known about Molina's life. Beyond his doctrine of middle knowledge and the years of his life and death, all that most students of Molina know is that he was a Catholic reformer, a member of the Jesuit order, a professor of philosophy and theology, and a Spaniard. Such a bare-bones list of facts is clearly inadequate to describe someone of Molina's influence. Moreover, these facts are misleading when taken in isolation, for they may give rise to various stereotypes that are not at all accurate in Molina's case. To illustrate, one might infer (wrongfully) from Molina's membership in the Jesuit order that he held the same theological convictions as Ignatius of Loyola (1491–1556) and Francis Xavier (1506–52), the cofounders of the Society of Jesus (Jesuits). In fact, Molina's coreligionists Enrique Henriquez (1536–1608) and Juan de Mariana (1536–1624) vehemently opposed Molina's 1588 magnum opus, the *Concordia*,[7] due to its deviance from the theology of Loyola and Xavier. Hence Molina did not subscribe to Loyola's famous maxim "That we may be altogether of the same mind and in conformity ... if the [Roman] Church shall have defined anything to be black which to our eyes appears to be white, we ought in like manner to pronounce it black."[8] To the contrary, Molina was drawn to the specific Jesuit community at Alcalá because of its recognition that the Roman Church stood in dire need of reform and that such reform must begin with the conversion of an individual's heart.

The reason for the general ignorance of the narrative of Molina's life is not hard to find. Until the present volume, no modern critical biography of Molina has been composed in any language, and no Molina biography of any significant length has ever been written. Apart from encyclopedia-length entries, the only other Molina biography is a short notice in the preface of the Cologne edition of his Latin treatise on social justice, *De justitia et jure* (*On Justice and Law*), published in 1733.[9] As a result, many students have

---

(Grand Rapids: Zondervan, 1996), 1:73–74; 2:17–23; although Williams does not use the phrase "middle knowledge," he clearly affirms the concept. Regarding the Catholic tradition, see Thomas P. Flint, *Divine Providence: The Molinist Account* (Ithaca, NY: Cornell University Press, 1998).

7. Its full Latin title is *Liberi Arbitrii cum Gratiae Donis, Divina Praescientia, Providentia, Praedestinatione et Reprobatione Concordia*, which translates to *The Compatibility of Free Choice with the Gifts of Grace, Divine Foreknowledge, Providence, Predestination, and Reprobation.*

8. Ignatius Loyola, "Rules for Thinking with the Church," in *Documents of the Christian Church*, 4th ed., ed. Henry Bettenson and Chris Maunder (Oxford: Oxford University Press, 2011), 263.

9. Gabriel Pinelo, "R. P. Ludovici Molinæ, e Societate Jesu, Vitæ Morumque Brevis Adumbratio," in Ludovici Molina, *De justitia et jure*, 5 vols. (Cologne: Marci-Michaelis Bousquet, 1733), 1:i–vi.

remained woefully content with the verdict of the twentieth-century Jesuit historian Johannes Rabeneck: "In the life of Molina ... there are few external facts worth being remembered, as is the case with many teachers who, far from the events and business of public life, move from the solitude of their room to the crowd of the lecture hall."[10] As this book will demonstrate, Rabeneck's verdict could not be further from the truth. It falsely presupposes that the only information that exists about Molina consists in the basic details of his life and severely underestimates the engagement Molina had with the significant happenings of his day. On its face, moreover, this verdict seems absurd, as no one would hastily generalize from the scholarly careers of Luther or Calvin that they lived boring, humdrum lives that did not significantly interact with public affairs; rather, one would assume the opposite unless proven otherwise. Likewise, we should begin with the hypothesis that Molina, who ranks among the foremost philosophical theologians in church history, naturally played an important role in the social and political life of the Iberian Peninsula.

This hypothesis is overwhelmingly confirmed by the textual evidence concerning Molina's life, evidence that is largely if not entirely unknown to students of Molina. Hence the story of Molina's life has lain buried in sixteenth-century primary sources, many of which remain in manuscript form. My purpose in this book is to bring the information from these sources to light for the first time, thus revealing a fuller picture of the exciting story of Molina's life and thought than has previously been available. The morsels of this story to which I have already alluded, including Molina's escape from the Spanish Inquisition and the political intrigue sparked by his writings, confirms that Molina's life was far from mundane. In fact, we will see that Molina's story proves just as captivating, edifying, and inspiring as the stories of Luther and Calvin.

---

10. "In vita Molinæ ... facta externa memoratu rara sunt, cum sicut multorum doctorum vita procul ab eventibus et a negotiis publicis intra cubicili solitudinem et auditorii frequentiam transierit" (Ioannes Rabeneck, "De vita et scriptis Ludovici Molina," *Archivium Storicum Societatis Iesu* [1950], 75).

CLEARING UP MISCONCEPTIONS

Telling the full story of Molina's life and thought will not only deepen our appreciation and admiration of him, but it will also clear up misconceptions that have prevented detractors of his thought from giving him a fair hearing. Here three misconceptions predominate, the first of which we have already treated briefly.

MISCONCEPTION 1: MOLINA FOR CATHOLICS ONLY

The first misconception alleges that Molina is relevant only to practitioners of the Roman Catholic tradition, or more modestly, that one needs to be a Catholic to embrace Molinism in its entirety. At this juncture we should emphasize that Molinism has been completely embraced by theologians representing a broad cross-section of Protestantism, namely, from the Lutheran, Reformed, Anabaptist, Wesleyan, and Pentecostal traditions. In the current literature, Protestant thinkers who reject Molinism in part or in whole have not done so because Catholic tendencies are somehow inherent to Molinist thought; rather, they reject Molinism either because of its conception of God's sovereignty, because of its doctrine of human freedom, or because of doubts that middle knowledge can be appropriately grounded so as actually to exist in the mind of God.

Furthermore, as we shall explore in greater detail in chapters 1 and 2, Molina himself was quick to question abuses in the Catholic Church. While he never remotely considered leaving the Church of Rome, Molina charted out a course that was neither mainline Catholic nor compatible with the Protestant Reformers' impulses. After joining a reform-minded Jesuit order at Alcalá at the age of eighteen, Molina praised the Catholic Church throughout his adult life on account of the progress he saw implemented by the Council of Trent (1545–63). He was especially encouraged that the Council remedied the major ethical abuses that precipitated the Protestant Reformation. In particular he lauded the Council's prohibition of the sale of indulgences, prevention of the buying and selling of church offices (simony), prohibition of bishops from holding church positions at which they would not work but from which they would draw a salary (absentee benefices), blockage of bishops and priests from holding more than one church position (benefice) at a time, and enforcement of biblical morality among the clergy (including the pope), monks, and nuns.[11] As a professor of philosophy and theology who also had a deep passion for improving the pastoral care received by the laity, Molina was especially gratified that the Council mandated the formal education of the clergy and established new seminaries for their pastoral training. Further, Molina heartily concurred with the Council's assertion of genuine human freedom, or the ability to choose between anything on the moral spectrum from spiritual and physical good to spiritual and physical evil. This was one teaching Molina regarded as firmly rooted in Scripture that many of his colleagues in the Protestant Reformation had either neglected or denied. Among the biblical warrants Molina often cited for this truth was Deuteronomy 30:11–19,[12] where Moses exhorted the Israelites before entering the Promised Land:

> Now what I am commanding you today is not too difficult for you or beyond your reach. It is not up in heaven, so that you have to ask, "Who will ascend into heaven to get it and proclaim it to us so we may obey it?" Nor is it beyond the sea, so that you have to ask, "Who will cross the sea to get it and proclaim it to us so we may obey it?" No, the word is very near you; it is in your mouth and in your heart so you may obey it.
>
> See, I set before you today life and prosperity, death and destruction. For I command you today to love the LORD your God, to walk in obedience to him, and to keep his commands, decrees and laws; then you will live and increase, and the LORD your God will bless you in the land you are entering to possess.
>
> But if your heart turns away and you are not obedient, and if you are drawn away to bow down to other gods and worship them, I declare to you this day that you will certainly be destroyed. You will not live long in the land you are crossing the Jordan to enter and possess.
>
> This day I call the heavens and the earth as witnesses against you that I have set before you life and death, blessings and curses. Now choose life, so that you and your children may live.

---

11. Friedrich Stegmüller, ed. and trans., *Geschichte des Molinismus: Neue Molinaschriften 1*, Beiträge zur Geschichte der Philosophie und Theologie des Mittelalters 32 (Münster: Aschendorffschen, 1935), 4*–8*.

12. Ludovici Molina, *Liberi Arbitrii cum Gratiae Donis, Divina Praescientia, Providentia, Praedestinatione et Reprobatione Concordia*, ed. Johannes Rabeneck (Madrid: Sumptibus Societatis Editorialis "Sapientia," 1953), 1.14.13.23.2.3.

Notwithstanding this progress that prompted Molina to continue to work for reform from within the Catholic Church, Molina was discouraged by the Council's endorsement of Thomas Aquinas's doctrine of grace. For he believed this to be a faulty view of grace as a kind of divine substance that empowered people to perform good works.[13] Instead, Molina agreed with Luther and Calvin in understanding grace as God's unmerited favor toward sinful humans and God's unmerited assistance in securing their regeneration and sanctification.[14] But unlike Luther and Calvin, Molina affirmed that God gives sufficient grace for salvation to every person that he creates, on the basis of biblical texts like 1 Timothy 2:4 ("[God our Savior] wants all people to be saved and to come to a knowledge of the truth") and 2 Peter 3:9 ("The Lord … is patient with you, not wanting anyone to perish, but everyone to come to repentance").[15] To navigate this middle ground between Aquinas on the one hand and Luther and Calvin on the other, Molina composed an ingenious commentary on Aquinas's *Summa Theologiae* between 1570 and 1573, which was less a commentary than a correction and reinterpretation of Aquinas's doctrines of grace and salvation in light of the emerging Protestant understanding of these doctrines.[16] This correction and reinterpretation did not endorse the Protestant views but navigated a middle ground between Tridentine Catholicism and Protestantism.

MISCONCEPTION 2: MOLINISM THE SAME AS ARMINIANISM

The second misconception that often prevents a full appreciation of Molina's thought is that Molina is a slightly more philosophically sophisticated version of Arminius.[17] Thus, for Reformed Christians, their rejection of Arminianism causes them to reject Molinism out of hand on the faulty

---

13. Ibid., 1.14.13.14.2.4; Ludovici Molina, *Commentaria in primam divi Thomae partem* (Venice, 1602), 1.43.3; 2.28; 3.14.13.7. Although Molina employs the traditional Scholastic categories of grace (e.g., *gratia operans* and *gratia cooperans*), the meaning he ascribes to these categories lies in terms of dispositions or new capacities that the Holy Spirit imparts to individuals rather than in terms of substances. One could rightfully conclude that Molina's conception of grace is more Augustinian than Thomistic.

14. Molina, *Concordia*, 1.14.13.8.5; 1.14.13.22.4; 7.23.4/5.4.2.

15. Ibid., 6.22.1.2.10; 7.23.4/5.1.6.22; 7.23.4/5.1.8.8.

16. Pinelo, "Molinæ," 1:v.

17. This misconception has sadly been perpetuated by Molinists themselves. Hence Eef Dekker answers affirmatively and without reservation the title question of his article, "Was Arminius a Molinist?" *The Sixteenth Century Journal* 27, no. 2 (1996): 337, 351–52.

assumption that the two are basically the same thing.[18] The truth of the situation is quite different. Molina differed from Arminius in profound ways, ways that are just as profound as those in which Molina differed from Calvin.[19] Moreover, Molina agreed with Calvin in profound ways, ways that are just as profound as those in which Molina agreed with Arminius.

To sum up, Molina was an original thinker whose theological system is not identical to Calvin's system or Arminius's system, such that Molinism agrees or disagrees with Calvinism at various points and agrees or disagrees with Arminianism at various points. Unfortunately, the misconception that Arminianism equals Protestant Molinism has a long history, stretching back to Arminius himself and the Reformed Synod of Dort (1618–19), which responded to Arminius's propositions. It would not be an exaggeration to say that this misconception forestalled Protestant interaction with Molinism for over 350 years, from 1619 to the 1970s. This is because Protestants who rejected Arminianism dismissed Molinism out of hand, and Protestants who embraced Arminianism did not investigate Molinism, supposing that their system was the same as Molinism. Due to this widespread ignorance of Molinism through either rejection of or alleged redundancy with Arminianism, it behooves us to tell briefly the story of how this misconception surfaced.

Profoundly troubled by Calvin's doctrine of double predestination (God's predestination of some to eternal life and others to eternal destruction), the Dutch theologian Jacob Arminius (1560–1609) formulated an alternative theological system of creation and providence that he implicitly claimed was consistent with Molina's doctrine of middle knowledge.[20] Arminius's claim is

---

18. Richard A. Muller, "Grace, Election, and Contingent Choice: Arminius's Gambit and the Reformed Response," in *The Grace of God, The Bondage of the Will: Historical and Theological Perspectives on Calvinism*, 2 vols., ed. Thomas R. Schreiner and Bruce A. Ware (Grand Rapids: Baker, 1995), 2:265–66.

19. Regarding Molina's conception of middle knowledge, Roger E. Olson correctly observes: "The claim that Arminius himself assumed God's middle knowledge and its role in providence and predestination is dubious. No one questions that Arminius occasionally but rarely said things that could be interpreted as Molinist.... For example, in his 'Public Disputation IV,' on the knowledge of God, Arminius mentioned 'middle knowledge' ... but the context does not seem to support the contention that he meant the same as Molina's ... version of middle knowledge.... the Dutch theologian rejected [Molina's version of] middle knowledge, especially as it might be used by God to predetermine decisions and actions of human persons," *Arminian Theology: Myths and Realities* (Downers Grove, IL: IVP Academic, 2006), 196.

20. As Richard Muller points out, Arminius made this claim in so many words, never explicitly citing Molina by name but vaguely citing "the schoolmen," by which he meant Molina, for his doctrine of middle knowledge (*God, Creation, and Providence in the Thought of Jacob Arminius* [Grand Rapids: Baker, 1991], 161). Unfortunately, Muller too quickly assumes from this claim that Arminius meant

highly ambivalent, for it depends on the narrowness or breadth of theological substance one ascribes to middle knowledge. On the one hand, if by middle knowledge one simply means God's knowledge of everything that would happen in any possible set of circumstances logically prior to his creation of the world, then Arminius's system is consistent with middle knowledge.[21] On the other hand, if by middle knowledge one also means, as Molina did, that God possessed this knowledge logically prior to making any decisions about the world, including whether he would create our world, then Arminius's system is inconsistent with middle knowledge.[22] In short, Arminius held to a different version of middle knowledge than Molina, as we shall see in chapter 10. Given the opportunity, it is certain that Molina would have accused Arminius of misunderstanding exactly what he meant by middle knowledge, since Molina anticipated Arminius's construal of middle knowledge and explicitly rejected it in the *Concordia*. (Molina had no such opportunity to directly rebut Arminius, since Arminius published his thoughts on middle knowledge in the decade following Molina's death.)

In Arminius's version of middle knowledge, logically prior to God's knowledge of what would happen in every possible set of circumstances, God had already made several choices. God had already decided to create this world, to appoint Christ as Redeemer, Mediator, and Savior of all future created persons, to save anyone who would receive Christ, and to give future persons the means (i.e., the Word, sacraments, and so forth) to believe in Christ.[23] Molina found this conception of "post–creative decisions middle

the same thing by "middle knowledge" as Molina. This assumption has been convincingly refuted by Olson (*Arminian Theology*, 196) and William G. Witt ("Creation, Redemption and Grace in the Theology of Jacob Arminius" [PhD diss., University of Notre Dame, 1993], 363–66).

21. In Arminius's two references to middle knowledge (*Public Disputations*, in *The Writings of Arminius*, 3 vols., trans. James Nichols and W. R. Bagnall [Grand Rapids: Baker, 1956], 1:448–49, and *Private Disputations*, in *Writings*, 2:38–39), middle knowledge serves the sole purpose of grounding God's foreknowledge of future contingents.

22. As we shall see, Arminius conceives of middle knowledge as logically posterior to God's decision to create our world, while Molina conceives of middle knowledge as logically prior to God's decision to create our world (or indeed any world).

23. Spelling out Arminius's interspersed succession of logical moments and divine decisions up to the creation of the actual world, I have written elsewhere: "First, not surprisingly, is God's *scientia naturalis* [natural knowledge], which [Arminius] defines as the knowledge 'by which God understands himself and all things possible' (*Public Disputations*, in *Writings*, 1:448). Having perceived all possible free individuals he could create, in his creative decree God chooses a particular subset of these individuals, which will, at the moment of creation, comprise the actual world (*Certain Articles to Be Considered and Weighed*, in *Writings*, 2:485). At this point God lovingly decrees to appoint Christ as Redeemer,

knowledge" incoherent on at least four counts, the third and fourth of which, ironically, are frequently registered today as objections to Molina's doctrine of middle knowledge.

First, God's decision to create the world was made, so to speak, before he knew whether this world (or indeed any world) would be worth creating. For all God knew at the logical moment of deciding to create our world, it might well be the case that the world contained no one who would freely receive Christ. (In fact, for all God knew at that logical moment, there might well exist no world of free creatures where anyone received Christ.) Yet God would be compelled to create the world despite its universal damnation.[24] Second, God lacked the freedom to create a world that did not feature the incarnation of the second person of the Trinity, which seems a denial of God's sovereignty. Certainly, Molina insisted, it lay within God's power to create a world where the incarnation did not occur, as the Logos's becoming flesh was a voluntary decision on the Logos's part.[25]

Third, Arminius's account of middle knowledge grounds middle knowledge on God's decision to create free creatures and, derivatively, on the potential free creatures themselves, many of whom will never actually exist. This consequence Arminius readily admitted: "That 'middle' kind of knowledge must intervene in things which *depend on* the liberty of a created will ... [that is], in things which *depend on* the liberty of created choice or pleasure."[26] But Molina believed that making middle knowledge depend on potential created beings undermined divine perfection, since it insinuates that God needs

---

Mediator, and Savior of all future created persons. Then God decrees both to save anyone who will receive Christ and to minister sufficiently and efficaciously the means ... for human appropriation of Christ (*Declaration of Sentiments*, in *Writings*, 1:247). Next comes God's *scientia media* [middle knowledge], by which he apprehends who would make good use of these means by freely receiving Christ and who, contrariwise, would freely reject Christ. Consequently, God decrees to save or damn particular persons based on his middle knowledge of who would or would not believe. Finally, simultaneous with the moment of creation is God's *scientia libera* [free knowledge], by which his logically prior knowledge of all individuals in the actual world and his freely decreed dealings with them are now converted into foreknowledge" (MacGregor, *Molinist-Anabaptist Systematic Theology*, 72).

24. Molina, *Concordia*, 7.23.3.15.
25. Ibid., 4.14.13.53.1.6–8; 7.23.4/5.1.11.41.
26. Arminius, *Public Disputations*, in *Writings*, 1:449; *Private Disputations*, in *Writings*, 2:39. Hence Richard Muller charges that since "God knows the future contingent relatively or hypothetically as a potential result of a prior creaturely act," middle knowledge "seems to introduce into the divine mind an element of potency or knowledge of possibility that is actualized by something external to God ... [which] raises a serious question about the extent of divine knowledge and its possible limitation" (*God, Creation, and Providence*, 156).

created beings to be omniscient. Interestingly, it is on this same score that many Reformed Christians reject middle knowledge, not realizing that they are denying a different version of middle knowledge than the one Molina proposed.[27] Moreover, Molina asserted that grounding middle knowledge upon potential free creatures, in reality, leaves God with no ground whatsoever for the vast majority of his middle knowledge. Since most of these creatures will never actually exist, there is no basis on which God can foresee what these creatures would do in any conceivable circumstances. Again, Molina's complaint is the single most common objection to middle knowledge in the contemporary philosophical and theological literature, appropriately known as the "grounding objection."[28] But Molina's doctrine of middle knowledge avoids this objection entirely, since he does not base middle knowledge on God's looking ahead and seeing what potential free creatures would do in various circumstances. Rather, Molina bases middle knowledge squarely on God's nature, specifically God's innate and timelessly present attribute of omniscience.[29] As Molina explains, "God does not get His knowledge from things, but knows all things *in* Himself and *from* Himself.... God has within Himself the means whereby He knows all things fully and perfectly."[30] Thus, logically prior to God's decision to create any world, God was still omniscient. Since being omniscient means knowing all truths, before his decision to create any world God must know all things that are true at this logical juncture. And since it has always been true that, if various sets of circumstances were to obtain, certain things would happen in them, God must know all such truths before he decided to create any world. God knows these truths innately simply by virtue of his nature, just as a human mind knows truths like the relationship between cause and effect innately simply

---

27. Thus Molina would agree with Norman Geisler's allegation that this version of middle knowledge "assumes that God must 'wait' to know things are true.... God's omniscience 'waits' to see what a free creature does 'before' he selects those who will be saved.... Hence, God must wait (from a logical standpoint) for the occurrence of free acts before he can know they are true" (*Baker Encyclopedia of Christian Apologetics*, s.v. "Molinism" [Grand Rapids: Baker, 1999], 493–94).

28. Robert M. Adams, "Middle Knowledge and the Problem of Evil," *American Philosophical Quarterly* 14 (1977): 109–17; Jennifer Jensen, "The Grounding Objection to Molinism," PhD diss. (University of Notre Dame, 2008).

29. In philosophical terminology, Arminius's version of middle knowledge is predicated on a perceptualist model of divine cognition, while Molina's version of middle knowledge is predicated on a conceptualist model of divine cognition.

30. Luis de Molina, *On Divine Foreknowledge*, trans. Alfred J. Freddoso (Ithaca, NY: Cornell University Press, 1988), 4.14.13.49.12, 11, emphasis his.

by virtue of its nature. Such innate knowledge includes what Molina terms *supercomprehension*, namely, God's unlimited intellectual capacity to perceive infinitely, within his own mind, the individual essence or pattern for every possible thing he could create.[31] Owing to God's perfect knowledge of his own imagination and, therefore, the possible things that he could create, God knows what the instantiation of each thing would freely do under any set of circumstances. Notice that the circumstances are not causes of what the instantiation of each thing would do, as there are no prior determining conditions for these agents' actions. Molina insists that such knowledge of what the instantiation of each thing would freely do stems *"not from the object*, but from the acumen and absolute perfection of his intellect."[32] So, for Molina, God's middle knowledge follows deductively from his omniscience and needs no further ground than that.[33]

Fourth, Arminius's claim that God decreed to save everyone who would receive Christ before apprehending his middle knowledge seemed to Molina a violation of God's sovereignty, as it meant that certain individuals could put an obligation on God to save them. God would then have no choice in the matter as to whether to save them, condemn them, or refrain from creating them, a consequence Molina found abhorrent.[34] For Molina was convinced that, for any possible person, the person would freely choose to accept Christ under some circumstances, freely choose to reject Christ under some other circumstances, and not exist at all under some other circumstances. On the one hand, Molina believed it was too high a view of human nature, fallen as it is, to think that anyone would accept Christ under every possible set of circumstances. On the other hand, Molina believed it was too low a view of

31. Here I disagree with Robert Adams's characterization of Molina's doctrine of supercomprehension as knowing more about something than there is to understand, on the basis of which he rejects supercomprehension as absurd ("Middle Knowledge," 111). However, if one reads Molina as Adams does, one can easily avert his objection by reducing supercomprehension to comprehension, namely, knowing everything about something that there is to understand. This is the move taken by William Lane Craig: "God comprehends an individual essence so completely that He knows what its exemplification would freely do under any circumstances" (*Divine Foreknowledge and Human Freedom*, 268).

32. Molina, *Foreknowledge*, 4.14.13.52.33; emphasis mine.

33. Scholars who find Molina's response unsatisfactory likely presuppose a theory of truth that requires that all true counterfactuals have truth-makers; such a theory I find utterly counterintuitive. For a potent critique of truth-maker theory as it relates to middle knowledge, see William Lane Craig, "Middle Knowledge, Truth-Makers, and the Grounding Objection," *Faith and Philosophy* 18 (2001): 337–52.

34. Molina, *Concordia*, 7.23.1/2.1.1–8.

human nature, made in the image of God, to think that anyone would reject Christ under every possible set of circumstances (where those circumstances include the assistance of God's grace).[35] In either case, it is absurd to think that anyone would exist under every possible set of circumstances. Molina believed it was essential to God's sovereignty that God would decide, for any possible individual, which set of circumstances would obtain. Thus God must choose whether each possible individual is freely saved, is freely lost, or fails to exist. Here Molina would concur with the judgment of contemporary scholars like Richard Muller in his criticism of a defective doctrine of middle knowledge, only protesting that such a doctrine was not his own:

> The effect of such a doctrine upon soteriology is to allow an area of human choice, prior to the effective operation of divine grace, the results of which condition the divine activity or operation *ad extra* [from the outside]. God can elect individuals on the basis of his foreknowledge of their freely willed acceptance of the promises given in Christ, and this election will be based on no antecedent willing or operation in God ... [which] limits the sovereignty of grace in the work of salvation.[36]

As one might guess from the preceding comments, Molina and Arminius read Romans 9 in diametrically opposite ways, where Molina knew and agreed with the interpretation of Calvin. This observation leads us to clear away the final misconception that predominates about Molina.

MISCONCEPTION 3: MOLINA STIFLED GOD'S SOVEREIGNTY

The third prevalent misconception surrounding Molina is that he attempted to diminish God's sovereignty. This misconception is based on the idea that God's sovereignty is inversely proportional to human freedom and randomness in the world, such that the more freedom humans have and the more randomness that exists in the world, the less sovereignty God has. It cannot be overemphasized that Molina rejected this idea absolutely. Indeed, Molina judged it a severe defect in the thought of Luther and Calvin that

---

35. Ibid., 7.23.4/5.1.4.13–18.
36. Richard A. Muller, *Dictionary of Latin and Greek Theological Terms* (Grand Rapids: Baker, 1985), 274.

God's sovereignty seemed threatened by human free choices and random events in the world.[37] Instead, Molina contended that God's sovereignty is directly proportional to human freedom and randomness in the world. Thus Molina believed that by maximizing human freedom and maximizing randomness, he would maximize God's sovereignty. It can be said that, no less than for Calvin, God's sovereignty was a major theme in Molina's theology and preaching. Far from diminishing God's sovereignty, Molina was preoccupied with enhancing the sovereignty of God. Molina insisted that his conception of God was more sovereign than Calvin's conception of God. That insistence can especially be seen in Molina's doctrine of predestination. Like Calvin, Molina interpreted Romans 9 as teaching God's sovereign predestination of each individual to salvation or condemnation. However, Molina asserted that a God who can infallibly bring about the salvation or condemnation of all individuals without compromising their absolute freedom is obviously superior to a God who can only bring about their eternal destinies if they lack absolute freedom and if he, in turn, premoves their bound wills toward his foreordained ends.[38]

Here it would be instructive to contrast Arminius's reading of Romans 9 with Molina's reading. Arminius regarded the predestination of Romans 9 as a group affair, in which each person freely joins the "children of the promise" through faith or the "children of the flesh" through unbelief.[39] Thus, in deciding to save anyone who would receive Christ before apprehending his middle knowledge, God, according to Arminius, predestined a group — the children of the promise — for salvation and gives each person the opportunity to join this group. Unfortunately, many leading proponents of Molinism have defended Arminius's exegesis of Romans 9, thereby implicitly retrojecting Arminius's exegesis back onto Molina. However, Molina agreed with Calvin (and contemporary Reformed Christians) that interpreting Romans 9 in this corporate way is a denial of God's sovereignty, since believers would compel God to save them by their placing faith in Christ. This leaves God no choice but to save various individuals! God plays no role, then, in deciding whether each person is saved or lost; each person makes this decision solely for himself

37. Molina, *Concordia*, 1.14.13.18.3; 5.19.6.3.11.
38. Ibid., 7.23.4/5.1.1, 4–5.
39. Jacob Arminius, *Analysis of the Ninth Chapter of Romans*, in *Writings*, 3:537.

or herself. To sum up, Molina objected that any system of salvation in which God is put in a position where creatures can compel God to save them constitutes a violation of God's sovereignty. For no creature, Molina declared, can compel God to save him or her; any creature's salvation is sheerly the result of God's free grace toward that creature.[40]

In his exegesis of Romans 9, Molina queried "whether the cause of predestination may be ascribed to the part of the predestinate [the elect]" and "whether the cause of reprobation may be ascribed to the part of the reprobate [the unbeliever]."[41] Contrary to those who follow "the errors of Origen and Pelagius,"[42] Molina answered both questions decidedly in the negative. Taking Romans 9:11–13[43] at face value, Molina declared that "foreseen faith cannot be the ground of justification or predestination."[44] So unlike Arminius but like Calvin, Molina asserted that God's decision to save Jacob and condemn Esau did not take into account their future decisions, such as whether each would believe in God. Molina asserted that this is the only natural reading of Romans 9: "Behold in what way Paul teaches concerning Jacob that it was not on account of his works or his merits that he was beloved and predestined by God, so likewise he affirms concerning Esau that it was not on account of his works that he was hated and reprobated."[45] Thus Molina held that God decides unconditionally to save certain individuals "with his holy calling, not according to our works, but according to his own purpose and grace which was given to us in Christ Jesus."[46] Likewise, God's decision that a particular individual is condemned or reprobated "is not because of foreseen sins, and truly [the reprobate person] has neither the cause nor the ground of reprobation within him."[47]

---

40. Molina, *Concordia*, 7.23.1/2.2.2.

41. "Utrum ex parte praedestinati detur causa praedestinationis.... Utrum ex parte reprobi detur causa reprobationis" (Molina, *Concordia*, 7.23.4/5.1.1; 7.23.4/5.4.1).

42. "Erroribus ... Origenis et Pelagii" (Molina, *Concordia*, 7.23.4/5.1.2.1).

43. "Yet, before the twins were born or had done anything good or bad—in order that God's purpose in election might stand: not by works but by him who calls ... [God said,] 'Jacob I loved, but Esau I hated.'"

44. "Fides praevisa non sit ratio iustificationis ac praedestinationis" (Molina, *Concordia*, 7.23.4/5.1.2).

45. "Ecce quemadmodum Paulus de Iacob docet non propter opera sive merita sua fuisse a Deo dilectum et praedestinatum ita quoque de Esau affirmat non fuisse propter opera odio habitum ac reprobatum" (Molina, *Concordia*, 7.23.4/5.4.1).

46. "Vocavit nos vocatione sua sancta, non secundum opera nostra, sed secundum propositum suum et gratiam quae data est nobis in Christo Iesu" (Molina, *Concordia*, 7.23.4/5.1.2.1).

47. "Ergo reprobatio non est propter peccata praevisa atque adeo nec causam nec rationem ex parte reprobi habet" (Molina, *Concordia*, 7.23.4/5.4.1).

For Molina, therefore, the cause and ground of any person's predestination to salvation (election) or to condemnation (reprobation) is God's sovereign will: "The total effect of predestination ... depends only on the free will of God."[48] Thus Molina emphasized that God could have predestined "any of the elect to have truly been reprobate" and any "of the reprobate to have truly been elect."[49] Any Calvinist would give a hearty "Amen" to Molina's reasoning from Romans 9:15 – 18 to substantiate this conclusion:

> Paul adds that God said to Moses: I will have mercy on whom I have mercy, and I will have compassion on whom I have compassion; that is, I will use mercy with whomever I wish and just as it gives pleasure to me. And Paul concludes: Therefore it is neither he who wills, nor he who runs, but God who shows mercy.... He has mercy on whom he wills, and whom he wills he hardens.... Therefore neither predestination nor reprobation is according to foreseen merits, but it leads back only to the free will of God.[50]

Remarkably, Molina believed that this face-value reading of Romans 9 was entirely consistent with human free will. Because Molina viewed no possible individual as bad enough so that she or he would freely spurn God's grace in every conceivable set of circumstances and no possible individual as good enough so that she or he would freely embrace God's grace in every conceivable set of circumstances, God's possession of middle knowledge logically prior to his making any decisions about this world, including who would be saved or lost, provides the key to God's sovereign individual predestination. Thus, for any possible individual, God has the power to elect (save) that individual by creating her or him in certain freedom-preserving circumstances where God already knows she or he would voluntarily embrace his grace. And God has the power to reprobate (condemn) that individual by creating her or him in other freedom-preserving circumstances where God

---

48. "Totius effectus praedestinationis ... ex sola libera Dei voluntate pendeat" (Molina, *Concordia*, 7.23.4/5.1.2).

49. "Illi electi ... hi vero reprobi fuerint ... illi reprobi ... hi vero electi fuerint" (Molina, *Concordia*, 7.23.4/5.1.2.4).

50. "Subiungit Paulus Deum dixisse Moysi: Miserebor cuius misereor; et misericordiam praestabo cui miserebor; hoc est, utar misericordia cum quocumque voluero et prout mihi placuerit. Concluditque Paulus: Igitur non volentis, neque currentis, sed miserentis est Dei.... cuius vult miseretur, et quem vult indurate.... Ergo sicut praedestinatio non est propter merita praevisa ita neque reprobatio, sed in solam liberam voluntatem Dei ea reducenda est" (Molina, *Concordia*, 7.23.4/5.4.2).

already knows she or he would voluntarily spurn his grace.[51] And God has the power not to create that individual at all by actualizing other circumstances where the individual does not exist. This choice of circumstances (leading to salvation, condemnation, or nonexistence) is unconditioned by anything about the individual but depends solely on the sovereign will of God.[52]

Now we can understand why Molina would ask "Which God is more sovereign?" when comparing his concept of God with Calvin's concept of God. Just as a human ruler who skillfully accomplishes his goals through the free choices of his subjects is more powerful than a dictator, so Molina found a God who can choose whether creatures possessing absolute freedom are saved or lost strictly on the basis of his good pleasure to be more sovereign than a God who can only determine their salvation or condemnation if these creatures lack absolute freedom.

OUTLINE OF THE BOOK'S CHAPTERS

Here unveiled for the first time, Molina's deeply inspirational and fascinating life serves as a model of faithful Christian service and heroism despite opposition. Chapter 1 paints the portrait of Molina's early life, his spiritual crisis that led him to enter the Jesuit order at Alcalá, and his profound conversion experience, which occurred through a series of directed meditations on the life of Christ.

Chapter 2 describes Molina's further studies at Coimbra in Portugal, specifically his disenchantment with Aquinas's doctrine of grace and the

---

51. Thus Edmond Vansteenberghe rightly summarizes Molina's doctrine of election and reprobation: "God knew an infinity of providential orders in which the non-predestined would freely arrive at eternal life and thus would have been predestined. But he also knew an infinity of providential orders in which the predestined would have freely lost beatitude and would have been reprobate. Yet he chose for the one and for the other the providential order in which he foresaw that the one would be saved and the other not (Dieu connaissait une infinité d'ordres providentiels dans lesquels les non prédestinés seraient librement arrivés à la vie éternelle, et donc auraient été prédestinés; il connaissait de même une infinité d'ordres providentiels dans lesquels les prédestinés auraient librement perdu la béatitude et auraient été réprouvés; et cependant il a choisi pour les uns et les autres l'ordre de providence, dans lequel il prévoyait que les uns seraient sauvés et les autres non)" ("Molinisme," in *Dictionnaire de théologie catholique* [ed. Alfred Vacant, Eugène Mangenot, and Émile Amann; Paris: Letouzey et Ané, 1929], 10.2.2168).

52. Molina, *Concordia*, 7.23.4/5.1.11.7. As William Lane Craig explains: "Molina held that God's choosing to create certain persons *has nothing to do with how they would respond to His grace*; He simply chooses the world order He wants to, and *no rationale for this choice is to be sought other than the divine will itself.* In this sense, predestination is for Molina *wholly gratuitous*, the result of the divine will, *and in no way based on the merits or demerits of creatures*" (*The Problem of Divine Foreknowledge and Future Contingents from Aristotle to Suarez*, Studies in Intellectual History 7 [Leiden: Brill, 1988], 204; emphasis mine).

beginnings of Molina's alternative approach for preserving both the suffi-ciency of grace and humanity's ability freely to embrace God's grace. Chapter 3 historically traces the steps in Molina's groundbreaking formulation of God's middle knowledge and shows how Molina expounded his scheme of natural, middle, and free knowledge in 1588. Chapters 4 and 5 explain how Molina employed this scheme in developing his doctrines of providence and predestination, respectively.

Similar to the furor in Germany over Luther's *95 Theses*, Molina's doc-trine of middle knowledge won him a groundswell of popular support and the enmity of leading Catholic authorities in Spain, due to its departure from the theology of Thomas Aquinas. Chapter 6 explains what happened when the authorities unleashed the Spanish Inquisition on Molina in 1591. Chapter 7 explores Molina's practical theology and his previously uncharted career as a pastor committed to the moral transformation of his flock, blend-ing truth with love in his firm yet compassionate spiritual direction.

Acutely aware of the political and economic difficulties plaguing Spain at the local and national levels, Molina eventually turned his scholarly atten-tion to issues of social justice, producing his five-volume *De justitia et jure* (*On Justice and Law*) in 1596. Chapter 8 displays Molina's vision of a just society, encompassing views of morality, national law, and economic ethics with which most evangelicals from a wide political spectrum would agree.

When the controversy elicited by middle knowledge refused to die down, in 1598 Pope Clement VIII convoked a special investigative commission dubbed the *Congregatio de auxiliis gratiae* (Congregation on the Help of Divine Grace). Chapter 9 recounts the dramatic swing from initial disap-probation (with Molina living out the rest of his days under constant fear that he would be burned at the stake as a heretic) to Pope Paul V's ultimate vindication of Molina's system as orthodox after Molina's death. Chapter 10 examines the continuing legacy of Molina for contemporary Christians in general and evangelicals in particular. Many evangelicals laud Molinism as the long-awaited rapprochement between Calvinism and Arminianism and the antidote to open theism. Moreover, the fruitful application of Molinism by Christian thinkers to a host of current philosophical and scientific prob-lems and Molinism's unlimited potential to handle future problems ensure Molina a permanent, prominent seat at the table of evangelicalism.

A CHALLENGE FOR THE JOURNEY

From his moving conversion experience to his theological genius to his faithfulness to Scripture in the face of the Spanish Inquisition to his pastoral brilliance to his championing of social justice, the tremendous relevance of Molina's life for us is quite obvious. We shall also learn valuable lessons from Molina's weaknesses in thought and action, as Molina was no less a product of his time than Luther and Calvin and so advocated various early modern political, economic, and cultural notions that we in the contemporary world do and should reject. These weaknesses can encourage us to take a more careful look at what may be our own political, economic, and cultural blind spots. With the exciting journey of exploring Molina's life in its religio-historical context ahead of us, let us pay careful attention to the many ways that Molina's theological and social ideas can strengthen the universal church in all its branches and reflect on how to implement those ideas.

CHAPTER 1

Early Years and Religious Conversion

❇   ❇   ❇

LUIS DE MOLINA WAS BORN into a noble family on September 29, 1535, at Cuenca, New Castile, Spain. His father, Don Diego de Orejón, was a wealthy merchant of honey, saffron, forest products, and minerals, all of which could be found in abundant supply in the Serranía de Cuenca, with its thick pine forests overlying a succession of intricate mountainous landforms.[1] In 1530 Orejón ascended to the nobility by purchasing a seat on the municipal council as a *veinticuatro* (alderman) for 7,000 ducats.[2] To enhance his social standing, in 1531 Orejón married Dona Ana García de Molina, who belonged to an established noble family in Cuenca that since the mid-fourteenth century had owned a massive sheep pasture responsible for the production of textiles.[3] The family possessed deep roots in Cuenca, having played a major military role in reclaiming Cuenca from the Moors in 1177.[4] Because the Molina family name, as old nobility, carried more prestige than the newly dignified Orejón name, all of the children from this marriage—Luis and his two younger brothers—were given the matrilineal name.[5]

---

1. Sara T. Nalle, *God in La Mancha: Religious Reform and the People of Cuenca, 1500–1650* (Baltimore: Johns Hopkins University Press, 1992), 7.

2. Baltasar Porreño, *Mapa del obispado de Cuenca*, in Biblioteca Nacional, Madrid, ms. 12961.7 (1622); Alonso de Andrade, *Varones illustres de la Compañia de Jesús* (Madrid, 1666), 5:785.

3. Paulino Iradiel Murugarren, *Evolución de la industria textil castellana en los siglos XIII–XVI* (Salamanca, Spain: Ediciones Universidad Salamanca, 1974), 24, 380; Antonio Franco, *Imagem da virtude em o Noviciado de Coimbra I* (Évora, 1719), 447.

4. Friedrich Stegmüller, ed. and trans., *Geschichte des Molinismus: Neue Molinaschriften 1*, Beiträge zur Geschichte der Philosophie und Theologie des Mittelalters 32 (Münster: Aschendorffschen, 1935), 2*.

5. Murugarren, *Evolución*, 327.

The young Molina grew up during an intense period of local religious enthusiasm and reform. Harking back to the proscription of Judaism and the capture of the last Muslim outpost in 1492, New Castile had entered a period of messianic expectations, kindled by both the oppressed *conversos* (forced Jewish converts to Christianity) and by the Christian populace. Rumors that the Messiah would quickly appear and lead either the *conversos* or the Christian common folk to the Promised Land swept through the region.[6] Among the professional classes and the nobility, an indigenous religious movement dubbed *Alumbradismo* (Illumination) arose, which rejected many of the external rites of the Roman Catholic Church, practiced mental prayer, and sought mystical union with God. Moreover, the elites also increasingly embraced Erasmus' criticisms of clerical abuses and popular superstition. Such criticisms found a ready audience in the new reform-minded bishop of Cuenca, Diego Ramírez de Villaescusa, who had been in Rome during the initial years of Martin Luther's break with the Catholic Church. Bishop Ramírez concurred with Luther's observations that the Roman Church financially preyed on its uninformed flock and exploited the flock's worry about the welfare of their relatives' souls in purgatory. As Bishop Ramírez sarcastically exclaimed at his installation: "How the bishopric of Cuenca is one of the most honored in these kingdoms! Because it has been forty years or more in the hands of Italian cardinals who have carried off its rent and promoted Italians to its benefices, that land has been completely lost."[7] Not only did Bishop Ramírez institute major administrative changes in Cuenca to prevent absenteeism (priests not being present at their parish churches), pluralism (priests holding, and drawing incomes from, more than one parish position at a time), and religious ignorance among the clergy, but he also launched a comprehensive program of lay reform. This program made an impact on Molina and his extended family.

When Molina was ten years old, his maternal grandmother, the Widow Molina, was brought before Bishop Ramírez on the charge of falling prey to superstitious customs. In 1545 the Widow Molina sought the help of the sorceress Juana de Sancta Fimia in compelling one of Molina's uncles, who had abandoned one of Molina's maternal aunts, to return to her through

---

6. Nalle, *God in La Mancha*, 20.
7. Felix G. Almedo, *Diego Ramírez de Villaescusa* (Madrid: Editora Nacional, 1944), 107.

love magic. But the Widow Molina was concerned with the orthodoxy of her actions and demanded from Sancta Fimia proof that what she did was "a good devotion," to which Sancta Fimia responded by laughing in her face and telling her a story about selling one's soul to the devil for love.[8] Frightened for her spiritual health, the Widow Molina departed without actually participating in the love magic. Bishop Ramírez compassionately abstained from turning the Widow Molina over to the Inquisition, despite her consorting with a sorceress, for which the Orejón-Molina family was quite grateful. Bishop Ramírez, however, insisted that the Widow Molina and the other members of her family acquire a much better understanding of Christian doctrine. Afterward, the Orejón-Molina family instilled into Luis the importance of keeping his formal obligations as a Christian, which included living a morally upstanding life, confessing his sins and partaking of the Eucharist at Easter, keeping Sunday as the Sabbath, and paying a tithe of whatever money or property he might receive.[9]

By the age of twelve, Molina's parents expressed their desire for him to become a lawyer, probably so that he could safeguard the legal interests of the family businesses. In traditional fashion, Molina underwent preparatory education at the cathedral school in Cuenca from 1547 to 1551, where he studied Latin grammar and literature.[10]

MOLINA'S SPIRITUAL JOURNEY

Molina then matriculated at the University of Salamanca in 1551 to study law.[11] Less than a year into his studies, Molina encountered the *Spiritual Exercises* of Ignatius of Loyola, cofounder of the Society of Jesus (the Jesuit order). A Jesuit community had been established at Salamanca in 1548, and its priests disseminated literature to students at the university.[12] Molina felt particularly disturbed by Loyola's taxonomy of the three classes of rich people, all of which desire to save their souls. For Loyola the first class fails

---

8. Nalle, *God in La Mancha*, 17.

9. Ramírez de Villaescusa, *Constituciones sinodales del obispado de Cuenca* (1545), fols. 12v, 15r.

10. Stegmüller, *Geschichte des Molinismus*, 3*.

11. Andre A. Alves and Jose M. Moreira, *The Salamanca School*, Major Conservative and Libertarian Thinkers 9 (New York: Continuum, 2010), 19.

12. J. M. S. Daurignac, *History of the Society of Jesus from Its Foundation to the Present Time*, 2 vols., trans. James Clements (Cincinnati: Walsh, 1865), 1:63.

in this endeavor because they obstinately refuse to rid themselves of their wealth under any circumstances before the hour of death. The second class fails because, in spite of their desire to give up their wealth, they feel addicted to the earthly security their money affords. Hence "they do not decide to give up the sum of money in order to go to God, though this would be the better way for them."[13] The third class succeeds in finding salvation because they rid themselves of all attachment to their wealth and seek the will of God as to how they will discharge their wealth, either relinquishing it entirely or personally administering it to advance the well-being of others rather than their own self-interest. In 1552 the seventeen-year-old Molina identified himself as belonging to the second class, which prompted the realization that keeping the moral requirements of the Christian faith was not enough.[14] Concerning salvation, Molina concluded that Jesus was not interested in law-keeping as an end in itself. Although Catholic theologians never taught this idea, it was common among laypeople to think in these terms, overemphasizing works by dissolving faith into ritual or moral requirements. Rather, Molina concluded that Jesus was interested in people's committing (*committere*) their lives to him and surrendering (*tradere*) their possessions and desires to his will.[15] As Molina later wrote, people must "surrender the right hand of their hearts and despise themselves, for the sake of God, in order to receive his assistance."[16]

This moment of recognition was profound in Molina's understanding of faith, which parted company with the widespread understanding in sixteenth-century Spain. Stemming from Thomas Aquinas, the prevailing understanding held that faith was an epistemological category, or way of knowing, complementary to reason that consisted in intellectual assent to doctrines not provable by reason. Molina rejected this intellectualist understanding of faith in favor of a relational understanding harmonious with the longstanding tradition of Christian mysticism. Hence Molina described faith as a relation to

---

13. Ignatius of Loyola, *The Spiritual Exercises*, trans. Louis J. Puhl (New York: Vintage, 2000), §150–55.

14. Pedro de Ribadeneira, *Illustrium Scriptorum Religionis Societatis Iesu Catalogus* (Lyons, 1609), 142–43.

15. Andrade, *Varones illustres de la Compañia de Jesús*, 5:788; this understanding was also evident in Molina's later treatises (Stegmüller, *Geschichte des Molinismus*, 149, 273, 595). In the terminology of current debates in evangelical theology, Molina was an unremitting advocate of "Lordship salvation" from his early manhood.

16. "Tradi desterius cordis sui, ae derelinqui, despicio, a Deo, ea magis, quo magis auxilia" (Ludovici Molina, *Commentaria in primam divi Thomae partem* [Venice, 1602], 14.13.10).

which every person is called, leading some to freely convert and others not to convert: "All are equally called to faith by God, to the same kind of relation. For some solely in their freedom fall into this relation by embracing this faith; however, others fall out of this relation by showing contempt. When these show contempt, it is not to be attributed to what grace alone had anticipated. But from the hearing of the gospel, some convert and others do not convert."[17] We need only recall the Catholic mysticism of Teresa of Ávila (1515–82) and John of the Cross (1542–91) prevalent during Molina's day on the Iberian Peninsula to see that Molina was not a lone Catholic voice in opting for a relational understanding of faith over against an intellectualist one.[18]

Here it would be fruitful to place Molina's conception of faith in conversation with the conceptions articulated by Luther and Calvin and by the evangelical Anabaptists. Luther often described faith in terms of a spiritual marriage, which implies personal commitment to Christ: "[Faith] unites the soul with Christ as a bride is united with her bridegroom."[19] Such unification causes the believer naturally to issue forth a life of devotion to Christ and love of humanity, just as a good tree naturally bears good fruit: "We conclude, therefore, that a Christian lives not in himself, but in Christ and in his neighbor. Otherwise he is not a Christian. He lives in Christ through faith, in his neighbor through love. By faith he is caught up beyond himself into God.... he always remains in God and in his love."[20] Like Molina, Luther rejected the popular understanding of faith as intellectual assent: "It is not enough or in any sense Christian to preach the works, life, and words of Christ as historical facts, as if the knowledge of these would suffice for the conduct of life."[21] In a later publication Molina explicitly voiced agreement with Luther on this point: "Luther rightly understood that it is not the right of the intelligence that through grace we are now the children who already possess the

---

17. "De eodem modo affectis, aequaliter a Deo ad fidem vocatis: pro sola namque eorum libertate porest euenire, ut unus amplectatur fidem, alter vero eandem contemnat. Quo fit, ut non soli gratiae praeuenienti tribuendum fit, quod ex audientibus Euangelium quidam conuertantur, quidam non conuertantur" (Molina, *Commentaria*, 14.13.12).

18. Ann L. Mackenzie, "Further *Studies of the Spanish Mystics*: Allison Peers on Miguel de Molinos' *Spiritual Guide*," in *Spain and Its Literature: Essays in Memory of E. Allison Peers*, ed. idem; Hispanic Studies Textual Research and Criticism 15 (Liverpool: Liverpool University Press, 1997), 122–24.

19. Martin Luther, *The Freedom of a Christian*, in *Luther's Works*, American ed., 55 vols., ed. Jaroslav Pelikan (St. Louis: Concordia, 1955–86), 31:352.

20. Ibid., 31:372.

21. Ibid., 31:357.

supernatural dignities."[22] Elsewhere in the same section, however, Molina condemned Luther for his doctrine of providence, thus distancing himself from any Protestant interpretation of his endorsement. Following Luther, Calvin implied that commitment to following Jesus in a life of discipleship was an indispensable part of faith. This is evident in his delineation of the relationship between faith and repentance: "Now it ought to be a fact beyond controversy that repentance not only constantly follows faith, but is also born of faith."[23] Due to faith's production of repentance, Calvin insisted that "no one can embrace the grace of the gospel without betaking himself from the errors of his past life into the right way, and applying his whole effort to the practice of repentance."[24]

The ideas of commitment and surrender to Christ implicit in Luther and Calvin found explicit expression in the evangelical Anabaptists. Balthasar Hubmaier, arguably the foremost theologian of evangelical Anabaptism, defined faith as a person's having "committed himself already in his heart henceforth to change and amend his life.... Now this person surrenders himself to the rule and teaching of Christ, the physician who has made him whole, from whom he received life."[25] The German Anabaptist preacher Jacob Kautz spoke for the entire movement when he affirmed, "Jesus Christ of Nazareth has not suffered for us or made satisfaction for us in any way unless we stand in his footsteps, walk the way he blazed before us, and follow the command of the Father as the Son, everyone in his measure. Whoever speaks, understands, or believes differently about Christ makes an idol out of Christ, which all the scribes and false evangelists and the whole world do."[26] We may therefore conclude that, although feeling no sympathy for either Protestantism or Anabaptism, Molina began his spiritual pilgrimage by coming to a realization about the nature of biblical faith that seems logically consistent with their doctrines of faith.

---

22. "Lutheri recte adnotauit, intelligendum non est de ius, qui per gratiam facti sunt iam filii, dignitatorum possident" (Molina, *Commentaria*, 14.13.10).

23. John Calvin, *Institutes of the Christian Religion*, ed. John T. McNeill, trans. Ford Lewis Battles (Philadelphia: Westminster, 1960), 3.3.1.

24. Ibid.

25. Balthasar Hubmaier, *Summa of the Entire Christian Life*, in *Balthasar Hubmaier: Theologian of Anabaptism*, trans. and ed. H. Wayne Pipkin and John H. Yoder (Scottdale, PA: Herald, 1989), 85.

26. Jacob Kautz, *The Seven Articles*, in *Anabaptism in Outline: Selected Primary Sources* ed. Walter Klaassen (Scottdale, PA: Herald, 1981), 48.

However, this realization did not break the grip that wealth had on the young man, to which he had grown quite reliant. Molina had the desire to entrust himself fully to Christ, but he found himself too weak to carry out this desire. Therefore Molina became seized with the fear of hell, which he imagined in line with Loyola's portrayal as an abode containing souls enclosed with bodies of fire who perpetually wailed and howled in agony, smelled smoke, sulfur, filth, and corruption, and experienced the palpable absence of Christ's love.[27] Molina thus found himself in a spiritual crisis every bit as terrifying as Luther's thunderstorm experience. For even Molina's fear of hell did not alter his soul so as to forsake his wealth; rather, it only served to produce a deep sense of foreboding. In the midst of this crisis, Molina came upon a biblical text in the lectionary that resonated directly with his situation, 1 John 4:18: "There is no fear in love. But perfect love drives out fear, because fear has to do with punishment. The one who fears is not made perfect in love."[28] Molina observed from this text that only perfect love for Christ could transform his soul, empowering him voluntarily to renounce all worldly possessions and surrender himself fully to Christ. As he later recalled, he needed to be "so strengthened by faith and love that he would be set on fire in order to gain a perfect love" and thus "be adopted as among the sons of God by means of grace making gracious."[29] Molina believed that this perfect love was a gift of the Holy Spirit that would cause him to imitate Jesus and, in the words of Loyola's *Spiritual Exercises*, to "desire and choose poverty with Christ poor, rather than riches; insults with Christ loaded with them, rather than honors ... to be accounted as worthless and a fool for Christ, rather than to be esteemed as wise and prudent in this world."[30] Seeking this spiritual gift, or charism, of love from the Spirit, Molina believed, was the only way to honor the goal for which he was created, namely, the praise of God and the salvation of his soul.

Molina pursued the Spirit's pure love by engaging in a series of directed meditations on the life of Jesus, from his baptism to his ascension. These

---

27. Andrade, *Varones illustres de la Compañia de Jesús*, 5:789; cf. Loyola, *Spiritual Exercises*, §65.

28. Franco, *Imagem*, 450.

29. "Immo quibus in fide roborantur adeoque caritate inflammantur ut perfecta caritas foras mittat timorem ... quod sint filii Dei per gratiam gratum facientem adoptati" (Molina, *Concordia*, 3.14.13.44.10). Here "grace making gracious" (*gratiam gratum facientem*) refers to the Christ-infused spiritual capacity of fallen humans to exercise faith by which the sinner may be justified, a phrase used by Molina as a synonym for "prevenient grace" (*gratia praeveniens*).

30. Franco, *Imagem*, 452; Loyola, *Spiritual Exercises*, §169.

meditations numbered forty and followed consecutively the twelfth through fifty-first "mysteries of the life of our Lord" spelled out by Loyola.[31] Molina found deep admiration for Jesus' resistance of the devil's temptation, "All this I will give you ... if you bow down and worship me" (Matt. 4:9), as this was precisely the temptation that Molina strove to overcome.[32] Molina took note of Jesus' order when he sent the apostles out to preach, "Do not get any gold or silver or copper" (Matt. 10:9). Molina was also deeply moved by the fact that "with a whip of cords" Jesus "overturned the tables and scattered the money of the wealthy money changers who were in the Temple."[33] In meditating on the Sermon on the Mount, Molina was struck by his observation that the blessed include "the poor in spirit," "the meek," "those who hunger," and "those who are persecuted" (Matt. 5:3, 5, 6, 10; cf. Luke 6:20–23). He was also captivated by Jesus' love for his enemies and his instruction to "do good to those who hate you" (Luke 6:27).[34] Unlike the fear of hell that had formerly left him paralyzed, Molina was touched and empowered by Jesus' compassion for his disciples when they faltered, gently asking his terrified disciples upon calming the storm, "You of little faith, why are you so afraid?" (Matt. 8:26).[35] Likewise, Molina sympathized with Peter when at Jesus' command he walked on the water and approached Jesus, but when he doubted he started to sink. If Jesus reached out and saved Peter when he could not summon the inner strength to obey Jesus' difficult command, Molina hoped, Jesus would do the same thing for him.[36] As an extremely gifted student, Molina gravitated toward Jesus' concern for the life of the mind, commanding his disciples to be as wise as serpents but at the same time to show intellectual integrity by being as innocent as doves.[37] So significant was the impact of this command on Molina that the balance between sharp, tough-minded dialectic and careful, honest consideration of the objections, both actual and possible, to be raised against his views would prove a hallmark of Molina's scholarship throughout his career.

Through these meditations, Molina's love for Jesus increasingly grew to

31. Franco, *Imagem*, 455; Loyola, *Spiritual Exercises*, §261.
32. Franco, *Imagem*, 456; Loyola, *Spiritual Exercises*, §274.
33. Franco, *Imagem*, 457; Loyola, *Spiritual Exercises*, §277.
34. Franco, *Imagem*, 457; Loyola, *Spiritual Exercises*, §278.
35. Franco, *Imagem*, 458; Loyola, *Spiritual Exercises*, §279.
36. Franco, *Imagem*, 460; Loyola, *Spiritual Exercises*, §280.
37. Andrade, *Varones illustres de la Compañia de Jesús*, 5:792; Loyola, *Spiritual Exercises*, §281.

the point that he found himself able to commit his life to Jesus and to surrender his worldly possessions and desires to Jesus' will. The tipping point that moved Molina from ability to conversion seems to have occurred during his meditation on the conversion of the sinful woman (whom Molina, following early modern exegesis, mistook for Mary Magdalene) in Luke 7:36–50. As Molina later observed, through the divinely assisted power of love for Jesus, the sinful woman and others in church history freely renounced their former lifestyles and found salvation: "With the help of God they were able more intensely or less intensely to cooperate of their own free will, which seems to have been praised in the Magdalene by Christ when he said [Luke 7:47]: Many sins are forgiven her because she has loved much."[38] The phrase "more intensely or less intensely" indicates the waxing and waning of a spiritual journey, a journey of love containing highs and lows that ultimately leads to the desired destination of personal relationship with Christ. The account of the sinful woman brought Molina full circle with the passage that launched his journey, 1 John 4:18. For Molina felt that he was in the same position as the sinful woman. He could now fall down at Jesus' feet in adoration. He could hear Jesus declare that his sins had been forgiven and that his faith, made effective through love, had saved him.[39] It should be emphasized that Molina, in contradistinction to many of his Spanish Catholic contemporaries, henceforth possessed full assurance of salvation, with no indication of worry about whether he had done enough or acquired sufficient merit before God.[40] While Molina was not at this juncture thinking in terms of the doctrine of justification, his reasoning implies a view of justification as a definitive, once-for-all event of reconciliation with Christ occurring at the moment of surrender to Christ and not as a lifelong process. We shall see in chapter 2 that this implication would be borne out when Molina expressed his own thoughts on justification.

---

38. "Potuerunt ... cooperante intensius aut minus intense ipsorum arbitrio cum auxilio Dei; id quod laudasse in Magdalena videtur Christus dum dixit [Lc 7, 47]: Remittuntur ei peccato multa, quoniam dilexit multum" (Molina, *Concordia*, 4.14.13.53.4.14).

39. Andrade, *Varones illustres de la Compañia de Jesús*, 5:793–94.

40. Not a trace of salvific doubt can be found, for example, in Molina's description of "he himself finding the essence of the divine rapture (ipse in raptu diuinam essentiam vidifiet)," when the state of being "in the rapture of his own soul strikes while in the body (in raptu anima ipsius fuerit in corpora)" (Molina, *Commentaria*, 12.11.4).

MOLINA'S ENTRANCE INTO THE SOCIETY OF JESUS

Molina's profound conversion experience led him to give up the study of law at the University of Salamanca in December 1552, as law was a profession he desired for the wealth it would bring him.[41] However, he retained an interest in theoretical issues of jurisprudence, particularly the relationship between the law and justice, throughout his life. Because of his reliance on Loyola's *Spiritual Exercises* throughout his spiritual journey, Molina desired to join a Jesuit order that emphasized the security found in knowing the love of Christ. At first Molina investigated the Society of Jesus in Salamanca. To his chagrin, he found a community that seemed oblivious to the problems in the Roman Catholic Church that Bishop Ramírez had striven to remedy and stressed unflinching obedience to the church and the pope under any circumstances.[42] In the course of his investigation, however, Molina heard about a reform-minded Jesuit order at Alcalá de Henares. Morally, this Jesuit order was committed to putting a stop to the whoring, gaming, and ignorance prevalent among its parish priests. In so doing, it aimed to restore the laity's trust in the church, such that they would treat the church with the respect it was due as the body of Christ.[43] As things stood, the laity treated the church with scarcely a modicum of respect, flagrantly abusing the canon laws dealing with adultery and marriage. On this score, Sara Nalle observes: "Fiances cohabited, people married within prohibited degrees of consanguinity, couples separated and lived freely with other partners. Many believed that one could separate legally from his or her spouse simply by going to the town notary and obtaining a so-called letter of separation. Others, who sought to annul their marriages, found witnesses willing to lie for them."[44] The Society of Jesus in Alcalá de Henares believed that the Roman Church, from head to members, stood in urgent need of reform. This Jesuit order also displayed a bent toward biblical mysticism, maintaining that such reform could not be enforced through external rules but must spring from the conversion of the hearts of individuals, both clergy

---

41. Stegmüller, *Geschichte des Molinismus*, 4*.
42. Daurignac, *History of the Society of Jesus*, 1:63–67.
43. Villaescusa, *Constituciones*, fols. 51v–53v.
44. Nalle, *God in La Mancha*, 28.

and lay.[45] The perspective of the Alcalá order fit perfectly with the stages of Molina's spiritual quest, namely, his insight that law keeping was insufficient to become a Christian and the gradual awakening of his heart to love Jesus to the point of personal commitment and surrender.

Thus in 1553 Molina became a novice of the Jesuit order at Alcalá de Henares at the age of eighteen. This entailed Molina's total renunciation of private ownership of property, which he regarded as an outward sign of his inward commitment to follow Christ. Although unhappy with his decision, Molina's parents seem to have resigned themselves to it.[46] During his novitiate, Molina grew acutely aware of the need for Christians to think about and actively engage issues of social justice for all persons, regardless of religion or ethnicity. When an outbreak of the plague struck Alcalá that year, Molina and his fellow brothers carried plague victims on their shoulders, encouraged them with gentle words of hope, and watched and attended day and night by the beds of the sick and dying.[47] The Alcalá Jesuits cared not only for Catholic victims but also for Muslim and *morisco*[48] victims of the plague, which stood in sharp contrast to the efforts of the Inquisition to eliminate Islam from Spain. For those victims who were homeless, the order set up a makeshift hospital in its monastery to provide them with lodging and medical treatment. This experience fostered in Molina a deep sense of pastoral sensitivity.

Moreover, during his novitiate Molina exhibited a voracious appetite for philosophy and theology, as he spent hours in the communal library poring over the works of Augustine, Bernard of Clairvaux, Thomas Aquinas, Thomas à Kempis, Gabriel Biel, and other patristic and medieval thinkers. Molina appreciated both positive theology (*theologia positiva*), which affirmed and explained the central truths of the Christian faith, and scholastic theology (*theologia scholastica*), which defended Christian truths in logical debate with adversaries. Molina's talents in philosophy and theology were too obvious to be ignored; his superiors soon made plans to send Molina for further

---

45. Andrade, *Varones illustres de la Compañia de Jesús*, 5:796.
46. Franco, *Imagem*, 465.
47. Daurignac, *History of the Society of Jesus*, 1:148.
48. *Moriscos* were forced Muslim converts to Christianity, whom the Inquisition always suspected (sometimes with justification) of being nominal Christians who secretly practiced Islam.

studies upon completion of his novitiate.[49] Hence the Jesuit order's strong emphasis on education proved a perfect fit for Molina.[50]

In 1554 Molina successfully finished his novitiate and became a full-fledged member of the Society of Jesus. The new Jesuit pointed to two passages from Thomas à Kempis's famous devotional work *Imitatio Christi* (*The Imitation of Christ*), passages that summed up his personal journey and spiritual growth up to that point. The first text stressed the grace of God in Molina's life over against his own works: "Is there anything exceptional in being happy and feeling devout when God's grace touches you? Everybody looks forward to such a time. The man who is carried along by God's grace indeed rides smoothly, and it is no wonder that he feels no drag since he is supported by the Almighty and led by the Supreme Guide.... When God gives you some spiritual consolation, accept it with thanksgiving and realize that it is a gift from God and not due you because of any merit on your part."[51] The second text concisely summarized Molina's spiritual journey toward obedience to Christ, which he formally vowed at his reception into the order: "The sooner you resign yourself with your whole heart to God, and no longer seek anything according to your own will or pleasure, but totally place yourself in His hands, the sooner you will find that you are united to God and are at peace. Nothing will make you happier or please you as much as being obedient to the divine will."[52] This twofold experience of divine grace and the resulting life of joyful obedience rooted in love for God would accompany Molina throughout his life, informing his theological inquiry and pastoral work.

---

49. Balthazar Telles, *Crónica de Companhia de Jesus da Província de Portugal* (Lisbon, 1647), 2:462–63.

50. Molina's interests matched precisely those of the ideal Jesuit, as laid out by Loyola: "We should praise both positive theology and that of the Scholastics. It is characteristic of the positive doctors, such as St. Augustine, St. Jerome, St. Gregory, and others, to rouse the affections so that we are moved to love and serve God our Lord in all things. On the other hand, it is more characteristic of the scholastic doctors, such as St. Thomas, St. Bonaventure, the Master of the Sentences, and others, to define and state clearly, according to the needs of our times, the doctrines that are necessary for eternal salvation, and that more efficaciously help to refute all errors and expose all fallacies" (*Spiritual Exercises*, §363).

51. Thomas à Kempis, *The Imitation of Christ*, ed. and trans. Joseph N. Tylenda (New York: Vintage, 1998), 2.9; Franco, *Imagem*, 467. Molina would later quote this passage in the *Concordia* (3.14.13.44.7), demonstrating its continued impact on Molina's spirituality.

52. Thomas à Kempis, *Imitation*, 4.15.3; Franco, *Imagem*, 467. Molina also quoted this passage in the *Concordia* (3.14.13.44.9), indicating that he henceforth thought of it as an abridgement of his religious experience.

SIGNIFICANCE OF MOLINA'S
EARLY LIFE (1535 – 54)

In this chapter, we have seen Molina's transformation from a rich teenager and aspiring law student to a devoted follower of Christ who renounced his wealth and developed a lifelong passion for philosophy and theology. Through the efforts of his hometown bishop, Bishop Ramírez, Molina recognized from his youth that there existed major problems in the Roman Church, including flagrant immorality among clergy and a lack of religious education among the laity so that they could not discern true from false doctrine. In Cuenca Molina was thus raised in a climate of reform. However, this reform only caused the teenage Molina to follow various moral and ritual rules. But soon after matriculating as a law student at the University of Salamanca, the seventeen-year old Molina was powerfully influenced by Ignatius of Loyola's *Spiritual Exercises*, which led him to realize that he had made money his god, preventing him from truly being a Christian. Moreover, the *Spiritual Exercises* led Molina to reconceive of faith in terms of commitment and surrender to Christ rather than assent to the truths of the gospel. Yet neither this new understanding of faith nor attempts to scare himself out of clinging to wealth by pondering the horrors of damnation were sufficient to break Molina's attachment to money.

After reading 1 John 4:18, which indicated to Molina that perfect love of Jesus would empower him to forsake all for Jesus and give him a sense of security that would forever cast out the fear of damnation, Molina began a period of deep mediations on the life of Jesus, leading to an intense attraction to the person and teachings of Jesus. He was especially drawn to Jesus' compassion for those who like Molina himself were seeking spiritual peace, and Jesus' commitment to a rigorous and honest intellectual life. Eventually, precipitated by his meditation on the account of the sinful woman in Luke 7:36 – 50, Molina committed his life and surrendered his aspirations and possessions to Jesus, at which point he believed his faith had saved him and that he possessed peace with God.

Leaving behind his law studies, Molina entered the Society of Jesus at Alcalá, which shared his reform-mindedness and convictions about the relation between love and good works. During his novitiate, Molina's insatiable appetite for philosophy and theology was joined by an enduring sense of pastoral sensitivity and concern for social justice. In 1554 Molina completed his novitiate and became formally inducted into the Jesuit order at Alcalá. At his initiation, Molina affirmed the truth that only surrender to Christ brings true fulfillment, based sheerly on the grace of God and not on works.

CHAPTER 2

Philosophical and
Theological Pilgrimage

⌗ ⌗ ⌗

IN 1554 MOLINA'S SUPERIORS in the Society of Jesus at Alcalá de Henares, aware of Molina's obvious abilities for philosophy, sent him to the University of Coimbra in Portugal to study philosophy. In addition to having a Jesuit college that was founded in 1541, the university arguably possessed the top philosophical faculty on the Iberian Peninsula.[1] At Coimbra, Molina studied primarily under Pedro da Fonseca (1528–99), a Jesuit philosopher whose scholarship in logic and metaphysics earned him wide esteem among his contemporaries as "the Portuguese Aristotle."[2] Molina loved Fonseca, praising him as a charismatic and effective teacher.[3] Molina undertook a four-year program in philosophy leading to a master's degree, each year containing three trimesters.

During the first trimester of year one (1554–55), Molina studied the *De re dialectica libellus* (*Book on Dialectics*) of the fifteenth-century Renaissance philosopher George of Trezibond and the *Isagoge* (*Introduction to Aristotle's Categories*) of the third-century Neoplatonic philosopher Porphyry.[4] The

---

1. J. M. S. Daurignac, *History of the Society of Jesus from Its Foundation to the Present Time*, 2 vols., trans. James Clements (Cincinnati: Walsh, 1865), 1:39–40. The University of Coimbra proved an even better choice for Molina than his superiors planned, as in 1555 the College of Arts of Coimbra was given to the Jesuits by the Portuguese king John III.

2. João Madeira, "Pedro da Fonseca's *Isagoge Philosophica* and the Predicables from Boethius to the *Lovanienses*," PhD diss. (Katholike Universiteit Leuven, 2006), 2.

3. Amândio A. Coxito and Maria L. C. Soares, "Pedro da Fonseca," in *História do Pensamento Filosófico Português v. II, Renascimento e Contra-Reforma*, ed. Pedro Calafate (Lisbon: Caminho, 2001), 456–57.

4. David A. Lines, "Moral Philosophy in the Universities: Medieval and Renaissance Europe," in *History of Universities, Volume XXII*, ed. Mordechai Feingold (Oxford: Oxford University Press, 2005), 56.

Dialectica functioned as a primer on how to carry out rational discourse on controversial subjects in a rhetorically persuasive manner. It presented Cicero as the model philosopher-orator for students to emulate, since he had the power to seize constantly changing and extraordinarily complex situations and adapt to them so as to steer the course of events through the force of speech.[5] George of Trezibond's work gave Molina an abiding respect for portions of Cicero's *De officiis* (*On Duties*), especially the insight that God has bestowed on humans nothing more divine than their consciences.[6] For Molina this insight entailed that the objective moral truths our consciences apprehend collectively constitute the interpretive lens through which God expects us to read Scripture. Hence the deliverances of natural revelation, including our perception of objective moral values and duties, serve as a necessary hermeneutical tool for properly interpreting special revelation.[7] The *Isagoge* was the standard sixteenth-century textbook on logic and raised, at Fonseca's urging, the question in Molina's mind as to the relation between universals, or common characteristics or relations (for instance, humanity), and particulars, or individual things that bear these characteristics or relations (for instance, specific humans). On this question, Molina adopted the position of conceptualism or moderate realism, which asserted the existence of universals as ideas in the mind of God.[8] This led Molina to affirm that all similar objects that do not exist at any particular place or time but rather exist as a type of thing (like numbers, sets, propositions, and essences) possess objective reality as the concepts of God's mind. So things like universals, numbers, sets, propositions, and essences exist neither independently of God nor outside of God but only within the mind of God. In modern philosophical terminology, such things are referred to as abstract objects.[9]

Molina embraced conceptualism over against its two principal rivals, realism (or Platonism) and nominalism. According to realism, abstract objects

5. John Monfasani, *George of Trezibond: A Biography and a Study of His Rhetoric and Logic* (Leiden: Brill, 1976), 294.

6. Balthazar Telles, *Crónica de Companhia de Jesus da Província de Portugal* (Lisbon, 1647), 2:465; cf. Cicero, *On Duties* (*De officiis*), trans. Walter Miller, Loeb Classical Library 30 (Cambridge: Harvard University Press, 1913), 3.10.44.

7. Molina draws this implication in *Commentaria in primam divi Thomae partem* (Venice, 1602), 16.1.1.

8. Ibid., 15.1.2.1.

9. For an excellent discussion of abstract objects, see J. P. Moreland and William Lane Craig, *Philosophical Foundations for a Christian Worldview* (Downers Grove, IL: InterVarsity, 2003), 184.

exist independently of God, such that God, no less than humans, is simply confronted by their necessary existence. According to nominalism, abstract objects do not have any objective existence at all but are just useful fictions devised by humans through their observation of particular things.[10] Molina's adoption of conceptualism brought him to an insight that would have profound implications for his future work: the essences or natures of things are known by God before God produces them. Since the essences or natures of things are ideas in the mind of God, and it is logically impossible for an omniscient God to exist without his ideas, God knows the essences or natures of all possible things before he chooses to create some of these things (namely, before he chooses to instantiate a certain set of these essences or natures). As Molina would later put it: "The natures of things are known by God before the things are produced ... the natures are known by God and used as patterns, so that by imitating them things are produced. For he intended to produce things among the natures that he preconceived, and the production is done by him such that the preconceptions of the agent who intends their production are imitated by the things themselves."[11] That all created things imitate God's preconceptions of them affords God with a means of choosing which preconceived things to create, as he already knows how they would turn out if actualized.

MOLINA AND ARISTOTLE

Molina formally launched into an extended study of Aristotle during the second trimester of year one, reading the *Predicamenta* (*Categories*) and *De interpretatione* (*On Interpretation*). The *Predicamenta* attempts to treat all the possible kinds of things that can be the subject or the predicate of a proposition by placing objects of human apprehension under one of ten categories. Most significant for the development of Molina's thought was the first category: substance. From Aristotle's distinction between primary substances (e.g., a particular human, a particular tree) and secondary substances (e.g.,

---

10. Ibid., 210–14, 504–5; Earle E. Cairns, *Christianity through the Centuries: A History of the Christian Church*, 3rd rev. ed. (Grand Rapids: Zondervan, 1996), 229–32.

11. "Naturis rerum cognitis a Deo antequam producantur.... Quia sunt objectum a Deo cognitum ad cuius imitationem res producuit; tales quippe intendit producere, quales eas praeconcipit, quo fit, ut, cum producuntur, ex intentione agentis seipsas ut praeconceptas imitentur" (Molina, *Commentaria*, 15.1.2.2).

humanity, treeness), Molina derived the notion of individual essences. For Molina an individual essence is the "whatness" of any particular entity that makes it the unique thing that it is and differentiates it from all other things of the same kind.[12] So each human exemplifies a separate individual essence that is foreknown to God, as opposed to God's only foreknowing the general essence (or kind essence) of humanity. This means that God creates each person not simply according to the generic pattern "humanity" but according to a unique and unrepeated pattern that includes the common property "humanity."[13] *De interpretatione* comprehensively explores the relationship between language and logic, drawing a series of rudimentary conclusions about terms, nouns, verbs, propositions, negations, and quantities. Of greatest importance to Molina was Aristotle's discussion of modal propositions, namely, the issue of whether propositions are necessarily true or possibly true. Propositions are necessarily true if it is logically impossible for them to be false under any circumstances. Thus the proposition "2 + 2 = 4" is necessarily true, since there is no state of affairs where two and two do not add up to four. However, propositions are possibly true if it is logically possible for them to be true under some circumstances and false under other circumstances. Many future propositions, such as "A sea battle will take place tomorrow," fall under this description. Since the sea battle might just as easily happen as not happen given the free decisions of the relevant agents, the proposition "A sea battle will take place tomorrow" is classified as contingent.[14] Hence Molina observed that reality is so constituted that, for any contingent proposition, it may issue in either of two opposite possibilities. Molina rejected the fatalistic argument that, since it is true today and was true yesterday that either "a sea battle will take place tomorrow" or "a sea battle will not take place tomorrow," the sea battle's occurrence or nonoccurrence is necessary. For the fact that a future contingent proposition has a truth value in the present or past does nothing to determine what that truth value is. The relevant agents have the power to choose whether the event identified by the future contingent

---

12. Ibid., 15.1.2.4.

13. Ibid., 16.3.1.

14. Aristotle, *Categories and De interpretation*, trans. J. L. Ackrill, Clarendon Aristotle Series (Oxford: Oxford University Press, 1975), 9; Friedrich Stegmüller, ed. and trans., *Geschichte des Molinismus: Neue Molinaschriften 1*, Beiträge zur Geschichte der Philosophie und Theologie des Mittelalters 32 (Münster: Aschendorffschen, 1935), 272.

proposition will or will not happen, and whichever way the agents freely act, it is their future action that stands logically prior (though not chronologically prior) to the truth value the proposition holds in the present or past.[15] In the third trimester, Molina read Aristotle's *Analytica Priora* (*Prior Analytics*), which explores the process of discovering facts through deductive reasoning expressed in syllogisms. To develop his rhetorical skills for public debate, Molina also read the *Institutio Oratoria* (*Institutes of Oratory*) of the first-century Roman rhetorician Quintilian.[16]

During his first trimester of year two (1555–56), Molina studied Aristotle's *Analytica Posteriora* (*Posterior Analytics*) and books 1 through 3 of his *Ethica Nicomachea* (*Nicomachean Ethics*). Unlike the *Analytica Priora*, which only considered the appropriate forms of syllogisms (the ways validly to move from premises to a conclusion), the *Analytica Posteriora* took up the matter of syllogisms, or the propositions of which they are composed. These propositions may be true or false, probable or improbable. Molina learned that a sound dialectical syllogism is one whose logic is valid and whose premises are more probably true than false.[17] From the *Ethica*, Molina latched onto the assertion that moral virtue is conscious choice. Therefore only voluntary actions can be praised or blamed, in contradistinction to coerced or necessary actions. This insight undergirds Molina's later definition of freedom: "Freedom can be understood in the first place insofar as it is opposed to coercion.... But freedom can also be understood insofar as it is opposed to necessity. Thus an agent is called free who, with all the prerequisites for action taken into account, is able to act and able not to act, or is able to do something in such a way that s/he is also able to do some contrary thing."[18] In modern terminology, Molina strongly advocated the doctrine of libertarian freedom.[19] When applied to humans, it denotes their unconstrained ability to choose between opposites in both the physical and spiritual realms. For Molina no circumstances exist that

---

15. Stegmüller, *Geschichte des Molinismus*, 273–75.

16. Lines, "Moral Philosophy," 56.

17. Molina, *Commentaria*, 28.3.3.

18. "In primis enim sumi potest, ut opponitur coactioni.... Alio vero modo accipi potest, ut opponitur necessitati. Quo pacto illud agens liberum dicitur quod positis omnibus requisitis ad agendum potest agere et non agere aut ita agere unum ut contrarium etiam agere possit" (Ludovici Molina, *Liberi Arbitrii cum Gratiae Donis, Divina Praescientia, Providentia, Praedestinatione et Reprobatione Concordia*, ed. Johannes Rabeneck [Madrid: Sumptibus Societatis Editorialis "Sapientia," 1953], 1.14.13.2.2–3).

19. Hence, while Molina never used the term *libertarian*, he clearly affirmed the concept the term signifies.

could determine a person's choices, and if a person chooses to do a particular thing, she or he could have done otherwise or could have refrained from acting at all.[20] Hence Molina opposed the doctrine that may be styled the theological version of compatibilist human freedom, or the freedom to choose between the options compatible with one's nature.[21] Advanced by Luther and Calvin, this doctrine held that unregenerate humans, while possessing the freedom to choose between opposites in the physical realm (in matters below), lack the ability to choose between spiritual good and evil (in matters above) due to original sin. Just as bad trees can bear bad fruit or no fruit at all, unregenerate humans can either perform spiritual wickedness by actively rebelling against God or do nothing spiritual at all by displaying passivity toward God; their nature precludes them from performing spiritual good.[22] Molina opposed this version of compatibilist human freedom on the grounds that God gives all humans sufficient grace to overcome any causal restraints imposed on them by the fall. This grace Molina styled both as prevenient grace (*gratia praeveniens*), in full conformity with the theology of Thomas Aquinas, and as grace making gracious (*gratia gratum faciens*); hence Molina took prevenient grace and grace making gracious as synonyms. This stood in partial agreement with Aquinas's theology.[23] For Aquinas used the term

---

20. Alfred J. Freddoso, "Introduction," in Ludovici Molina, *On Divine Foreknowledge*, trans. Alfred J. Freddoso (Ithaca, NY: Cornell University Press, 1988), 24.

21. This theological version is based on the more conventional philosophical definition of compatibilist freedom that free will is compatible with determinism, specifically, with the will's actions being determined by one's beliefs, desires, character, and other aspects of one's nature. It follows from this that one's choices are determined by one's nature. Where the theological version differs from the philosophical one is that the theological version affords the individual a range of options (i.e., the choice must come from an incomplete set containing many members), while the philosophical version typically affords the individual only a single option (i.e., the choice must come from an incomplete set containing one member).

22. As Luther famously stated concerning free will, "If we do not want to drop this term altogether—which would really be the safest and most Christian thing to do—we may still in good faith teach people to use it to credit man with 'free-will' in respect, not of what is above him, but of what is below him" (Martin Luther, *The Bondage of the Will*, trans. James I. Packer and O. R. Johnston [Grand Rapids: Revell, 1957], 107). Similarly, Calvin expressed the doctrine of compatibilist freedom in this assessment of the spiritual choices made by unregenerate humanity: "Man will then be spoken of as having this sort of free decision, not because he has free choice equally of good and evil, but because he acts wickedly by will, not by compulsion.... The chief point of this distinction, then, must be that man, as he was corrupted by the Fall, sinned willingly, not unwillingly or by compulsion; by the most eager inclination of his heart, not by forced compulsion; by the prompting of his own lust, not by compulsion from without. Yet so depraved is his nature that he can be moved or impelled only to evil. But if this is true, then it is clearly expressed that man is surely subject to the necessity of sinning" (John Calvin, *Institutes of the Christian Religion*, ed. John T. McNeill, trans. Ford Lewis Battles [Philadelphia: Westminster, 1960], 2.2.7; 2.3.5).

"grace making gracious" as a category that included prevenient grace but was not identical to it. The category also included the soul's willing the good, the soul's successfully doing the good that it wills, the soul's persevering in the good, and the soul's attaining the glory of salvation.[24]

The second and third trimesters of year two saw Molina explore Aristotle's *Topoi* (*Topics*), *De sophisticis elenchis* (*Sophistical Refutations*), and books 4 through 7 of the *Ethica*.[25] The *Topoi* taught Molina the art of dialectic, which Aristotle defined as the invention and discovery of arguments in which the premises rest on commonly held opinions. Moreover, this work stimulated Molina's thinking about properties or attributes, specifically the distinction between essential attributes and relative attributes, the distinction between permanent attributes and temporary attributes, the relationship between essential and permanent attributes, and the relationship between relative and temporary attributes. While essential attributes must be permanent attributes, permanent attributes are not necessarily essential attributes. For example, we can conclude from God's essential goodness that God is permanently good. But we cannot conclude from God's permanent willing to create our universe that God's willing to create our universe is one of his essential attributes, as God could have just as easily permanently willed to create a different universe than ours or even no universe at all.[26] While relative attributes are not necessarily temporary attributes, temporary attributes must be relative attributes. Thus God's permanently willing to create our universe is a relative attribute of God (it could have been otherwise) but is clearly not a temporary attribute of God. However, the second person of the Trinity's assuming a human nature is a temporary attribute of his, which he did not possess either temporally or logically prior to the incarnation,[27] and is therefore a

23. Molina, *Commentaria*, 14.13.7, 43.3.1.

24. Thomas Aquinas, *Summa Theologiae*, trans. Fathers of the English Dominican Province (New York: Benziger Brothers, 1947), 2.1.111.1–5.

25. Lines, "Moral Philosophy," 56.

26. Molina, *Commentaria*, 2.3.1.

27. The notion of "temporally prior" should be clear enough, as the Logos did not possess a human nature in, for example, 100 BC. There was a point in time at which the Logos assumed a human nature (c. 5 BC), which Paul described as "the set time" (κρόνος) (Gal. 4:4). I also use the phrase "logically prior" because, whatever one's view of God's relationship to time, God existed "before time began" (1 Cor. 2:7), and at this juncture the Logos did not possess a human nature. For a full treatment of God's relationship to time, see William Lane Craig, *Time and Eternity: Exploring God's Relationship to Time* (Wheaton: Crossway, 2001).

relative attribute. There was no logical necessity for the second person of the Trinity to become incarnate, as this was a free choice on his part, which he could have just as easily not undertaken.[28] In addition to advancing Molina's understanding of properties, the *Topoi* taught Molina the numerous strategies that could be used to defend and attack a definition and the techniques of organizing and delivering a verbal disputation. These skills would prove most useful throughout Molina's theological career.

From *De sophisticis elenchis*, Molina learned to identify thirteen fallacies in reasoning, comprising the six verbal fallacies (accent or emphasis,[29] ambiguous grammatical structures,[30] equivocation of terms, composition,[31] division,[32] and figures of speech) and the seven material fallacies (applying general rules to irrelevant situations,[33] affirming the consequent,[34] calling for a generalization to apply to all cases, drawing an irrelevant conclusion that fails to address the issue at hand, begging the question,[35] false cause,[36] and the fallacy of

---

28. Molina, *Commentaria*, 32.1.1.

29. This fallacy designates using emphasis to suggest a meaning different from the actual content of a proposition. For instance, Bob, seeking revenge on his coworker Sally, says, "Sally was sober today," thereby falsely suggesting that Sally is usually drunk.

30. This fallacy, which Aristotle termed *amphibology*, occurs when more than one possible meaning can be drawn from a statement or a short discourse. For instance, the statement, "Old people shouldn't be allowed to drive; it's getting too dangerous on the streets," could mean either that old people are in danger from others on the streets or that old people are causing the danger on the streets.

31. This fallacy occurs when one infers that something is true of the whole from the fact that it is true of some part or all parts of the whole. For instance, "The tooth of an elephant isn't heavy; therefore the elephant isn't heavy," commits the fallacy of composition.

32. Conversely to the fallacy of composition, this fallacy arises when one infers that something is true of some part of the whole or all parts of the whole from the fact that it is true of the whole. For instance, "The elephant is heavy; therefore the tooth of the elephant isn't heavy," commits the fallacy of division.

33. This fallacy, which Aristotle termed "the fallacy of accident," occurs in an argument that follows the laws of logic but is unsound by ignoring one or more clear exceptions to a generalization. For instance, the argument "Punching someone in the face is a crime; boxers punch people in the face; therefore boxers are criminals," commits this fallacy by ignoring the many exceptions to the generalization that punching someone in the face is a crime (e.g., prize-fighting, self-defense, police apprehension of suspects, and so forth).

34. For two propositions A and B, this fallacy takes the form "If A, then B; B; therefore A." Just because B is true does nothing to prove that A is true, since A is not necessarily the only sufficient condition for B. For instance, the argument "If Halley is a cat, then Halley is a mammal; Halley is a mammal; therefore Halley is a cat," is fallacious because there are several other ways for Halley to be a mammal than by being a cat.

35. Known in Latin as *petitio principii*, this fallacy occurs when the premises of an argument include the claim that the conclusion is true or directly or indirectly assume that the conclusion is true. For instance, in the argument, "The Bible was written by God; everything God writes is true; the Bible says that God exists; therefore God exists," the premises "The Bible was written by God" and "everything God writes is true" assume what is to be proved (that God exists) and therefore beg the question.

36. This fallacy arises when a cause is incorrectly identified, such as when a correlation between independent variables is taken to indicate that one variable is the cause of the other.

many questions[37]). From books 5 through 7 of the *Ethica*, Molina deduced that true social justice entailed that which is equitable or fair to all parties involved. Regarding justice and the civil law, Molina agreed with Aristotle that "whatever is unfair is lawless, but not everything lawless is unfair" and that "it would seem that to be a good man is not in every case the same thing as to be a good citizen."[38] As Diego Alonso-Lasheras points out, Molina employed his own experience as a law student at Salamanca in expanding upon Aristotle's understanding: "Molina had studied law for a year in Salamanca prior to becoming a Jesuit. He had to honor his previous studies in his development of a doctrine on justice."[39] In particular, Molina appropriated from the Roman legal tradition a conception of justice that required fairness in the distribution of social goods and actively cultivated individual morality. Hence for Molina, justice manifests itself in formulation of good laws, equitable division of social benefits, and cultivation of the virtues necessary for the common good.[40]

During the first and second trimesters of year three (1556–57), Molina read Aristotle's *Physica* (*Physics*) and was influenced by his theory of causation. According to Aristotle, there are four types of cause: material cause, explaining what something is made of; formal cause, explaining the form or pattern an entity follows to become that entity; efficient cause, explaining the actual source of change; and final cause, explaining the intended purpose of change. Regarding efficient cause, Molina subdivided this notion into primary causation, particular (direct) causation, and general (universal or indirect) causation. Molina held that God is the primary cause of everything that occurs; in the words of Alfred Freddoso, God "created the original constituents of the universe *ex nihilo*, and no creature can exist or possess causal power through any interval of time unless God conserves it and its powers in being at every instant in that interval."[41] However, this does not mean that,

---

37. This fallacy occurs when a loaded question is posed, namely, a question containing a hidden assumption that the respondent becomes committed to when the respondent gives any direct answer. For instance, any direct answer to the question "Have you stopped beating your wife?" implies that one has beaten one's wife.

38. Aristotle, *The Nicomachean Ethics*, trans. Roger Crisp, Cambridge Texts in the History of Philosophy (Cambridge: Cambridge University Press, 2000), 5.2; Molina, *De justitia et jure*, 5 vols. (Cologne: Marci-Michaelis Bousquet, 1733), 1.1.4, 10.

39. Diego Alonso-Lasheras, *Luis de Molina's De Iustitia et Iure: Justice as Virtue in an Economic Context*, Studies in the History of Christian Traditions 152 (Leiden: Brill, 2011), 188.

40. Molina, *De justitia*, 1.1.6.

41. Freddoso, "Introduction," 16.

for everything that occurs, God determines it or is morally responsible for it. Molina maintained that God is the particular or direct cause when God does determine something (for which thing he would be morally responsible) by producing an effect by himself, since God's causal power by itself controls the specific nature of the effect.[42] But Molina insisted that creatures possess authentic causal power as well and are therefore particular yet secondary causes. Nonetheless, for creatures to exercise their causal power, God must simultaneously and indirectly cooperate with them to produce the intended effect. When God so cooperates with creatures, God acts as a general cause of the effect, and Molina dubbed God's simultaneous and indirect action his general concurrence (*concursus generalis*).[43] The term *general* indicates that the specific nature of the effect (i.e., good or evil) is in no way attributable to God's causal contribution, although that contribution is necessary in order for any effect to be produced at all. Rather, the goodness or badness of the effect is due solely to the creatures, who are the particular causes of the effect.

To illustrate, Molina observed that the sun causally contributes to human acts of sin by providing heat and light on earth, without which humans could do nothing. Hence the sun is a general or indirect cause of human sin. Obviously, however, the sun is not morally responsible for human sin, for none of its causal input determined the production of sinful actions. Human beings freely choose to channel the sun's causal input toward sinful actions and are therefore solely responsible for them.[44] In exactly the same way, Molina averred, creatures channel the causal input of God's general concurrence toward sinful actions, despite that God absolutely does not will for his general concurrence to be so used. So like the sun, God is a general cause of human sin (and everything else that humans do) but without determining it or being morally responsible for it. As Freddoso nicely puts it, for Molina "God is the paradigmatic indeterministic cause."[45] Closely tied to Molina's understanding of divine causation was his analysis of Aristotle's distinction between potentiality and actuality. Molina contended that for every individual essence, God knows from eternity whether and when each of its potentialities would be actualized, either by itself or by some external agent, under any given

---

42. Molina, *Concordia*, 2.14.13.25.
43. Ibid., 2.14.13.26.1.
44. Ibid., 2.14.13.26.12.
45. Freddoso, "Introduction," 19.

circumstances.[46] Many of these individual essences, if instantiated, would operate in some measure indeterministically, including those that possess libertarian freedom like human and angelic essences and those that display natural randomness or spontaneity like earthquake and tornado essences.[47] Reporting the comments he originally made while studying the *Physica*, years later Molina delineated further instances of natural randomness:

> When commenting on Part I–II, q. 13, a. 2, and on Book IV of Aristotle's *Physics*, we claimed to find contingency, of the sort found in the shattering of a vase full of water, by which the water, if it were frozen and there were no external atmosphere, would rush out to fill the vacuum. For in such a case, if the vase were in all its parts uniform and of entirely equal resistance, then since there would be no more reason it should shatter in this part rather than that part — though it would necessarily have to shatter, lest there be a vacuum — clearly, the fracturing's occurring in a given part will be said to happen by chance or fortune and hence contingently.... The same thing will be true of the snapping of a cord that is very slender and equally resistant in each part, if its ends should be pulled apart in opposite directions with an application of maximal force. Likewise, if a beast were presented with two objects so well suited to and in keeping with its appetite that it was equally attracted to both of them, then there would likewise be no more reason it should be moved in one direction rather than the other by the combined force of the desire, of the objects and of the other attendant circumstances. In all these instances we claimed that effects would emanate from the causes in question, since in the proposed cases it would be ridiculous to assert that the vase and the cord would not break, or that the beast would not move. But since there is no more reason why the fracture should occur at one point in the vase or cord rather than another, or why the motion of the beast should follow the one path rather than the other, we claimed that these effects would occur contingently in such a way that chance would prevail.[48]

---

46. Molina, *Commentaria*, 12.1.2.

47. In view of modern scientific knowledge, examples of individual essences displaying natural randomness or spontaneity comprise essences of quantum vacuums, which if created would indeterministically generate virtual particles, and essences of radioactive isotopes, which if created would indeterministically decay. However, I am not here implying any relation between physical indeterminacy and libertarian human freedom. Personally, I do not feel that physical indeterminacy is a sufficient condition for libertarian freedom.

48. Molina, *Foreknowledge*, 4.13.47.13.

In view of Molina's conceptualism, individual essences do not exist as objects independent of God but exist solely as concepts within the mind of God. God's knowledge of how each potentiality of any individual essence would be actualized under any given circumstances Molina denominated supercomprehension.[49] Accordingly, God possesses epistemic certainty, or certainty of knowledge, regarding states of affairs apart from metaphysical certitude, or certainty of existence.[50] The doctrine of supercomprehension would prove a necessary pillar in Molina's later formulation of middle knowledge.

In the third trimester of year three, Molina turned to Aristotle's *De coelo* (*On the Heavens*) and *De generatione et corruptione* (*On Generation and Corruption*). Chief among Aristotle's cosmological works, *De coelo* supplied Molina with an argument for the existence of God from motion or change. Based on the reduction of potency to act, Molina perceived that if something is moved from one state to another, it must be moved by something already moving. But since an infinite regress is impossible, the thing, upon tracing back the causal chain, must ultimately be moved by an unmoved mover, who is God.[51] On a related note, *De generatione* helped Molina perceive the distinction between contingent being and necessary being. Contingent being can come into existence and pass out of existence, while necessary being simply exists and can neither come into existence nor pass out of existence. In other words, it is logically possible for contingent being not to exist, but it is logically impossible for necessary being not to exist.[52] This distinction enabled Molina to propose a second argument for God's existence based on contingency and necessity. Molina reasoned that since contingent being, by definition, cannot bring itself into existence, there must be a reason why contingent being exists. Hence contingent being must have been brought

---

49. Molina, *Commentaria*, 14.13.18.

50. Freddoso, "Introduction," 52.

51. Molina dismissed the possibility of an infinite regress of past causes with these words: "The generations of things shall not be able to exist from all eternity (Generationes rerum esse non potuerunt ex aeternitate)" (*Commentaria*, 2.3). As Molina acknowledged, his argument is roughly equivalent to Aquinas's first of "five ways (quinque viae)" or proofs for the existence of God (*Summa Theologiae*, 1.2.3).

52. Here Molina's inference may well have gone beyond what Aristotle intended, for Aristotle probably meant simply that necessary being was immune to generation and corruption but not that it was logically indispensable. In modern philosophical terms, Aristotle was likely speaking of factual necessity, which means that given the existence of necessary being, it is impossible for it to come into or pass out of existence.

into existence by necessary being, which Molina identifies as God.[53] The conditional demands that which is absolute.

During all three trimesters of year four (1557–58), Molina investigated the *Metereologica* (*Metereology*), *De anima* (*On the Soul*), and *Metaphysics*.[54] The *Metereologica* was Aristotle's treatise on the earth sciences, and *De anima* treats the types of souls possessed by different types of living things. Historically speaking, the *Metaphysics* is the first major work of philosophy on the study of being or reality and the kinds of things that are real. While reading *De anima*, Molina found that he differed from Aristotle on the concept of soul. For Aristotle posited that the soul was the form or essence of any living thing, not a substance distinct from the body. Thus it is the possession of a soul that makes an organism an organism, and the notion of a body without a soul or a soul in the wrong type of body is a contradiction in terms. As a result, Aristotle proposed that plants, animals, and humans have souls. Plant souls have the capability to take in food, obtain energy from it, grow, adapt to their environment, and reproduce. Such capabilities, averred Aristotle, represented the minimum that must be possessed by any living organism.[55] In addition to these capabilities, animal souls possess the powers of sense perception and self-motion.[56] Human souls possess all these powers as well as reason.[57] By contrast, Molina believed that the soul was a living immaterial substance possessing personhood, self-consciousness, reason, libertarian freedom, intentionality, and the ability to perceive immaterial realities like mathematical objects and objective moral values.[58] This ability could be called spiritual sight, the soul's ability to see abstract objects resident in the mind of God. On Molina's view, only humans, angels, and God have, and are, souls. God and angels are unembodied souls, while humans are embodied souls. As Descartes would assert a century later, Molina held that animals are not souls but are irrational

---

53. Molina, *Commentaria*, 2.3; idem., *Concordia*, 2.14.13.28.3; cf. Aristotle, *De generatione et corruptione*, trans. C. J. F. Williams, Clarendon Aristotle Series (Oxford: Oxford University Press, 1982), 2.8–9. This argument strongly resembles Aquinas's third "way" for God's existence (*Summa Theologiae*, 1.2.3).

54. Lines, "Moral Philosophy," 56.

55. Aristotle, *De anima*, 2.1–4.

56. Ibid., 2.5–6.

57. Ibid., 3.5–7.

58. Molina, *Commentaria*, 2.3; 9.2.2.

brutes identical to their bodies.[59] However, Molina thought, contrary to Descartes, that animals were conscious or sentient beings, but he did not think that consciousness required the existence of the soul but could be generated by the brain alone. While souls indeed possess consciousness, so do living brains, and the combination of souls and brains in the case of humans produces an enriched experience of consciousness. For Molina it is the factors of personhood, self-consciousness, reason, libertarian freedom, intentionality, and "spiritual sight" that are exclusive properties of the soul, not consciousness.[60]

We may here illustrate Molina's position by way of analogy. For human beings, the relationship between soul and brain resembles that between an organist and a partially "player" and partially "manual" organ. Based on the human's genetic makeup and the input of the five senses, this organ performs a range of involuntary acts on its own, some of which cannot be controlled by the organist (heart beating, digestion, and so forth), corresponding to the "player" keyboards. Other keyboards play themselves only at the times the organist does not touch them—thus, to mix metaphors, such keyboards are either on "automatic pilot" or controlled by the organist at any given time. Like a player piano, the main keyboard generates the "score" of music from the human's genetic makeup and the input of the five senses; however, unlike a player piano, the score does not automatically play, but the organist has the libertarian freedom to play the score, to play something entirely different, or not to play anything at all. But animals are entirely "player" organs without any organists or selves; they are not persons. Animals universally lack the freedom to reject the "score" of music generated by their genetic makeup and the input of their five senses, a score that includes sensations, thoughts, desires, purposes, and beliefs. Animals must act in accord with this information. Thus animals are electro-chemical automatons that are largely determined to act in the ways they do by their genetic influences and sensory data.[61]

By the end of May 1558, Molina had earned his master's degree in

---

59. Ibid., 4.2.2; hence Molina consistently refers to animals as "brute animals" (*Foreknowledge*, 14.13.47.7–9). Cf. René Descartes, *Letter to More (5 February 1649)*, in *Descartes' Philosophical Letters*, trans. Anthony Kenny (Oxford: Clarendon, 1970), 243.

60. Molina, *Commentaria*, 19.4.2.

61. Kirk R. MacGregor, *A Molinist-Anabaptist Systematic Theology* (Lanham, MD: University Press of America, 2007), 146.

philosophy from the University of Coimbra, a degree that firstly displayed mastery and engagement with the work of Aristotle. To sum up Aristotle's profound influence on Molina, Molina often used Aristotle's thought as a springboard and driving force for his own philosophical reflections. Using Aristotle's distinction between primary and secondary substances, Molina developed the notion of individual essences and went on to claim that God foreknows every individual essence as an abstract object conceptually grounded in his own mind. From Aristotle's analysis of modal propositions, Molina discerned the role of future contingent propositions in his conception of reality and reasoned that the chronologically prior truth value of a future contingent proposition does nothing causally to determine that truth value. Like a shadow that precedes the object casting it, the truth values of future contingents "foreshadow" the free decisions of the relevant agents who "cast" the aforesaid truth values. So the free decisions of the relevant agents are logically prior to the truth values of future contingents about those agents. Based on Aristotle's demand that only free actions, not coerced or necessary actions, can be praised or blamed, Molina championed the doctrine of libertarian human freedom as opposed to the theological compatibilism of Luther and Calvin. Aristotle provoked Molina's insights about properties and attributes, particularly the distinctions and relationships between essential and relative attributes as well as between permanent and temporary attributes. Synthesizing Aristotelian ethics with his prior legal training, Molina formulated a concept of justice that encompassed the outworking of good laws, the fair dividing of social benefits, and the nurturing of virtues indispensable to the commonweal. Adopting Aristotle's fourfold theory of causation, Molina broke down the idea of efficient causation into primary causation, particular (direct) causation, and general (indirect) causation. Molina declared that God is the primary cause, either direct or indirect, of all that occurs, and that God is exempt from moral responsibility for any event he indirectly causes. Molina termed God's indirect causal input, which may be freely used by creatures for either good or ill, as his general concurrence. Given Aristotle's discussion of potentiality and actuality, Molina surmised that for each individual essence, God timelessly knows how each of its potentialities would be actualized under any given circumstances, which knowledge Molina called supercomprehension. This conclusion is remarkable because many of these essences, at least in part, act indeterministically, such as human essences and various natural phenomena. Finally, Molina used what he deemed as Aristotle's defective understanding of soul as a launching pad for his own definition of soul as a living immaterial substance possessing personhood, self-consciousness, reason, libertarian freedom, intentionality, and the ability to perceive immaterial realities. On this definition, only humans, angels, and God possess souls.

It should be emphasized, as João Madeira has ably demonstrated, that Molina's supervisor Pedro da Fonseca guided Molina to read Aristotle in such a way as to be most profitable for the study of Scholastic theology.[62] This fact is abundantly evident in the distinctly theological nature of the contributions Aristotle made to Molina's thought.

MOLINA AS A CATHOLIC BETWEEN AQUINAS AND THE PROTESTANT REFORMERS

Due to Molina's strong theological interests and high intellectual acumen, Fonseca encouraged Molina to continue his studies at Coimbra by pursuing a doctorate in theology and ordination to the priesthood. Agreeing with his beloved teacher, Molina had independently reached the point, through his studies, where he felt it was his life's vocation to be a priest who served primarily as a professor of theology and philosophy. Hence, from 1558 to 1562, Molina completed a second four-year course of study under Fonseca, leading to ordination in 1561 and the doctoral degree in 1562.[63] Containing both breadth and depth, this academic program furnished Molina with a generalist's knowledge of patristic, medieval, and contemporary theology (including the major works of the Protestant Reformers) and with a specialist's knowledge of the Bible and the theology of Thomas Aquinas. Regarding Aquinas, this program was aimed at producing mastery of Aquinas's two major works, the *Summa Theologiae* and the *Summa contra Gentiles*, and mastery of several of Aquinas's minor works, particularly the *Scriptum super libros Sententiarum* (*Commentary on the Sentences of Peter Lombard*), *Quaestiones disputatae de malo* (*Disputed Questions on Evil*), *Quaestiones disputatae de potentia Dei*

---

62. Madeira, "Pedro da Fonseca's *Isagoge Philosophica*," 2–3.
63. Stegmüller, *Geschichte des Molinismus*, 4*.

(*Disputed Questions on the Power of God*), and *Questiones disputatae de Veritate* (*Disputed Questions on Truth*).[64]

Throughout his studies, Molina perceived tension between the Bible and Aquinas on the meaning of grace. Within a Catholic framework, Molina reached a parallel conclusion to Luther and Calvin in distinguishing grace in the Bible as God's unmerited favor toward sinful persons who deserve no favor but only punishment, which favor is freely given on God's part.[65] Pivotal to Molina's concept of grace as unmerited, freely given favor were three Pauline texts. In Romans 11:5–6, Molina discerned that grace is the opposite of merit based on works and that the people comprising the group of the saved are chosen purely by God's grace: "So too, at the present time there is a remnant chosen by grace. And if by grace, then it cannot be based on works; if it were, grace would no longer be grace."[66] Molina found in Romans 3:23–24 that salvation by grace is the opposite of salvation by human effort since grace is a freely given gift: "For all have sinned and fall short of the glory of God, and all are justified freely by his grace through the redemption that came by Christ Jesus."[67] Molina observed in Ephesians 2:8–9 that humans are totally unable to merit favor with God, such that the only way humans could be regarded as righteous is if God freely provides salvation for them by grace, completely apart from their work: "For it is by grace you have been saved, through faith—and this is not from yourselves, it is the gift of God—not by works, so that no one can boast." Molina here took the antecedent of the pronoun "this" (in the Latin Vulgate, *hoc*) to be the fact or state of affairs that "it is by grace you have been saved, through faith," thus splitting the horns of the later Calvinist-Arminian dilemma as to whether "this" referred to "grace" or "faith."[68]

---

64. Jerónimo Nadal, *Instructiones Conimbricae de Cursu Artium Datae (1561)*, in *Monumenta paedagogica Societatis Iesu*, 5 vols., ed. Ladislaus Lukács (Rome: Institutum Historicum Societatis Iesu, 1965), 2:59.

65. Molina, *Commentaria*, 14.13.7, 10, 12.

66. Molina, *Concordia*, 3.14.13.46.20; 7.23.4/5.1.5.1.

67. Ibid., 3.14.13.46.20, 7.23.4/5.2.3, 20.

68. Molina, *Concordia*, 1.14.13.8.5; 1.14.13.22.4; 7.23.4/5.1.5.2. Molina's exegesis seems to be well supported in both the Latin and the original Greek. For in both languages, the pronoun "this" (*hoc*/ τοῦτο) is neuter and does not agree in gender with either the feminine noun "grace" (*gratia*/χάριτι) or the feminine noun "faith" (*fidem*; πίστεως). Hence, as Andrew T. Lincoln confirms, "τοῦτο is probably best taken, therefore, as referring to the preceding clause as a whole, and thus to the whole process of salvation it describes" (*Ephesians*, Word Biblical Commentary 42 [Dallas: Word, 1990], 112).

Molina also concurred with Luther and Calvin in understanding biblical grace as God's unmerited assistance toward humans in procuring their regeneration and sanctification.[69] That grace helps people to become regenerate Molina detected in Acts 18:27, which states that when Apollos arrived at Achaia, "he was a great help to those who by grace had believed." So by grace the Achaian Christians believed and were accordingly regenerated.[70] The aid of grace in the process of sanctification was discerned by Molina in Acts 4:33–35, where grace enabled the earliest community of Jesus' followers to periodically sell their property to meet the needs of the poor in their midst: "And God's grace was so powerfully at work in them all that there were no needy persons among them. For from time to time those who owned land or houses sold them, brought the money from the sales and put it at the apostles' feet, and it was distributed to anyone who had need."[71] Molina also saw the divine assistance of grace in increasingly causing Paul to conform to the image of Jesus through his missions work: "But by the grace of God I am what I am, and his grace to me was not without effect. No, I worked harder than all of them—yet not I, but the grace of God that was with me" (1 Cor. 15:10).[72] In summary, Molina interpreted grace as God's undeserved favor toward sinners and the free and unmerited help that God gives sinners to become adopted children of God who are continually made more liberated from sin and more like Christ in our actual lives.[73]

On the other hand, Molina found in Aquinas a conception of grace as a kind of divine substance on which the soul feeds. In discussing the Old

69. Molina, *Concordia*, 1.14.13.8.5; 1.14.13.22.4; 7.23.4/5.4.2; cf. Robert Koester, "Grace as Taught by Augustine and Luther," *Lutheran Synod Quarterly* 35/36 (1995): 84; Cornelis P. Venema, *Accepted and Renewed in Christ: The Twofold Grace of God and the Interpretation of Calvin's Theology* (Göttingen: Vandenhoeck & Ruprecht, 2007), 95–98.

70. Molina, *Commentaria*, 14.13.7, 42.

71. Ibid., 14.13.3.4.

72. Ibid., 14.13.39.

73. Hence Craig unwittingly draws a false dichotomy when he claims, "As a Catholic Counter-Reformer, Molina did not profit from Luther's insight into the nature of grace as the unmerited favor of God, but instead thought of grace as a sort of divine assistance or power given to men to enable them to perform certain acts, which they in their corrupted natural state could not do, that lead in turn to their meriting salvation" (William Lane Craig, *The Problem of Divine Foreknowledge and Future Contingents from Aristotle to Suarez*, Studies in Intellectual History 7 [Leiden: Brill, 1988], 204–5). Molina thought of grace as both the unmerited favor of God and a divine assistance or power that enabled persons to perform acts they could not naturally perform; Molina simply did not see these two concepts as opposed to each other but thought of them as complementary. Moreover, Molina denied that persons can merit salvation.

Testament sacrifices, Aquinas stated that "oil betokens the grace of Christ."[74] Aquinas went on to identify grace as the hidden manna described in the book of Revelation: "Thus anyone may know he has grace, when he is conscious of delighting in God, and of despising worldly things, and inasmuch as a man is not conscious of any mortal sin. And thus it is written (Apoc. 2:17): 'To him that overcometh I will give the hidden manna ... which no man knoweth, but he that receiveth it.' "[75] In line with the idea of grace as substance, Aquinas examined "when God infuses grace into a soul," how "God guards man immediately by infusing into him grace," the "magnitude of grace" a soul possesses, and the "supernatural endowment of grace."[76] According to Aquinas, grace is a type of physical stuff: "For grace by its physical reality is in the soul."[77] The ceremonies of the Old Testament, such as circumcision, proved ultimately ineffective "from the fact that they do not contain grace within themselves," unlike the sacraments of the New Testament: "Consequently it was becoming that the grace [which] flows from the incarnate Word should be given to us by means of certain external sensible objects."[78] So Aquinas stated succinctly, "Grace resides instrumentally in the sacraments of the New Law."[79] Employing the language of instillation of a substance, Aquinas declared that the new covenant "derives its pre-eminence from the spiritual grace instilled into our hearts."[80] For Aquinas the physical reality that is grace causes "a certain transmutation of the human soul," such that "from this inward grace, whereby the flesh is subjected to the Spirit, certain external works should ensue."[81] To give a modern analogy, grace is like spiritual gasoline that empowers the engine of the soul to do good works. Hence Aquinas stated, "The right use of grace is by means of works of charity," and claimed that without the soul's food of grace it cannot perform actions worthy of eternal life: "Hence it is that no created nature is a sufficient principle of an act meritorious of eternal life, unless there is added a supernatural gift,

74. Aquinas, *Summa Theologiae*, 2.1.102.3; cf. Molina, *Commentaria*, 43.3.
75. Aquinas, *Summa Theologiae*, 2.1.112.5; cf. Molina, *Commentaria*, 112.1.
76. Aquinas, *Summa Theologiae*, 2.1.112.2, 4; 2.1.95.1; 2.1.113.1; cf. Molina, *Commentaria*, 112.1, 113.1. Similarly, Aquinas asserted that "we could not conceive the remission of guilt, without the infusion of grace" (*Summa Theologiae*, 2.1.113.2).
77. Aquinas, *Summa Theologiae*, 2.1.112.5; cf. Molina, *Commentaria*, 112.1.
78. Aquinas, *Summa Theologiae*, 2.1.103.2; 2.1.108.1; cf. Molina, *Commentaria*, 43.3.
79. Aquinas, *Summa Theologiae*, 1.43.6; cf. Molina, *Commentaria*, 43.3.
80. Aquinas, *Summa Theologiae*, 2.1.107.1; cf. Molina, *Commentaria*, 107.1.
81. Aquinas, *Summa Theologiae*, 2.1.113.3; 2.1.108.1; cf. Molina, *Commentaria*, 113.1.

which we call grace."[82] The soul, on Aquinas's view, cannot survive without the food of grace: "things pertaining to the health of the soul are ordained to grace."[83] Like gasoline put into a car, God gives grace to people because he foreknows that they will make good use of it: "God gives grace to a person, and pre-ordains that He will give it, because He knows beforehand that He will make good use of that grace, as if a king were to give a horse to a soldier because he knows he will make good use of it.... He pre-ordained to give grace to merit glory."[84]

Given the teaching of Scripture, Molina took issue with this statement on two fronts. First, Molina denied that God gives grace only to those people whom he foreknows will put it to good use. Rather, Molina insisted, in view of 1 Timothy 2:4 ("[God our Savior] wants all people to be saved and to come to a knowledge of the truth") and Ezekiel 18:23 ("Do I take any pleasure in the death of the wicked? declares the Sovereign LORD. Rather, am I not pleased when they turn from their ways and live?"), that God gives sufficient grace for salvation to every person that he creates, regardless of how he foreknows they will respond to it. Thus Molina declared concerning divine grace: "God wills for all humans to be saved. Of the same truth God even affirms under oath ... that he does not will the death of the wicked but wills that the wicked should be converted and live. And all humans are under the same state and without exception are invited by God to eternal life. In addition, Christ is given for the redemption of all so that all, if such does not stand opposed by the persons themselves, arrive at eternal life."[85] Likewise, Molina commented on 2 Peter 3:9 ("[The Lord] is patient with you, not wanting anyone to perish, but everyone to come to repentance") that God's grace "refers back to the only end, that in which all humans are directed toward beatitude by the providence of God."[86] Second, Molina rejected as antithetical to the very

---

82. Aquinas, *Summa Theologiae*, 2.1.108.2; 2.1.114.2; cf. Molina, *Commentaria*, 108.1.

83. Aquinas, *Summa Theologiae*, 2.1.106.3; cf. Molina, *Commentaria*, 43.3.

84. Aquinas, *Summa Theologiae*, 1.23.5; cf. Molina, *Commentaria*, 23.4/5.1.4.

85. "Deum velle omnes homines salvos fieri. De eodem etiam statu sub iureiurando affirmat.... Deus non esse voluntatis suae mortem impii, sed ut convertatur et vivat. Atque in eodem statu omnes sine exceptione invitantur a Deo ad vitam aeternam. Christus praeterea omnibus in redemptorem datus est ut omnes, si per ipsos non staret, in vitam aeternat pervenirent" (Molina, *Concordia*, 7.23.4/5.1.8.8); cf. Molina, *Commentaria*, 12.6.4.

86. "In finem respicit tantum, unde per Dei providentiam omnes homines, ad beatitudinem ordinantur" (Molina, *Commentaria*, 22.1.2); cf. Molina, *Concordia*, 6.22.1.2.10; 7.23.4/5.1.6.22; 7.23.4/5.1.8.8.

concept of grace that people could use grace to merit salvation, as Scripture diametrically opposes grace and merit. If something is by grace, then it, by definition, is not by merit. Thus Molina deemed self-contradictory Aquinas's assertion that "by the gift of grace men can merit glory in such a degree as to be equal to the angels, in each of the angelic grades,"[87] for no one can merit anything by the unmerited favor and assistance of God, which is grace.[88]

In his opposition to Aquinas's teaching that God gives sufficient grace for salvation to those whom he foreknows will utilize it to merit glory, Molina concurred with Luther and Calvin.[89] But on a deeper level, Molina dissented from Luther and Calvin, whom he felt committed *mutatis mutandis*, the same error as Aquinas. For like Aquinas, Luther and Calvin maintained that grace was given discriminately to some persons, not indiscriminately to all persons. Hence Luther contrasted the recipients and nonrecipients of grace: "According to His own counsel, [God] ordains such persons as He wills to receive and partake of the mercy preached and offered.... ungodly persons, who, being born in ungodliness, and staying so, and being damned ... are compelled by natural necessity to sin and perish."[90] Calvin expressed the point in even more straightforward terms: "We shall never be clearly persuaded, as we ought to be, that our salvation flows from the wellspring of God's free mercy until we come to know his eternal election, which illumines God's grace by this contrast: that he does not indiscriminately adopt all into the hope of salvation but gives to some what he denies to others."[91] On Molina's assessment, the only difference between Aquinas and Luther/Calvin consisted in the reason why God bestows sufficient grace only on some and not on all. For Aquinas it is because God foreknows that only some will utilize grace well. For Luther and Calvin it is because of God's inscrutable or hidden will, without respect to his foreknowledge of the way anyone would use grace. Hence Luther stated that God directly accomplishes the death of persons on whom he has chosen not to bestow grace: "But God hidden in Majesty neither deplores nor takes away death, but works life, and death, and all in all.... He wills [the death of

---

87. Aquinas, *Summa Theologiae*, 2.1.108.8.
88. Molina, *Commentaria*, 22.1.2.
89. Paul Althaus, *The Theology of Martin Luther*, trans. Robert C. Schultz (Minneapolis: Fortress, 1966), 274–75; Charles Partee, *The Theology of John Calvin* (Louisville: Westminster John Knox, 2008), 250–52.
90. Luther, *Bondage of the Will*, 169, 314.
91. Calvin, *Institutes*, 3.21.1.

a sinner] by his inscrutable will."[92] Calvin maintained that persons on whom God has chosen to bestow grace receive it without regard to foreseen works and in order that they would be holy, which obviates the possibility that God bestowed grace on them based on their foreseen holiness:

> "He called us," Paul says, "with a holy calling, not according to our works, but according to his own purpose, and the grace that was given to us by Christ before time began." [II Tim. 1:9].... Say: "Since he foresaw that we would be holy, he chose us," and you will invert Paul's order. Therefore you can safely infer the following: if he chose us that we should be holy, he did not choose us because he foresaw that we would be so.... The fact that they were elected "to be holy" [Eph. 1:4b] plainly refutes the error that derives election from foreknowledge.[93]

Molina judged that this differential treatment of people in receiving grace both contradicted God's universal salvific will plainly attested in Scripture and disingenuously tried to explain it away using theological double-talk about how God's revealed will differed from God's hidden will.[94] For Molina this was tantamount to saying that God lied in what he revealed to humanity, which contradicted the essential truthfulness of God.[95] Moreover, Molina averred that the notion of God's hidden will was predicated on a misapplication of the attribute of God's incomprehensibility. Molina disavowed any definition of incomprehensibility that posited that humans can never really know what God is like. Rather, Molina defined incomprehensibility as meaning that humans, as finite beings, can never fully apprehend the infinite set of propositional truths about God but can only apprehend a finite subset of those propositional truths.[96] Included in that finite subset are truths revealed in Scripture and the natural order plus truths that humans can discover through philosophical and theological investigation. Moreover, the finite subset of propositional truths that humans do apprehend about God must be logically consistent with the full infinite range of propositional

---

92. Luther, *Bondage of the Will*, 170.

93. Calvin, *Institutes*, 3.22.3, 2.

94. Molina, *Commentaria*, 14.13.9.

95. Ibid., 16.1.

96. Hence Molina (*Commentaria*, 12.5.1) affirmed that those who respond affirmatively to God's grace will always face the exhilarating project, in both time and eternity, of continuing to learn increasingly more objective truths about God, never being able to exhaust the limitless set of such truths.

truths about God; one divine truth cannot contradict another divine truth. So Molina emphasized that there cannot be anything in what humans do not know about God that stands opposed to what humans do know about God, as clearly would be the case if according to God's revealed will God wanted all people to be saved but if according to God's hidden will God ultimately wanted some people to be damned.[97]

On grace, Molina thus found himself on middle ground, agreeing with Luther and Calvin over against Aquinas on the character of grace as unmerited divine favor given unconditionally but disagreeing with Luther, Calvin, and Aquinas on the limitedness of grace's recipients. During his doctoral studies, Molina wrote personal notes on the *Summa Theologiae* in dialogue with the developing Protestant understanding of grace. In these notes, Molina expressed his own Catholic but non-Thomistic doctrine of grace and worked out a Catholic doctrine of justification that lay between Aquinas on the one hand and Luther and Calvin on the other hand. These notes later served in 1570 as the basis of a major commentary on the *Summa Theologiae*, which Molina completed in 1573. Regarding justification, Molina argued that justification was the act of God whereby persons who have committed their lives to God and surrendered their possessions and desires to his will are declared to be in the right before God and regenerated by God.[98] For Molina regeneration is a necessary component of justification that cannot be separated from it into a separate event, as Luther and Calvin had done.

Recall from chapter 1 that personal commitment and surrender to God constituted Molina's definition of biblical faith. Hence Molina affirmed in conversation with Paul's statements in Romans, "With the heart, he says, that is to say, the will, we believe unto justification."[99] So for Molina people are indeed justified by faith alone, once faith is properly construed as a free choice of personal commitment and surrender. However, Molina insisted that faith is not a work by which humans merit justification; rather, it is simply the means of receiving justification: "From grace humans are justified by faith, because faith is the foundational receptor of human salvation, the root of all justification, without which it is impossible to please God. But it is not

---

97. Molina, *Commentaria*, 19.6.2.
98. Ibid., 14.13.44.
99. "Corde, inquit, id est, voluntate, creditur ad iustitiam" (Molina, *Commentaria*, 1.6).

the case that any of those things which precede justification, whether faith or works, merit the grace of justification itself, because if it is a grace, it is no more of works. Otherwise grace, as the Apostle [Paul] says ... is not grace."[100] Molina found damnable the notion, which he took to be the position of many of Luther's followers (though not Luther himself), that people are justified by faith alone when faith is taken simply to mean intellectual belief in certain truths about God. Thus Molina wrote, "We reject and condemn the Lutheran errors as deadly illusions, which claim that faith alone justifies without explaining the nature of justifying faith in Scripture."[101]

In addition to declaring his committed followers to be in the right before him, God regenerates his followers via justification. According to Molina, here the third person of the Trinity—the Holy Spirit—performs a beneficial operation directly on the soul of each believer. This operation strips the power away from the soul's desire to live ultimately for self and greatly empowers the soul's desire to live ultimately for God and others. Consequently, followers of Jesus are supernaturally transformed into persons who ultimately desire to carry out the will of God and display love to others, a way of life that constitutes their new modus operandi. In Molina's words, "having been remade wonderfully according to their reformation," such persons will "display a noble character and the performance of virtues ... so as to appear like him [Christ]."[102] Molina thus held that, in justification, persons are ontologically translated from being merely children of Adam into adopted as children of God: "Justification ... is the translation from the state in which humans are born first as the children of Adam into a state of grace and adoption as children of God through the Second Adam, Jesus Christ our Savior."[103]

Molina's doctrine of justification is similar to Aquinas's doctrine in

---

100. "Iustificari hominem per fidem et gratis: quia fides est humane salutis putium fundamentum, et radix omnis iustificationis, sine qu impossible est placere Deo, et ad filiorum eius consortium peruenire. Gratis vero, quia nihil eorum, que iustificatione praecedunt, siue fides, siue opera, ipsam iustificationis gratiam promerentur: quia si gratia est, iam non est ex operibus: alioquin gratia, ut ibidem Apostolus ait, iam no est gratia" (Molina, *Commentaria*, 14.13.44).

101. "Rejecere ac damnare pestiferum illu Lutheranorum errorum, quo afferebat solam fidem iustificare simule explanare, in quo sensu iustificatio interdu in Scripturis factis fideitribuat" (Molina, *Commentaria*, 14.13.44).

102. "Mirabilius in secundo reformanit ... nobilitate morum executionem virtutum ... ut quando apparuerit qualis sit" (Molina, *Commentaria*, 62.3).

103. "Iustificationem.... Est translatio ab eo statu, in quo homo nascitur filius primi Adae, in statum gratiae & adoptionis filiorum Dei per Secudem Adam Iesum Christum Salvatorem nostrum" (Molina, *Commentaria*, 14.13.44); cf. Molina, *Concordia*, 7.23.4/5.1.5.2; 1.14.13.15.14; 7.23.4/5.1.6.15.

that both predicate an individual's justification on that individual's freely responding to God's prevenient grace with a biblical faith that expresses itself through love (Gal. 5:6). As Aquinas remarked:

> No one comes to the Father by justifying grace without a movement of the free will.... Hence for the justification of the ungodly a movement of the mind is required, by which it is turned to God. Now the first turning to God is by faith.... Hence a movement of faith is required for the justification of the ungodly.... The movement of faith is not perfect unless it is quickened by charity.... in the justification of the ungodly [is] the movement of the free will towards God, which is an act of faith quickened by charity.[104]

However, Molina's doctrine of justification is different from Aquinas's doctrine in that Molina considered justification as a definitive, once-for-all transformative event occurring at the outset of an individual's journey of discipleship that causes the individual's soul to thereafter generate the desires necessary for following Christ. Even though the individual has not done good works yet, given the individual's transformed nature it is logically necessary that the individual will perform good works. By contrast, Aquinas considered justification as a lifelong process in which the sinner, through the performance of good works, is gradually transformed into a saint.[105] In this way, Molina differentiated justification from sanctification, while Aquinas regarded the two concepts as synonymous. To show where Molina's position falls on the Catholic spectrum, his doctrine of justification is, to all appearances, identical to that of contemporary Catholic theologian Peter Kreeft. Molina would have concurred with the entirety of Kreeft's statement that "a. we are neither justified (forgiven) nor sanctified (made holy) by intellectual faith alone (belief); b. we *are* justified by will-faith, or heart-faith alone; c. but this faith will necessarily produce good works; d. and we are not sanctified by faith alone, in either sense, but only by faith plus good works."[106]

Molina's doctrine of justification is similar to the doctrine of Luther and Calvin in that justification is, in part, a declarative act of God that the sinner

---

104. Aquinas, *Summa Theologiae*, 2.1.113.3–4; 3.85.6.
105. Ibid., 2.1.113.1; Molina, *Commentaria*, 14.13.44.
106. Peter J. Kreeft, *Catholic Christianity* (San Francisco: Ignatius, 2001), 25–26.

is in the right before God.[107] Resembling Luther and Calvin in this respect, Molina held that the basis of this divine declaration is God's infusion of the perfect righteousness of Christ into the sinner. This infusion occurs in addition to and simultaneously with the sinner's regeneration. While not regarding grace as a substance, Molina did regard Christ's perfect righteousness as a spiritual substance, as evident by his consistent language of Christ's righteousness being "infused" or "poured into" (*infundere*) the soul of the person who has placed faith in Jesus.[108] This spiritual substance is made up of the three theological virtues—faith, hope, and love—the attributes which in perfect measure constituted Christ's righteousness. Hence, Christ's "supernatural believing, hoping, and loving ... these theological virtues are dispensed by justification, which are infused by God."[109] Though functionally equivalent, Molina here differed from the view of Luther and Calvin in that the latter did not regard Christ's righteousness as a spiritual substance but as merit, or the moral value of Christ's actions. Hence Luther and Calvin maintained that Christ imputes (*imputare*) his righteousness to the believing sinner such that the person legally possesses the merits of Christ's perfect obedience, not that a spiritual substance has been poured into the person's soul.[110] But in either case, whether by virtue of possessing a Christ-generated holy spiritual substance in the soul or possessing Christ's merit, God declares the sinner righteous. Moreover, God justly forgives the sins of the believer. Hence God, for Molina, Luther, and Calvin alike, is just in declaring the sinner to be in the right before him and the justifier of the one who has biblical faith in Christ.[111]

Unlike Luther and Calvin, however, Molina held that the sinner's placing faith in Christ to obtain justification is a free decision on the sinner's part, such that the sinner could have done otherwise. Hence Molina stressed that "the consent of our will to God exciting, enticing, and calling by means of his

---

107. It would be incorrect to think of Molina's understanding of justification as forensic, since Molina held regeneration to be a necessary component of justification. The ethical transformation that justification accomplishes via regeneration sharply distinguishes Molina's doctrine from the doctrines of Luther and Calvin, in which justification is purely a legal declaration.

108. Molina, *Commentaria*, 14.13.38, 44.

109. "Supernaturales credendi, sperandi, diligendi ... ad iustificationem.... Theologalium virturem disponunt, illique a Deo infunduntu" (Molina, *Commentaria*, 14.13.44).

110. Althaus, *Theology of Martin Luther*, 227; Partee, *Theology of John Calvin*, 227.

111. Molina, *Concordia*, 3.14.13.46.18; Martin Luther, *Commentary on Romans*, trans. J. Theodore Mueller (Grand Rapids: Kregel, 1976), 79; Calvin, *Institutes*, 3.11.3.

prevenient grace" is not coerced but "is nothing other than the influx of our free will, as well as the cooperation with the help of grace in this same supernatural act," where this consent and cooperation with prevenient grace "are the dispositions for justification."[112] By contrast, Luther made the claim that because God determines his foreknowledge by the force of his will,[113] everything humans do, including putting faith in Christ, is done necessarily and not by their own free will. As Luther delineated concerning God: "If He wills what He foreknows, His will is eternal and changeless, because His nature is so. From which it follows, by resistless logic, that all we do, however it may appear to us to be done mutably and contingently, is in reality done necessarily and immutably in respect of God's will ... then, on reason's own testimony, there can be no 'free-will' in man.... knowing that salvation does not depend on 'free-will.'"[114] Moreover, Calvin averred that God gives the elect irresistible grace, which logically necessitates that they place faith in Christ:

> The Lord corrects our evil will, or rather extinguishes it.... He substitutes for it a good one for himself.... God's activity does not produce a possibility that we can exhaust, but an actuality to which we cannot add.... He does not move the will in such a manner ... that it is afterward in our choice either to obey or resist the motion—but by disposing it efficaciously. Therefore one must deny that oft-repeated statement of Chrysostom: "Whom he draws he draws willing." ... For the apostle [Paul] does not teach that the grace of a good will is bestowed upon us if we accept it, but that He wills to work in us. This means nothing else than that the Lord by his Spirit directs, bends, and governs our heart and reigns in it as his own possession. Indeed, he does not promise through Ezekiel that he will give a new Spirit to his elect only in order that they may be able to walk according to his precepts, but also that they may actually so walk [Ezek. 11:19–20; 36:27]. Now can Christ's saying ("Every one who has heard ... from the Father comes to me" [John 6:45; cf. Vg.]) be understood in any other way than that the grace of God is efficacious of itself.[115]

---

112. "Consensum arbitrii nostri Deo excitanti, allicienti, ac vocanti per auxilium gratiae praeuenientis non esse aliud, quam liberum nostri arbitrii influxum, et cooperatione cum eodem gratiae auxilio ad supernaturales actus ... qui dispositiones sunt ad iustificationem" (Molina, *Commentaria*, 14.13.38).

113. As we will see in chapter 3, Molina would agree with this sentiment in one sense but disagree with it in another sense.

114. Luther, *Bondage of the Will*, 80, 318, 313.

115. Calvin, *Institutes*, 2.3.7, 10.

While Molina would disagree with these conclusions of Luther and Calvin, he did concur with one aspect of Calvin's reasoning. Molina agreed that the impact of original sin upon humanity was so great that it incapacitated their mental faculty to choose freely to do spiritual good, including positively responding to Christ's offer of salvation.[116] As a result, Molina deduced, along with Calvin, that humans left to their own devices could not freely choose salvation. But *contra* Calvin, Molina believed that God's sufficient grace for salvation given to all humans by the Holy Spirit — namely, God's prevenient grace — supernaturally restored their mental faculty to choose spiritual good. Hence Molina's doctrine of justification maintained that while any human being could freely embrace Christ, this was only possible through the grace of God, without which no one could embrace Christ.[117]

To sum up Molina's Catholic but non-Thomistic doctrines of grace and justification, which he developed during his doctoral studies, we observe that fallen humans, apart from God's universally given prevenient grace, would have possessed the theological version of compatibilist free will; but in fact, God does universally give prevenient grace, thereby establishing libertarian free will. In other words, apart from God's unmerited supernatural assistance, fallen creatures would only have the ability to choose between good and evil in matters below, or in physical matters that we humans typically regard as good (e.g., saving someone's life) and evil (e.g., committing murder). But they would not have the ability to choose anything spiritually good, namely, to perform any act with the pure, altruistic motives requisite to making the act worthwhile in God's sight. Their range of spiritual options would be limited to choosing between some form of spiritual evil (lying on a spectrum between physically good deeds performed for selfish motives and physically evil deeds performed for selfish motives) or doing nothing spiritual at all. But because of the universality of God's grace, Molina was able to retain his belief in libertarian human freedom. So for Molina, his belief in libertarian human freedom is logically dependent on his doctrine of grace. Through that grace, all humans have the ability to commit their lives to God and thereby receive once and for all time justification, a gift of God including right standing

---

116. Molina, *Commentaria*, 14.13.6, 38.
117. Accordingly, Molina asserted that, in and of itself, human "free will is not sufficient without grace (liberum arbitrium … non sufficere sine gratia)" (*Commentaria*, 14.13.3.4).

before him, regeneration, forgiveness of sins, and the infusion of Christ's righteousness composed of his faith, his hope, and his love.[118]

MOLINA AS PROFESSOR OF PHILOSOPHY AND THEOLOGY

In 1562 Molina earned his doctorate of theology at the University of Coimbra, having already been ordained as a Jesuit priest a year earlier.[119] On the recommendation of his doctoral father Fonseca, Molina was hired as a professor of philosophy and theology at Coimbra in 1563, at which post he served until 1567. During this time, Molina interacted heavily with the final edition of Calvin's *Institutes of the Christian Religion* (1559), particularly with book 3, chapters 21 through 25.[120] These chapters present Calvin's doctrine of double predestination, namely, of the elect to salvation and of the reprobate to damnation. While Molina disagreed with Calvin that God's foreknowledge played no role at all in his making a choice of who is saved and who is damned, Molina came to concur with the central point in Calvin's exegesis of Romans 9. For Molina as for Calvin, Romans 9 revealed God's sovereign predestination of each individual that he creates to salvation or damnation.[121] Using the word *election* to refer to God's sovereign choice and opposing the term *predestination* to *reprobation*, Molina concluded, "Therefore a double election is to be found in God.... Predestination is that whereby certain persons obtain eternal life and are destined from eternity by God to the same, which is well known from Sacred Scripture.... Reprobation is the contrary decision, to exclude and not in any way ... to make someone worthy to be admitted."[122] We shall return to this issue in chapter 5.

With the denouement of the Council of Trent in 1563, Molina eagerly took

---

118. Molina's doctrine of infusion cannot be equated with the Reformed doctrine of imputation. Infusion means that a spiritual substance has been poured into a believer's soul, while imputation means that the believer is given legal possession of Christ's merit.

119. Frank Bartholomew Costello, *The Political Philosophy of Luis de Molina, S.J. (1535–1600)* (Spokane: Gonzaga University Press, 1974), 6–7.

120. Stegmüller, *Geschichte des Molinismus*, 436–40.

121. Molina, *Commentaria*, 23.4/5.1.11; 23.4/5.3; 14.13.10.

122. "Duplex ergo electio est in Deo meditanda.... Praedestinatione esse, qua ij, qui vitam aeternam consequentur ad id ipsum ex aeternitate a Deo sunt destinati, ex sacris Scripturis notissimu est.... Reprobatio approbationi opponitur, non quocunque modo ... exclusione illius ... quasi digna admittitur" (Molina, *Commentaria*, 23.1/2.1; 23.3).

note of the numerous reforms it proposed for the Roman Catholic Church. He was quite gratified with the ethical and educational reforms on which the Council embarked, all of which he henceforth championed in his writings and in the classroom. Molina believed that the Council effectively remedied the main ethical abuses that triggered the Protestant Reformation.[123] Hence Molina praised the Council's proscription of the sale of indulgences and of simony, or the buying and selling of ecclesiastical offices. He extolled the Council for prohibiting bishops and priests from holding absentee benefices, or positions at churches where they would not work but from which they would draw a salary, and from holding more than one benefice, or church position, at a time. Any clergy currently holding more than one benefice was required to resign all but one of them. Molina acclaimed the Council for its enforcement of biblical morality among the clergy, from parish priests to pope, by implementing a system for defrocking them for the crimes of concubinage, solicitation in the confessional, bribery, misappropriation of church funds, violation of civil law, teaching false doctrine, refusing to preach from the Scriptures, dueling, and perpetuating popular superstition concerning the magical power of images.[124] As the Council mandated, "Privileges will no longer avail anyone for an impure and wicked life or for evil and pernicious teaching; no crime will go unpunished."[125]

Due to Molina's passion for improving the pastoral care received by the laity, Molina applauded the Council's mandate of formal theological education for priestly ordination and its institution of several new seminaries for the training of candidates to the priesthood. Indeed the Council made financial provisions that every cathedral and metropolitan church was to have near it a seminary for preparing young men for the clergy. It also drew up the *Catechism of the Council of Trent* to ensure the proper theological and homiletical instruction of parish priests and thereby eliminate the previously common situation of illiterate, untrained clergy who could not preach the Word of God.[126] The Council's emphasis that priests preach the Word of God, on pain of excommunication, was heartily welcomed by Molina.

123. Franco, *Imagem*, 472.

124. Molina, *Commentaria*, 14.13.15.

125. *The Canons and Decrees of the Council of Trent*, trans. H. J. Schroeder (Rockford, IL: TAN Books and Publishers, 1978), 262.

126. Kenneth Scott Latourette, *A History of Christianity*, rev. ed., 2 vols. (New York: Harper & Row, 1975), 2:872.

On theological grounds, Molina found the proclamations of the Council a mixed bag. Molina vigorously agreed with the Council's declaration of libertarian human freedom. Considering it solidly rooted in the Bible, this constituted the primary teaching Molina was outraged to see either overtly denied (Luther and Calvin) or implicitly deemphasized (Melanchthon and Bucer) by the Protestant Reformers. Exceptionally thankful for the Council's reclamation of this doctrine, Molina would go on to list in support no less than twenty biblical passages that he judged to affirm libertarian human freedom after the fall. Hence Molina appealed to Genesis 4:6–7, where God lays out before Cain the choice of spiritual good (that which will be accepted by God) and spiritual evil: "Then the LORD said to Cain, 'Why are you angry? Why is your face downcast? If you do what is right, will you not be accepted? But if you do not do what is right, sin is crouching at your door; it desires to have you, but you must rule over it."[127] Moreover, Molina cited Ezekiel 18:30–32 as definitive proof that every human being has the freedom to turn from sin and give his or her life to God, at which point God will justify the person and give the person a new heart and a new spirit in regeneration. Thus God pleaded with the Israelites to avoid his judgment and receive justification and regeneration: "Therefore, you Israelites, I will judge each of you according to your own ways, declares the Sovereign LORD. Repent! Turn away from all your offenses; then sin will not be your downfall. Rid yourselves of all the offenses you have committed, and get a new heart and a new spirit. Why will you die, people of Israel? For I take no pleasure in the death of anyone, declares the Sovereign LORD. Repent and live!"[128] Notwithstanding the Council's strong affirmation of libertarian freedom, Molina was discouraged by the Council's endorsement of Aquinas's doctrine of grace. He felt that this decision perpetuated a substantive understanding of grace as a balm for the soul. Moreover, Molina agreed with the Council's statement on justification in one sense but disagreed with it in another sense. The Council declared that persons are saved by grace alone through faith and works. On the one hand, Molina agreed that good works were a logically

---

127. Molina, *Concordia*, 1.14.13.23.2.1.

128. Ibid., 1.14.13.23.2.7. The other Scriptures Molina quoted to substantiate libertarian human freedom included Deuteronomy 30:11–19; Joshua 24:13–15; Psalm 119:108–9; Proverbs 1:24–33; Isaiah 5:4; Jeremiah 8:3–5; 26:2–3; Ezekiel 18:21–22; Zechariah 1:2–4; Matthew 19:17; 23:37; Mark 13:34; John 1:12; Acts 5:4; 1 Corinthians 7:37; 1 Timothy 2:4; Revelation 2:21; 3:18–20.

necessary condition to salvation, such that it is impossible for anyone to possess salvation without good works. On the other hand, Molina denied that works were a causally necessary condition to salvation, such that works are not the means by which salvation is achieved.[129]

In 1568 Molina and Fonseca heeded the call of their Jesuit superiors to relocate to the new University of Évora, founded in 1559 by Cardinal Infante Dom Henrique (the future King Henry of Portugal) and Pope Paul IV and bequeathed to the Society of Jesus.[130] Unlike his position as a relatively unknown professor within a large department who fell into a long historical line of faculty members at the already established University of Coimbra, Molina found himself instantly thrust into the spotlight as Évora's star professor of theology and philosophy and head of both departments. It was at Évora that, over the next two decades, Molina would make a name for himself as one of the greatest philosophical theologians in all Europe.[131] Moreover, Molina would construct such a fine theology faculty at Évora that, by the late 1580s, the department rivaled that at Coimbra as the standard bearer of religious education on the Iberian Peninsula.[132] Between 1570 and 1573, Molina collated his notes placing Aquinas in conversation with Luther and Calvin and formulating his own, strikingly modern-seeming Catholic views of grace and justification, which stood between Trent and Protestantism. Molina thus proved a forerunner to post–Vatican II Catholic doctrines of grace and justification. To his notes he added an abundance of new material interacting with the entire First Part of Aquinas's *Summa Theologiae*. Molina's effort came to fruition in 1573 as an ingenious commentary on the *Summa Theologiae*, which was less a commentary than a correction and reinterpretation of Aquinas's doctrines of grace and justification.[133] While employing Aquinas's Scholastic terms, the meanings Molina imparted to these terms

---

129. Molina, *Commentaria*, 1.3.3; 14.13.43.

130. Feingold, ed., *History of Universities*, 57–58, 78.

131. As Notker Hammerstein muses, "In Luís de Molina, Évora had a teacher with a fame and influence reaching far beyond Portugal" ("Relations with Authority," in *A History of the University in Europe, Volume II: Universities in Early Modern Europe (1500–1800)*, ed. Hilde de Ridder-Symeons, gen. ed. Walter Rüegg [Cambridge: Cambridge University Press, 1996], 133).

132. Jorge Araûjo, "Luís de Molina regressa a Évora. Alocução de abertura das Jornadas," in *Luís de Molina: regressa a Évora: actas das jornadas, Évora, 13, 14 de junho 1997* (Évora: Fundação Luís Molina, 1998), 13–14.

133. Gabriel Pinelo, "R. P. Ludovici Molinæ, e Societate Jesu, Vitæ Morumque Brevis Adumbratio," in Molina, *De justitia et jure*, 1:v. Molina would publish a revised edition of this commentary in 1593.

was strikingly different. For instance, *gratia operans* (operating grace) was no longer the spiritual substance resident in the soul that kept a person on the track toward justification (i.e., in a state of grace), as it was for Aquinas. Rather, it was for Molina the disposition or capacity freely to perform spiritual good that the Holy Spirit restored to the souls of fallen individuals through prevenient grace. Likewise, *gratia cooperans* (cooperating grace) was no longer Aquinas's divine empowerment to perform spiritual good whereby a person progressed on the track toward justification. Rather, for Molina it became the Spirit-engendered disposition of the regenerate person's soul to do the will of God and serve others. This disposition made the greatest joy and deepest desire of believers to carry out Jesus' two great commandments to love God maximally and to love neighbor as oneself.[134]

After the publication of his commentary, Molina proceeded to occupy the next fifteen years with resolving the precise dispute that he rightly perceived as underlying the Reformation polemics over justification and which, even after the Council of Trent, still divided his nascent Society of Jesus from the Dominicans and other like-minded religious orders. This dispute concerned the perennial theological question of how best to reconcile the doctrine of human freedom with the interrelated doctrines of divine grace, foreknowledge, predestination, and providence.[135] Opposing himself to what he considered the central error of the Protestant Reformation—the explicit or implicit denial of genuine human freedom in virtue of God's sovereignty and omniscience—Molina framed an explanatory order among the various logical moments of omniscience. The power and ingenuity of Molina's order revolves around the schematic placement and content of the second moment. Denominating this moment as *scientia media* (middle knowledge) since it fell between the first and the concluding third moment, Molina insisted that it provided the key to avoiding the Protestant error of obliterating libertarian human freedom without relinquishing divine sovereignty in the process.[136] Via his proposed resolution of this ancient tension, Molina boldly professed the ability consistently to affirm both divine sovereignty and libertarian human freedom in his seven-volume *Liberi Arbitrii cum Gratiae Donis, Divina*

---

134. Molina, *Commentaria*, 14.13.40.
135. MacGregor, *Molinist-Anabaptist Systematic Theology*, 14–15.
136. Molina, *Foreknowledge*, 4.14.13.52.9.

Praescientia, Providentia, Praedestinatione et Reprobatione Concordia (*The Compatibility of Free Choice with the Gifts of Grace, Divine Foreknowledge, Providence, Predestination, and Reprobation*), better known as the *Concordia* and published in 1588. The next three chapters will analyze the central teachings of Molina's magnum opus, specifically his conception of middle knowledge and his derivative doctrines of providence and predestination.

CHAPTER 3

Molina's Conception of Middle Knowledge

❖   ❖   ❖

UNQUESTIONABLY A MAJOR TURNING POINT (and arguably *the* decisive moment) in the extensive history of theological and philosophical reflection on how to reconcile divine omniscience and human freedom is Luis de Molina's groundbreaking conception of middle knowledge (*scientia media*). In short, middle knowledge is God's prevolitional knowledge of all true counterfactuals. That is to say, it is a type of knowledge God possessed logically or explanatorily prior to his willing to create the world or his making of any decisions about what kind of world, if any, he would create. In this knowledge, God apprehended the truth value of all counterfactuals, or conditional propositions in the subjunctive mood. Counterfactuals take the following form: if something *were* the case (when in fact it may or may not be the case), then something else *would be* the case. To illustrate, the propositions "If I were to drive a yellow Lamborghini on the interstate, I would get pulled over by a police officer for speeding," "If the Supreme Court had declared Al Gore the winner of the 2000 presidential election, the United States would not have invaded Afghanistan and Iraq," and "If there were a quantum vacuum, it would produce a virtual particle at such and such a time," are all counterfactuals. And according to middle knowledge, God knows which of these propositions are true and which are false before deciding to make this world or any world. It is important to notice, per the three examples, that many counterfactuals involve agents with libertarian free will or events that take place utterly at random and by chance. Thus, included in God's middle knowledge is God's awareness of what all possible individuals with libertarian freedom would freely do in any set of circumstances in which they find themselves as well as how completely random, chance events would turn out in any possible set of circumstances. William Lane Craig rightly observes that the doctrine of middle knowledge, if accurate, "is one of the most fruitful theological ideas ever conceived."[1] For it, among other things, would explain God's knowledge of the future and make it possible for God to know truly contingent future propositions. Molina delineated the doctrine of middle knowledge and its logical implications for divine providence and predestination in his 1588 magnum opus, the *Concordia* (full title *Liberi Arbitrii cum Gratiae Donis, Divina Praescientia, Providentia, Praedestinatione et Reprobatione Concordia*, translated *The Compatibility of Free Choice with the Gifts of Grace, Divine Foreknowledge, Providence, Predestination, and Reprobation*).[2]

This chapter traces the steps in Molina's development of the doctrine of middle knowledge. It first discusses how Molina found in the Bible God's counterfactual knowledge. It then proceeds to disclose Molina's argument that, in order for God's counterfactual knowledge to harmonize with biblical texts teaching human free choice, such knowledge must lie logically prior to God's decree concerning which world, if any, to create. It finally shows how Molina expounded his scheme of natural, middle, and free knowledge, today called Molinism.

BIBLICAL EVIDENCE FOR GOD'S COUNTERFACTUAL KNOWLEDGE

Molina believed the Bible was replete with texts whose literal exegesis demanded that God possesses counterfactual knowledge. An account frequently cited by Molina portrayed David inquiring of Yahweh through an ephod, a divining device containing the Urim and Thummim (differently colored stones respectively connoting an affirmative or negative reply) and out of which one of those stones would be drawn.[3]

---

1. William Lane Craig, *The Only Wise God: The Compatibility of Divine Foreknowledge and Human Freedom* (Grand Rapids: Baker, 1987), 127.

2. Only book 4 (*De Praescientia Dei*) of the seven-volume *Concordia* has been translated into English. This translation was made quite skillfully by Alfred J. Freddoso as *On Divine Foreknowledge* (Ithaca, NY: Cornell University Press, 1988).

3. Ludovici Molina, *Commentaria in primam divi Thomae partem* (Venice, 1602), 14.13.14; idem, *Foreknowledge*, 4.14.13.49.9; 4.14.13.53.10.

When David learned that Saul was plotting against him, he said to Abiathar the priest, "Bring the ephod." David said, "LORD, God of Israel, your servant has heard definitely that Saul plans to come to Keilah and destroy the town on account of me. Will the citizens of Keilah surrender me to him? Will Saul come down, as your servant has heard? LORD, God of Israel, tell your servant."

And the LORD said, "He will."

Again David asked, "Will the citizens of Keilah surrender me and my men to Saul?"

And the LORD said, "They will."

So David and his men, about six hundred in number, left Keilah and kept moving from place to place. When Saul was told that David had escaped from Keilah, he did not go there. (1 Sam. 23:9–13)

In this text David queries whether Saul would attack Keilah, where David was stationed, and whether the citizens of the city would deliver David over to Saul. Both times the ephod yielded the Urim for an affirmative answer, leading David to flee the city, such that the predictions did not in fact come to pass. As early as 1573 Molina recognized that the knowledge mediated here did not constitute predictions of the future (foreknowledge), for Saul never actually came to Keilah, and the citizens of Keilah never actually handed David over to Saul. Since God is infallible, we cannot construe the given answers as mistakes on God's part, as they would be if the information David received comprised instances of foreknowledge. Neither was the information a description of mere possibilities, as David already knew that Saul *could* come to Keilah and that the citizens of Keilah *could* hand him over to Saul. David wanted to know what Saul *would* do if he stayed at Keilah. So rather than foreknowledge or knowledge of possibilities, it follows that God was imparting to David counterfactual knowledge. God was letting David know that if he *were* to remain at Keilah, then Saul *would* come to get him, and that if Saul *were* to come to get David, then the townspeople *would* hand David over to Saul. Hence the divinely provided answers were correct despite their nonoccurrence, as they revealed what would occur under different circumstances than the circumstances which in fact obtained.[4]

---

4. Molina, *Foreknowledge*, 4.14.13.49.9.

In his commentary on Aquinas's *Summa Theologiae,* Molina pointed to other prophecies that also convey counterfactual knowledge rather than categorical declarations of simple foreknowledge.[5] Of these Jeremiah 38:17–18 is representative: "Then Jeremiah said to Zedekiah, 'This is what the LORD God Almighty, the God of Israel, says: "If you surrender to the officers of the king of Babylon, your life will be spared and this city will not be burned down; you and your family will live. But if you will not surrender to the officers of the king of Babylon, this city will be given into the hands of the Babylonians and they will burn it down; you yourself will not escape from them." ' " Hence we find that God, as an omniscient being, knew the Babylonians' free creaturely response to whichever course of action Zedekiah freely chose. As evidenced by the Babylonian exile, Zedekiah refused to submit and was subsequently killed by Nebuchadnezzar. However, God also knew the counterfactual truth that if Zedekiah had instead submitted to Nebuchadnezzar's officials, then Zedekiah and the city of Jerusalem, which was in fact razed to the ground, would have been spared.[6]

Molina found statements of counterfactual knowledge on the lips of Jesus as well. Perhaps the most complete and theologically wide-ranging example is Jesus' denunciation of Chorazin, Bethsaida, and Capernaum:

> Then Jesus began to denounce the towns in which most of his miracles had been performed, because they did not repent. "Woe to you, Chorazin! Woe to you, Bethsaida! For if the miracles that were performed in you had been performed in Tyre and Sidon, they would have repented long ago in sackcloth and ashes. But I tell you, it will be more bearable for Tyre and Sidon on the day of judgment than for you. And you, Capernaum, will you be lifted to the heavens? No, you will go down to Hades. For if the miracles that were performed in you had been performed in Sodom, it would have remained to this day. But I tell you that it will be more bearable for Sodom on the day of judgment than for you." (Matt. 11:20–24; cf. Luke 10:13–15)[7]

---

5. Molina, *Commentaria,* 14.13.16, 38.

6. Kirk R. MacGregor, *A Molinist-Anabaptist Systematic Theology* (Lanham, MD: University Press of America, 2007), 43.

7. Molina, *Commentaria,* 14.13.14; idem, *Liberi Arbitrii cum Gratiae Donis, Divina Praescientia, Providentia, Praedestinatione et Reprobatione Concordia,* ed. Johannes Rabeneck (Madrid: Sumptibus Societatis Editorialis "Sapientia," 1953), 1.14.13.9; 7.23.4/5.1.4.13; 7.23.4/5.1.11.41.

Here Jesus articulated his knowledge that if he had performed his miracles in different spatio-temporal locations than in those where he actually performed them, then certain groups of individuals who had not in fact repented and were damned would have repented and been saved. This statement significantly touches on divine predestination, which we shall explore in chapter 5. Thus God was aware that he could have created different worlds, specifically, a world where Jesus performed his miracles in the Gentile cities of Tyre and Sidon and a world where Jesus' incarnation took place in around the nineteenth century BC and he performed his miracles in Sodom. In these worlds, some of the same individuals who are reprobate in our world would have been elect. Notwithstanding this fact, God chose to create the actual world instead. As Molina explained, "God knows that there would have been repentance in sackcloth and ashes among the Tyronians and Sidonians on the hypothesis that the wonders that were worked in Chorazin and Bethsaida should have been worked in Tyre and Sidon.... But because the hypothesis on which it was going to occur was not in fact actualized, this repentance never did and never will exist in reality—and yet it was a future contingent dependent on the free choice of human beings."[8] For Molina the remarkable statement of Matthew 11:20–24 not only proved Christ's possession of counterfactual knowledge, but it also revealed that the reprobate citizens of Tyre, Sidon, and Sodom possessed the ability to appropriate salvation. Molina therefore identified this statement as a direct refutation of the position of Luther and Calvin that the reprobate lacked the freedom to receive salvation.[9]

Molina held that Jesus also claimed counterfactual knowledge concerning people's salvation in John 15:22–24, "If I had not come and spoken to them, they would not be guilty of sin; but now they have no excuse for their sin.... If I had not done among them the works no one else did, they would not be guilty of sin. As it is, they have seen, and yet they have hated both me and my Father."[10] In a fascinating converse to the Matthean text, Jesus disclosed that the Jewish religious leaders (the "they" in Jesus' remarks)

8. Molina, *Foreknowledge*, 4.14.13.49.9.

9. Friedrich Stegmüller, ed. and trans., *Geschichte des Molinismus: Neue Molinaschriften 1*, Beiträge zur Geschichte der Philosophie und Theologie des Mittelalters 32 (Münster: Aschendorffschen, 1935), 430, 440, 481; cf. Molina, *Concordia*, 1.14.13.1.20, where he charged that "Calvin persists in the error of Luther (Calvinus in errore persistit Lutheri)."

10. Molina, *Concordia*, 1.14.13.7.4; 1.14.13.23.1.3.

would have been innocent of wrongdoing if he had not spoken to them and if he had not performed his deity-attesting miracles among them. But due to Jesus' self-disclosure through his words and actions as a divine as well as human person, the religious leaders hated both him and his Father, thereby placing themselves under God's wrath. Molina also believed that, when interrogated by Pilate, Jesus divulged counterfactual knowledge concerning what his followers would have done if his messianic program had been political in character: "My kingdom is not of this world. If it were, my servants would fight to prevent my arrest by the Jewish leaders. But now my kingdom is from another place" (John 18:36).[11] So Jesus knew the counterfactual truth that, if his kingdom were the expected political and military quest to liberate Israel from Rome, his disciples would use violence to prevent his capture. Moreover, Molina perceived the divine possession of counterfactual knowledge in Paul, who described what would have happened if the Jewish leaders and Pilate had understood the divine wisdom of Jesus' messiahship: "None of the rulers of this age understood it, for if they had, they would not have crucified the Lord of glory" (1 Cor. 2:8).[12] Here we have a divinely inspired statement that if the powers of Jesus' day had understood God's wisdom, they would not have engineered Jesus' crucifixion. Molina argued that the foregoing statements from Jesus and Paul, like the prophecy given to David through the ephod, are not reducible to either foreknowledge or knowledge of possibilities. For if these statements were assertions of foreknowledge, they would self-contradictorily be mistakes on the part of a God who cannot err, since the consequent or "then" clause of these statements did not come to pass. On the other hand, these statements cannot be stating mere possibilities, since they affirm what *would* happen, not what *could* happen, under certain conditions different than those which in fact materialized. Therefore Molina declared it was indisputable that the God of the Bible possesses counterfactual knowledge.[13]

---

11. Molina, *Commentaria*, 22.1.

12. Ibid., 14.13.19.5.

13. Molina, *Foreknowledge*, 4.14.13.52.8. In addition to the texts cited by Molina, William Lane Craig points out several other examples of counterfactual knowledge in Scripture: "Indeed, when we construe certain prophecies as counterfactual warnings, rather than as categorical declarations of simple foreknowledge, we can explain how it is that in Israel the test of a true prophet is the fulfillment of his predictions (Deut 18:22) and yet some predictions given by true prophets do not actually come to pass because the people forewarned responded in an appropriate way (Is 38:1–5; Amos 7:1–6; Jon 3:1–10). In such cases, the prophecy from God was counterfactual knowledge of what would happen under the prevailing circumstances; but were intercessory prayer or repentance to occur, then God would not

"WHEN" DID GOD OBTAIN HIS COUNTERFACTUAL KNOWLEDGE?

The disputed issue between Molina and his interlocutors was when, in the logical order of God's decrees, God possessed his counterfactual knowledge. To understand this issue, we must first place it in its early modern theological context. Early modern theologians like Molina, Luther, and Calvin shared a common view on the basic logical structure of divine omniscience. This structure was first proposed by Thomas Aquinas (a fact of which Molina was aware but Luther and Calvin were unaware) and was mediated to Molina, Luther, and Calvin as a staple of the Catholic theological curriculum.[14] Not surprisingly, the Thomistic logical blueprint of omniscience was vigorously defended by the Dominicans following the Council of Trent. On each logical side of God's decree to create the actual world, Aquinas placed one moment within God's timeless act of knowledge. Logically prior to the divine creative decree, Aquinas claimed that God apprehended his *scientia simplicis intelligentiae* (knowledge of simple intelligence), by which God perfectly knows himself as well as all logical possibilities. Such exhaustive knowledge furnishes God with a range of possible worlds (i.e., logically consistent sets of possible circumstances), from which he chooses to actualize one world in his creative decree. Logically posterior to the divine creative decree, Aquinas held that God perceives his *scientia visionis* (visionary knowledge), by which he knows all past, present, and future tense truths in the world he has freely created.[15] Aquinas emphasized that his logical sequence of moments in no way implies any temporal priority or succession in God's omniscience, as an omniscient

---

carry out what had been threatened. We also find counterfactual knowledge exhibited by Christ. For example, he tells Peter, 'Go to the sea and cast a hook; take the first fish that comes up; and when you open its mouth, you will find a coin; take that and give it to them for you and me' (Mt 17:27). This passage is most naturally understood as an expression of Jesus' knowledge that if Peter were to carry out Jesus' instructions, he would find things as the Lord predicted. Again, Jesus commands the disciples, after a futile night of fishing, 'Cast the net to the right side of the boat, and you will find some [fish]' (Jn 21:6). The miraculous catch that ensued shows that Jesus knew exactly what would happen if the disciples obeyed his command. Sometimes Jesus makes counterfactual statements himself.... 'Woe to that one by whom the Son of Man is betrayed! It would have been better for that one not to have been born' (Mt 26:24)" (William Lane Craig, "The Middle-Knowledge View," in James K. Beilby and Paul R. Eddy, *Divine Foreknowledge: Four Views* [Downers Grove, IL: InterVarsity, 2001], 124).

14. Reinhold Seeberg, *Text-Book of the History of Doctrine*, 4 vols., trans. Charles E. Kay (Grand Rapids: Baker, 1956), 2:185.

15. Thomas Aquinas, *Summa contra Gentiles*, 1.66.4; idem, *Summa Theologiae*, trans. Fathers of the English Dominican Province (New York: Benziger Brothers, 1947), 1.14.5–8.

being cannot know more or less at one point in time than at another but must possess complete knowledge at every point in time. However, Aquinas equally insisted that his progression is no figment of the imagination, but exists in the same mode as the progression between various premises in a syllogism. Just as the antecedent premises are explanatorily prior to the conclusion, such that the conclusion follows as a result of the conditions posited by the antecedent premises, so the knowledge of simple intelligence furnishes the necessary ground for the divine creative decree, which in turn jointly furnishes the necessary ground for visionary knowledge.[16] The idea that God's knowledge of all possible worlds preceded his creative decree and that God's exhaustive foreknowledge about the actual world followed his creative decree was therefore common stock for Molina, Luther, and Calvin.

However, absent from Aquinas's ordering of divine cognitive events was God's knowledge of all counterfactual truths, because he believed that its apprehension was a motion parallel to and simultaneous with the divine apprehension of visionary knowledge. In other words, Aquinas proposed that God, as part of his divine creative decree, freely assigned truth values to all counterfactual statements.[17] Thus both divine knowledge of all tensed facts (visionary knowledge) and divine knowledge of all counterfactuals follow immediately from God's combined awareness of his creative decree and of his almighty power to bring about that decree.[18] While Aquinas asserted that his view of counterfactuals in no way undermined genuine human freedom, Luther, Calvin, and Molina alike perceived that the dependence of counterfactuals on God's decree eradicated the libertarian type of freedom, as it is God who determines what all creatures would do in every set of circumstances in which they found themselves. Hence Luther, Calvin, and Molina either explicitly or implicitly saw that libertarian freedom is rendered impossible by placing God's counterfactual knowledge logically posterior to the divine creative decree, thus yielding the following logical order: (1) God's knowledge of all possible worlds (knowledge of simple intelligence), (2) the divine creative decree, and (3) God's knowledge of past, present, and future truths about the actual world (visionary knowledge) along with God's

---

16. Harm J. M. J. Goris, *Free Creatures of an Eternal God: Thomas Aquinas on God's Infallible Foreknowledge and Irresistible Will*, Thomas Instituut te Utrecht 4 (Leuven: Peeters, 1996), 274.

17. Aquinas, *Summa Theologiae*, 1.14.13.

18. MacGregor, *Molinist-Anabaptist Systematic Theology*, 19.

counterfactual knowledge. The difference between Luther and Calvin on the one hand and Molina on the other hand is whether they endorsed this placement of counterfactual knowledge after the divine creative decree or altered it.

Endorsing this placement of counterfactuals after the divine creative decree, Luther and Calvin denied humans the ability to choose otherwise in the circumstances in which they find themselves, at least in their dealings with God, and followed the lead of the great patristic theologian Augustine in reducing creaturely freedom to mere spontaneity of choice and voluntariness of will.[19] Because the omnipotent God ordains all things that will occur in future circumstances and would occur under all other circumstances, Luther emphasized that whatever God foreknows happens necessarily: "It is, then, fundamentally necessary and wholesome for Christians to know that God foreknows nothing contingently, but that He foresees, purposes, and does all things according to His own immutable, eternal and infallible will. This bombshell knocks 'free-will' flat, and utterly shatters it.... Since then His will is not impeded, what is done cannot but be done where, when, how, as far as, and by whom, He foresees and wills."[20] For Luther, then, God does not know future contingents because there are no future contingents to be known. Since God chooses the content of his prescience (both future and counterfactual knowledge) and God has all power to bring about his prescience, humans do not have free choice or the ability to choose between the alternatives. As Luther summarized: "So the foreknowledge and omnipotence of God are diametrically opposed to our 'free-will.'"[21] For Luther the only human freedom permitted by the divine-human relationship is compatibilist in nature, namely, that the will chooses voluntarily and without external coercion, although whatever the will chooses it chooses necessarily. Hence Luther did not refrain from declaring that Judas betrayed Jesus necessarily.[22]

Calvin adhered to precisely the same train of thought as Luther, contending that human free choice is ruled out by the all-encompassing will of God as to foreknowledge and counterfactual knowledge. In his definition of

19. Ibid., 15.

20. Martin Luther, *The Bondage of the Will*, trans. James I. Packer and O. R. Johnston (Grand Rapids: Revell, 1957), 80–81.

21. Ibid., 217.

22. Ibid., 213.

providence, Calvin declared that nothing can happen unless God has by his will decreed it and by his power brought it to pass.

> Providence means not that by which God idly observes from heaven what takes place on earth, but that by which, as keeper of the keys, he governs all events. Thus it pertains no less to his hands than to his eyes. And indeed, when Abraham said to his son, "God will provide" [Gen. 22:8], he meant not only to assert God's foreknowledge of a future event, but to cast the care of a matter unknown to him upon the will of Him who is wont to give a way out of things perplexed and confused. Whence it follows that providence is lodged in the act; for many babble too ignorantly of bare foreknowledge.... But we make God the ruler and governor of all things, who in accordance with his wisdom has from the farthest limit of eternity decreed what he was going to do, and now by his might carries out what he has decreed. From this we declare that not only heaven and earth and the inanimate creatures, but also the plans and intentions of men, are so governed by his providence that they are borne by it straight to their appointed end. What then? you will ask. Does nothing happen by chance, nothing by contingency? I reply ... that "fortune" and "chance" are pagan terms, with whose significance the minds of the godly ought not to be occupied. For if every success is God's blessing, and calamity and adversity his curse, no place now remains in human affairs for fortune or chance.... In fine, Augustine commonly teaches that if anything is left to fortune, the world is aimlessly whirled about.... For this reason he excludes, also, the contingency that depends upon men's will.[23]

Clearly for Calvin, sovereignty is equated with complete control, such that God cannot be sovereign save for his determination of every event in the physical and spiritual realms.[24]

In contrast to Luther and Calvin, Molina placed God's counterfactual knowledge logically prior to the divine creative decree. As we saw in chapter 2, Molina insisted that a literal exegesis of more than twenty biblical passages, such as Genesis 4:6–7; Deuteronomy 30:11–19; and Ezekiel 18:30–32, demand that postfall humans possess libertarian freedom, though not

---

23. John Calvin, *Institutes of the Christian Religion*, ed. John T. McNeill, trans. Ford Lewis Battles (Philadelphia: Westminster, 1960), 1.16.4, 8.

24. On this score, Calvin asserted "that nothing at all in the world is undertaken without [God's] determination" (*Institutes*, 1.16.6).

intrinsically but by virtue of prevenient grace.[25] By exempting counterfactual truths from the divine creative decree, Molina made room for libertarian human freedom and all other instances of genuine contingency. Just as logically necessary truths like $1 + 1 = 2$ are logically before and so independent of the divine creative decree, so for Molina all counterfactual truths—including what every possible libertarian free creature would choose to do in any set of circumstances in which they find themselves as well as how utterly random, chance events would turn out in any possible set of circumstances—are logically before and so independent of the divine creative decree.[26] Hence counterfactual knowledge, Molina averred,

> is indeed in God before any free act of His will, and that it is a knowledge of *all* effects in general, not only (i) of those effects that are in fact going to exist because of the faculties of choice that He has decided to create within the order of things and circumstances that He chose to establish, but also (ii) of those effects that would have been going to exist (whether because of these very same faculties of choice or because of the infinitely many others that He could have created) if any of the circumstances had been altered within the order of things He chose to establish or if any other order of things had existed from among the infinity upon infinity of orders of things that He could have created.[27]

---

25. Here Molina (*Concordia*, 1.14.13.23.33) declared himself in full agreement with the position of the prominent medieval Cistercian reformer Bernard of Clairvaux: "Bernard affirms this same freedom of choice in his treatise *On Grace and Free Will*. Note the spot where he said, among other things [11.33]: The Creator endowed his rational creature with this prerogative of his dignity, that even as he himself was independent and controller of his own will and therefore not good by any necessity, so the creature was also made controller of his own will in order that he would become evil only by his will and so rightly be condemned, or stay good by his will and rightly be saved. Not that his will alone could ever be able to attain salvation, but he would never have the opportunity to gain salvation without his consent. No one is unwillingly saved (Eandem arbitrii libertatem affirmat Bernardus in tractatu De Gratia et Libero Arbitrio. Quo loco inter alia ait: Hac dignitatis praerogativa rationalem singulariter creaturam conditor insignivit ut quemadmodum ipse sui iuris erat ita illa quoque suo quodammodo iuris in hac parte existeret, quatenus non nisi sua voluntate aut mala fieret et iuste damnaretur aut bona maneret et merito salvaretur. Non quod ei propria possit sufficere ad salutem voluntas, sed quod eam nullatenus sine sua voluntate consequerentur. Nemo quippe salvatur invitus)." Hence the positive reception of Bernard in the sixteenth century, which has been demonstrated to extend to Luther (Franz Posset, *Pater Bernhardus: Martin Luther and Bernard of Clairvaux* [Kalamazoo, MI: Cistercian Publications, 1999]), Calvin (Dennis E. Tamburello, *Union with Christ: John Calvin and the Mysticism of St. Bernard* [Louisville: Westminster John Knox, 1994]), and Balthasar Hubmaier (Kirk R. MacGregor, *A Central European Synthesis of Radical and Magisterial Reform: The Sacramental Theology of Balthasar Hubmaier* [Lanham, MD: University Press of America, 2006], 37–89), extended to Molina as well.

26. Craig, "Middle-Knowledge View," 122.

27. Molina, *Foreknowledge*, 4.14.13.53.11; emphasis in original.

Owing to the fact that counterfactual knowledge is, for Molina, independent of God's will, it falls logically outside the scope of God's omnipotence. In the same way as God's knowledge of necessary truths lies beyond his omnipotence and is simply given (God did not make 1 + 1 = 2 and could not have made 1 + 1 = 3), so God's knowledge of what would be the free choices or random actions of individual essences if instantiated in various circumstances lies beyond his omnipotence and is simply given.[28] This is not because there is anything defective in God's omnipotence, but solely because omnipotence constitutes the ability to do anything logically possible and not the ability to do the logically impossible. And it is logically impossible to *determine* that a libertarian creature *freely* does something such that it cannot do otherwise or to *determine* that a stochastic (i.e., utterly random) process *contingently* turns out in a certain way such that it could not turn out otherwise.[29]

To sum up, Molina concurred with Luther and Calvin that placing God's counterfactual knowledge after his creative decree would obliterate libertarian freedom, a consequence that Luther and Calvin accepted. But because Molina judged that this consequence ran contrary to the infallibility of Scripture, Molina placed God's counterfactual knowledge before the divine creative decree, thus rendering it logically impossible for God to control. Now certainly, Molina insisted, God could easily prevent a libertarian creature from freely doing something by not making that creature at all or by putting that creature in different circumstances where it would freely choose to do something else. *Contra* any form of determinism, the circumstances do not bring about or cause actions and therefore do nothing to dictate decisions. But there simply are contingent facts that in various circumstances, creatures would freely (i.e., indeterministically) do various things.[30] And God, as an omniscient being, knows these facts. Moreover, God could easily preclude a stochastic process from randomly generating an effect by not making that stochastic process at all or by putting that stochastic process in different

28. Ibid., 4.14.15.49.8, 11.

29. Ibid., 4.14.15.47.9. Molina did not use the modern term *stochastic* but clearly affirmed the concept that the term signifies.

30. Hence there is no logical or causal tie between circumstances and what creatures would freely do in them. To put it another way, Molina held that there are contingent facts of the following kind: for any set of circumstances C (where C includes the entire history of the world up to the moment of decision), there is some action A such that if a libertarian free agent L were in C, L would indeterministically do A. This is true even though C in no way caused L to do A or made L do A, and L could have done something entirely different than A in C.

circumstances. Notice again that the circumstances do nothing to produce, much less guarantee, effects; there are simply contingent facts known by God that in various circumstances, stochastic processes would randomly behave in various ways. Nonetheless, it is logically impossible for God to alter the contingent fact that if a libertarian creature were placed in a certain set of circumstances, then it would freely choose to perform a particular action, even though it could have chosen to do otherwise in those circumstances. And it is logically impossible for God to alter the contingent fact that if a stochastic process were placed in a certain set of circumstances, then it would randomly generate a particular behavior, even though it could have randomly generated a different behavior in those circumstances.[31]

Having located God's acquisition of counterfactual knowledge logically prior to the divine creative decree, Molina then fit counterfactual knowledge into the basic structure of omniscience inherited from Aquinas. We recall that this structure comprised, in sequence, God's knowledge of simple intelligence, the divine creative decree, and God's visionary knowledge. Hence Molina needed to place counterfactual knowledge either logically before, simultaneous with, or after God's knowledge of simple intelligence. Since what *would* happen in particular circumstances (counterfactual knowledge) is logically subsequent to what *could* happen in particular circumstances (knowledge of simple intelligence), Molina placed counterfactual knowledge after God's knowledge of simple intelligence, thereby positioning it between God's knowledge of simple intelligence and the divine creative decree. So while on Aquinas's view there were two moments of divine knowledge, one on either side of the creative decree, on Molina's view there were three moments of divine knowledge, two before the creative decree and one after.[32]

MOLINA'S THREEFOLD STRUCTURE OF DIVINE KNOWLEDGE

We are now in a position to spell out Molina's revolutionary threefold structure of omniscience alongside its theological implications. Molina began by renaming the knowledge of simple intelligence and visionary knowledge to

---

31. Molina, *Foreknowledge*, 4.14.15.49.13.
32. Ibid., 4.14.15.52.19; 4.14.15.53.2.22.

better reflect their roles in the divine cognition, dubbing the former *scientia naturalis* (natural knowledge) and the latter *scientia libera* (free knowledge). Because God's apprehension of counterfactual knowledge comes logically between these two moments, Molina called it God's *scientia media* (middle knowledge).[33]

In natural knowledge, the first logical moment of Molina's structure, God knows all possibilities, including all necessary truths (e.g., the laws of logic), all the possible individuals and worlds he might create, as well as everything that every possible individual *could* freely do in any set of circumstances in which that individual found itself and everything that every possible stochastic process *could* randomly do in any set of circumstances where it existed. Molina insisted that God does not determine his natural knowledge by willing certain possibilities to be true, as this first logical moment precedes any decision or decree of the divine will. Rather, God knows his natural knowledge, as Molina's nomenclature suggests, as indispensable to his very nature, such that God could not lack this knowledge and still be God.[34]

In middle knowledge, the second logical moment of Molina's structure, God knows all counterfactual truths, including that which every possible individual *would* freely do in any set of circumstances in which that individual found himself or herself and that which every possible stochastic process *would* randomly do in any set of circumstances where it existed.[35] To illustrate the distinction between the first two moments of divine omniscience, God knew in his natural knowledge that Peter, if placed in the courtyard of the Sanhedrin, could freely affirm or deny Christ, but God discerned in his middle knowledge that Peter would freely deny Jesus under those circumstances. As previously indicated, that is not because the circumstances compelled him to deny Jesus — for Molina all sets of circumstances are necessarily

---

33. Ibid., 4.14.15.52.9.
34. Ibid., 4.14.15.53.3.2.
35. Ibid., 4.14.15.52.10. In his middle knowledge, God does not apprehend counterfactual truths about what he himself would do in any set of circumstances, since this would prevent God from being able to make any free choices about what he would subsequently do. All of God's subsequent decisions would be determined by his own prior middle knowledge of himself! In other words, God's having middle knowledge of himself would destroy his own free will, which is impossible. Therefore Molina stated that "just as human beings and angels do not know, before the determination of their own wills, which part they are going to turn themselves toward ... so too neither does God know, before He determines His own will, which part it is going to be turned toward" (4.14.15.52.11). We shall return to this topic in chapter 6.

freedom-preserving in character—but rather that God knew which way Peter would freely choose.[36] Because the content of middle knowledge does not lie within the scope of God's will or omnipotence, God cannot control what he knows via middle knowledge, any more than he can control what he knows via natural knowledge. In Molina's words, "All contingent states of affairs are, I repeat, represented to God *naturally, before* any act or free determination of the divine will; and they are represented not only as being *possible* but also as being *future*—not *absolutely future*, but *future under the condition and on the hypothesis* that God should decide to create this or that order of things and causes with these or those circumstances."[37] This means that middle knowledge allows for there to be genuine future contingents, not simply things that seem contingent to us humans but are in fact determined by God. Moreover, it also allows for God to know future contingents, a claim which is today denied by open theists. Molina held that God's middle knowledge, like his natural knowledge, is essential to God's nature. In order for God to be God, the omniscient being, he must know all counterfactual truths logically prior to his creative decree. But unlike natural knowledge, the content of middle knowledge is not essential to God. Since libertarian creatures could choose differently and stochastic processes could behave differently, God's middle knowledge would be different if they were to do so.[38]

Because much of God's middle knowledge is contingent on what various libertarian individual essences and stochastic individual essences, if instantiated, would do in various circumstances, it follows that God discerns countless worlds in his natural knowledge—worlds logically possible in and of themselves—that are impossible for God to create because in none of the possible worlds that God would want to actualize would the individual essences freely or randomly cooperate. Notice that what these essences would do in various circumstances comprise contingent properties of these essences,

---

36. Molina, *Foreknowledge*, 4.14.15.51.1, 17, 19.

37. Ibid., 4.14.15.50.15; emphasis in original.

38. Craig, *Only Wise God*, 131. This is why Molina explained, "Therefore, it should be said (i) that *middle* knowledge partly has the character of *natural* knowledge, since it was prior to the free act of the divine will and since God did not have the power to know anything else, and (ii) that it partly has the character of *free* knowledge, since the fact that it is knowledge of the one part rather than of the other derives from the fact that free choice, on the hypothesis that it should be created in one or another order of things, would do the one thing rather than the other, even though it would indifferently be able to do either of them" (*Foreknowledge*, 4.14.15.52.10; emphasis in original).

not parts of the essences themselves. Hence there is no "essence fatalism" going on here, as one's essence does not determine what one would freely do in various circumstances; nor, as we have seen, do the circumstances determine what one would freely do.[39] For example, there are logically possible worlds where Peter freely affirms Jesus, flees from the courtyard, or does any of a number of things other than denying Jesus in precisely the same circumstances where Peter in fact denied Jesus, along with a logically possible world where Peter denies Jesus in those circumstances. But in light of the counterfactual truth that if Peter were in those circumstances, then he would freely deny Jesus, none of the logically possible worlds on our list except for the last is possible for God to create. Now this does not mean that God could not prevent Peter from denying Jesus, for he could easily do this by putting Peter in different circumstances or not making Peter at all. But God cannot control the fact that if he were to instantiate Peter's individual essence in the aforementioned circumstances, then Peter would freely deny Jesus. This is not because Peter's essence made him deny Jesus in these circumstances, since "denying Jesus in such-and-such circumstances" is not part of Peter's essence. Nor do the circumstances determine Peter's denial. But there remains a contingent fact of the matter that if Peter's essence were instantiated in these circumstances, then Peter would indeterministically deny Jesus.[40] Thus God's middle knowledge serves to reduce the range of worlds logically possible in and of themselves to those logically possible for him to create given libertarian freedom and genuine randomness. To avoid confusion, contemporary philosophers of religion designate the former as possible worlds and the latter as feasible worlds.[41] Not only does middle knowledge, Molina proclaimed, allow for human freedom and stochastic processes, but it also furnishes God a means of choosing which feasible world to create. For by knowing what instantiated individual essences would do under any circumstances, God can choose a feasible world where his ultimate purposes are achieved through free creaturely decisions and random processes. Upon making an "absolutely

39. Accordingly, Molina would deny any characterization of an essence as a "locked-in" set of psychological makeup, choices, desires, and ideas, fixed before our birth and predetermining our actions. Rather, an essence is simply the "whatness" or quiddity of something, and for each human, that quiddity includes libertarian freedom.

40. Molina, *Foreknowledge*, 4.14.15.52.30; Craig, "Middle-Knowledge View," 123.

41. Thomas P. Flint, "The Problem of Divine Freedom," *American Philosophical Quarterly* 20, no. 3 (1983): 257.

complete and unlimited deliberation" about which feasible world to create, God chooses one of these worlds to be actual in his creative decree.[42]

In free knowledge, the third logical moment of Molina's structure, God fully knows the actual world, including his foreknowledge of everything that will happen therein. This includes not only the circumstances God will directly cause and the decisions he will make, but also the free decisions that humans will make, the random actions of stochastic processes, and the contingent circumstances that will result from those decisions and actions. Called "free knowledge" because this knowledge is predicated on God's free decision of which feasible world to create, God has control over which statements are true and false in free knowledge.[43] Hence Molina could verbally agree with Luther that God "determines" his foreknowledge by the force of his will in the sense that God chooses what his foreknowledge will be, though not in the sense intended by Luther that God directly causes the full content of his foreknowledge to transpire.[44] By choosing to create another world, God would have brought it about that his foreknowledge would be different, as statements that are true in the actual world would be false and statements that are false in the actual world would be true. For instance, if God had created a world where Peter had never existed, then all the true statements about things he actually did would be false. Moreover, if God had decided not to make any world at all, then God would not even possess free knowledge.[45] Therefore neither the content nor even the existence of free knowledge is necessary to God, as God could lack such knowledge and still be God.[46]

We may now illustrate Molina's structure of omniscience with the following enumeration of its logical moments:

1. Natural knowledge: God's knowledge of all possible truths and therefore of all possible worlds (*i.e.*, logically consistent sets of possible circumstances).

42. Molina, *Foreknowledge*, 4.14.15.52.13.

43. Ibid., 4.14.15.52.9.

44. Ibid., 4.14.15.53.3.

45. Ibid., 4.14.15.53.4.3. This is correct, Molina warned, only if discussing positive states of affairs; if the assessment is extended to negative states of affairs, we would affirm God's possession of a free knowledge comprised entirely of negative propositions (e.g., "There will be no actual world," "Peter will never exist," and the like).

46. MacGregor, *Molinist-Anabaptist Systematic Theology*, 38.

2. Middle knowledge: God's knowledge of all counterfactual truths and therefore of all feasible worlds (*i.e.*, logically consistent sets of circumstances compatible with the decisions springing from libertarian freedom and the actions springing from natural randomness).

→ *Divine creative decree*

3. Free knowledge: God's knowledge of all actual truths (past, present, and future) in the world he has chosen to create.[47]

Notice that middle knowledge plays the crucial role of grounding God's foreknowledge, which would seem to lack any ground if God lacked middle knowledge. For if one adopts the commonsensical view of time in which temporal becoming is real—where only the present moment exists while the past is what did exist and the future does not yet exist but is a realm of unactualized possibility—then apart from middle knowledge, God cannot know the future since future events are not actually present for God to look ahead and see.[48] But if God has middle knowledge, then he knows what every possible creature would do under any circumstances and therefore in every feasible world. When God, in his creative decree, selects one of these feasible worlds to be the actual world, then his middle knowledge of what would happen were he to create this world is transformed into foreknowledge of what will happen in this world. So God foreknows, completely without reference to anything outside himself, what the future will be. Hence, as Craig nicely puts it, "Given middle knowledge and the divine decree, foreknowledge follows automatically as a result."[49]

---

47. Craig, *Only Wise God*, 131; idem, "Middle-Knowledge View," 123.

48. This commonsensical view of time is also known as the tensed theory of time or the A-Theory of time. However, one could ground divine foreknowledge if one abandoned this view in favor of a tenseless theory of time, also known as the B-Theory of time. (The labels "A-Theory" and "B-Theory" were introduced by John M. E. McTaggart in *The Nature of Existence*, ed. C. D. Broad [Cambridge: Cambridge University Press, 1927], 5:33.) According to the B-Theory, temporal becoming is an illusion of human consciousness, and all events on the timeline (past, present, and future) are equally existent. So for the people in 1945, that moment is now and we are in the future, but for the people in 2180, that moment is now and we are in the past. The universe is a four-dimensional space-time block that exists tenselessly, and there is no privileged present moment that alone actually exists. On the B-Theory, it is easy to ground foreknowledge by positing that God resides outside the four-dimensional space-time universe in an "eternal now" and looks into the universe, perceiving all moments on the timeline as equally present. However, I concur with Craig in advocating the A-Theory and in maintaining that the B-Theory faces insuperable difficulties. For a thorough analysis of these two theories of time, see William Lane Craig, *The Tensed Theory of Time: A Critical Examination*, Synthese Library 293 (Dordrecht: Kluwer Academic, 2000); and idem, *The Tenseless Theory of Time: A Critical Examination*, Synthese Library 294 (Dordrecht: Kluwer Academic, 2000).

49. Craig, "Middle-Knowledge View," 133.

At this juncture the question could be posed as to how God could have middle knowledge since counterfactual truths are not present for God to look ahead and see, and most of them will never actually be present. Here it should be stressed that Molina's doctrine of middle knowledge carries with it a conceptualist model of divine cognition rather than a perceptualist model of divine cognition. On the perceptualist model, God derives his knowledge by looking and seeing what exists. This model is tacitly affirmed when people talk of God foreseeing the future or possessing foresight of events in the future. However, Molina insisted that God does not derive his knowledge by anything resembling perception. Instead, God's knowledge is self-contained and should be construed on the analogy of a mind's knowledge of innate ideas. Thus Molina stated concerning middle knowledge that "God acquires no knowledge *from things* but instead knows and comprehends everything He knows in His own essence."[50] So God's knowledge is discerned completely from within God's intellect and not by anything outside himself.[51] As the omniscient being, God essentially possesses the attribute of knowing all truths; there exist counterfactual truths; therefore God knows all counterfactual truths. Craig has shown that one can employ this fact about omniscience to construct a philosophical argument that, if successful, proves that God has middle knowledge. The argument, in modified form, runs as follows:

1. If there exist counterfactual truths about the actions of libertarian creatures (known as "counterfactuals of creaturely freedom") and counterfactual truths about stochastic processes (which we may call "counterfactuals of natural randomness"), then the omniscient God knows these truths.

2. There exist counterfactual truths about the actions of libertarian creatures and stochastic processes.

3. If God knows counterfactual truths about the actions of libertarian creatures and stochastic processes, then God knows them either logically prior to the divine creative decree or only logically posterior to the divine creative decree.

50. Molina, *Foreknowledge*, 4.14.15.52.19; emphasis in original.
51. Craig, *Divine Foreknowledge and Human Freedom*, 240; Craig, "Middle-Knowledge View," 133.

4. Counterfactual truths about the actions of libertarian creatures and stochastic processes cannot be known only logically posterior to the divine creative decree.

5. Therefore God knows counterfactual truths about the actions of libertarian creatures and stochastic processes (from 1 and 2).

6. Therefore God knows counterfactual truths about the actions of libertarian creatures and stochastic processes either logically prior to the divine creative decree or only logically posterior to the divine creative decree (from 3 and 5).

7. Therefore God knows counterfactual truths about the actions of libertarian creatures and stochastic processes logically prior to the divine creative decree (from 4 and 6), which is the sum and substance of middle knowledge.[52]

Although Molina did not explicitly formulate this argument, he did implicitly endorse all of its premises. I shall now briefly say something in defense of premises 1 through 4, from which the rest of the argument deductively follows.

Premise 1 follows necessarily from the definition of omniscience, namely, knowing all truths and believing no falsehoods. As Molina put it, "God has within Himself the means whereby He knows all things fully and perfectly."[53] So if there are counterfactual truths about libertarian creatures and stochastic processes, then the omniscient God must know them.

Premise 2 is intuitively obvious, as statements of the form "if libertarian creature L were in circumstances C, then L would freely do action A" and "if stochastic process S were in circumstances C, then S would randomly generate action A" are either true or false, even if we do not know which one, by the law of bivalence. (Here the circumstances C are thoroughly well-defined and include the entire history of the relevant possible world up until the moment of action.)[54] The law of bivalence is the logical principle that states that every proposition has precisely one truth value, either true or false. Now clearly some of the above statements are true, since L has to do *something* in C (even if L chooses to remain exactly as L was before) and S has to do *something* in C

52. Craig, "Middle-Knowledge View," 136–37.
53. Molina, *Foreknowledge*, 4.14.15.49.12.
54. That such statements are either true or false is presupposed in Molina, *Foreknowledge*, 4.14.15.49.11.

(even if *S* randomly remains in a static state). That *L* or *S* is in *C* means that no nonaction is logically possible. Hence there indeed exist counterfactual truths about the actions of libertarian creatures and stochastic processes.

Premise 3 simply states logically exhaustive possibilities, namely, that if God knows counterfactuals of creaturely freedom and natural randomness, then God knows them either logically before or only after his creative decree. One could not say that God knows counterfactuals of creaturely freedom and natural randomness only simultaneous with his creative decree, because the creative decree is not itself a moment of divine knowledge. So either God's knowledge of counterfactuals logically originates prior to or following the divine creative decree.[55]

Premise 4 is true because, as we have seen, if counterfactuals of creaturely freedom and natural randomness were known only following the divine creative decree, then it is God who determined what every creature would do and how every stochastic process would behave in every set of circumstances. (Recall that this was a point of unanimity between the major sixteenth-century reformers of each confession.) In that case, we would have the self-contradiction of counterfactuals of creaturely *freedom* being *determined* by God, such that they would no longer be free in a libertarian way![56] By definition, counterfactuals of creaturely freedom cannot be "of creaturely freedom" if God determined them. Hence Craig rightly observes that "if God knows counterfactual truths about us only posterior to his decree, then there really are no counterfactuals of creaturely freedom."[57] On top of that, we would have the self-contradiction of counterfactuals of natural *randomness* being *determined* by God, such that they would no longer be random in a stochastic way. By definition, counterfactuals of natural randomness cannot be "of natural randomness" if God determined them.

---

55. Craig, "Middle-Knowledge View," 143.

56. In refuting the position of thirteenth-century theologian John Duns Scotus that "the free determination of the divine will is the whole explanation and basis for the fact that God knows with certainty which things are contingently future *absolutely* and *in an unqualified way*," Molina insisted that this position was both self-contradictory and perilous to the omnibenevolent character of God taught by the Christian faith: "I take it to be sufficiently obvious that this position of Scotus's is more than dangerous from the point of view of the faith. For it destroys the freedom of choice which ... we demonstrated from Sacred Scripture and from experience itself, and it makes God the cause by which our free choice is turned toward and determined to those sinful acts by which we offend Him and break His law" (*Foreknowledge*, 4.14.15.50.7; emphasis in original).

57. Craig, "Middle-Knowledge View," 143.

Given the truth of premises 1 through 4, it follows that logically prior to the divine creative decree, God knows all true counterfactuals of creaturely freedom and natural randomness, which means that God has middle knowledge. This argument from omniscience goes to refute the single most frequent objection to middle knowledge in the contemporary philosophical and theological literature, namely, the grounding objection. The grounding objection holds that there is no ground or basis on which God could have middle knowledge.[58] But this argument shows that the ground of middle knowledge is God's omniscience, from which middle knowledge follows deductively. The omniscient God knows all truths; counterfactuals of creaturely freedom and natural randomness are true logically prior to God's creative decree; therefore God knows counterfactuals of creaturely freedom and natural randomness logically prior to his creative decree. So, for Molina "the depth and perfection of the divine knowledge" includes innate knowledge of all truths, and God simply discerns counterfactuals of creaturely freedom and natural randomness as part of his omniscience.[59]

At this point, Molina's contemporaries were apt to query as to the precise means by which God discerns his middle knowledge. Although the foregoing argument, if successful, shows that God has middle knowledge even if we can never know or understand the means by which he has it, Molina proposed an answer: supercomprehension, namely, "an *absolutely profound and absolutely preeminent comprehension.*"[60] To understand this answer, we must first observe that on Molina's conceptualist model of divine cognition, God knows all truths that are independent of his will and omnipotence (i.e., the truths he apprehends in his natural and middle knowledge) innately simply by virtue of his nature. This innate knowledge encompasses supercomprehension, which Molina construes as God's unlimited intellectual capacity to perceive infinitely, within his own mind, the individual essence (or pattern) for every possible thing he could create. Remember from chapter 2 that, for Molina,

58. For well-known presentations of the grounding objection, see Robert M. Adams, "Middle Knowledge and the Problem of Evil," *American Philosophical Quarterly* 14 (1977): 109–17; William Hasker, *God, Time, and Knowledge* (Ithaca, NY: Cornell University Press, 1989), 29–52; David Paul Hunt, "Middle Knowledge: The 'Foreknowledge Defense,'" *International Journal for Philosophy of Religion* 28, no. 1 (1990): 1–24; Timothy O'Connor, "The Impossibility of Middle Knowledge," *Philosophical Studies* 66, no. 2 (1992): 139–66.
59. Molina, *Foreknowledge*, 4.14.15.49.11.
60. Ibid., 4.14.15.52.11; emphasis in original.

these individual essences exist neither independently of God nor outside of God but only as designs within the mind of God. In other words, these individual essences are solely the product of God's imagination—mental patterns or designs for things he knows in his infinite creativity and artistry he could create if he so willed.

Hence we see immediately that God obtains no knowledge at all from the creatures that could or would be created from these patterns or designs.[61] Rather, Molina insisted that God's knowledge comes solely from the individual essences (the patterns or designs) themselves, which only exist as the thoughts of God's own mind. In short, "God does not get His knowledge from things, but knows all things *in* Himself and *from* Himself."[62] So, for Molina all God's knowledge is self-contained, a doctrine which redounds to the aseity—the absolute self-existence, self-sufficiency, independence, and autonomy—of God.[63] Since each individual essence is the product of the divine imagination, and God perfectly understands his own imagination, it follows for Molina that God can infinitely perceive each essence. This infinite perception includes knowing what each essence, if instantiated, would do (whether freely in the case of libertarian essences, randomly in the case of stochastic essences, and deterministically in the case of other essences) in any possible set of circumstances in which it existed.[64] As Molina stated in the case of libertarian essences:

---

61. This is an issue on which many detractors of middle knowledge, especially from the Reformed tradition, misunderstand Molina. As noted in the introduction, this misunderstanding springs from the mistaken assumption that Arminius's doctrine of middle knowledge was the same as Molina's. While Arminius explicitly stated (Jacob Arminius, *Public Disputations*, in *The Writings of Arminius*, 3 vols., trans. James Nichols and W. R. Bagnall [Grand Rapids: Baker, 1956], 1:449; *Private Disputations*, in idem, 2:39) that God obtains his middle knowledge from creatures, Molina vehemently rejected this notion as undermining God's aseity and perfection (*Foreknowledge*, 4.14.15.52.19). Hence Molina would agree with his contemporary Reformed detractors that any theory of divine omniscience that predicates God's knowledge of counterfactuals of creaturely freedom on creatures is hopelessly defective.

62. Molina, *Foreknowledge*, 4.14.15.49.12; emphasis in original.

63. This is a point emphasized by Craig: "A second notion in Molina's account of God's knowledge of future contingents that merits comment is his claim that God knows future contingents in Himself. Molina wishes to insist as strongly as Aquinas that God does not acquire His knowledge from external sources. He asserts, ' ... God acquires no knowledge *from things* but instead knows and comprehends everything He knows in His own essence and in the determination of His own will ...' [*Concordia*, 4.14.15.52.19]. In His essence He knows the content of His natural and middle knowledge, while the determination of His creative will furnishes the basis of His free knowledge" (William Lane Craig, *The Problem of Divine Foreknowledge and Future Contingents from Aristotle to Suarez*, Studies in Intellectual History 7 [Leiden: Brill, 1988], 178).

64. In the case of libertarian and stochastic essences, what these essences would do in any set of circumstances is not part of these essences but rather constitute contingent properties of these essences, i.e., properties that could have been different with the essence remaining unchanged.

In Himself[God] comprehends all the things that exist *eminently in Him* and thus the free choice of any creature whom He is able to make through His omnipotence. Therefore, before any free determination of His will, by virtue of the depth of His ... knowledge, by which He infinitely surpasses each of the things *He contains eminently in Himself,* He discerns what the free choice of any creature would do by its own innate freedom, given the hypothesis that He should create it in this or that order of things with these or those circumstances or aids—even though the creature could, if it so willed, refrain from acting or do the opposite, and even though if it was going to do so, as it is able to freely, God would foresee *that* very act and *not* the one that He *in fact* foresees would be performed by that creature.[65]

So logically prior to his choice to create anything, the Designer knows all of his unactualized designs or patterns of possible individuals (of which a tiny minority would ever be actualized) so perfectly well to know how each (if possessing libertarian freedom) would freely behave in any state of affairs if he proceeded to create it.

Here we detect a further refutation of the grounding objection, as we may say that Molina grounded middle knowledge in God's cognitive ability to comprehend perfectly his own creative aptitude and power. As Molina declared concerning God, "Thus, what was in itself uncertain [counterfactuals of creaturely freedom] He knew with certainty, a certainty that stemmed *not from the object,* but from the acumen and absolute perfection of His intellect."[66] Indeed, Molina declared that

it would be insulting to the depth and perfection of the divine knowledge—and indeed impious and not at all compatible with so great a comprehension of the free choice of each creature—to assert that God is ignorant of what I would have done by my freedom of choice (i) if He had created me in some other order of things, or (ii) if, in this very order of things in which He has created me, He had decided to confer on me more or fewer aids than He in fact decided to give me, or (iii) if He had granted me a longer life or handed me over to more serious temptations. So it follows that even before He created anything by His free will, He knew

65. Molina, *Foreknowledge,* 4.14.15.49.11; emphasis added except in the last clause, where emphasis is found in the original.
66. Ibid., 4.14.15.52.33; emphasis added.

all future contingents with certainty ... *not absolutely speaking* but rather *on the hypothesis* that He Himself should decide to create this or that order of things with these or those circumstances.... Therefore, God does not need the existence of those things in His eternity in order to know them with certainty.[67]

Here we should point out the clear distinction Molina made between certainty and necessity. For Molina certainty is an attribute of persons and has no relationship to the truth or falsity of propositions. This is evident from the fact that a person can be absolutely certain that some proposition is true that turns out to be false. So to say that God knows something with certainty is only to affirm that God feels sure that some proposition is true. It is not to put any type of a constraint on the truth value of the proposition. By contrast, necessity is a logical constraint carried by some propositions that prohibits them from even possibly being false.[68] To illustrate, a mathematical theorem may be necessarily true, which means that it is logically impossible for the theorem to be false.[69]

Molina was quick to emphasize that God knows the content of his middle knowledge with certainty and not with necessity.[70] In other words, God feels sure that his middle knowledge is true, even though he knows that his middle knowledge could have been different than it in fact is. Much of what God knows via his middle knowledge is contingently, not necessarily, true, such that there is nothing to constrain or make it true logically. The fact that God knows his middle knowledge with certainty in no way determines that counterfactuals of creaturely freedom are true, any more than our knowledge of counterfactuals of creaturely freedom about other persons determines those counterfactuals to be true. For example, I know with certainty that if I were to offer my wife a glass of Dr Pepper and a glass of Pepsi, she would choose the glass of Dr Pepper. But the certainty of my knowledge of this counterfactual does not determine it to be true; the counterfactual is just as contingent as if I had no knowledge whatsoever about it. Obviously, my knowledge in no way compels her to choose the glass of Dr Pepper were I to put her in the

67. Ibid., 4.14.15.49.11; emphasis in original.
68. Ibid., 4.14.15.52.4–6, 34–37.
69. Craig, "Middle-Knowledge View," 127.
70. Molina, *Foreknowledge*, 4.14.15.52.35.

position of having to make the choice between the two glasses. In exactly the same way, Molina declared that the certainty of God's middle knowledge does not make counterfactuals of creaturely freedom true, and God's middle knowledge in no way compels free creatures to choose in particular ways were God to put creatures in the position of having to make various choices.

In view of this insight, Molina was able to offer an account of divine foreknowledge that does not lead to fatalism. For when God converts his middle knowledge of certain propositions into foreknowledge by deciding to create the circumstances assumed by those propositions, that foreknowledge places no constraint on free creatures or stochastic processes to do the things he knows with certainty will happen; they could still do otherwise. In Molina's words, "it is a foreknowledge that imposes *no necessity* ... on future things, but rather leaves them as uncertain in themselves and in relation to their causes as they would be if there were no such foreknowledge."[71] To sum up, Molina insisted that knowledge is not causally determinative. That is to say, God's knowledge of what a person would do in some set of circumstances exerts no causal power on the person to act as God knows, just as human knowledge of what other humans would do exerts no causal power over their choices.

SUMMARY OF THE DEVELOPMENT OF MIDDLE KNOWLEDGE

Molina's doctrine of middle knowledge was formulated through the conjunction of biblical infallibility and logical inference. A staunch defender of biblical infallibility, Molina believed that the literal (today we would say grammatico-historical) exegesis of several passages necessitated that humans have libertarian freedom and that God possesses counterfactual knowledge. The question for Molina was how these truths could be harmonized with each other. To answer this question, Molina turned to logical inference. Logically, God must have first apprehended his counterfactual knowledge either before or after his creative decree. But as Molina (as well as Luther and Calvin) saw, if God apprehended his counterfactual knowledge after his creative decree, this would obliterate libertarian human freedom, as it would be God who determined what every person would do in any possible

---

71. Ibid., 4.14.15.52.36; emphasis in original.

set of circumstances. Since humans according to Scripture have libertarian freedom, it follows by *reductio ad absurdum* (i.e., proof by contradiction) that God apprehended his counterfactual knowledge before his creative decree. Hence God's counterfactual knowledge of what individual essences *would* do in any set of circumstances logically falls between, or in the middle of, what individual essences *could* do in any set of circumstances (natural knowledge) and what those individual essences that God has chosen to actualize *will* do in the circumstances making up the actual world (free knowledge). (What creatures *would* do in possible circumstances is logically dependent on what they *could* do in those circumstances, and what creatures *will* do in actual circumstances is logically dependent on what they *would* do if certain possible circumstances were made actual.) Therefore Molina called God's counterfactual knowledge his middle knowledge.

Molina asserted that God's middle knowledge was grounded in his omniscience and apprehended by means of his supercomprehension. Because knowledge, divine or human, of what some other free creature would do in no way causes the creature to do it, Molina held that middle knowledge (and free knowledge) rendered fatalism impossible. On the basis of his nonfatalistic or indeterministic model of human choices and random processes, Molina put forward a provocative account of divine providence, the details of which we shall unpack in the next chapter.

CHAPTER 4

Molina's Doctrine of Providence

∷ ∷ ∷

MOLINA MAINTAINED THAT THE BIBLE just as emphatically teaches an extremely strong conception of divine sovereignty as it teaches libertarian human freedom, entailing the responsibility of humans for their actions. Harmonizing these two doctrines without undermining either has proven extremely difficult throughout the history of Christianity. However, Molina's conception of middle knowledge provides a stunning solution to this quandary. Primarily employing the presently untranslated books 5, 6, and 7 of Molina's *Concordia*, this chapter delineates how Molina used middle knowledge to formulate his ingenious doctrine of divine providence. According to Molina, God causes everything to happen by concurring with the choices of free individuals and stochastic processes in producing their effects. However, God does this in a way that preserves contingency, including human freedom and indeterminacy in the natural world. The key to this reconciliation between sovereignty and contingency lies in Molina's differentiation between God's absolute and conditional will. While God's absolute will is for each individual to find salvation freely, for no individual to sin freely, and for no natural evil to occur, it is logically impossible for God to create a world where this scenario would transpire. To use the terminology of the previous chapter, such a world is a possible world but not a feasible world. Hence God's absolute will can be thwarted. However, God's conditional will cannot be thwarted, since it depends on his middle knowledge and thus takes into account what every possible individual would freely do and how every stochastic process would randomly behave in any conceivable circumstances. In his conditional will, God permits several actions by free individuals and stochastic processes that he does not absolutely will. But the infinitely wise God providentially orders which circumstances transpire (i.e., by choosing to create a feasible world comprising those circumstances) so that his purposes are achieved notwithstanding, and even through, sinful human decisions and natural evils. Because God knows prior to his creative decree what any possible libertarian creature and stochastic process would do in any possible circumstances, God in deciding what creatures and stochastic processes to create and which circumstances to bring about or permit—namely, what feasible world to create—ultimately controls and directs the course of history to his ordained purposes, and yet without violating in any way the freedom of creatures or the randomness of natural processes.[1]

THE BIBLICAL BASIS FOR ALL-ENCOMPASSING PROVIDENCE

Molina defined providence as God's ordering of things to their intended good purposes either directly by his own action or indirectly by secondary causes. As Molina explained, "Divine providence is therefore nothing other than the reason or conception existing in the divine mind to order things to their ends by himself or even to be committed to the execution of the intervention of secondary causes to bring about his purposes, or ... is itself the very divine reason that disposes all things to their highest aims."[2] Molina believed that this all-encompassing providence over all events, whether good or evil, toward their highest purposes was seen most clearly in four biblical texts. First was Acts 4:27–28: "Indeed Herod and Pontius Pilate met together with the Gentiles and the people of Israel in this city to conspire against your holy servant Jesus, whom you anointed. They did what your power and will had decided beforehand should happen."[3] Here Molina detected an overwhelming providence over human affairs. For the wicked and complex

---

1. William Lane Craig, *The Problem of Divine Foreknowledge and Future Contingents from Aristotle to Suarez*, Studies in Intellectual History 7 (Leiden: Brill, 1988), 200.

2. "Est ergo providentia divina non aliud quam ratio seu conceptio ordinis rerum in suos fines in mente divina existens cum proposito eum per se vel etiam interventu causarum secundarum executioni mandandi, aut ... est ipsa divina ratio in summo omnium principe constituta qua cuncta disponit" (Ludovici Molina, *Liberi Arbitrii cum Gratiae Donis, Divina Praescientia, Providentia, Praedestinatione et Reprobatione Concordia*, ed. Johannes Rabeneck [Madrid: Sumptibus Societatis Editorialis "Sapientia," 1953], 6.1.1).

3. Ibid., 5.19.6.2.2.

human plot to crucify Jesus freely, which included the Jews and the Romans in Jerusalem at the time and, in particular, Herod and Pilate who tried Jesus, is asserted to have occurred by what God's power and will had decided beforehand — namely, by God's providence.[4] And God took this wicked and complex plot, which he despised, and made it the means by which human- ity would find forgiveness of sins and salvation. A second text that asserts that God so arranges things that even the sinful acts of humans advance his benevolent purposes is Genesis 50:20, where Joseph said to his brothers, "You intended to harm me, but God intended it for good to accomplish what is now being done, the saving of many lives."[5] Thus the heinous crime of Joseph's brothers selling him into Egyptian slavery was intended by God for the good purpose of saving the lives of the Egyptians, the children of Israel, and the neighboring people groups in the ancient Near East. The third text Molina called attention to was Ephesians 1:11, where Paul explained that in Christ "we were also chosen, having been predestined according to the plan of him who works out everything in conformity with the purpose of his will."[6] Molina observed that God works out *all things* in keeping with the intent of his will, or providence, such that not even a single event in creation lies beyond God's providence.[7] Finally, Molina saw the all-encompassing character of God's providence for the good of believers in Romans 8:28, "And we know that in all things God works for the good of those who love him, who have been called according to his purpose."[8] Not just in good circumstances but in *all circumstances*, Molina perceived, God providentially works for the benefit of his children in order to accomplish his ultimate, benevolent ends for human history.[9]

Based on this biblical evidence, the pressing question for Molina became, how can God cause or ordain good and evil acts alike without becoming the author of evil? In other words, how can we understand God's providence without saying God resorts to the immoral principle of the ends justifying the means? At this point, Molina drew on what contemporary philosophers

---

4. William Lane Craig, "The Middle-Knowledge View," in James K. Beilby and Paul R. Eddy, *Divine Foreknowledge: Four Views* (Downers Grove, IL: InterVarsity, 2001), 134.

5. Molina, *Concordia*, 5.19.6.2.3.

6. Ibid., 7.23.4/5.1.4.18.

7. Ibid., 7.23.4/5.2.1, 11.

8. Ibid., 7.23.1/2.3.3.

9. Ibid., 7.23.4/5.1.11.36.

call the distinction between strong and weak actualization (or causation).[10] An agent strongly actualizes (or strongly causes) an event if and only if the agent causally determines the event's obtaining. In this case, the agent directly causes the event and is therefore morally responsible for that event. By contrast, an agent weakly actualizes (or weakly causes) an event if and only if the agent strongly actualizes a situation in which another agent would strongly actualize an event. For example, suppose a teacher left his classroom for a few minutes during an exam to test his students' honesty, hoping that all the students would keep their eyes on their own papers and not cheat. Hence the teacher strongly actualizes the situation of the exam's being temporarily unproctored. But suppose that in this situation, one of the students decides to cheat by copying answers from his neighbor's paper. The student strongly actualizes the event of cheating. Obviously the student is morally responsible for the cheating, and the teacher bears no moral responsibility for the cheating. Nevertheless, the teacher did weakly cause the cheating by placing the student in circumstances where, despite the teacher's intentions to the contrary, the student freely chose to cheat. Hence in the case of weak causation, an agent indirectly causes various things to happen by bringing about the circumstances in which someone or something else would directly do those things. Although the agent causes the events in the limited sense that they never would have happened without the agent's generating the relevant circumstances, the agent is in no way morally responsible for the events. Molina recognized that the Bible, as a narrative record of God's dealings with humanity and not a philosophical treatise, makes no distinction between strong and weak causation. Thus when the Bible states that God does, causes, or ordains something, it is the case that God could do this thing either strongly or weakly. It is therefore up to Christians, as part of loving God with all their minds, to use their God-given ethical sensibilities and philosophical capacities to figure out which is which.[11]

Recall from chapter 2 Molina's distinction between God's particular or direct causation and God's general concurrence. God's particular or direct causation is the same as his strong causation, while God's general concurrence

---

10. For a thorough discussion of these modes of actualization see Alvin Plantinga, *The Nature of Necessity* (Oxford: Clarendon, 1974), 172–73.

11. Molina, *Concordia*, 3.14.13.40.25.

is the same as his weak causation. It is a fundamental facet of Molina's doctrine of providence that God causes everything in the world, either strongly or weakly. Regarding weak causation or general concurrence, we remember that, in any set of circumstances, for a creature to exercise its causal power God must simultaneously and indirectly cooperate with it by sustaining the creature and its causal power in being. It is important to note that the term *cooperate* (*cooperatio*), for Molina, does not in any way imply "to agree with" but conveys its literal meaning, to "co-operate," or to operate in conjunction with a creature.[12] So just as the sun cooperates, or operates in conjunction, with sinners by providing them with the heat and the light, which they use to sin, God cooperates with sinners by providing them with the existence and the causal power they use to sin. Neither the sun nor God is morally responsible for their sin. With this in mind, we are now able fully to delineate Molina's conception of weak causation.[13] God's weak causation means to cause indirectly by bringing about the circumstances—which include sustaining an agent's existence and causal power—where that agent directly (i.e., strongly) does something. Based on the fact that God's nature is the paradigm of goodness, Molina insisted that every evil act is weakly caused by God, whereas every good act is either weakly or strongly caused by God. Hence God causes, either indirectly or directly, every action without being the author of evil or standing morally responsible for evil.[14]

In describing what God's providence is and is not morally responsible for, Molina distinguished between two senses in which agents are related to actions or events, the *sensus divisius* (divided sense) and the *sensus compositus* (composite sense).[15] The divided sense analyzes each realm of reality (e.g., what happens on earth, what happens in heaven) in and of itself and takes other realms into account only when they determine, or place causal restraints on, what happens in the realm in question. It is an inherently moral sense, in that anyone who does something in the divided sense directly causes and is therefore morally responsible for that thing. Thus if a man killed a woman, the man committed homicide in the divided sense, since he directly caused her

---

12. Ibid., 2.14.13.28.6; 2.14.13.29.3–5.
13. Ibid., 2.14.13.25.
14. Ibid., 2.14.13.33.3–5.
15. Luis de Molina, *On Divine Foreknowledge*, trans. Alfred J. Freddoso (Ithaca, NY: Cornell University Press, 1988), 4.14.13.52.30.

death, and God did not make him kill her or put any causal restraints on him that necessitated his killing her. The man could have done otherwise and let the woman live. Therefore, in the divided sense, God did not commit homicide or cause the homicide. By contrast, the composite sense examines the full scope of reality by taking all of its realms into account as well as the interplay between the various realms, regardless of whether such interplay stems from cause and effect relationships. It is an inherently nonmoral sense, in that it says nothing about the moral responsibility for an action. One may or may not be responsible for what one does in the composite sense, as the composite sense makes no distinction between indirect and direct action.[16] Since God knew, via his middle knowledge, that were the man in certain circumstances (which include God's sustaining the man's existence and his causal power) the man would kill the woman, if God proceeds to create a world containing those circumstances, then, in the composite sense, God commits homicide or causes the homicide. But this says nothing about whether God directly committed the homicide or is morally responsible for it; indeed we already know that because God did not commit the homicide in the divided sense, he did not directly commit it and is not morally responsible for it.[17]

Molina returned to his oft-cited example of Peter's denying Jesus to differentiate between the divided and the composite senses. Even though one could say that God caused Peter to deny Jesus in the composite sense, for God chose to create a world in which Peter freely denies Jesus, one could not say that God caused Peter to deny Jesus in the divided sense. In the divided sense, Peter was the sole cause of his sin. Concerning the error of inferring from the composite sense that Peter was powerless but to deny Jesus, Molina protested:

> We should not claim that because the divine foreknowledge already existed beforehand, Peter is in reality not able not to sin, as if because of the preexisting divine knowledge he has lost something of his freedom and power not to sin in reality should he so will. For I would not hesitate to call this sort of interpretation an error from the point of view of the faith. Indeed, even though that knowledge did exist beforehand, it was just as truly within his power not to sin as it would have been had that knowledge not existed,

---

16. For a complete examination of the divided and composite senses, see Alfred J. Freddoso, "Accidental Necessity and Logical Determinism," *Journal of Philosophy* 80 (1983): 257–58.

17. My illustration is inspired by Molina's similar illustration in *Foreknowledge*, 4.14.13.53.16, 18.

and he was just as truly able to refrain from the act in light of which he was foreknown to be a future sinner as he would have been had that knowledge not existed.... And so that knowledge, which would not have existed if, as is possible, Peter were not going to sin, does not in any way prevent Peter's now being able in the divided sense not to sin, in just the way he would have been able not to sin had such knowledge not existed beforehand.[18]

Here Molina reiterated the claim made while discussing fatalism that knowledge is not causally determinative, such that neither God's middle knowledge nor his foreknowledge cost anyone a shred of their libertarian freedom. On the same score, God's causing an act in the composite sense does not necessitate that the act occur or take away any of the freedom of the direct agent. The direct agent could still freely choose not to perform the act, just as much as if God had never caused it in the composite sense.

THE EXPLANATORY POWER OF MOLINA'S DOCTRINE OF PROVIDENCE

On Molina's doctrine of providence, then, God does all of the world's activities in the composite sense.[19] This follows inescapably from God's creative decree, precipitated upon his middle knowledge. But God only does a tiny minority of the world's activities in the divided sense. That tiny minority encompasses God's direct acts of intervention in the natural order, such as miracles, prophecy, and above all, the life of Jesus. Notice that everything God does in the divided sense is good, as required by God's character. It is morally impossible for God to do anything evil in the divided sense. These conclusions about providence functioned for Molina as a hermeneutical lens through which Scripture must be read. In other words, any good act the Bible attributes to God is caused by God in the composite sense and may or may not be caused by God in the divided sense, depending on the situation. All good acts fall under the rubric of God's absolute will. But any evil act that the Bible attributes to God is caused by God in the composite sense and is not caused by God in the divided sense; rather, in the divided sense it is caused by creatures. All evil acts fall under the rubric of God's permission, meaning

---

18. Molina, *Foreknowledge*, 4.14.13.52.30.
19. Molina, *Concordia*, 5.19.6.2.1.

that God allows them to occur by his conditional will to enable creaturely freedom even though they violate his absolute will. Hence Molina declared, "It is not always the case that God wills (i.e., absolutely wills) by virtue of his conditional will. This conclusion ... is manifest. God wills for all humans to be saved in accord with their volition, yet nevertheless all do not attain salvation. He also wills that his precepts and counsels be observed, and yet they are everywhere disregarded."[20] One cannot therefore assume that because something is permitted by God's conditional will, it is approved of or desired by God. Certainly such is not true concerning the damnation of unbelievers or the breaking of God's commandments.

This hermeneutic nicely explained the four core texts on which Molina's doctrine of providence was based as well as many other perennially difficult texts. Regarding Acts 4:27–28, the evil plot to crucify Jesus did occur in the composite sense by what God's power and will had decided beforehand. For God knew that if the relevant Jewish and Roman agents were in various circumstances, including his empowering their existence and libertarian freedom, they would freely engineer Jesus' crucifixion. And yet God willed to create a world containing these circumstances. But God had nothing to do with the plot to crucify Jesus in the divided sense, as demonstrated by Jesus' plaintive cry, "Father, forgive them, for they do not know what they are doing" (Luke 23:34), and by Jesus' remark to his opponents that "this is your hour—when darkness reigns" (Luke 22:53).[21] Genesis 50:20 illustrates how God, in his conditional will, can intend that Joseph endure hardship in Egypt for the good purpose of saving lives even though Joseph's hardship contradicted God's absolute will and was not intended for good by its direct perpetrators. According to Molina, this text made an extremely important point about God's conditional will.[22] Via his conditional will, the infinitely wise God permits many evil acts and intends them for good purposes utterly contrary to the nefarious intentions for which creatures committed them, so that God's end or *telos* for human history is achieved in spite of and even through the evil free choices of creatures. Hence God's conditional will

---

20. "Non semper impletur quod Deus voluntate condicionali vult. Conclusio haec ... est manifesta. Vult enim eiusmodi volitione omnes hominess salvos fieri, nec tamen omnes salutem assequuntur. Vult item sua praecepta et consilia observari quae tamen passim contemnuntur" (ibid., 5.19.6.2.6).

21. Ibid., 5.19.6.2.2.

22. Ibid., 5.19.6.2.3.

factors all creaturely evils into the proverbial equation and still accomplishes God's *telos*, which entails that God's conditional will cannot be frustrated by creatures.[23] Molina observed that precisely this fact was affirmed by Ephesians 1:11, as God works out everything, good and bad, in conformity with the *telos* of his conditional will, and presupposed by Romans 8:28, as God works out everything for the good of believers.[24]

Other difficult texts which this hermeneutic successfully elucidates include God's hardening the heart of Pharaoh (Exod. 4:21; 7:3; 14:4; Rom. 9:17–18), God's inciting David to take a census of the Israelites (2 Sam. 24:1), and God's sending evildoers in the end times a powerful delusion so that they will believe the lie and be condemned (2 Thess. 2:11–12). For Molina God hardened Pharaoh's heart in the composite sense and not in the divided sense. Even though God never willed for Pharaoh's heart to be hardened, God placed Pharaoh in various circumstances where Pharaoh freely hardened his own heart. As Molina insisted, "Thus it is agreed concerning the hardness of heart that it was not the taking away of the faculty of doing from Pharaoh, a faculty that persisted because his hardness of heart was able to be defeated by it, if he willed."[25] Given Pharaoh's free choice to do evil, God, in his conditional will, intended to use Pharaoh's choice for the good purpose of gaining glory for himself and increasing the knowledge of himself throughout the earth (Exod. 9:16; 14:4; Rom. 9:17). Similarly, God did not incite David sinfully to take a census in the divided sense but only in the composite sense, as 1 Chronicles 21:1 reveals that Satan was responsible for inciting David to take the census in the divided sense. In other words, God chose to create a world in which Satan would freely and successfully tempt David to take the census. Though God did not want David to take the census, God knew that David would violate his will. That such an act constituted a violation of God's will is evident from David's words in 2 Samuel 24:10: "I have sinned greatly in what I have done. Now, LORD, I beg you, take away the guilt of your servant. I have done a very foolish thing." It is also evident from God's sending a plague on Israel as punishment for conducting the census (2 Sam. 24:15–16).

---

23. William Lane Craig, *Divine Foreknowledge and Human Freedom: The Coherence of Theism: Omniscience*, Studies in Intellectual History 19 (Leiden: Brill, 1990), 241.

24. Molina, *Concordia*, 7.23.4/5.2.11; 7.23.4/5.1.11.36.

25. "Constat ergo per obdurationem illam non fuisse sublatam facultatem a Pharaone faciendi id circa quod obdurato persistebat corde potuisseque duritiam illam vincere, si vellet" (ibid., 1.14.13.10.8; cf. 7.23.4/5.4.2).

Regarding 2 Thessalonians 2:11–12, Molina argued that God will send end-time evildoers a powerful delusion in the composite sense and not in the divided sense; in the divided sense Satan and the man of sin, or Antichrist, are the cause of the delusion. God is only its cause in the sense that he chose to create a world in which Satan freely uses the Antichrist to send the delusion on those who freely delight in wickedness, a delusion so attractive for them that they freely believe the lie and so find condemnation. As Molina explained the text: "Therefore that operation of error which God sends is nothing other than the future seduction of the Antichrist whose advent is not according to the operation of God, but according to the operation of Satan; thus it is said there how God permits the offense of the sins of the world."[26] However, it is God's will for the end-time evildoers not to believe the lie but to receive salvation and come to the knowledge of the truth (1 Tim. 2:4; 2 Peter 3:9). And it remains within their power, even after the delusion comes, not to believe the Antichrist's lie and to find salvation. So Molina concluded that in the cases of Pharaoh, David, and the end-time evildoers, God did not will for them to sin, as he is a loving God whose desire for them and for all his creatures is that they always choose good.[27] In the circumstances in which Pharaoh and David found themselves and in which the end-time evildoers will find themselves, they were or will be truly free to select from opposite courses of action. The aforementioned texts, and ones like it, are simply examples of Scripture's following its consistent pattern of attributing to God events that he weakly actualizes by setting in motion courses of free creaturely action which he knows, if instantiated, would indeterministically lead to the pertinent events.[28]

26. "Quare operatio illa erroris quam Deus immittet non est alia quam seductio quae futura est per Antichristum cuius adventus non erit secundum operationem Dei, sed secundum operationem satanae, ut ibi dicitur, quam Deus propter delicta huius saeculi permittet" (ibid., 2.14.13.34.11).

27. Ibid., 1.14.13.10.13.

28. Other texts that Molina expounds according to the same hermeneutic include God's giving people over to the sinful desires of their hearts, shameful lusts, and a depraved mind (Rom. 1:24, 26, 28), the rhetorical question "When disaster comes to a city, has not the LORD caused it?" (Amos 3:6); the affirmation that God creates darkness and disaster (Isa. 45:7); the turn of events from God whereby Rehoboam did not listen to the people of Israel (1 Kings 12:15); God's hardening of the Israelites' hearts so that they did not revere him (Isa. 63:17); and God's depriving the earth's leaders of their reason (Job 12:24–25). Molina proclaimed that his hermeneutic is necessary to preserve the goodness of God in all these texts, since it shows how God did not directly cause any of the evils described but indirectly caused them by his permission (ibid., 2.14.13.34.1, 6, 9–11).

THE PROCESS AND RESULTS OF GOD'S PROVIDENCE

Molina claimed that on his account of divine providence, the traditional tension between divine sovereignty and genuine human freedom evaporates. This is due to the fact that the process of God's providence occurs through a combination of knowledge beyond God's control and a cornucopia of decisions under God's control. By possessing middle knowledge of how persons would freely choose in any feasible world and knowing the various ways he could freely sustain relationships with them and react to their choices, God, in deciding which feasible world will be actual, undergoes what Molina called an "absolutely complete and unlimited deliberation."[29] This deliberation is the unimaginably complex planning stage of the world, in which God weighs all the possibilities of the different creatures (including persons and stochastic processes) existing and acting in various circumstances as well as the various ways he could relate to different persons and respond to their actions. Through his unlimited reflection on all these factors, God plans down to the last detail the feasible world he will create and does so without obliterating libertarian freedom or contingency, for God already knows what free creatures and stochastic processes would do in any feasible world. Thus, in making his creative decree, which looks at first glance like only one decision, God in fact makes an incomprehensibly vast array of decisions concerning the creatures that will exist, the circumstances they will find themselves in, how they will contingently act in those circumstances, his future relationships with persons, and his future reactions to their choices. These last two items show that God, in his creative decree, commits himself to taking various courses of action in the world as opposed to other available courses of action.

Allow me to illustrate the incomprehensibly nested nature of the decision that is the divine creative decree: in this decree God decides, among a plethora of other things, that he will instantiate the individual essences of Adam and Eve (and not some other individual human essences), that he will place Adam and Eve in the garden of Eden despite that they will rebel against him there, and that he will react to this rebellion by expelling Adam and Eve from the garden instead of letting them stay in the garden. In sum, because

---

29. Molina, *Foreknowledge*, 4.14.15.52.13.

God possesses middle knowledge and makes a cornucopia of free decisions as part of his choice concerning which feasible world to create, God possesses complete foreknowledge as to how those creatures will act and tremendous control over their actions, in the sense that any act they carry out is either willed or permitted by God. Nevertheless, since the knowledge that underlies God's sovereign planning (i.e., middle knowledge) is not itself a product of God's choice or control, human actions are genuinely free, not the puppet-like effects of God's causal determination.[30]

Let's look at an example of how God is provident over particular actions at this point. Take the action of Ian's buying a dog in certain circumstances *C*. According to Molina, God has foreknowledge of and control over this action.[31] Before creation, God first by his natural knowledge apprehended infinitely many truths about Ian's individual essence, including the possibility of Ian's individual essence, if instantiated, buying a dog. Then by his middle knowledge, God knew that Ian's individual essence, if instantiated and placed in *C*, would freely buy a dog, even though it could have done otherwise. Thus "Ian's individual essence buying a dog in *C*" is not part of Ian's individual essence. But this knowledge obviously left God with countless options prior to his creative decree. He could instantiate Ian's individual essence and place Ian in *C*. He could instantiate Ian's individual essence and place Ian in a plethora of other circumstances, only in some of which Ian would freely buy a dog. In many of these circumstances, however, Ian would freely not buy the dog. In some Ian would freely buy a cat; in others Ian would freely buy a hamster; in others Ian would freely refrain from purchasing any animal. Or God could choose not to instantiate Ian's individual essence at all. Whichever of these myriad options God chooses with respect to Ian, God knows via his middle knowledge precisely how the world would turn out if he selected that option. Hence God exercises tremendous control over Ian. Whatever Ian does (if there is an Ian to do anything in the first place), Ian will do only because God knowingly actualizes a world in which that precise choice is freely made by Ian. Assessing these myriad options, God issues his creative decree, a nested decision that includes the decision to instantiate Ian's

---

30. Thomas P. Flint, *Divine Providence: The Molinist Account* (Ithaca, NY: Cornell University Press, 1998), 44.

31. Molina, *Concordia*, 6.22.2.1, 3–5.

individual essence and place Ian in *C.* As its immediate results, this creative decree yields God's foreknowledge that Ian will buy the dog and Ian's being in *C,* which in turn leads to his freely buying the dog. Middle knowledge is therefore the key to God's providence, as it provides God both foreknowledge of and control over Ian's free decision.[32]

Here we see that the results of God's providence—including his planning and decision making—are foreknowledge and control of contingent events. Thus far from compromising divine sovereignty, Molina attempted to enhance God's sovereignty such that, on his doctrine of providence, God is actually more sovereign than he is on Calvin's doctrine of providence.[33] For, as Molina insisted, it is obvious that a God who can infallibly control every libertarian free creaturely action and random natural event without compromising that freedom and randomness is more sovereign than a God who can only control every creaturely action or natural event if creatures lack libertarian freedom and natural processes lack randomness. While on Calvin's view God is threatened by libertarian freedom and randomness and cannot permit either in order to remain sovereign, on Molina's view God's sovereignty is not threatened by either libertarian freedom or randomness but is rather augmented by his ability to control the effects of both.[34] Accordingly, Molina held that his view issues in praise and adoration of God for his breathtaking sovereignty "so that it should be exclaimed with Paul [Rom. 11:33–35]: O, the depth of the riches of the wisdom and knowledge of God, how incomprehensible are his judgments, and how inscrutable his ways!"[35] That Molina's view is the only one on offer that permits the conjunction of an all-encompassing providence and libertarian freedom is recognized by a good many philosophers and theologians.[36] Even the philosopher William Hasker,

32. My example of Ian buying the dog closely follows Flint's example (*Divine Providence*, 44) of the fictional Cuthbert buying an iguana.

33. Molina, *Concordia*, 7.23.4/5.1.1, 4–5.

34. God's ability to control the effects of both is one reason why, as Kenneth Keathley points out (*Salvation and Sovereignty: A Molinist Approach* [Nashville: Broadman & Holman Academic, 2010], 5–6), several staunch Arminians like Roger Olson and Robert Picirilli reject Molinism as being too Calvinistic. For this critique, see Roger E. Olson, *Arminian Theology: Myths and Realities* (Downers Grove, IL: IVP Academic, 2006), 194–99; and Robert E. Picirilli, *Grace, Faith, Free Will* (Nashville: Randall House, 2002), 62–63.

35. "Exclamandum est cum Paulo [Rom 11, 33–35]: O altitudo divitiarum sapientiae et scientiae Dei, quam incomprehensibilia sunt iudicia eius, et investigabiles viae eius!" (Molina, *Concordia*, 7.23.4/5.1.13.4; cf. 7.23.4/5.1.11.13).

36. Representative of these thinkers are William Lane Craig ("Middle-Knowledge View," 135),

a prominent open theist and anti-Molinist, admits, "If you are committed to a 'strong' view of providence, according to which, down to the smallest detail, 'things are as they are because God knowingly decided to create such a world,' and yet you also wish to maintain a libertarian conception of free will—if this is what you want, then Molinism is the only game in town."[37]

To get a very small handle on the depth of God's wisdom and knowledge asserted by Molina's doctrine of providence, consider, in Craig's words, "the unimaginably complex and numerous factors that would need to be combined in order to bring about through the free decisions of creatures a single human event."[38] As a case in point, let us take the establishment of the doctrine of the Trinity (three divine persons comprising the one God) as the official teaching of the universal Christian church at the Council of Constantinople in 381. For, through his middle knowledge, God knew exactly what Gregory of Nazianzus, if archbishop of Constantinople, would freely maintain concerning the distinction between the three persons (*hypostases*) and the one divine nature or being (*ousia*); what Gregory of Nyssa, if bishop of Nyssa, would freely believe concerning Gregory of Nazianzus's distinction; what Basil the Great, if bishop of Caesarea Mazaca, would freely write in opposition to the Arians (who denied the deity of Christ) and the Pneumatomachians (who denied the deity and personality of the Holy Spirit); what Theodosius I, if the Roman emperor, would freely decide regarding the calling of an ecumenical council; and which persons, if bishops of prominent churches in the Roman Empire, would freely vote in favor of the Niceno-Constantinopolitan Creed (what is today called the Nicene Creed).[39] Craig sums up the situation nicely: "Knowing all the possible circumstances, persons and permutations of those circumstances and persons, God decreed to create just those circumstances and just those people who would freely do what God willed to happen."[40]

Thomas P. Flint (*Divine Providence*, 75–76), Alvin Plantinga (*God, Freedom, and Evil* [New York: Harper & Row, 1974], 29–44), Kenneth Keathley (*Salvation and Sovereignty*, 6), Alfred J. Freddoso ("Introduction," in Molina, *Foreknowledge*, 53–62, 80–81), and Bruce A. Little (*A Creation-Order Theodicy: God and Gratuitous Evil* [Lanham, MD: University Press of America, 2005], 146–48).

37. William Hasker, "Response to Thomas Flint," *Philosophical Studies* 60, no. 1/2 (1990): 117–18.

38. William Lane Craig, *The Only Wise God: The Compatibility of Divine Foreknowledge and Human Freedom* (Grand Rapids: Baker, 1987), 135.

39. For a full discussion of the circumstances surrounding the Council of Constantinople, see Everett Ferguson, *Church History, Volume One: From Christ to Pre-Reformation* (Grand Rapids: Zondervan, 2005), 206–10.

40. Craig, "Middle-Knowledge View," 134. Although Craig wrote this summation with a different example in mind, it is equally applicable to our example of the official codification of Trinitarian doctrine.

Hence the entire situation unfolded according to the plan of God. All of this is utterly mind-dizzying. When we consider that the various circumstances and persons involved were themselves the result of a plethora of prior free decisions on the part of these and other persons (including the decisions leading up to and generating the Council of Nicea in 325), and these in turn of still other preceding contingent events, and so forth, we perceive that only an infinite, omniscient mind could providentially lead a world of free creatures and random natural events toward his sovereignly chosen ends.[41]

At this juncture Molina reiterated that although God's providential planning of and predetermination to create the actual world encompasses everything that happens, this does not entail that God positively wills everything that happens. In other words, just because God controls everything that happens (by choosing to create a world where it contingently happens) does not mean that God wills everything he controls. Rather, Molina maintained that while God indeed positively wills every good creaturely choice, every evil creaturely choice he does not will but simply permits. As we have previously seen, God permits them through his general concurrence, genuinely willing that creatures employ that concurrence not to make evil choices but good choices. Moreover, Molina postulated that God permits each particular evil for the sake of a greater good.[42] For God is cognizant, in his middle knowledge, that only if creatures freely committed that evil would some greater good freely come about. Hence God permitted Joseph's brothers freely to sell him into slavery because God knew that it was the only way that Egypt and the surrounding Near Eastern nations would freely be saved from the ensuing famine. Molina drew together the threads of his reasoning in the following passage:

> Finally, we claim that all *good* things, whether produced by causes acting from a necessity of nature or by free causes, depend on divine predetermination (of the sort we have just explicated) and providence in such a way that each is *specifically intended* by God through His predetermination and providence, whereas the *evil* acts of the created faculty of choice are subject as well to divine predetermination and providence to the extent that the causes from which they emanate and the general concurrence on God's part required to elicit them are granted through divine predetermination

41. Ibid., 135; idem, *Only Wise God*, 135.
42. Craig, *Problem of Divine Foreknowledge and Future Contingents*, 200.

and providence—though not in order that *these particular acts* should emanate from them, but rather in order that *other, far different, acts* might come to be, and in order that the innate freedom of the things endowed with a faculty of choice might be preserved for their maximum benefit; in addition, evil acts are subject to that same divine predetermination and providence to the extent that they cannot exist in particular unless God by His providence *permits them in particular* for the sake of some greater good. It clearly follows that all things without exception are *individually* subject to God's providence and will, which intends certain of them *as particulars* and permits the rest *as particulars*. Thus, the leaf hanging from the tree does not fall, nor does anything else whatever happen without God's providence and will either *intending* it *as a particular* or *permitting* it *as a particular*. This is the greatest consolation of the righteous, who place all their hope in God and rest comfortably in the shadow of the wings of His providence, desiring that in both prosperity and adversity God's will with regard to them might always be fulfilled.[43]

In sum, God's all-encompassing providence, by which he intends each particular good act and permits each particular evil act for the sake of a greater good, furnishes believers with tremendous confidence that through all things, whether good or evil, God's loving purposes for them will ultimately be accomplished.

APPLICATIONS OF MOLINA'S DOCTRINE OF PROVIDENCE

Molina recognized that his doctrine of providence carries profound ramifications for many features of the divine-human relationship, especially prophecy and prayer. Regarding prophecy, let us return to Molina's favorite example of Peter's threefold denial of Jesus. Prior to Peter's denial, Jesus famously prophesied: "Truly I tell you ... today—yes, tonight—before the rooster crows twice you yourself will disown me three times" (Mark 14:30). The question for Molina was whether when Jesus uttered these words, he determined that Peter would deny him such that Peter could not do otherwise. The same question arises with God's prophesying any other future

---

43. Molina, *Foreknowledge*, 4.14.15.53.3.17; emphasis in original.

event in Scripture: does God thereby determine it to occur so that nothing else could have occurred in its place? According to Molina, the answer to this question is no. For God employs his middle knowledge in deciding when he will communicate to creatures knowledge of future events. Here Molina took a similar train of thought to that of will and permission with regard to God's prophecy of good and evil acts, which we shall treat in reverse order. A necessary (but not sufficient) condition for God to prophesy evil acts is when he apprehends in his middle knowledge that his prophecy would not causally contribute to their commission and that the prophecy itself would accomplish some future good. Now God doesn't prophesy every evil act that meets this condition, but God in his sovereignty chooses only to prophesy evil acts that do meet this condition.[44] So, in the case of Peter, Jesus prophesied Peter's threefold denial because Jesus knew in his middle knowledge that Peter's individual essence, if instantiated, would freely deny Jesus three times (even though it could have done otherwise) regardless of whether Jesus prophesied it and that the prophecy would accomplish the future good of leading Peter to repent of his sin (Mark 14:72; Luke 22:32) and of convincing Peter and persons down through history to believe in Jesus as deity (John 14:29).[45]

Notice the importance, in God's prophesying evil acts, of God's middle knowledge that his prophecy would not somehow bring about the evil. In other words, Jesus would not have prophesied Peter's denial if he knew that Peter would not deny him unless Jesus first prophesied it and so planted, as it were, the seed of the denial in Peter's mind. For this, as Craig observes, would constitute a "divine sting operation" utterly contrary to God's morally perfect character and to God's will that creatures always, in every set of circumstances, choose the good.[46] Hence Molina emphasized that "God is able to influence our free choice in whatever way He wants to, except toward sin — for that would involve a contradiction."[47] So it is a prerequisite for Jesus' prophecy of Peter's denial that Jesus middle-knew Peter would freely deny him in the absence of the prophecy (thus not contributing to sin) and that the prophecy would not alter Peter's future free denial (thus ensuring the truthfulness of the prophecy).

---

44. Molina, *Concordia*, 6.22.4.8.
45. Molina, *Foreknowledge*, 4.14.15.51.19; 4.14.15.52.8.
46. Craig, *Only Wise God*, 134.
47. Molina, *Foreknowledge*, 4.14.15.52.10.

By contrast, with regard to God's prophecy of any good act, Molina held that God may prophesy it under either of two conditions. Either God middle-knew that the good act would come to pass regardless of the occurrence or nonoccurrence of the prophecy or, intriguingly, God middle-knew that the prophecy itself would causally contribute to the good act, such that in the absence of the prophecy the good act would not come to pass.[48] Let us furnish an example of each condition. On the one hand, God middle-knew that the Persian emperor Cyrus would freely liberate the Jewish people from the Babylonian exile in 538 BC regardless of the presence or absence of any prophecy to this effect. Yet, through the prophet Isaiah over a century in advance, God prophesied that Cyrus would accomplish this liberation (Isa. 45:1–13). That the prophecy made no causal contribution to its fulfillment is evidenced by the fact that Cyrus was a pagan emperor who knew nothing of Isaiah's prophecy and did not follow the biblical God. This is stated in the prophecy itself, where God says of Cyrus, "You do not acknowledge me.... You have not acknowledged me" (Isa. 45:4–5). On the other hand, Jesus middle-knew that his followers would carry out the prophecy, "you will be my witnesses in Jerusalem, and in all Judea and Samaria, and to the ends of the earth" (Acts 1:8), only if he made the prophecy. Here the prophecy functioned as an exhortation for the original disciples to evangelize not only their fellow Jews, which they might have done in any case, but to evangelize Samaritans and the Gentile nations, which ran contrary to their Jewish modes of thinking and which they would not have done without Jesus' prompting. Moreover, the prophecy continues to function as an exhortation for Christians to carry out the task of world evangelization and has prompted the work of many missionaries throughout history and today.

Molina's doctrine of providence also has much to say concerning prayer. Because God middle-knew how each possible individual would freely pray in any set of circumstances, God uses this information providentially to order the world in such a way that at least some of our prayers make a profound difference in the history of the world. As part of the cornucopia of free decisions God makes in his decree to create this world, God decides to respond to some of our prayers in such a way that prayers change the course of the future. Suppose God middle-knew that Ben, if created, would pray for certain

---

48. Molina, *Concordia*, 6.22.2.1–5.

things. God can then decree to actualize a feasible world where Ben exists and where the future course of events includes some of the things Ben prays for, which come about either through the course of free creaturely decisions or through direct supernatural intervention. But suppose God middle-knew that Ben, if created, would want but not pray for the things in question. God could then decree to actualize another feasible world where Ben exists (say, a world with the same history as the first up to the moment of Ben's decision not to pray) and where none of these things Ben wanted would occur, namely, a world with a different future course of free creaturely decisions not leading to the things Ben wanted and lacking any direct supernatural intervention to accomplish the things Ben wanted. Since our prayers or lack thereof are already factored into the equation of God's providential planning, they prove to be the deciding factor in whether God actualizes a future where some of the things we desire either do or do not happen. Thus we truly have a reciprocal relationship with God through prayer.

Molina pointed out that many events in the natural world, such as births, happen and that many people are saved, both physically and spiritually, as a result of the prayers of the righteous: "Here is the proof, insofar as the righteous through their own prayers ... received from God many natural blessings. In fact, the prayers of Isaac made Rebecca fertile out of her state of barrenness. Through prayer Hannah received her son Samuel and Zechariah received John the Baptist. And the prayers of the righteous obtained and will obtain in the future many natural blessings and greatly contribute to the salvation of many."[49] In response to his middle knowledge of these persons' prayers, God providentially arranges the natural order in a different way than how he would have ordered it apart from their prayers or supernaturally intervenes in a way that he would not have done apart from their prayers. So Molina argued that had it not been for the prayer of Isaac, Rebecca would have remained barren (Gen. 25:21); had it not been for the prayer of Hannah, Samuel never would have been born (1 Sam. 1:10–20); and had it not been for the prayer of Zechariah, John the Baptist would never have been born (Luke 1:13). If at any of these links of the chain making up our world the

---

49. "Probatur, quoniam multa naturalia iusti suis orationibus ... a Deo obtinuerunt. Isaac enim preces Rebeccam ex sterili foecundam reddiderunt, Anna Samuelem filium, Zacharias Ioannem Baptistam et pleraque alia naturalia iusti orationibus a Deo impetrarunt impetrabunt que in posterum quorum multa ad salutem plurimorum maxime conferunt" (Molina, *Concordia*, 7.23.4/5.2.5).

relevant persons did not pray, the world would be a radically different place than it in fact is. If Rebecca had remained barren, there would not have been a Hannah, since Hannah was a descendant of Rebecca. And if Samuel had never been born, there would probably have not been a Zechariah (and thus no John the Baptist), since without Samuel's leadership the nation of Israel would likely have been obliterated by the Philistines (1 Sam. 7:7–13).[50] Regarding salvation of body and/or soul, we may point to Moses' prayer to spare the Israelites following the golden calf incident (Exod. 32:9–14). Had Moses not prayed, God would have wiped out the Israelites, causing the lot of them to be physically and spiritually lost, but because of Moses' prayer, the Israelites were spared and some of them received eternal life, including Aaron, Miriam, Joshua, and Caleb. Moreover, had Hezekiah not prayed for Israel's deliverance from the attack of the Assyrian king Sennacherib, Israel would have been physically destroyed in 701 BC, which would have caused many future individuals either not to exist or to exist and not find spiritual salvation. But because of Hezekiah's prayer, God supernaturally intervened by sending the angel of the Lord to defeat the Assyrian armies (2 Kings 19:14–36; Isa. 37:14–37). We may also point to Stephen's dying prayer for his slayers, "Lord, do not hold this sin against them" (Acts 7:60), which God answered through his conversion of the chief persecutor, Saul/Paul of Tarsus (Acts 9:1–19), who became the foremost theologian and evangelist of early Christianity.[51] In these ways, we, through our prayers, are cocreators of the world with God.

At this point, an even more provocative question arises: does middle knowledge make it possible for God to respond to some of our prayers in such a way that prayers affect the course of the past? This is a question not directly taken up by Molina, but Thomas Flint has argued that middle knowledge allows for a select few of our prayers causally to impact the past.[52] Now, no prayer can causally impact the past in a contradictory fashion; I cannot successfully pray that something had happened that would preclude a present

---

50. Among the other natural events Molina also could have cited here is Hezekiah's prayer for deliverance from a fatal illness, which God answered by effecting his healing through the application of a poultice of figs and allowing him to live for fifteen additional years. Without Hezekiah's prayer, he would have died from the illness (2 Kings 20:1–7; Isa. 38:1–21).

51. Molina, *Concordia*, 7.23.4/5.1.7.16.

52. Flint, *Divine Providence*, 229–50.

reality or that a past event had never occurred. (Thus I cannot successfully pray that something happened that would preclude my own existence or that World War II never happened.) In other words, I cannot pray to *change* the past.[53] But barring those things that preclude present realities or past events, I can pray for something to have happened such that God in the past would have brought about precisely that event, and if I did not pray for that event to have happened, God in the past would not have brought about that event.[54] So while the event is chronologically prior to the prayer, my prayer is logically prior to the event. To illustrate, suppose there was a multicar pileup on I–55 just outside Chicago. In his middle knowledge, God knows that if he were to permit this evil event (because he knows he could work through it to bring about a greater good), then when the pileup would be reported on the news a few minutes later, a mother would freely pray that her son was not in the pileup. Consequently, in his creative decree God decides to actualize a feasible world where God permits the pileup but protects the son from the accident. But had God instead middle-known that if he were to permit the pileup, then when the pileup would be reported on the news the mother would not freely pray for her son, God in his creative decree may well decide to actualize a different feasible world with exactly the same history as the aforementioned world up to the moment of the pileup but where the son is involved in the accident. Hence even though I cannot *change* the past, through prayer I can *effect* the past. I can pray in such a way that had I not prayed, the past would have been different than it in fact is. Even though this is not backward causation (making the past no longer the past), it is what I have called in another place a "functional equivalent to backward causation."[55] For it accomplishes, in a noncontradictory way, the aim of causally impacting the past without altering the past. The past cannot be altered, but the reason the past is the way it is consists in my divinely middle-known prayer in the present or future. Consequently, on Molinism, the past is not counterfactually closed, an observation Molina implied in reflecting on the scriptural truth that God

---

53. Ibid., 230.
54. Counterfactuals of this form are known among philosophers of religion as backtracking counterfactuals; for further discussion of backtracking counterfactuals, see Craig, *Divine Foreknowledge and Human Freedom*, 185–86, 191–93, 197, 212–21.
55. Kirk R. MacGregor, *A Molinist-Anabaptist Systematic Theology* (Lanham, MD: University Press of America, 2007), 89.

knows the end from the beginning (Isa. 46:10).[56] Through prayer, then, we do have some degree of counterfactual power over the past.[57]

Molina's doctrine of providence also goes to solve the personally troublesome problem of unanswered prayer faced by all followers of Christ. According to Molina, there are four possible reasons why God does not answer an individual's prayer. First, answering a prayer may be logically impossible for God and therefore lies outside the bounds of divine omnipotence.[58] For example, it is logically impossible for God to answer someone's prayer that an enemy was never born, that the Holocaust never happened, or that God would commit evil so the individual could get revenge on someone. Second, answering a prayer may be logically infeasible for God—namely, logically possible in and of itself but logically impossible given God's will to enable libertarian human freedom and stochastic processes.[59] For example, a father may pray that his daughter turn from a life of sin to a life of Christian discipleship. But since the envisioned conversion entails a free choice on the part of the daughter, it is not solely up to God whether the prayer is answered. As Flint rightly notes, "God may do all he can—indeed, may do more than he would have done in the absence of the prayer—and yet find his best efforts rebuffed by his free creature."[60] Hence there may not be a feasible world that God could have created where the daughter exists and is saved, even given the increased divine assistance garnered by her father's prayer.

Third, God may middle-know that answering a prayer would not be ultimately advantageous to the individual.[61] Suppose God, in his middle knowledge, apprehends that if the essences of a particular girl and boy were actualized, then the girl would pray that the boy would freely marry her. Suppose God also apprehends that in every feasible world he could create where the boy freely marries the girl, the boy cheats on the girl and ruins her life, prompting her to abandon her belief in God. Finally, suppose God

---

56. Molina, *Concordia*, 5.19.6.2.1.

57. Flint (*Divine Providence*, 243) calls this type of power "weak counterfactual power" and states that an agent has weak counterfactual power over a particular truth if and only if for some event the agent can directly cause that event, in the absence of which the truth would not be true.

58. Molina, *Concordia*, 2.14.13.26.14; Ludovici Molina, *Commentaria in primam divi Thomae partem* (Venice, 1602), 25.3.

59. Molina, *Concordia*, 7.23.4/5.1.13.6; idem, *Commentaria*, 25.4.

60. Flint, *Divine Providence*, 216.

61. Molina, *Concordia*, 6.22.4.10; 7.23.4/5.1.14.8–10.

apprehends that there are feasible worlds he could create where the boy freely refuses to marry the girl, such that she then in turn goes on to marry a committed Christian boy who is perpetually faithful to her. Assuming God chooses to create the girl, bad boy, and Christian boy, due to his goodness and middle knowledge God will not answer the girl's prayer but will instead steer her toward the Christian boy who will bring her true happiness and increased faith. In other words, God will choose to create a feasible world including the girl, bad boy, and Christian boy where the bad boy freely rejects her and where the Christian boy freely embraces and marries her.

Fourth, God may middle-know that answering a prayer would not be ultimately advantageous to other people or even to the world at large.[62] Craig points out that on Molinism, the all-good and all-loving God's overriding desire is to achieve an optimal balance between saved and lost, namely, to create a world containing no more of the lost than necessary to achieve the maximal number of the saved.[63] Hence God chooses to create one of the infinity of feasible worlds satisfying this condition, an observation to which we will return in the next chapter. This sheds light on a wide range of unanswered prayers for good to befall a particular individual, as these prayers may be ultimately disadvantageous to the ultimate good of the optimal salvific balance. For instance, suppose a mother prays that her son would be cured of cancer. If God apprehends in his middle knowledge that answering this prayer through either natural means or supernatural intervention would result in a world not containing the optimal salvific balance, then God will not answer the prayer. For in the ultimate scheme of things, the temporary separation of body and soul for one person (which will be forever rejoined in the general resurrection), while bad, pales in comparison to the eternal loss of another person or persons. Suppose God middle-knows that only if the son dies, at the funeral someone would place his faith in Christ who would otherwise have been eternally lost, and then that person would lead many others to Christ who would otherwise have been eternally lost, and then one of those others would be the next Billy Graham and lead thousands to Christ

62. Ibid., 7.23.4/5.1.6.23.
63. William Lane Craig, "Politically Incorrect Salvation," in *Christian Apologetics in the Postmodern World*, ed. Timothy R. Phillips and Dennis Okholm (Downers Grove, IL: InterVarsity, 1995), 84; idem, "'No Other Name': A Middle Knowledge Perspective on the Exclusivity of Salvation through Christ," *Faith and Philosophy* 6 (1989): 176.

who would otherwise have been eternally lost. It's obvious that, in this case, for the ultimate good of others God does not answer the mother's prayer.

All four of these reasons why God may not answer prayer were, for Molina, suggested by Matthew 7:7 – 11, "Ask and it will be given to you; seek and you will find; knock and the door will be opened to you. For everyone who asks receives; the one who seeks finds; and to the one who knocks, the door will be opened. Which of you, if your son asks for bread, will give him a stone? Or if he asks for a fish, will give him a snake? If you, then, though you are evil, know how to give good gifts to your children, how much more will your Father in heaven give good gifts to those who ask him!" Here Molina called attention to Jesus' assertion that the Father will give *good* gifts to those who ask him.[64] Jesus did not say that the Father will give his children gifts that are logically impossible, logically infeasible, bad for his children, or beneficial for his children at other people's expense. In all of these cases, the gifts are not objectively good. Rather, the Father will give his children gifts that are objectively good, which Molina interpreted as the meaning of the conjunction of "good and perfect" in James 1:17, "Every good and perfect gift is from above, coming down from the Father of the heavenly lights."[65] So Molina argued that God actually gives us *everything* we ask for that is objectively good, and those things we ask for and do not receive fall under one of the aforementioned four categories.[66] Flint captures the gist of Molina's reasoning when he states, "Perhaps God does always give us the good things we request. Perhaps the prayers he doesn't answer are cases where what we have prayed for wouldn't have been good, for ourselves or for others."[67] So Christians can always be confident that God will employ his middle knowledge to answer all and only their prayers that will accomplish objective good. When they pray Christians need never fear, "Be careful what you wish for, because you just might get it," or worry that they brought about some

---

64. Molina, *Commentaria*, 38.1/2.1.

65. Molina, *Concordia*, 1.14.13.24.5; 5.19.6.2.1 – 2.

66. Although not cited by Molina, he could have used 1 John 5:14 – 15 ("This is the confidence we have in approaching God: that if we ask anything according to his will, he hears us. And if we know that he hears us — whatever we ask — we know that we have what we asked of him") to make the same point, defining the phrase "ask anything according to [God's] will" as "ask for anything which is objectively good" since God's will, for Molina, is to accomplish the objectively good (*Foreknowledge*, 4.14.15.53.3.17).

67. Flint, *Divine Providence*, 217.

tragedy through some emotionally charged prayer. Hence the psalmist had no chance of causing multiple infanticides when he angrily prayed against his Babylonian captors, "Happy is the one who seizes your infants and dashes them against the rocks" (Ps. 137:9). Molina's doctrine of providence thus affords Christians a tremendous level of comfort that they can safely lay bare their emotions before God in prayer, knowing that God will only act on those sentiments that will bring about objective good.

SUMMARY OF THE MOLINIST CONCEPTION OF PROVIDENCE

For Molina providence constituted God's ordering of things to their intended good purposes either directly by his own action or indirectly by secondary causes and God's performance of all the world's activities, either in the composite sense alone or in both the composite and divided senses. In the nonmoral and indirect composite sense, God accomplishes everything that happens simply by setting in motion a world where he middle-knew how its history would transpire. Hence God does everything in the world by getting the proverbial ball of world history rolling, without which prime motion nothing would occur. But in the moral and direct divided sense, God only does good things. Accordingly, any good act which Scripture attributes to God is caused by God in the composite sense and may be caused by either God or creatures in the divided sense. Moreover, God absolutely wills all good acts, whether directly caused by God or creatures. However, any evil act which Scripture attributes to God (e.g., hardening Pharaoh's heart, deceiving the followers of the Antichrist) is caused by God only in the composite sense and not in the divided sense; in the direct, morally relevant divided sense it is caused by creatures. All evil acts violate God's absolute will, yet God permits them to occur by his conditional will that creatures possess genuine freedom.

Essential to God's ordering of things to their intended good purposes is God's absolutely complete and unlimited deliberation, which occurs logically between his middle knowledge and his creative decree. In this inconceivably complex planning stage of the world, God weighs all the possibilities of the different creatures existing and acting in various circumstances as well as the various ways he could interact with different persons and their actions.

By his unlimited reflection on this host of factors, God plans down to the last detail which feasible world he will choose to create, but without in any way annihilating creaturely freedom or natural randomness, since these elements are already factored into his planning. Hence God's creative decree is an unimaginably complex nested decision, comprising a vast array of decisions regarding the creatures that will exist, the circumstances they will find themselves in, how they will contingently act in those circumstances, and his relationships with creatures. In these ways, God decrees to bring about his ultimate purposes through free creaturely decisions and the random products of stochastic processes.

Molina's doctrine of providence contains profound implications for prophecy and prayer. God's prophecy is grounded squarely on his middle knowledge. For God to prophesy any evil act, he must middle-know that the prophecy would not causally contribute to the act's commission and that the prophecy itself would accomplish some future good. For God to prophesy any good act, God must middle-know either that the act would occur regardless of the presence or absence of the prophecy or that the prophecy itself would causally contribute to the good act, such that in the absence of the prophecy the good act would not come to pass. As in the case of prophecy, God's middle knowledge supplies the key to his answering of prayer. Because God middle-knew how each possible individual would freely pray in any set of circumstances, God uses this information providentially to order the world in such a way that we receive all the objectively good things for which we pray, whereas if we had not prayed, God would have providentially ordered the world in such a way that we may well not have received these same goods. Further, it is possible to pray for some past events as well—namely, objective goods that do not involve the contradictions of altering past or present realities. While we cannot change the past, we can pray in such a way that had we not prayed, God would have ordered the past differently than it is in fact ordered. Since we receive all the objective goods for which we pray, Molina held that anything we pray for and do not receive cannot be objectively good but falls into at least one of four categories. These categories include things that are logically impossible for God, things that are logically infeasible for God, things that God middle-knows not to be ultimately advantageous to the person praying, and things that God middle-knows not to be ultimately advantageous to other people or the world at large. Regarding the fourth category, God may middle-know it not to be ultimately disadvantageous in the sense that it would disallow the world's obtaining an optimal balance between saved and lost (i.e., a balance where the world contains no more of the lost than necessary to achieve the maximal number of the saved). We shall further explore the issues surrounding salvation and damnation when analyzing Molina's doctrine of predestination in the next chapter.

CHAPTER 5

Molina's Doctrine of Predestination

✠   ✠   ✠

MOLINA DEFINED PREDESTINATION as that segment of God's providence pertaining to eternal life.[1] In formulating his doctrine of predestination, Molina attempted to reconcile three sets of biblical texts—passages affirming sovereign individual predestination, passages affirming libertarian human freedom, and passages affirming God's universal salvific will. Four features of Molina's attempted reconciliation are immediately noteworthy. First, Molina did not find any contradiction between these sets of texts. Even though it is baffling for many people how all three sets can simultaneously be true, nevertheless, Molina pointed out that there is no logical inconsistency between them. Nor can there be any logical inconsistency between them, because they are all God's errorless Word.[2] Second, Molina interpreted each set of texts literally and straightforwardly, in line with its face-value meaning. Hence Molina staunchly rejected any interpretive strategy that pitted the texts affirming individual predestination against those affirming libertarian freedom and the divine salvific will or that pitted the texts affirming libertarian freedom and the divine salvific will against those affirming individual predestination. Now Molina recognized that hardly anyone in the history of exegesis had explicitly pitted some biblical texts against others, as this would

---

1. Ludovici Molina, *Liberi Arbitrii cum Gratiae Donis, Divina Praescientia, Providentia, Praedestinatione et Reprobatione Concordia*, ed. Johannes Rabeneck (Madrid: Sumptibus Societatis Editorialis "Sapientia," 1953), 7.23.1/2.1.1, 8; William Lane Craig, *Divine Foreknowledge and Human Freedom: The Coherence of Theism: Omniscience*, Studies in Intellectual History 19 (Leiden: Brill, 1990), 241.
2. Molina, *Concordia*, 5.19.6.1.19; 7.23.4/5.1.6.25.

exhibit an unseemly disregard for various parts of Scripture. Nevertheless, Molina maintained that many in the history of exegesis, including most of his contemporaries, implicitly took the approach of pitting some biblical texts against others.[3] In the fashion of Calvin, some exegetes interpreted the freedom and salvific will texts not according to their face-value meaning but through the hermeneutical lenses of the predestination texts, thus for Molina negating the plain meaning of the freedom and salvific will texts and denying biblical inerrancy. And in the fashion of Arminius, other exegetes interpreted the predestination texts not according to their face-value meaning but through the hermeneutical lenses of the freedom and salvific will texts, thus for Molina negating the plain meaning of the predestination texts and also denying biblical inerrancy.[4]

Third, Molina believed that the way to reconcile these three sets of biblical texts was not exegetical but philosophical. In other words, sound exegesis of each set leaves us only with three noncontradictory puzzle pieces which themselves do not fit together. As part of loving God with all our minds, Molina insisted we use philosophical reflection to detect the larger puzzle into which all three pieces fit.[5] Fourth, Molina sought to avoid what he regarded as two failed philosophical attempts to detect the puzzle prevalent in various eras of church history. Prior to Augustine, Molina characterized the prevalent patristic approach as basing predestination on foreknowledge, such that God predestined those persons to be saved whom he foreknew would freely believe in Christ.[6] However, this approach was shown inadequate by the early fifth-century heretic Pelagius, who inferred from it the error that persons could believe in Christ on their own initiative without the aid of prior grace. Hence Augustine responded to Pelagius by claiming that by his unmerited grace, God moved the wills of certain individuals to believe in Christ. As Molina saw things, Augustine's realization swung the philosophical pendulum to the opposite extreme in the medieval era, whose prevalent approach was to make predestination an arbitrary gift of God unconnected to his foreknowledge.[7]

---

3. Ibid., 7.23.4/5.1.2.1–4; 7.23.4/5.1.7.28.

4. Ibid., 7.23.4/5.1.5.1–2; 7.23.4/5.1.11.25; 7.23.4/5.1.14.6. While Molina does not cite Arminius by name (as Arminius's writings postdated Molina's), Molina refers specifically to the exegetical approach taken by Arminius.

5. Ibid., 7.23.4/5.1.11.30–3, 35–36.

6. Ibid., 7.23.4/5.1.14.4.

7. Ibid., 7.23.4/5.1.6.1–5; 7.23.4/5.1.14.5.

Consequently, the patristic and medieval attempts formed the horns of the following dilemma, which confronted all Reformation thinkers: "With regard to the doctrine of predestination, one seemingly has to hold either that predestination is based on the foreknowledge of human merits or else that predestination is wholly wrought by God without any considerations of human free decision."[8] Through the doctrine of middle knowledge, Molina endeavored to split the horns of this dilemma. Accordingly, we shall analyze Molina's doctrine of predestination, relying mainly on the currently untranslated book 7 of the *Concordia* devoted to this topic.

MOLINA'S EXEGESIS OF THE PERTINENT SCRIPTURAL TEXTS

Molina believed that Exodus 33:19; Ezekiel 11:19 – 20; 36:26 – 27; Malachi 1:2 – 3; Romans 8:29 – 30; 9; Ephesians 1:4 – 5; 1:11; 2 Timothy 2:20; and 1 Peter 1:1 – 2 comprised the set of texts affirming God's sovereign individual predestination. In other words, Molina claimed these texts teach that, for each individual, God has freely chosen from before the foundation of the world whether that individual would be saved (elect) or damned (reprobate). This was conclusively demonstrated for Molina by several verses in Romans 9. Molina asserted that the example of Jacob and Esau in Romans 9:11 – 13 strictly referred to those two individuals, such that Jacob and Esau were not, as Arminius claimed, representatives of two different groups.[9] In Romans 9:15 (a Pauline quotation of Exodus 33:19), "I will have mercy on *whom* I have mercy, and I will have compassion on *whom* I have compassion" (emphasis added), Molina called attention to the fact that the pronouns "whom" are singular (*cuius* in the Vulgate) rather than plural (*quorum*), thus indicating God's merciful and compassionate election of specific individuals.[10] That God not only elects specific individuals but also reprobates specific individuals Molina found clear in Romans 9:18, "Therefore God has mercy on *whom* he wants to have mercy, and he hardens *whom* he wants to harden"

---

8. William Lane Craig, *The Problem of Divine Foreknowledge and Future Contingents from Aristotle to Suarez*. Studies in Intellectual History 7 (Leiden: Brill, 1988), 203.

9. Molina, *Concordia*, 7.23.4/5.4.1, 22 – 23.

10. Ibid., 7.23.4/5.4.2, 24. Molina's observation equally applies to the original Greek of Romans 9:15, which uses the singular ὅν rather than the plural ὅντινα.

(emphasis added). Again, Molina argued that this conclusion was guaranteed by the verse's use of singular pronouns for "whom" (*cuius* and *quem* in the Vulgate) rather than plural pronouns (*quorum* and *quos*).[11] One specific individual God reprobated, or hardened, was Pharaoh, as described in Romans 9:17.[12] That some are predestinated to salvation and others reprobated to eternal destruction was made even more evident for Molina by Romans 9:13 (a Pauline quotation of Malachi 1:2–3); 9:20–23; and its parallel in 2 Timothy 2:20. Thus Molina claimed that the reality of individual predestination and reprobation

> is so clear from the Holy Scriptures that it cannot be denied without prejudice to the faith. For it says in Malachi 1:2–3 and in Romans 9:13: Jacob I have loved, but Esau I have hated. In showing that no injustice can be charged to God on account of the fact that he predestined some and that he reprobated others, Paul adds [in Romans 9:20–23]: Shall the thing formed say to him that formed it, Why have you made me thus? Or, moreover, has not the potter power over the clay, over the lump to make one vessel unto honor and another in reproach? What if God, willing to show his wrath and to make his power known, endured with much patience the vessels of wrath, fitted for destruction, in order that he might make known the riches of his glory to the vessels of mercy, which he had prepared beforehand unto glory.... And 2 Timothy 2:20 says concerning the predestined and the reprobate that in a great house there are not only vessels of gold and silver but also vessels of wood and earth—some to honor and some to dishonor.... Since, therefore, God is not in time but has been in existence from eternity, with God the eternal reprobation of some takes place, and similarly the eternal predestination of many others takes place.[13]

11. Ibid., 7.23.4/5.4.2. On precisely the same linguistic grounds as Romans 9:15 (ὅν rather than ὅντινα), Molina's argument also applies to the original Greek of Romans 9:18.

12. Ibid.

13. "Ex Scripturis Sanctis adeo est manifestum ut salva fide negari non possit. Dicitur enim Mal 1,2.3 et Rom 9,13: Iacob dilexi, Esau autem odio habui, ostendensque Paulus nullam iniquitatem esse in Deo propterea, quod quosdam praedestinaverit, alios vero reprobaverit, subiungit [Rom 9,20.23]: Numquid dicit figmentum ei, qui se finixit: Quid me fecisti sic? An non habet potestatem figulus luti ex eadem massa facere aliud quidem vas in honorem, aliud vero in contumeliam? Quod si Deus volens ostendere iram, et notam facere potentiam suam, sustinuit in multa patentia, vasa irae, apta in interitum, ut ostenderet divitias gloriae suae in vasa misericordiae, quae praeparavit in gloriam.... Et 2 Tim 2,20 de praedestinatis et reprobis agens: In magna, inquit, domo non solum sunt vasa aurea, et argentea, sed et lignea, et fictilia: et quaedam quidem in honorem, quaedam autem in contumeliam.... Cum ergo id Deus non ex tempore, sed ex aeternitate constituerit, fit ut sit apud Deum aeterna reprobatio quorundum, sicut etiam apud eundem est quorundam aliorum aeterna praedestinatio" (Molina, *Concordia*, 7.23.3.18).

To the possible objection that Romans 9:20–23 (paralleled by 2 Timothy 2:20) teaches corporate predestination because it refers to two groups (the vessels of wrath/dishonor and the vessels of mercy/honor), Molina responded that the context of individual predestination running throughout Romans 9 and leading up to verses 20–23 necessitates that these verses mean God chose the specific individuals for election and reprobation who made up the two groups.[14]

The eternal nature of God's predestination was confirmed for Molina by Ephesians 1:4–5, "For he [the Father] chose us in him [Jesus Christ] before the creation of the world to be holy and blameless in his sight. In love he predestined us for adoption to sonship through Jesus Christ, in accordance with his pleasure and will." Before God created the world, and thus before time began, God predestined, according to his pleasure and will alone, various individuals to be his adopted, holy, and blameless children in and through Christ.[15] Molina's conviction that God's predestination was a subcategory of God's providential plan arose from Ephesians 1:11: "In him we were also chosen, having been predestined *according to the plan of him* who works out everything in conformity with the purpose of his will" (emphasis added).[16] Molina insisted that because of the effects of the fall, no one can come to Christ by their own devices.[17] Rather, for anyone to come to Christ, God must first give that individual a new, soft heart and a new spirit to replace the old, stony heart and dead spirit wrought by the fall. Hence prior grace given by the Holy Spirit, which Molina called prevenient grace, sufficient grace, or grace making gracious, is necessary for anyone to receive Christ. Such grace draws people to follow Christ.[18] Molina claimed that this was the inescapable conclusion of Ezekiel 36:26–27: "I will give you a new heart and put a new spirit in you; I will remove from you your heart of stone and give you a heart of flesh. And I will put my Spirit in you and move you to follow my decrees and be careful to keep my laws" (cf. Ezek. 11:19–20).[19] As a result, Molina

---

14. Molina, *Concordia*, 7.23.4/5.1.6.4.

15. Ibid., 7.23.1/2.1.2; 7.23.1/2.2.4; 7.23.4/5.1.8.25; 7.23.4/5.1.11.12.

16. Ibid., 7.23.4/5.1.4.18; 7.23.4/5.2.1, 11.

17. Hence Molina strenuously rejected the claim of the Dominican theologian Domingo de Soto (1494–1560) and the Franciscan theologian Andreas de Vega (d. 1560) that human free will alone without the special help of prevenient grace was sufficient for repentance and belief (*Concordia*, 3.13.13.39.1–8).

18. Molina, *Concordia*, 2.14.13.35.8.

19. Ibid., 7.23.4/5.1.6.15.

maintained that it is "necessary for our conversion" that "God stir and move our faculty of choice by the assistance of supervening grace."[20]

Molina then came to Romans 8:29–30 and 1 Peter 1:1–2, two texts that had historically been used to teach that predestination was based on God's foreknowledge of who would freely place their faith in Christ. This was because Romans 8:29 ("For those God foreknew he also predestined to be conformed to the image of his Son") places foreknowledge logically prior to predestination, and 1 Peter 1:1–2 ("To God's elect ... who have been chosen according to the foreknowledge of God the Father") makes some kind of foreknowledge a factor in election. While affirming these clear observations, Molina rejected the inference from these observations to the historic interpretation of the texts on two fronts.

First, Molina declared that the historic interpretation is ruled out by the wider context of Scripture, especially the data in Romans 9. For if our freely believing in Christ is the reason why God predestines us, then it is we who, in effect, predestine ourselves by our faith rather than God's predestining us. We force God's hand in predestining us by performing the spiritually meritorious act of placing faith in Christ. Conversely, the reprobate force God's hand in reprobating them by refusing to place faith in Christ. In such a case, none of the elect could have been reprobate or vice versa; election and reprobation amount to the choices of human beings rather than God. All of this, Molina asserted, is directly contradictory to Romans 9, and Scripture cannot contradict Scripture.[21] Hence Molina rhetorically asked "whether the cause of predestination may be ascribed to the part of the predestinate [the elect]" and "whether the cause of reprobation may be ascribed to the part of the reprobate."[22] He answered both questions decidedly in the negative, claiming that any positive answer amounted to following "the errors of Origen and Pelagius."[23] On the basis of the Pauline statement, "Yet, before the twins were born or had done anything good or bad—in order that God's purpose in election might stand: not by works but by him who calls.... Jacob

---

20. Luis de Molina, *On Divine Foreknowledge*, trans. Alfred J. Freddoso (Ithaca, NY: Cornell University Press, 1988), 4.14.13.53.1.8.

21. Molina, *Concordia*, 7.23.4/5.1.2.3–4.

22. "Utrum ex parte praedestinati detur causa praedestinationis.... Utrum ex parte reprobi detur causa reprobationis" (Molina, *Concordia*, 7.23.4/5.1.1; 7.23.4/5.4.1).

23. "Erroribus ... Origenis et Pelagii" (Molina, *Concordia*, 7.23.4/5.1.2.1).

I loved, but Esau I hated" (Rom. 9:11 – 13), Molina declared that "foreseen faith cannot be the ground of justification or predestination,"[24] as affirming otherwise would undermine the face-value implication that God's decree to elect Jacob and reprobate Esau did not take into account any future good or evil acts on their part, such as belief or unbelief. Thus Molina deduced that God elects persons "with his holy calling, not according to our works, but according to his own purpose and grace which was given to us in Christ Jesus."[25] Likewise, the reprobate person "is not reprobated because of foreseen sins, and truly he has neither the cause nor the ground of reprobation within him."[26] Molina insisted that such constitutes the only exegetically defensible reading of Romans 9, which cannot be overturned by a possible but far from obvious reading of Romans 8:29 – 30 and 1 Peter 1:1 – 2. Regarding Romans 9, Molina proclaimed: "Behold in what way Paul teaches concerning Jacob that it was not on account of his works or his merits that he was beloved and predestined by God, so likewise he affirms concerning Esau that it was not on account of his works that he was hated and reprobated."[27] For Molina, therefore, God elects or reprobates individuals not in theory (i.e. God's putting his stamp of approval or disapproval on our foreseen belief or unbelief) but in fact (i.e., God's actually making the choice to save or damn), such that the cause and ground of any person's election or reprobation is God's sovereign will. Since "the total effect of predestination ... depends only on the free will of God,"[28] God could have predestined "any of the elect to have truly been reprobate" and any "of the reprobate to have truly been elect."[29] Molina proof-texted Romans 9:15 – 18 to substantiate this conclusion:

> Paul adds that God said to Moses: I will have mercy on whom I have mercy, and I will have compassion on whom I have compassion; that is, I

---

24. "Fides praevisa non sit ratio iustificationis ac praedestinationis" (Molina, *Concordia*, 7.23.4/5.1.2).

25. "Vocavit nos vocatione sua sancta, non secundum opera nostra, sed secundum propositum suum et gratiam quae data est nobis in Christo Iesu" (Molina, *Concordia*, 7.23.4/5.1.2.1).

26. "Ergo reprobatio non est propter peccata praevisa atque adeo nec causam nec rationem ex parte reprobi habet" (Molina, *Concordia*, 7.23.4/5.4.1).

27. "Ecce quemadmodum Paulus de Iacob docet non propter opera sive merita sua fuisse a Deo dilectum et praedestinatum ita quoque de Esau affirmat non fuisse propter opera odio habitum ac reprobatum" (Molina, *Concordia*, 7.23.4/5.4.1).

28. "Totius effectus praedestinationis ... ex sola libera Dei voluntate pendeat" (Molina, *Concordia*, 7.23.4/5.1.2).

29. "Illi electi ... hi vero reprobi fuerint ... illi reprobi ... hi vero electi fuerint" (Molina, *Concordia*, 7.23.4/5.1.2.4).

will use mercy with whomever I wish and just as it gives pleasure to me. And Paul concludes: Therefore it is neither he who wills, nor he who runs, but God who shows mercy.... He has mercy on whom he wills, and whom he wills he hardens.... Therefore neither predestination nor reprobation is according to foreseen merits, but it leads back only to the free will of God.[30]

Consequently, Molina was a firm believer in unconditional election, holding that God elects purely according to his pleasure without regard to any foreseen faith or good works and reprobates without regard to any foreseen unbelief or sins.[31]

Second, Molina argued that the historic interpretation of Romans 8:29–30 and 1 Peter 1:1–2 anachronistically understood the terms "foreknew" and "foreknowledge" in light of patristic and medieval philosophical distinctions that were unknown and thus foreign to the intent of Paul and Peter. According to Molina, biblical writers like Paul and Peter did not differentiate between the species of God's prescience (such as knowledge of simple intelligence and visionary knowledge), but simply classified all instances of prescience under the term "foreknowledge" and its derivatives.[32] However, patristic and medieval thinkers understood only visionary knowledge (which Molina dubbed "free knowledge") as constituting foreknowledge in the philosophical sense (i.e., knowledge of the future), while knowledge of simple intelligence (which Molina dubbed "natural knowledge") was only God's knowledge of what could happen, yielding no information about what actually will happen. Moreover, most of the possibilities apprehended by God in his knowledge of simple intelligence will never occur in the future. Consequently, most patristic and medieval exegetes read "knowledge of the future" back into the terms "foreknew" and "foreknowledge" in Romans 8:29–30 and 1 Peter 1:1–2. But Paul and Peter could have just as easily denoted natural or middle knowledge by these terms as they could have denoted free knowledge (foreknowledge in the strict philosophical sense), as they did not distinguish between these

30. "Subiungit Paulus Deum dixisse Moysi: Miserebor cuius misereor; et misericordiam praestabo cui miserebor; hoc est, utar misericordia cum quocumque voluero et prout mihi placuerit. Concluditque Paulus: Igitur non volentis, neque currentis, sed miserentis est Dei.... Cuius vult miseretur, et quem vult indurate.... Ergo sicut praedestinatio non est propter merita praevisa ita neque reprobatio, sed in solam liberam voluntatem Dei ea reducenda est" (Molina, *Concordia*, 7.23.4/5.4.2).

31. Kirk R. MacGregor, *A Molinist-Anabaptist Systematic Theology* (Lanham, MD: University Press of America, 2007), 66–68.

32. Molina, *Concordia*, 7.23.4/5.1.11.36.

three types of knowledge. So all that sound exegesis of Romans 8:29 – 30 and 1 Peter 1:1 – 2 can establish is that some species of prescience (natural, middle, or free knowledge) is logically prior to predestination and that some species of prescience is a factor in election.[33] Since Romans 9 rules out the possibility of free knowledge (as this would make us the determiners of our election or reprobation), the principle of comparing Scripture with Scripture leaves us with either natural knowledge or middle knowledge as the precise referent of Romans 8:29 and 1 Peter 1:1 – 2. Here, Molina contended, philosophical analysis must be integrated with hermeneutics to discern the answer.[34] In the case of both texts, Molina believed that natural knowledge was eliminated by *reductio ad absurdum*. For God apprehends in his natural knowledge that it is logically possible for anyone to be saved. But if, in the case of Romans 8:29, God predestined those he knew simply *could* be saved and if, in the case of 1 Peter 1:1 – 2, God elected those he knew simply *could* be saved, then everyone would be predestined to salvation. But universalism (the view that God saves all persons) is explicitly denied throughout Scripture, including Romans 9, which presents Esau, Pharaoh, and the vessels of wrath as eternally condemned. By process of elimination, then, the foreknowledge described in Romans 8:29 – 30 and 1 Peter 1:1 – 2 must be middle knowledge.[35] Hence, in some way God predestined and elected those he knew *would* be saved under various circumstances of his choosing.

Molina was aware of two other interpretations of the foreknowledge described in these texts, one of which he rejected and the other of which he believed implied his own interpretation. The rejected interpretation took foreknowledge to be synonymous with foreordination, a view first put forward by Augustine and, in Molina's day, advanced by Calvin.[36] Thus God knows

33. Ibid., 7.23.4/5.1.3.9.

34. Ibid., 7.23.4/5.1.8.25.

35. Ibid., 7.23.4/5.1.3.9; 7.23.4/5.1.11.38.

36. Augustine, *De Spiritu et Littera* (*On the Spirit and the Letter*), in Nicene and Post-Nicene Fathers, vol. 5, First Series, trans. Peter Holmes, Robert Ernest Wallis, and Benjamin B. Warfield, ed. Philip Schaff (repr. ed., Peabody, MA: Hendrickson, 2004), 85 – 86; idem, *De Gestis Pelagii* (*On the Proceedings of Pelagius*), in Nicene and Post-Nicene Fathers, vol. 5, First Series, trans. Peter Holmes, Robert Ernest Wallis, and Benjamin B. Warfield, ed. Philip Schaff (repr. ed., Peabody, MA: Hendrickson, 2004), 186; *De Correptione et Gratia* (*On Rebuke and Grace*), in Nicene and Post-Nicene Fathers, vol. 5, First Series, trans. Peter Holmes, Robert Ernest Wallis, and Benjamin B. Warfield, ed. Philip Schaff (repr. ed., Peabody, MA: Hendrickson, 2004), 480 – 81; John Calvin, *Institutes of the Christian Religion*, ed. John T. McNeill, trans. Ford Lewis Battles (Philadelphia: Westminster, 1960), 3.22.8 – 10.

in advance which persons will be saved because he makes those persons be saved, giving them irresistible grace, which it is logically impossible for them to oppose. Cognizant of the intentions of his will and his omnipotence, God foreknows that all his intentions shall be accomplished.[37] Molina charged this interpretation with contradicting the set of over twenty biblical texts treated in chapter 2 affirming that humans possess libertarian freedom after the fall (including Gen. 4:6–7; Deut. 30:11–19; Ezek. 18:30–32). But God's making certain persons be saved obliterates their libertarian freedom: "For if, having no idea of what created free choice was going to do in its freedom, God by the free eternal determination of His will and by His influence determines it to whatever He wills, and if, as long as that determination and divine influence remain, free choice is able to do nothing other than that to which it is so determined, then I do not at all see in what sense it remains genuinely free to strive after what it wills."[38] Due to libertarian freedom, it is logically impossible for God to make any human be saved. This consequence led Molina to deny that prior or prevenient grace is irresistible. Rather, prevenient grace restores to persons their mental faculty to choose spiritual good (a faculty that had been eviscerated in the fall) and thus supplies persons with their libertarian freedom. In addition, it draws people to place their faith in Christ.[39] Significantly, since the aforementioned set of scriptural texts attests that all humans possess libertarian freedom (even giving specific examples of people who possessed libertarian freedom but are known to be eternally lost, such as those Israelites who committed idolatry), it followed for Molina that God gives all humans prevenient grace. For they could not possess libertarian freedom without it.[40] Therefore Molina averred that God's predestination is not his decision to give some people irresistible prior grace and withhold it from others (for everyone receives prior grace, and it is not irresistible), but it must be his decision to do something else in unconditionally choosing certain persons to be elect and others to be reprobate.[41]

Originally proposed by Bernard of Clairvaux, the interpretation that

---

37. William Lane Craig, "The Middle-Knowledge View," in James K. Beilby and Paul R. Eddy, *Divine Foreknowledge: Four Views* (Downers Grove, IL: InterVarsity, 2001), 135.

38. Molina, *Foreknowledge*, 4.14.13.50.9.

39. Molina, *Concordia*, 3.14.13.40.2–17.

40. Ibid., 3.14.13.40.18–27.

41. Ibid., 7.23.1/2.1.5, 8.

Molina felt implied his own was that the foreknowledge described in Romans 8:29–30 and 1 Peter 1:1–2 amounted to God's prior relational knowledge of the persons whom he would predestine.[42] For if God had prior relational knowledge of the persons whom he would predestine before those persons existed, that relational knowledge would technically be of their individual essences, which existed as ideas in the mind of God. And full relational knowledge of someone's individual essence would encompass knowing everything that individual essence, if instantiated, would freely do under any set of circumstances.[43] This fact is evident by analogy from human experience, as the partial relational knowledge one person has of another person encompasses knowing some things the latter person would freely do under some sets of circumstances. Hence the complete relational knowledge God has of possible persons must extend to all free decisions those persons would make, including whether they would be saved, under any set of circumstances. Thus Molina held that complete relational knowledge does not exclude but rather entails complete factual knowledge.[44] As Steven C. Roy puts it, "An understanding of divine foreknowledge in this context as involving God's prior intimate, covenant love does not preclude his factual knowledge of his people. If God's foreknowledge is linked to his predestination (Rom 8:29) that his people come to faith in Christ and are ultimately conformed to his image, God's relational foreknowledge also includes his factual foreknowledge of them and their decisions and actions."[45] Hence God knows the individual essence of each possible individual so intimately that he knows under what conditions they would and would not freely be saved, and it is this prior, counterfactual knowledge that is related by the texts under consideration.

In addition to the sets of texts affirming individual predestination and libertarian freedom, Molina identified Ezekiel 18:23–32; 33:11; 1 Timothy 2:4; 2 Peter 3:9; and Revelation 3:20 as comprising the set of texts teaching God's universal salvific will, or God's absolute desire that every person he

42. Bernard of Clairvaux, *Sermones super Cantica Conticorum*, in *Sämtliche Werke* V–VI (Innsbruck: Tyrolia-Verlag, 1995), 21.7; cf. idem, *De gratia et libero arbitrio*, in *Sämtliche Werke* I (Innsbruck: Tyrolia-Verlag, 1990), 14.51; idem, *De gradibus humilitatis et superbiae*, in *Sämtliche Werke* II (Innsbruck: Tyrolia-Verlag, 1990), 10.36.

43. Ludovici Molina, *Commentaria in primam divi Thomae partem* (Venice, 1602), 15.1.2.4; 16.3.1.

44. Molina, *Concordia*, 7.23.4/5.1.11.18.

45. Steven C. Roy, *How Much Does God Foreknow? A Comprehensive Biblical Study* (Downers Grove, IL: InterVarsity, 2006), 82.

creates receives his salvation.[46] For 1 Timothy 2:4 describes God as the one "who wants all people to be saved and to come to a knowledge of the truth," and 2 Peter 3:9 presents God as "not wanting anyone to perish, but everyone to come to repentance."[47] Likewise, in Ezekiel 18 and 33 God categorically states that he takes no pleasure in the death of the wicked but wants them to find salvation.[48] Hence God literally pleads with lost persons to turn from their evil ways and be saved:

> "Do I take any pleasure in the death of the wicked? declares the Sovereign LORD. Rather, am I not pleased when they turn from their ways and live?...
>
> "Repent! Turn away from all your offenses; then sin will not be your downfall. Rid yourselves of all the offenses you have committed, and get a new heart and a new spirit. Why will you die, people of Israel? For I take no pleasure in the death of anyone, declares the Sovereign LORD. Repent and live!...
>
> "'As surely as I live, declares the Sovereign LORD, I take no pleasure in the death of the wicked, but rather that they turn from their ways and live. Turn! Turn from your evil ways! Why will you die, people of Israel?'"
> (Ezek. 18:23, 30–32; 33:11)

Notice the charge to all the Israelites to "get a new heart and a new spirit," where a new heart and a new spirit constitute precisely the description of various potential effects of prevenient grace in Ezekiel 11:19–20 and 36:26–27. Putting these passages from Ezekiel together, it followed for Molina that anyone could freely choose to cooperate with prevenient grace, which itself supplied their libertarian freedom, and thereby receive its benefits of new spiritual birth (the new heart and new spirit).[49] All persons may cooperate with prevenient grace by availing themselves of its opportunity to place their faith in Christ, a situation excellently depicted by Revelation 3:20. There Jesus knocks on the door of everyone's soul (representing the work of prevenient grace in drawing each person to Jesus) and invites anyone to open the door, which will result in a saving relationship with him: "Here I am! I stand

---

46. Molina, *Concordia*, 1.14.13.10.1; 1.14.13.23.2.7–8; 7.23.4/5.1.8.8, 6.
47. Ibid., 5.19.6.1.19–21; 6.22.1.2.10; 7.23.4/5.1.6.23.
48. Ibid., 5.19.6.1.26.
49. Ibid., 7.23.4/5.1.7.25.

at the door and knock. If anyone hears my voice and opens the door, I will come in and eat with that person, and they with me."[50] With the scriptural data on the table, Molina now turned to philosophical analysis for the task of disclosing the larger puzzle into which the data fit.

A MIDDLE-KNOWLEDGE BASED PHILOSOPHICAL ANALYSIS OF PREDESTINATION

Molina began his analysis by proposing various factors that went into God's absolutely complete and unlimited deliberation—namely, the intricately complex planning stage of which feasible world God would create—following and thus based on the information gleaned from his middle knowledge. Confronted with his middle knowledge of what every possible individual would freely do in every conceivable set of circumstances, God commits himself, out of his love, to consider for creation only those feasible worlds in which he offers sufficient grace for salvation (i.e., prevenient grace) to each individual. Thus, in keeping with the set of texts asserting God's universal salvific will, God eliminates from consideration any feasible world in which he offers prevenient grace only to some individuals, thereby moving their wills alone in a salvific direction.[51] As Craig explains, "Molina rejects as Calvinistic and heretical the view ... that God gratuitously chooses certain persons to be saved and others to be damned and then premoves each elect person's will to produce saving faith, while leaving the non-elect in sin, so that the elect are subjects of predestination while the non-elect are subjects of reprobation."[52] While never stated in these terms by Molina, various comments of Molina imply that God also commits himself, out of his goodness, to consider for creation only those feasible worlds that obtain an optimal balance between salvation and damnation, containing no more of the lost than are necessary to achieve the greatest salvation.[53] According

---

50. Ibid., 3.14.13.45.4, 16.
51. Ibid., 7.23.4/5.1.6.23.
52. Craig, *Problem of Divine Foreknowledge and Future Contingents*, 203.
53. Molina, *Concordia*, 7.23.4/5.1.8.6–8. Craig states things in these terms in "Politically Incorrect Salvation," in *Christian Apologetics in the Postmodern World*, ed. Timothy R. Phillips and Dennis Okholm (Downers Grove, IL: InterVarsity, 1995), 84, and "'No Other Name': A Middle Knowledge Perspective on the Exclusivity of Salvation through Christ," *Faith and Philosophy* 6 (1989): 176. Were we to query whether God's choice of a world based on salvific optimality diminishes God's sovereignty,

to Molina, within the range of those feasible worlds in which God gives prevenient grace to all and that obtain to the optimal salvific balance—a range that is infinite—God perceives from his middle knowledge that there is at least one feasible world where each possible individual exists and would freely receive salvation. And God likewise middle-knows that there is at least one feasible world where each possible individual exists and would freely spurn salvation, so being lost. And God likewise middle-knows that there is at least one feasible world where each possible individual does not exist at all. Aside from the obvious point that all possible individuals are contingent (that no created person necessarily exists), contained within this scenario are two important and complementary claims. On the one hand, Molina was claiming that no possible individual, made in the image of God, is depraved enough so that, given prevenient grace, she or he would freely spurn God's offer of salvation in all available circumstances. On the other hand, Molina was also claiming that no possible individual, prone to sin, is good enough so that, given prevenient grace, she or he would freely accept God's offer of salvation in all available circumstances.[54]

Molina believed these claims followed as inferences from personal moral introspection and from Scripture. Regarding personal moral introspection, Molina felt that if persons were truly honest with themselves, any believer could perceive circumstances in which he or she would not have believed in Christ and any unbeliever could perceive circumstances in which he or she would have believed in Christ.[55] Regarding Scripture, Molina insisted that Jesus explicitly taught that certain persons (the inhabitants of Tyre, Sidon, and ancient Sodom) who are freely lost in the actual world would have been saved in a feasible world containing different circumstances:

Molina would respond in the negative. This is due to three factors. First, God's choice of a salvifically optimal world, for Molina, follows deductively from God's choice to create humans in the *imago Dei* and God's omnibenevolence. So given God's choice to create divine image-bearers, Molina believed it was logically impossible for God, in view of his all-goodness, to desire a world containing less than an optimal salvific balance. It is no compromise of divine sovereignty that God cannot do the logically impossible. Second, Molina held that there is an infinite range of salvifically optimal worlds. So God has an infinity of equally good worlds from which to choose. Third, there may well be other factors that God takes into account when choosing a world, factors about which we may know nothing. To say that salvific optimality is a necessary factor does not imply that there are not other contingent factors based sheerly on God's will.

54. Molina, *Concordia*, 7.23.4/5.7.1.1.
55. Ibid., 1.14.13.12.6; 3.14.13.40.13.

Then Jesus began to denounce the towns in which most of his miracles had been performed, because they did not repent. "Woe to you, Chorazin! Woe to you, Bethsaida! For if the miracles that were performed in you had been performed in Tyre and Sidon, they would have repented long ago in sackcloth and ashes. But I tell you, it will be more bearable for Tyre and Sidon on the day of judgment than for you. And you, Capernaum, will you be lifted up to the heavens? No, you will go down to Hades. For if the miracles that were performed in you had been performed in Sodom, it would have remained to this day. But I tell you that it will be more bearable for Sodom on the day of judgment than for you." (Matt. 11:20–24)

Here Jesus furnished two stunning pieces of divine middle knowledge. The reprobate citizens of Tyre and Sidon would have been elect in the feasible world where Jesus performed his miracles in those cities. Moreover, the reprobate citizens of Sodom would have been elect in the feasible world where Jesus' incarnation occurred in around the nineteenth century BC instead of the first century AD and where he performed his miracles in Sodom.[56]

It should be pointed out at this juncture that Molina would have regarded as false and unbiblical what many people take to be the "Molinist" doctrine of transworld damnation. Formulated by William Lane Craig and held by several contemporary Molinists, the doctrine of transworld damnation affirms that God has so providentially ordered things that anyone who is lost in the actual world would have been lost in any feasible world that God could create.[57] Craig himself acknowledges that Molina did not accept transworld damnation but instead maintained that had the lost "been put in different circumstances or given other helps, they would freely have responded to God's grace and been predestined to salvation."[58] While God's possession of middle knowledge is necessary for the doctrine of transworld damnation to be true, middle knowledge does not imply the doctrine of transworld

56. Ibid., 7.23.4/5.1.4.13; 7.23.4/5.1.11.41; idem, *Foreknowledge*, 4.14.13.49.9.

57. Craig, "No Other Name," 184. Other prominent Molinists who subscribe to transworld damnation include Thomas Flint (*Divine Providence: The Molinist Account* [Ithaca, NY: Cornell University Press, 1998], 119), Paul Copan (*"True for You, but Not for Me": Overcoming Objections to Christian Faith*, rev. ed. [Bloomington, MN: Bethany House, 2009], 212), and Bruce Little (*A Creation-Order Theodicy: God and Gratuitous Evil* [Lanham, MD: University Press of America, 2005], 154–55). The notion of transworld damnation is based on Alvin Plantinga's idea of transworld depravity, according to which there are certain possible persons who would produce moral evil in every feasible world in which they exist (*Nature of Necessity*, 186–88).

58. Craig, *Problem of Divine Foreknowledge and Future Contingents*, 204.

damnation. That is to say, without middle knowledge God could not arrange things so that anyone actually lost would have been lost in every feasible world. But God's possession of middle knowledge in no way entails that God actually arranged things in this way. In fact, proponents of transworld damnation who believe in biblical infallibility are forced to interpret Matthew 11:20–24 in a manner different from its face-value meaning, as they admit that a straightforward reading rules out transworld damnation. Hence Craig argues that "the passage in Matthew 11 is probably religious hyperbole meant merely to underscore the depth of the depravity of the cities in which Jesus preached."[59] But Craig offers no exegetical substantiation for this assertion, which in my judgment falls outside the mainstream of Matthean scholarship. For instance, Matthean commentator D. A. Carson points out that one of the "three large theological propositions … presupposed by Jesus' insistence that on the Day of Judgment, when he will judge, things will go worse for the cities that have received so much light than for the pagan cities … is that the Judge has contingent knowledge: he knows what Tyre and Sidon would have done under such-and-such circumstances."[60] Accordingly, while transworld damnation is a possible modification of the Molinist scheme for those who find the hyperbolic interpretation of Matthew 11:20–24 persuasive, transworld damnation is not part of the Molinist scheme.

For Molina himself, at this logical point in God's complete and unlimited deliberation, God is faced with an infinite range of feasible worlds in which he grants all persons sufficient grace to be saved and which obtain to the optimal salvific balance. Within this infinity of worlds is at least one world where any particular possible individual would freely attain salvation, at least one world where any particular possible individual would freely reach damnation, and at least one world where any particular possible individual would not exist. It is here that the genius of Molina's doctrine of predestination is exposed. Basing his thought on Romans 9, Molina insisted that predestination was unconditional. He proposed that God's unconditional predestination is

59. William Lane Craig, *The Only Wise God: The Compatibility of Divine Foreknowledge and Human Freedom* (Grand Rapids: Baker, 1987), 137.

60. D. A. Carson, "Matthew," in *The Expositor's Bible Commentary*, 12 vols.; gen. ed. Frank E. Gaebelein (Grand Rapids: Zondervan, 1984), 8:273. Carson's verdict is also implicit in the relevant statements from Robert H. Gundry's magisterial commentary on Matthew (*Matthew: A Commentary on His Handbook for a Mixed Church under Persecution*, 2nd ed. [Grand Rapids: Eerdmans, 1994], 214–15).

accomplished when, in making his sovereign providential choice of which of these equally good feasible worlds to create, God does not take into consideration any particular individual's salvation, damnation, or nonexistence. Without regard for any possible individual's salvific status or existence, God chooses the feasible world he desires as a sheer act of his sovereignty.[61] Any individual who would freely choose to embrace God's offer of salvation in the world God selects is thus predestined to salvation and so elected by God, even though God could have just as easily selected an equally good world in which that same individual would freely choose to reject God's offer of salvation or a different equally good world in which that same individual would not exist. Any individual who would freely choose to reject God's offer of salvation in the world God selects is reprobated by God, even though God could have just as easily chosen an equally good world in which that same individual would freely choose to embrace God's offer of salvation or a different equally good world in which that same individual would not exist.[62] Hence Molina claimed we may finally understand why Paul insisted that, in predestination, there is no injustice with God: "What then shall we say? Is God unjust? Not at all!... One of you will say to me, 'Then why does God still blame us? For who is able to resist his will?' But who are you, a human being, to talk back to God?" (Rom. 9:14, 19–20). God cannot be gainsaid for electing some people and reprobating others, since all feasible worlds available to him at this stage are equally good, and God's electing some and reprobating others is simply the logically unavoidable consequence of his choice to create a world at all. Therefore the only way God can avoid electing some and reprobating others is by choosing not to create any world.[63]

Let us unpack the implications of this account. On Molina's view, predestination, comprising election and reprobation, is logically simultaneous with the divine creative decree, as predestination, in the words of Craig,

61. Molina, *Concordia*, 7.23.4/5.1.11.7. Here we recall that each feasible world in the infinite array of worlds from which God sovereignly chooses obtains an optimal salvific balance. Lest we think it diminishes God's sovereignty to say that God could not choose a world obtaining worse than the optimal salvific balance (i.e., where more people are lost than need to be lost to achieve the greatest salvation), Molina would argue that it is no diminution of God's sovereignty that God cannot choose to sin, and choosing a world obtaining worse than the optimal salvific balance and so containing gratuitous damnation would be sin, a violation of God's good and loving nature.

62. Molina, *Concordia*, 7.23.4/5.1.11.8–16.

63. Ibid., 2.14.13.31.4; 7.23.4/5.4.3, 25–27.

"involves God's willing that aspect of the world comprising the natural circumstances and supernatural gifts of grace which form the milieu in which a person freely responds to God's gracious initiatives."[64] For by choosing which feasible world to actualize, God predestines to salvation, or elects, every individual in that world who would freely accept his prevenient grace, and he predestines to damnation, or reprobates, every individual in that world who would freely reject his prevenient grace. Such is the meaning of Romans 8:29–30 and 1 Peter 1:1–2, which affirm that predestination is according to (namely, it corresponds with) God's prior counterfactual knowledge of the conditions under which each possible individual would and would not freely be saved. This is not to say that the circumstances making up the feasible world determine whether one is saved or lost, as all such circumstances are freedom-preserving in character. Rather, God middle-knows the essence of each possible individual in that world so well that he knows which way the individual, if instantiated, would freely choose even though it could choose otherwise. Far from being some form of determinism based on essence, this is simply to say that God knows the essence of each possible individual so well that he knows its contingent properties, properties that do not form part of the essence or in any way shape the essence. Thus Molina's doctrine of predestination is entirely harmonious with libertarian human freedom, and the respective sets of biblical texts teaching individual predestination and human freedom may be simultaneously affirmed at face value.

However, we must not therefore think that predestination, for Molina, depends on human free choice. For every elect person, God could have just as easily chosen another feasible world in which the same individual would have freely rejected his saving grace or not existed at all. Likewise, for every reprobate person, God could have just as easily chosen another feasible world in which the same individual would have freely embraced his salvation or not existed at all. Molina insisted that no reason can be given concerning why God selected one feasible world over a host of others except for his sovereign will.[65] Since this predestinary choice is in no way predicated on how any person in that world would respond to his grace, Molina's doctrine of predestination champions the doctrine of unconditional election. This is the clear teaching

---

64. Craig, *Problem of Divine Foreknowledge and Future Contingents*, 206.
65. Molina, *Concordia*, 7.23.4/5.1.11.7–10.

of Romans 9 (especially verses 11–13, "Yet, before the twins were born or had done anything good or bad—in order that God's purpose in election might stand: not by works but by him who calls.... 'Jacob I loved, but Esau I hated,'" and verse 18, "Therefore God has mercy on whom he wants to have mercy, and he hardens whom he wants to harden") and 2 Timothy 2:20. Hence Craig observes, "Molina held that God's choosing to create certain persons has nothing to do with how they would respond to His grace; He simply chooses the world order He wants to, and no rationale for this choice is to be sought other than the divine will itself. In this sense, predestination is for Molina wholly gratuitous, the result of the divine will, and in no way based on the merits or demerits of creatures."[66] Thus God's choosing to elect or reprobate certain individuals by creating a world in which they would or would not attain to salvation rather than another world where they would freely do the opposite or not even exist has nothing to do with their freely chosen belief or unbelief; God simply, in his absolute sovereignty, selects the world he wants.[67]

At this juncture it must be emphasized that God is not guilty of foisting a divine sting operation on the reprobate, as the circumstances in the world he chooses to actualize (as well as every other feasible world) are freedom-preserving and do nothing to cause either the reprobate to spurn prevenient grace or the elect to embrace it. Hence no one could legitimately complain before the throne of God, "Since I rejected you because of my unfortunate life circumstances, my condemnation is unfair." In this case, God would reply, "While you freely chose to reject me in a world where you experienced various circumstances, those circumstances were irrelevant to your choice; you could have just as easily chosen to accept me under those same circumstances. So your condemnation is entirely fair as well as self-incurred."[68] Consistently with his justice, then, God does not "set up" anyone for damnation in choosing to create a certain feasible world, as no feasible world is salvifically unfair. Edmond Vansteenberghe succinctly captures Molina's synthesis of unconditional election, libertarian freedom, and God's universal salvific will:

---

66. Craig, *Problem of Divine Foreknowledge and Future Contingents*, 204.

67. Consequently, Molina contended that if the doctrine of middle knowledge, which undergirds his doctrine of predestination, had been discovered in the first three centuries of church history, then neither Pelagianism (which claimed that humans freely merit their own predestination) nor Lutheranism nor Calvinism (both of which asserted that predestination precludes libertarian freedom) would have emerged (*Concordia*, 7.23.4/5.1.14.6).

68. MacGregor, *Molinist-Anabaptist Systematic Theology*, 78.

Predestination does not depend upon the individual, because it consists in the choice God made to create an order of things wherein he foresaw that this individual will obtain salvation. Precisely here is the subtle point, "the impenetrable depths of the designs of God": God knew an infinity of providential orders in which the non-predestined would freely arrive at eternal life and thus would have been predestined. But he also knew an infinity of providential orders in which the predestined would have freely lost beatitude and would have been reprobate. Yet he chose for the one and for the other the providential order in which he foresaw that the one would be saved and the other not. God did this by his will alone and without consideration of their acts, but without injustice because he has provided all of them the means of obtaining eternal life.[69]

As was previously alluded to, Molina's doctrine of predestination not only reconciles the three sets of biblical texts affirming sovereign individual predestination, libertarian human freedom, and God's universal salvific will, but it also reconciles probably the seemingly most knotty discrepancy within the set of texts affirming individual predestination. This is the alleged discrepancy between Romans 8:29–30 and 1 Peter 1:1–2, which affirm that predestination *accords with* God's prior knowledge of free creaturely responses to prevenient grace, and Romans 9, which affirms that predestination is *not based on* God's prior knowledge of free creaturely responses to prevenient grace. Molina pointed out that there is no logical contradiction between these two affirmations. Predestination literally does accord or agree with God's prior knowledge of free creaturely responses to prevenient grace, since anyone who would freely accept God's grace in the feasible world God chooses to create is elect and anyone who would freely reject God's grace in the feasible world God chooses to create is reprobate. To express the same sentiment in

69. "Ce n'est pas à dire pour cela que la predestination dépende de l'individu, puisqu'elle consiste dans le choix fait par Dieu d'un ordre de choses dans lequel il prévoit que cet individu arrivera au salut. Là est précisément le point délicat, 'l'abime insondable des desseins de Dieu': Dieu connaissait une infinité d'ordres providentiels dans lesquels les non prédestinés seraient librement arrivés à la vie éternelle, et donc auraient été prédestinés; il connaissait de même une infinité d'ordres providentiels dans lesquels les prédestinés auraient librement perdu la béatitude et auraient été réprouvés; et cependant il a choisi pour les uns et les autres l'ordre de providence, dans lequel il prévoyait que les uns seraient sauvés et les autres non. Il l'a fait par sa seule volonté et sans tenir, compte de leurs actes, mais sans injustice, puisqu'il les a pourvus tous de moyens d'arriver à la vie éternelle" (Edmond Vansteenberghe, "Molinisme," in *Dictionnaire de théologie catholique*, ed. Alfred Vacant, Eugène Mangenot, and Émile Amann [Paris: Letouzey et Ané, 1929], 10.2.2168).

a negative way, no one who would freely accept God's grace in the feasible world God chooses is reprobate and no one who would freely reject God's grace in the feasible world God chooses is elect.[70] So there is full accordance or agreement between predestination and God's prior knowledge of free creaturely responses. However, predestination is not based on God's prior knowledge of free creaturely responses to prevenient grace. When Romans 9:11–13 says that "before the twins were born or had done anything good or bad—in order that God's purpose in election might stand: not by works but by him who calls.... 'Jacob I loved, but Esau I hated,'" it only affirms that election is *not based on* prior knowledge of their actions. It does not affirm that God *lacks prior knowledge* of their actions, and it seems that no one who affirms a traditional understanding of God's omniscience (as do Calvinists) could deny that God has prior knowledge of their actions. So while God has prior knowledge of what Jacob, Esau, and all other creatures would freely do in any feasible world, his predestination is not based on this knowledge. It does not take this knowledge into consideration. God's predestination of Jacob to salvation and Esau to condemnation is based sheerly on his sovereign choice to actualize a feasible world where Jacob is elect and Esau reprobate (i.e., where Jacob freely accepts his grace and Esau freely rejects God's grace) rather than a feasible world where Esau is elect and Jacob reprobate (i.e., where Esau freely accepts his grace and Jacob freely rejects God's grace) or a feasible world where Jacob is elect and Esau does not exist, Esau is elect and Jacob does not exist, or neither Jacob nor Esau exists. All such worlds are within God's power to create, and all are equally good. Hence nothing (such as prior knowledge of creaturely acts) influences God's choice of one world over the others, and the choice is based purely on God's good pleasure.[71]

We may now combine Molina's account of predestination with his view of what it meant to accept God's gracious offer of salvation and with his doctrine of justification. Recall that, for Molina, accepting God's gracious offer of salvation meant committing and surrendering one's life to God, which Molina understood as the biblical definition of faith. Molina believed that when an individual placed such faith in God, God responded by putting the individual in right standing with himself, regenerating the

---

70. Molina, *Concordia*, 7.23.4/5.1.2.9, 7.23.4/5.4.24.
71. Ibid., 7.23.4/5.1.11.8–16.

individual, forgiving the individual's sins, and infusing into the individual
Christ's righteousness composed of his faith, hope, and love. Regeneration
produced in the individual what Molina denominated a *habitus supernaturalis
fidei* (supernatural habit of faith), namely, a profound strengthening of the
individual's desire to live lovingly and selflessly for God and for neighbor.[72]
An individual possessing the supernatural habit of faith still has libertarian
freedom and thus has the ability to do anything on the spectrum between
spiritually good and spiritually evil acts. However, the individual's desires are
so profoundly inclined toward doing what is spiritually good that such acts
constitute her or his new standard mode of behavior. This is not to say that
the individual never sins, but it is to say that sinful actions occur much less
frequently than they did prior to the production of the supernatural habit of
faith and that sinful actions now comprise the exception that proves the rule
of God-centered and other-centered actions that dominate the individual's
life (1 John 3:9; 5:18). Accordingly, even though it is logically possible, it
is practically impossible for the individual to sin so consistently that she or
he falls away from the faith. And God middle-knows this practical impossibility.[73] Hence none of the predestined ever lose their salvation, a fact that
obtains due to the conjunction of libertarian freedom with the supernatural
habit of faith. In this way, Molina embraced the doctrine of eternal security or
the perseverance of the saints. On Molina's analysis of this doctrine, all who
place biblical faith in God freely persevere, even though it is logically possible
for them to fall away. In short, the elect contingently persevere, as the vast
majority of the time they freely do that which the supernatural habit of faith
renders their greatest joy—the will of God.[74] This is contrary to Calvin's
analysis, in which God makes the elect persevere via irresistible grace, such
that it is logically impossible for them to fall away.[75]

For Molina it followed that anyone who claims to have put their faith
in God but falls away from the faith never in fact committed her or his life
to God and was never elect. Such a person's "faith" was not biblical faith.

---

72. Ibid., 3.14.13.38.6; 7.23.4/5.1.5.2; 1.14.13.15.14; 7.23.4/5.1.6.15; cf. Craig, *Problem of Divine
Foreknowledge and Future Contingents*, 205. Here Craig understands Molina's description of the *habitus
supernaturalis fidei* somewhat differently than I do.
73. Molina, *Concordia*, appendix 3.56.
74. Ibid., 7.23.4/5.1.14.8.
75. Calvin, *Institutes*, 3.22.7; 3.24.6–11.

In other words, the person's "faith" was not surrender but mere intellectual assent, which does not issue in justification. Molina claimed this conclusion was explicitly drawn in 1 John 2:19, which describes persons who left the Christian faith: "They went out from us, but they did not really belong to us. For if they had belonged to us, they would have remained with us; but their going showed that none of them belonged to us." Since predestination accords with, but is not based on, middle knowledge of how individuals would use their free will, Molina held that God's middle knowledge of various persons' abandoning Christianity (a result of their never having true faith in the first place) precluded them from being predestined: "But that predestination was not made without prior knowledge of the future use of free will ... is affirmed ... where it is said ... they went out from us, but they were not of us, for if they had been of us, they would have remained with us [1 Jn. 2:19]. Those who will freely come out will freely fall. And because it is foreknown who will fall, these people are not predestined.... And by God's predestination many are caused to stand and no one is caused to fall."[76]

Molina's final comment is quite intriguing, as it exhibits the importance he attached to the priority of predestination to justification in Romans 8:30, "Those he predestined, he also called; those he called, he also justified." When God predestines someone in accord with, not because of, their middle-known biblical faith, he resolves to justify that person, which results in the new birth or supernatural habit of faith. Thus Molina held that predestination is the cause of the supernatural habit of faith, which indirectly though efficaciously causes many to stand and no one to fall.[77] Moreover, God's predestination does not cause the reprobate to fall. The reprobate are given sufficient grace for salvation, perhaps an even greater measure of grace than given the elect.[78] It is simply that the reprobate freely choose to reject God as the Lord of their lives.[79] Therefore Craig rightly says that "those who are not predestined have no one to blame but themselves. It is up to God whether we find ourselves

---

76. "Immo vero praedstinationem fuisse factam non sine praescientia usus liberi arbitrii future ... affirmat ... Illi de quibus dicitur: Ex nobis exierunt, sed non fuerunt ex nobis; si enim fuissent ex nobis, mansissent utique nobiscum, voluntate exierunt, voluntate ceciderunt. Et quia praesciti sunt casuri, non sunt praedestinati; essent autem praedestinati.... Ac per hoc praedestinatio Dei multis est causa standi, nemini labendi" (Molina, *Concordia*, 7.23.4/5.1.6.23; cf. 7.23.4/5.1.14.11).

77. Molina, *Concordia*, 3.14.13.38.5.

78. Vansteenberghe, "Molinisme," 10.2.2130.

79. Molina, *Concordia*, 7.23.3.11–13.

in a world in which we are predestined, but it is up to us whether we are predestined in the world in which we find ourselves.... No matter what world a person may be in, in that world God accords him sufficient grace for salvation; it is therefore up to each person whether in that world he is predestined or not."[80]

To put it another way, it is in the divided sense possible for the elect to be lost and the reprobate saved, since both the elect and reprobate in any world are entirely free to accept or reject salvation. Salvation therefore lies in each person's own hands. But given the truth of God's middle knowledge, it is in the composite sense impossible for the elect to be lost or for the reprobate to be saved; the elect will freely persevere to final salvation, while the reprobate will freely persevere in their resistance to God's prevenient grace until the moment of death.[81]

A SUMMARY OF MOLINIST PREDESTINATION

Molina's doctrine of predestination can be encapsulated as follows. Molina perceived no possible individual as bad enough so that she or he would freely reject God's offer of salvation in every conceivable circumstances and no possible individual as good enough so that she or he would freely accept God's offer of salvation in every conceivable circumstances. Accordingly, God's possession of middle knowledge logically prior to his making any decisions about the world, including who would be saved or lost, provides the key to God's sovereign individual predestination. For any possible individual, God can choose to elect that individual by creating a world of freedom-preserving circumstances in which God already knows that she or he would voluntarily commit her or his life to God. And God can choose to reprobate that individual by creating a different, equally good world of freedom-preserving circumstances in which God already knows that she or he would voluntarily refuse to commit her or his life to God. And God can choose not to make that individual at all by creating a different, equally good world of freedom-preserving circumstances where the individual does not exist. This choice between election, reprobation, and nonexistence is

80. Craig, *Divine Foreknowledge and Human Freedom*, 242.
81. MacGregor, *Molinist-Anabaptist Systematic Theology*, 79.

unconditioned by anything about the individual, but depends exclusively on the sovereign will of God.[82]

By coupling middle knowledge with the hypothesis that God could sovereignly actualize for any possible individual a state of affairs in which that person was freely saved, freely lost, or nonexistent, where the choice depends not at all on the possible individual but solely on God's good pleasure, Molina ingeniously reconciles full divine sovereignty, libertarian human freedom, and the universal divine salvific will without undercutting the face value meaning of any of these doctrines or the biblical texts supporting them. However, for Molina personally, the 1588 publication of the *Concordia*, containing this view of predestination and delineating the doctrine of middle knowledge on which it was based, proved both a blessing and a curse. We turn now to the intriguing story of the aftermath of the *Concordia*'s publication.

82. Ibid., 7.23.4/5.1.11.7. As Craig nicely puts it, "Since God chooses to create any world He wishes without respect to how any given person would respond to His grace, predestination is unmerited and gratuitous" (*Problem of Divine Foreknowledge and Future Contingents*, 206).

CHAPTER 6

Popularity and Escape from the Spanish Inquisition

⠶ ⠶ ⠶

MOLINA'S *CONCORDIA* HAD BARELY left the press and not yet appeared on the market when violent opposition emerged against it. Molina optimistically but naively thought his doctrine of middle knowledge would resolve the age-old dispute between the monergistic and synergistic doctrines of grace that separated the Dominican order from his Jesuit order. In fact, Molina surmised that the Pelagian controversy and its late-Augustinian[1] reaction never would have arisen if the doctrine of middle knowledge had been discovered in the first three hundred years of church history. Nor would Luther and Calvin have proposed their deterministic doctrines of predestination, as both were late-Augustinian in origin.[2] Hence Molina believed that middle knowledge could serve as a rapprochement between sixteenth-century Protestantism and the decrees of the Council of Trent. On all of these counts, Molina was tremendously disappointed during his lifetime. Within the Catholic community, the doctrine of middle knowledge proved impotent to halt the late-Augustinian predestinarianism of Michael Baius (1513–89), which later gave rise to the virtually Calvinistic theology of Cornelius Jansen (1585–1638). Because it dissented from Aquinas's doctrines of divine concurrence and divine freedom,

---

1. *Late-Augustinian* is a term used by Patristicists to denote ideas stemming from the third period of Augustine's literary output dominated by polemics provoked by the Pelagian controversy. During this period, Augustine shifted his view of human freedom from libertarian to compatibilist, or in his own words, from "free choice" (the ability to choose between spiritual good and evil) to "free will" (the will's voluntary doing of whatever it does, even though it lacks the ability not to sin).

2. Ludovici Molina, *Liberi Arbitrii cum Gratiae Donis, Divina Praescientia, Providentia, Praedestinatione et Reprobatione Concordia*, ed. Johannes Rabeneck (Madrid: Sumptibus Societatis Editorialis "Sapientia," 1953), 7.23.4/5.1.14.

the *Concordia* was rejected by leading Dominican theologians in Portugal and Spain, who endeavored to prevent its further publication by any means necessary. Ironically, this effort was joined by a few of Molina's fellow Jesuit theologians, because the *Concordia* opposed the doctrine of conditional election held by Loyola and Xavier.

But similar to the furor in Germany a generation earlier over Luther's *95 Theses*, Molina's *Concordia* also won him an outpouring of popular support from literate Portuguese and Spanish middle- to upper-class laity, who found the doctrine of middle knowledge intellectually satisfying. Each attempt at banning the book backfired, only whetting the public's hunger for it and making its publication quite lucrative for local printers.[3] At the public sermons Molina gave weekly as part of his professorial duties in the Évora university chapel, crowds ranging from approximately 700 to 1,900 people turned out following the release of the *Concordia*; previous attendance had averaged approximately 150 people.[4] This fact was all the more remarkable in that the *Concordia* was published just after the 1588 Easter season had ended. Molina observed that customarily when the sermons and works of Lent were concluded, most people inclined toward embracing carnal pleasures and relaxation rather than engaging new theological ideas.[5] A testimony of Molina's popularity despite official disapproval is that, one year later, in 1589, he was able to publish *Appendix ad Concordiam, continens responsiones ad tres objectiones et satisfactiones ad 17 animadversiones* (*Appendix to the Concordia, Containing Responses to Three Objections and Satisfactory Replies to 17 Negative Observations*), a defense of the *Concordia* that answered both major and minor objections to middle knowledge. In its chronicling of the clerical hostility and lay support toward Molina, this chapter will give a detailed account of the principal complaints lodged against middle knowledge by Molina's detractors juxtaposed with Molina's rebuttals to those complaints.

---

3. Marcelino Ocaña García, *Luis de Molina (1535–1600)*, Biblioteca Filosífica Colección Filósofos y Textos (Madrid: Ediciones del Orto, 1995), 20–24.

4. Friedrich Stegmüller, ed. and trans., *Geschichte des Molinismus: Neue Molinaschriften 1*, Beiträge zur Geschichte der Philosophie und Theologie des Mittelalters 32 (Münster: Aschendorffschen, 1935), 9*, makes the remarkable suggestion that Molina had left Évora in 1586 (due to an alleged falling out with the university chancellor Peter Paul Ferrer) and was living at Madrid at the time of the *Concordia*'s publication. However, this suggestion runs contrary to the positive documentary evidence that Molina was still in Évora in 1588.

5. Melquíades Andrés Martín, *La teología española en el siglo XVI* (Madrid: Biblioteca de Autores Cristianos, 1977), 461.

DOMINICAN OPPOSITION TO MIDDLE KNOWLEDGE

In 1588 the Dominican theologians Domingo Báñez (1528 – 1604) and Tomas de Lemos (1555 – 1629) emerged as the chief opponents of middle knowledge. Báñez and Lemos launched three major criticisms on the doctrine.[6] First, it contradicts Aquinas's understanding of God's general concurrence. For Aquinas general concurrence constituted God's sovereign generation of events by acting directly on secondary agents (e.g., humans), premoving them and so working through them to bring about those events. So as to make God the author of only good and not evil events, Aquinas drew a sharp distinction between efficacious and inefficacious concurrence. Efficacious concurrence occurs when secondary agents produce effects that God purposes for them to generate; in this case, God's power on the agents is infallibly and irresistibly directed toward the production of its intended effects. Inefficacious concurrence occurs when secondary agents produce effects that God does not purpose for them to generate; in that case, God's power on the agents is enough or sufficient for those agents to produce the effects God intended but is not infallibly or irresistibly directed toward those effects. Hence defective creatures redirect God's power toward the production of sinful events, which could not transpire apart from that power. On Aquinas's view, then, efficacious concurrence is intrinsically efficacious, and inefficacious concurrence is intrinsically inefficacious. While efficacious concurrence inevitably yields effects God positively wills, inefficacious concurrence inevitably yields effects God does not intend but simply permits. In contrast to Aquinas, Molina declared that general concurrence amounted to God's sovereign causation of events by acting directly on those events and not on secondary agents. He therefore denied that secondary agents must be moved by God to use their causal power. Further, Molina argued that, intrinsically, God's general concurrence is neither efficacious nor inefficacious. Rather, it is intrinsically neutral and is extrinsically made efficacious or inefficacious by the pertinent secondary agents.[7]

---

6. Robert Joseph Matava, "Divine Causality and Human Free Choice: Domingo Báñez and the Controversy *de Auxiliis*," PhD diss. (University of St. Andrews, 2010), 1 – 24.

7. Alfred J. Freddoso, "Introduction," in Luis de Molina, *On Divine Foreknowledge*, trans. Alfred J. Freddoso (Ithaca, NY: Cornell University Press, 1988), 18 – 19.

Second, Báñez and Lemos charged that middle knowledge entailed passivity in God, since making divine concurrence intrinsically neutral seemed to render God related in precisely the same way to both good and evil creaturely actions. In the words of Réginald Garrigou-Lagrange, "God would be no more the author of good than of bad acts, at least as regards their intrinsic and free determination, because neither good nor bad acts would come from Him, at least as regards the performance of these acts."[8] Consequently, God's essence as *actus purus* (pure actuality), as Aquinas defined it, would be jeopardized by God's not decreeing what free creatures would do in every set of circumstances but instead sitting by like an impotent bystander and seeing what would take place.[9] Third, Báñez and Lemos alleged that middle knowledge eviscerated God's freedom, as God would thereby know what he would freely do in any set of circumstances in which he found himself.[10] Finding these criticisms persuasive, the vast majority of contemporaneous Dominicans followed Báñez and Lemos in denouncing Molina.

Regarding divine concurrence, Molina defended his position by asserting the incoherence of the Thomistic alternative held by his Dominican interlocutors on three grounds. First, the Dominicans could not explain the detailed knowledge God possesses of evil events. While the Dominican position had the ability to delineate God's detailed knowledge of good events as well as God's general knowledge that good events would not occur in various circumstances (based on his decisions to concur inefficaciously rather than efficaciously with creatures), Molina contended that the Dominican position lacked an explanation of how God knows precisely which evil events would happen instead.[11] Freddoso illustrates Molina's point with the following example:

> Take the state of affairs of Peter's remaining loyal to Christ in *H*, where *H* is the situation in which Peter in fact freely denies Christ. Given that

8. Réginald Garrigou-Lagrange, *The One God*, trans. Bede Rose (St. Louis: Herder, 1943), 466.

9. William Lane Craig, *Divine Foreknowledge and Human Freedom: The Coherence of Theism: Omniscience*, Studies in Intellectual History 19 (Leiden: Brill, 1990), 270.

10. Domingo Báñez, Pedro Herrera, and Didacus Alvarez, *Apologetica fratrum prædicatorum in provinciâ Hispaniæ sacræ theologiæ professorum, adversus novas quasdam assertiones cujusdam doctoris Ludovici Molinæ nuncupati* (Madrid, 1595), 3.25; Tomas de Lemos, *Acta omnia Congregatioum et disputationum, quae coram SS. Clemente VIII et Panlo V Summis Pontificibus sunt celebratae in causa et controversia illa magna de auxiliis divinae gratiae* (Louvain, 1702), 8.5.

11. Ludovici Molina, *Appendix ad Concordiam, continens responsiones ad tres objectiones et satisfactiones ad 17 animadversiones* (Lisbon, 1589), 4–7.

God's concurrence with Peter in H is in itself merely sufficient to produce the intended effect of Peter's remaining loyal, it follows only that Peter will not remain loyal. But there are any number of ways in which Peter might deny Christ, any number of intentions he might act on, different degrees of cowardice or outright malice his act might evince, different words he might use. How can God know all the relevant details with precision, given only His prior resolution not to causally predetermine Peter's remaining loyal in H?[12]

Second, Molina charged that the radical asymmetry proposed by the Dominicans between God's causal contribution to good and evil events was nonsensical. For an evil event may differ from its good analogue only by virtue of some historical circumstance. On this score, Molina pointed out that the very same act of sexual intercourse, with all its physical and psychological features, is good if the partners are married but evil if they are not. Imagine that the history of the couple's relationship in both cases is exactly the same except for the short visit to a priest where the marriage ceremony was performed. Is it not preposterous, Molina queried, to suppose that God's intrinsically efficacious concurrence is necessary in the one case but not the other? If creatures are able to perform the act without intrinsically efficacious concurrence when it is evil, why are they not similarly able to perform the same act without intrinsically efficacious concurrence when it is good?[13]

Third, Molina argued that on the Dominican view, God cannot really intend the virtuous events he elects not to predetermine by his intrinsically efficacious concurrence. For instance, if God truly intends for Judas to repent after betraying Jesus, and if God can effectuate this repentance simply through efficacious concurrence, then why does God refuse to grant such concurrence? In general, Molina maintained that the Dominicans made it impossible to blame creatures for their evil acts, since those acts necessarily resulted from the absence of God's efficacious concurrence. Sins then become acts of God's omission, making God just as much the author of sins as if they were accomplished by God's commission. Hence Molina declared:

---

12. Freddoso, "Introduction," 39.

13. Ibid., 40; Luis de Molina, *On Divine Foreknowledge*, trans. Alfred J. Freddoso (Ithaca, NY: Cornell University Press, 1988), 4.14.13.53.2.13.

Again, what grievance will God have on Judgment Day against the wicked, since they were unable not to sin as long as God did not efficaciously incline and determine them to the good, but rather solely by His own free will decided from eternity not so to determine them? Most assuredly, if this position is accepted, then our freedom of choice is altogether destroyed, and God's justice with respect to the wicked vanishes, and a manifest cruelty and wickedness is discerned in God. That is why I regard this position as extremely dangerous from the point of view of the faith.[14]

For these reasons, Molina concluded that if divine concurrence were intrinsically efficacious or inefficacious rather than, as he insisted, intrinsically neutral, then ostensibly free creatures would be nothing more than marionettes controlled by God, who alone possesses freedom.[15]

In response to Báñez and Lemos's second charge that middle knowledge entailed divine passivity, Molina asserted that it does so only if one conceives of God in a Thomistic vein as pure actuality, the determining cause of all that occurs. But Molina insisted that one should abandon the doctrine of pure actuality as philosophically incoherent and as contradictory to Scripture. For if God is pure actuality, then God's attributes are not distinct from one another. But surely, for example, God's omnipotence and God's omnibenevolence denote two distinct properties, each of which is irreducible to the other.[16] This can be seen conceptually by observing that an entity could be all-powerful without being all-loving, and an entity could be all-loving without being all-good. However, both of these attributes are philosophically necessary to God's status, *pro* Anselm, as the greatest conceivable being, and both of these attributes are biblically affirmed (e.g., Gen. 17:1; 1 John 4:8).[17]

Instead of pure actuality, Molina believed that God should be understood

14. Molina, *Foreknowledge*, 4.14.13.50.14.

15. The Dominicans did not feel they were denying libertarian human freedom. Indeed, they alleged that creatures possess libertarian freedom, albeit without using the modern phrase. But Molina found this allegation philosophically incoherent and concluded that despite themselves, the Dominicans ended up with compatibilist freedom.

16. However, Molina also held that neither God's omnipotence nor God's omnibenevolence is separable from God's essence. So I don't think the evidence enables us to conclude what Molina's position was (or even if he had a position) concerning divine simplicity. It seems to me that Molina's doctrine is compatible with either divine simplicity (the mainstream Christian view) or divine univocity (the minority view held, e.g., by Scotus), depending on whether one thinks the doctrine applies on the level of essence or on the level of attributes.

17. Molina, *Concordia*, 1.14.13.19.2.10.

as essentially infinite and tripersonal, an understanding that precluded divine passivity. God's infinity, or sum total of his great-making perfections, includes his omniscience, which in turn includes his middle knowledge. By availing himself of this knowledge, the tripersonal God chooses, in his creative decree, everything that will happen (the actual world) out of everything that would possibly happen given human freedom and natural indeterminism (the set of all feasible worlds). So far from sitting idly by on the sidelines, God is the active agent whose free decision is the indispensable factor bringing about all human actions.[18] And God's free decision brings about these actions indeterministically, such that God cannot be indicted as the author of sin. In fact, each of the three Trinitarian persons is grieved by sin (Gen. 6:6; Luke 19:41–44; Eph. 4:30).[19] This grief was so strong that it moved God to enter into human history and become incarnate as Jesus of Nazareth, to solve the problem of sin once and for all and so redeem all who place faith in him (Rom. 3:24–26; 8:3–4; Eph. 1:7; Titus 2:14).[20]

With respect to Báñez and Lemos's third charge that middle knowledge destroyed divine freedom, Molina emphasized that middle knowledge does not give God knowledge of what *he himself* would do under any set of circumstances. If God had such knowledge, Molina conceded, that would indeed obliterate divine freedom.[21] Middle knowledge only gives God knowledge of what any possible *creature* would freely do under any conceivable circumstances. Here Molina stressed that the means by which God has middle knowledge is supercomprehension, or his ability to infinitely perceive the individual essence or pattern of every possible creature that exists solely in his imagination prior to the divine creative decree. Because these individual essences are abstract, not concrete, objects and God perfectly understands his own imagination, supercomprehension follows inescapably as a result. But it is logically impossible for God to supercomprehend himself, since God is a concrete object (more than that, the only logically necessary concrete object), not an abstract object that exists within God's imagination. Nor is God's individual essence an abstract object that exists

18. Ludovici Molina, *Appendix ad Concordiam*, 26–27.
19. Molina, *Concordia*, 5.19.6.1.26.
20. Ibid., 3.14.13.46.18, 20.
21. Molina, *Foreknowledge*, 4.14.13.52.13.

within God's imagination, but it is one and the same as his existence.[22] In addition, Molina insisted that supercomprehension can occur only when the knower infinitely transcends in completeness or wholeness what is known. Since God cannot infinitely transcend his own perfection, the idea of God's supercomprehending himself again proves self-refuting. Drawing together the threads of his case, Molina asserted:

> God does not know, just by virtue of the knowledge that *precedes* the act of His will, which part *His own* will is going to determine itself to with regard to any object able to be created by Him, even though by virtue of that same knowledge He *does* know, on the hypothesis that His will should choose to determine itself to one or another order of things and circumstances, what each *created* faculty of choice would in its freedom will or do within that order. Now the reason for this is that while the divine intellect and knowledge surpass in perfection by an infinite distance each *created* faculty of choice which they contain eminently in themselves and which for this reason they comprehend in a certain infinitely more eminent way than that in which it is knowable [i.e., to itself[23]], they do not likewise surpass the *divine* will in perfection or comprehend it in a more eminent way than that in which it is knowable in itself. Yet, as has been said, it is *this* sort of comprehension that is required to know regarding free choice, before it determines itself, which part it is going to determine itself to in its freedom under any given hypothesis.[24]

Molina went on to affirm that in choosing to create the actual world, God freely decides what all his future actions in that world will be. These actions are not determined in any way by God's prevolitional knowledge but are entirely up to God in his liberty. Hence God knows everything that he will do in the world in his free knowledge, not in his middle knowledge. In other

---

22. Here Molina split a Thomistic hair, since Aquinas believed the notion of God as pure actuality was logically equivalent to the identity between God's essence and his existence. Molina takes these as two entirely different notions, interpreting pure actuality as God's all-determining actualization of all that happens and the identity between essence and existence as the Anselmian claim that the idea of God in the mind, even God's mind, cannot exist apart from the concrete reality of God (*Appendix ad Concordiam*, 13, 36, 41).

23. This reflexive understanding of "it is knowable" is implicit both in the immediate context and in the Latin construction "quodam eminentiori modo, quam illud sit cognoscibile" (*Concordia*, 4.14.13.52.13).

24. Molina, *Foreknowledge*, 4.14.13.52.13.

words, God has foreknowledge of his own actions in the actual world not by middle-knowing what he would do in every conceivable circumstance but by knowing what he has, in his creative decree, decided to do in every forthcoming circumstance by his almighty power to carry out his freely chosen will.[25]

MINORITY JESUIT OPPOSITION TO MIDDLE KNOWLEDGE

Joining the Dominicans Báñez and Lemos in their opposition to middle knowledge were Enrique Henriquez (1536–1608) and Juan de Mariana (1536–1624), two of Molina's Jesuit brethren. Although the vast majority of the Jesuits sided with middle knowledge, Henriquez and Mariana objected on the grounds that Molina's corollary doctrine of predestination taught unconditional election of persons to salvation or damnation.[26] Recall from chapter 5 that on Molina's view, for any possible individual, God could have created either a feasible world where that individual freely embraces God's salvation, an equally good feasible world where that individual freely rejects God's salvation, or an equally good feasible world where that individual does not exist. God makes his decision of which world to actualize entirely without regard to that individual's salvation, damnation, or nonexistence. Henriquez and Mariana had two problems with this perspective. First, it seemed too Calvinistic.[27] Unconditional election had been practically ruled out by the Council of Trent, which decreed: "If any one shall say, that the grace of justification only befalleth those who are predestined unto life; but that all others who are called, are called indeed, but receive not grace, as being, by the divine power, predestined unto evil; let him be anathema."[28] Thus Trent identified as heretical the notion that, while God generally calls all humans to salvation (a call which is itself inadequate to accomplish their salvation), God effectually calls to salvation only the predestinate, so guaranteeing their

---

25. Freddoso, "Introduction," 52.

26. Enrique Henriquez, *Theologiæ Moralis Summa* (Salamanca, Spain, 1593), 1.4.18; Juan de Mariana, *Tractatus VII: Theologici et historici* (Cologne, 1609), 2.5.

27. Ironically, many contemporary thinkers who only know Arminius's modified version of middle knowledge and anachronistically retroject it back onto Molina object to middle knowledge precisely on the basis that it denies unconditional election and is not Calvinistic enough!

28. *The Canons and Decrees of the Council of Trent*, trans. H. J. Schroeder (Rockford, IL: TAN Books and Publishers, 1978), 44.

beatitude without respect to their foreseen works or merits. Although Molina did not appeal to Calvin's distinction between general calling and effectual calling, Henriquez and Mariana viewed Molina's teaching on predestination as functionally equivalent. For on their reading of Molina, God's creating a world and giving all persons within that world sufficient grace for salvation was not enough to secure their salvation, just as Calvin's general call was not enough. But, like Calvin's effectual call, God's choosing to actualize a world in which a person finds herself/himself predestined was enough to secure that individual's salvation.[29]

Second, Henriquez and Mariana contended that Ignatius of Loyola and Francis Xavier, cofounders of the Jesuit order, held to the doctrine of conditional election. On their reading of Loyola and Xavier, predestination is based on foreknown merits, as God looks out over the sweep of time, sees who will persevere on the path of justification, and then elects them on that basis.[30] In support of this interpretation, Henriquez and Mariana quoted Rule 15 from Loyola's "Rules for Thinking with the Church," which they claimed only made sense given conditional election: "If in some way and at some times one speaks ... of predestination ... let him so speak that the common people may not come into any error, as sometimes happens, saying: Whether I have to be saved or condemned is already determined, and no other thing can now be, through my doing well or ill; and with this, growing lazy, they become negligent in the works which lead to the salvation and the spiritual profit of their souls."[31] Further, Henriquez and Mariana averred that Xavier's renowned missionary zeal for the conversion of multitudes in the Far East was compatible exclusively with conditional election. For given that God wants to save the heathen (1 Tim. 2:4; 2 Peter 3:9), if unconditional election were true, God could elect them without the labors of missionaries. Only if election is conditioned by certain grounds, such as knowledge and acceptance of the Christian faith, were the past labors of Xavier and the current missionary efforts of the Jesuit order not in vain.[32]

29. Henriquez, *Theologiæ Moralis Summa*, 1.6.3; Mariana, *Tractatus VII: Theologici et historici*, 2.8.

30. Henriquez, *Theologiæ Moralis Summa*, 1.7.1; Mariana, *Tractatus VII: Theologici et historici*, 2.5.

31. Here I cite the more literal translation of Loyola provided by Elder Mullan in *The Spiritual Exercises of St. Ignatius of Loyola* (Raleigh, NC: Hayes Barton, 2009), 105. Elsewhere I continue to employ Puhl's more dynamic translation.

32. Hernandez, *Theologiæ Moralis Summa*, 1.8.5; Mariana, *Tractatus VII: Theologici et historici*, 2.11.

In response to Henriquez and Mariana's allegation that Molinist election was functionally equivalent to Calvinist election, Molina asserted that this charge could only be sustained if one looked at the world exclusively from the *sensus compositus* (composite sense). However, if one looked at the world from both the *sensus compositus* and the *sensus divisius* (divided sense), then the key difference between Molinist and Calvinist election immediately emerges.[33] We remember from chapter 4 that the composite sense looks from a distance at the full scope of reality, while the divided sense analyzes each realm of reality in and of itself. It is true that, looking only at the final state of affairs, God's granting a person sufficient grace does not guarantee his salvation, while God's predestining a person does guarantee his salvation. But viewing things only at this composite level would be too facile, as one must analyze the specific things or factors that go to bring about those outcomes. Failing to do this would eviscerate all moral discriminations. For instance, looking only at the final state of affairs would render killing someone in self-defense equivalent to murdering someone with premeditation, as the person wound up dead in both cases. In the divided sense, looking specifically at the human will and any causally determining influences on it, Molina insisted that neither God's granting a person sufficient grace nor God's predestining a person guarantees that person's salvation. Neither is intrinsically efficacious; both are extrinsically efficacious.[34] When God gives a person sufficient grace, that grace can indeed be, and often is, used by the individual to take hold of salvation, *contra* Calvin's general calling, which cannot actually be used by anyone to appropriate salvation. If the individual freely uses sufficient grace to take hold of salvation, that grace is efficacious, and extrinsically so. If the individual freely rejects sufficient grace and fails to appropriate salvation, that grace is inefficacious, and extrinsically so. That, for Molina, there is no difference in the quality of sufficient grace between efficacious and inefficacious grace is seen in the fact many persons who ultimately end up nonbelievers receive far greater gifts of sufficient grace than do those who end up believers. It is just that the former freely reject and the latter freely accept that grace.[35]

Likewise, Molina held that when God predestines a person, this exerts no

---

33. Molina, *Foreknowledge*, 4.14.13.52.30; 4.14.13.53.2.6.
34. Molina, *Appendix ad Concordiam*, 38.
35. Ibid., 57–58.

causal power at all over whether a person accepts sufficient grace and finds salvation or rejects sufficient grace and is lost.[36] Causally speaking, it is irrelevant whether a person is elect or reprobate. For Molina being elect does not "make sure" that one freely accepts sufficient grace, and being reprobate does not "make sure" that one freely rejects sufficient grace. It is entirely possible for the elect to reject sufficient grace and be lost and for the reprobate to accept sufficient grace and be saved. Both are treated equally by God. Indeed, freely accepting sufficient grace "makes sure" that one is elect, and freely rejecting sufficient grace "makes sure" that one is reprobate (cf. 2 Peter 1:10).[37] It is up to the individual if one is elect or reprobate in the world in which one finds oneself. So in the divided sense, predestination does nothing to guarantee salvation, quite unlike Calvin's effectual call, which causally guarantees salvation. Lest it be objected here that creatures determine God's predestination, Molina emphasized that for any elect creature, God could have reprobated him by creating a world where he would freely reject sufficient grace, or God could have not made him at all by creating a world where he would not exist. And for any reprobate creature, God could have elected him by creating a world where he would freely accept sufficient grace, or God could have not made him at all by creating a world where he would not exist.[38] So it is up to God if one finds oneself in a world in which one is elect or reprobate or if one is not found in a world. For Molina there is no such thing as transworld salvation, transworld damnation, or transworld existence.

The only sense in which predestination guarantees a creature's salvation is in the composite sense that it is logically impossible for God to be mistaken about his middle knowledge that if a creature were actualized, that creature would freely embrace sufficient grace in the feasible world God eventually creates. Therefore, viewed from a distance, the elect creature's salvation is guaranteed from the moment of the world's creation.[39] But this logical impossibility is impotent to make the creature freely embrace sufficient grace in the world; the creature could freely reject sufficient grace in that very same world. It is simply that God knows, in point of fact, that the creature will there embrace sufficient grace and will do so contingently. And this

---

36. Ibid., 60–61.
37. Molina, *Concordia*, 7.23.4/5.1.11.39; idem, *Foreknowledge*, 4.14.13.52.39.
38. Molina, *Appendix ad Concordiam*, 36.
39. Molina, *Foreknowledge*, 4.14.13.53.2.25.

infallible knowledge, just like any other knowledge, is logically powerless to cause anything. According to Molina, such a solution where predestination in the broadly composite sense but not, per Calvinism, in the causally determinative divided sense ensures salvation resolves the seeming paradox of 1 Peter 1:1–2, in which "God's elect … have been chosen according to the foreknowledge of God." By taking middle knowledge and not simple foreknowledge (i.e., free knowledge) to be the referent to "foreknowledge," Molina pointed out that God's elect were indeed gratuitously chosen by him (he could have chosen others or no one at all) and that middle knowledge served as the means according to which God noncausally and indeterministically guaranteed their election.[40]

Concerning Loyola and Xavier, Molina did not so much deny that these Jesuit founders personally believed in conditional election (a claim he felt amounted to unfalsifiable speculation) as he argued that nothing they wrote forbade one from holding to unconditional election. Molina began by pointing out that nothing could be logically deduced from Rule 15 of Loyola's "Rules for Thinking with the Church" or Xavier's tireless missionary efforts about their stance on conditional versus unconditional election. At best, a person could show his or her denial of the Calvinistic idea that election causally determined a person's salvation.[41] Since Molina's doctrine of unconditional election was not causally determinative, it proved acceptable within a Jesuit framework. Molina went on to assert that, in fact, the unwavering fidelity to Scripture required by the Jesuit order and its intellectual mandate to find reasons in support of all scriptural precepts demanded that one believe in and defend unconditional election.[42] For, Molina averred, Romans 9:15–18 plainly taught unconditional election, making it his intellectual duty as a Jesuit to reconcile this with the biblical affirmation of libertarian human freedom, stressed by the Council of Trent over against Lutheranism and Calvinism.[43]

Molina alleged that to say unconditional election undercuts missionary

---

40. Ibid., 4.14.13.53.2.13; idem, *Concordia*, 7.23.4/5.1.11.38.
41. Molina, *Appendix ad Concordiam*, 94–99; Melquíades Andrés Martín, *La teología española en el siglo XVI* (Madrid: Biblioteca de Autores Cristianos, 1977), 462.
42. Here Molina is paraphrasing the Ninth Rule of Loyola's "Rules for Thinking with the Church" (Mullan, *Spiritual Exercises*, 125).
43. Molina, *Concordia*, 7.23.4/5.4.2.

efforts was not even true on Calvinism, much less on his own view. On Calvinism, God uses means to execute his decrees in time. Among the means God employs in carrying out his decree to elect various individuals are other people and their preaching of the gospel. Thus far, Molina agreed entirely with Calvin.[44] The difficulty Molina had with Calvin lay in his further contention that God deterministically controls the means by which the salvation of the elect is accomplished. Calvin reasoned that God could not achieve with certainty the outcome of the elect's salvation unless he deterministically controlled the means on which the outcome hung.[45] But on Molinism, middle knowledge gave God the certainty of knowing what choice of world would contingently contain the means, including missionaries, that would in turn contingently bring about the salvation of the elect. Hence Molina charged Calvin with confusing certainty with necessity. As we saw in chapter 3, certainty is a property of persons that has nothing to do with truth, as evident by the fact that an individual can be entirely certain about something that turns out to be false. Necessity is a property of propositions, signifying that it is logically impossible for a proposition to be false.[46] It is true that God could not achieve *with necessity* the outcome of the elect's salvation — namely, he could not render it logically impossible for the proposition "The elect will be saved" to be false — unless he deterministically controlled the means of salvation. However, Molina asserted, middle knowledge afforded God the means to achieve *with certainty* the outcome of the elect's salvation without deterministically controlling its means. In other words, God knows via his middle knowledge that the proposition "The elect will be saved" is in fact true, even though it could have been false. In sum, it is certain that the elect will be saved contingently.[47]

44. Molina, *Appendix ad Concordiam*, 64.

45. John Calvin, *Institutes of the Christian Religion*, ed. John T. McNeill, trans. Ford Lewis Battles (Philadelphia: Westminster, 1960), 3.24.2.

46. William Lane Craig, "The Middle-Knowledge View," in James K. Beilby and Paul R. Eddy, *Divine Foreknowledge: Four Views* (Downers Grove, IL: InterVarsity, 2001), 127.

47. Molina, *Appendix ad Concordiam*, 36, 79.

MOLINA AND THE SPANISH INQUISITION

Despite Molina's responses to his detractors, in 1590 the protestations of Báñez, Lemos, Henriquez, and Mariana moved the theological faculty at the University of Salamanca to make an attempted block of any future publication of the *Concordia*. On behalf of the faculty, Báñez reported to Archduke Albert, Viceroy of Portugal (1559–1621), that the *Concordia* definitely contained thirteen assertions the Spanish Inquisition had proscribed.[48] Thereafter Albert sent the *Concordia* to the chief censor of the Holy Office of the Inquisition, Bartolomeu Ferreira (c. 1540–c. 1610). Ironically, not only did Ferreira find nothing wrong with the work, declaring that its assertions did not violate the Inquisition's ban, but Ferreira loved the *Concordia* and praised it with a glowing *imprimatur*. The *imprimatur* affirmed that in the *Concordia* "many passages from the Councils and Holy Scriptures were explained in a most satisfactory manner."[49] To the dismay of the Salamanca theological faculty, the new impetus gained by the *Concordia* triggered its positive reception in wide lay circles throughout Portugal and Spain, and scholarly interest in the work across the European continent led to the printing of new editions at Lyons, Antwerp, and Venice.[50] Further, the theological faculty at the University of Valladolid, while attempting to downplay the originality of Molina's doctrine, endorsed the *Concordia*'s solution to the age-old tension between divine predestination and human freedom. John Hardon summarizes the faculty verdict as follows: "The book contained nothing fundamentally new that could not be found in Augustine and Thomas Aquinas; yet ... Molina was the first to treat of the reconciliation of grace and freedom at such length and with so much detail, by solving the difficulties that theologians needed to meet the crises of Protestantism."[51]

Molina's successes proved incendiary to the rise of stiffer opposition in 1591. Exploiting his friendship with several leading censors of the Spanish Inquisition, Báñez repeatedly insisted that the *Concordia* be included in a supplement that the Inquisition was preparing to its *Index of Prohibited Books*.

---

48. Matava, "Divine Causality and Human Free Choice," 68.
49. John Hardon, *History and Theology of Grace: The Catholic Teaching on Divine Grace* (Washington, DC: Catholic University of America Press, 2006), 332.
50. Guido Stucco, *The Catholic Doctrine of Predestination from Luther to Jansenius* (Bloomington, IN: Xlibris, 2014), 81.
51. Hardon, *History and Theology of Grace*, 333.

While delaying formal judgment on the *Concordia*, the Inquisition issued a provisional denunciation of Molina on the assumption, gleaned from Báñez, that Molinism was incompatible with the decrees of the Council of Trent.[52] This was more than enough to jeopardize Molina's academic standing at the University of Évora and to put him in danger of bodily harm. Anticipating betrayal by his colleagues and fearing for his own safety, Molina retreated to his hometown of Cuenca, where he knew he would receive protection from the local magistrates. These magistrates had formally approved of the *Concordia*, even publishing a new edition of the work on the city's printing press. Moreover, on theological matters the city was remarkably tolerant. Following the spirit of the Renaissance, the Code of the city affirmed the "dignity and prerogative of freedom" of religion, giving a "guarantee" of "royal protection ... to all the inhabitants of Cuenca." The city magistrates believed that such an open exchange of ideas would only serve to honor "Holy Mother Church" and bring "the increase of the Catholic faith," as the faith could only flourish when people obeyed and thought about God in an uncoerced fashion. Accordingly, religious liberty amounted to a corollary of Matthew 11:28–30, "for God living and true ... whose yoke is soft and his load light," people must "serve in freedom."[53] At Cuenca, Molina served as a parish priest, preaching weekly and hearing confession at the Iglesia de San Miguel (Church of Saint Michael) and performing deeds of charity throughout the city. In addition to his pastoral duties, Molina began preparing for print a defense of middle knowledge called the *Apologia Concordiae*, featuring a point-by-point response to each of his principal critics in letter, or epistolary, form. He also launched into an extended study of issues related to social justice and politics, especially as they touched on the spiritual lives of his parishioners.[54]

---

52. Matava, "Divine Causality and Human Free Choice," 106.

53. *The Code of Cuenca*, trans. James F. Powers (Philadelphia: University of Pennsylvania Press, 2000), 29.

54. Augustin de Backer and Carlos Sommervogel, *Bibliographie des éscrevains de la compagnie de Jésus*, 7 vols. (Liège, Belgium: Grandmont-Donders, 1853–97), 5:1167–70.

THE THEOLOGICAL "CIVIL WAR" BETWEEN JESUITS AND DOMINICANS

Notwithstanding the criticisms of Henriquez and Mariana, the Jesuit order as a whole rallied to the defense of Molina, arguing that the Dominicans misrepresented Molina's doctrine at numerous points. The Jesuits were not without justification in their argument, as Hardon reports about the *Concordia* that it seemed "no book ... since the invention of the printing press [had] been subjected to such minute and ruthless criticism in every line."[55] The debate between the Jesuits and Dominicans became so heated that, in Hardon's words, "a veritable civil war of theology was waged throughout Spain."[56] Chief among Molina's supporters in Spain was Gabriel Vásquez (1549–1604), and chief among Molina's supporters elsewhere on the European continent was the Flemish theologian Leonardus Lessius (1554–1623). Endorsing the substance of middle knowledge, Vásquez affirmed that contingents of creaturely freedom are conditionally future, namely, future only on the condition that God decides to create the agents and states of affairs they describe. Further, even after the divine creative decree (in free knowledge) these contingents are foreknown by God as conditionally future, as his concurrence with the choices of free agents is necessary to move them from the realm of possibility to the realm of actuality.[57] Vásquez thus maintained that Molina perspicuously reconciled human free choice with divine sovereignty, as no free creature can produce even the smallest effect apart from both God's will and God's general concurrence. Similarly, Lessius came out enthusiastically in favor of middle knowledge, endorsing especially Molina's view of extrinsically efficacious grace. While Lessius admitted with the Dominicans that any denial of efficacious grace per se was impossible for a biblically faithful Christian, he proclaimed that a denial of intrinsically efficacious grace was necessary for avoiding the Dominican theory of predetermination, which obliterated human free choice and thus proved harmful to the faith.[58]

55. Hardon, *History and Theology of Grace*, 340.
56. Ibid., 333.
57. J. Martin Bac, *Perfect Will Theology: Divine Agency in Reformed Scholasticism as against Suárez, Episcopius, Descartes, and Spinoza*. Series in Church History 42 (Leiden: Brill, 2010), 114.
58. Leonardus Lessius, *De perfectionibus moribusque divinis* (Amberes, Belgium, 1620), 4.2.7.

Debates between the Jesuit Molinists and the Dominican Thomists went on throughout Spain from 1591 to 1596. In 1594 a particularly acrimonious public debate occurred at Valladolid between the Jesuit theologian Antonio de Padilla (c. 1555–c. 1617) and the Dominican theologian Diego Nuûo (c. 1562–c. 1635).[59] Very much like Luther's absence from the Diet of Augsburg in 1530 on account of his having been declared an outlaw—someone free to be killed by anyone at any time—at the Diet of Worms, Molina was not present to see his position defended on account of potential capture by the Spanish Inquisition. Padilla charged that Thomism made God out to be the author of evil, while Nuûo charged that Molinism made God out to be impotent. Hence what should have been a complex and nuanced theological debate was reduced, and unfairly so, to simplistic yet misleading ideas that could trigger strong responses from the assembled laypeople. In short, both Padilla and Nuûo played to the crowd, throwing out red meat, which the audience could easily consume. Their heated exchange provoked a riot, with about two-thirds of the citizens present backing Padilla and about one-third backing Nuûo. Shortly after Molina got word of this development, he sent the *Apologia Concordiae* to the Cuencan printer in the hope that he would represent his opponents' positions fairly and refute them accurately in their strongest forms, thereby encouraging his supporters to do the same. For this reason, as Joseph Pohle states, "Molina commanded the respect and esteem of his bitterest adversaries.... His virtues were a source of edification to all who knew him."[60]

The most important contribution of the *Apologia Concordiae* (1594) was Molina's painstakingly thorough and detailed criticism of Báñez. No longer content merely to defend his own views, Molina went on the offense in attacking Báñez's doctrines of grace and free will, condemning them as irreconcilable with the Council of Trent. Trent maintained that the effects of the fall do not extinguish but rather weaken the power of human freedom; each person still has enough freedom to cooperate with God's prevenient grace and attain salvation.[61] But Báñez seemed to abnegate libertarian freedom by

59. Livinus de Meyer, *Historia Controversiarum de Divinae Gratiae Auxiliis* (Antwerp, Belgium, 1705), 245.

60. Joseph Pohle, "Luis de Molina," *The Catholic Encyclopedia*, 15 vols., ed. Charles G. Herbermann (New York: Robert Appleton, 1907–12), 10:437.

61. *Canons and Decrees of the Council of Trent*, 30, 32.

claiming that no one, apart from God's intrinsically efficacious concurrence, could attain salvation, rendering God's general concurrence insufficient for the salvation of all. Molina pointed out that Luther, in *The Bondage of the Will*, had started from the same precepts as Báñez and ended by denying human free choice.[62] To support this indictment, Molina compiled a list of texts from Luther's *Bondage of the Will* and Calvin's *Institutes* and placed them side by side with analogous texts from Báñez and his chief apologist, Francisco Zumel (1540–1607). Molina was here not too subtly implying that Báñez had actually drawn his ideas from the writings of Luther and Calvin, an implication for which the similarity of the texts at least made out a prima facie case. Molina finally accused Báñez of being the first Catholic theologian to introduce these Lutheran and Calvinistic ideas into Spain, a claim that is historically plausible but unprovable.[63] Although Molina's criticism was trenchant, it would be difficult to claim that he, like Padilla, had been shooting down a straw man.

Molina's efforts to bring a blend of rigor and fairness to the Jesuit-Dominican controversy proved to no avail, as rancorous debates continued to transpire at Salamanca, Saragossa, Cordova, and other cities in Spain. Because of the public disturbances that followed these debates, Pope Clement VIII (r. 1592–1605) declared a moratorium on any further discussion of what had become known as the controversy over grace. As Hardon notes, "A papal letter of August 15, 1594, was received by the two religious orders, instructing them not to discuss efficacious grace in public or private under penalty of excommunication."[64] Between 1594 and 1596, a massive report on the works of Molina and Báñez was prepared by the Spanish Inquisition and finally sent to Rome. This report conveyed the opinions of five bishops and four scholars, none of them Jesuits or Dominicans, on the relative merits of Molina and Báñez. The opinions were divided, with one bishop and two scholars solidly on the side of Molina, two bishops and one scholar solidly on the side of Báñez, and two bishops and one scholar condemning both Molina and Báñez for innovative and false doctrine.[65] Meanwhile, the controversy

---

62. Ludovici Molina, *Apologia Concordiae* (Cuenca, Spain, 1594), 3.1.
63. Ibid., 3.6; Hardon, *History and Theology of Grace*, 334.
64. Hardon, *History and Theology of Grace*, 335.
65. Meyer, *Historia Controversiarum*, 273.

continued to brew between the Jesuits and Dominicans throughout Spain despite the papal demand for silence, making potential excommunication an empty threat since it could not realistically be enforced en masse. Hence in 1596 Clement VIII attempted to take matters into his own hands. He ordered that all the relevant documents, including the writings of Molina, Báñez, Lemos, Henriquez, Mariana, Vásquez, and Lessius, be sent to the Vatican. He also instructed the Jesuits and Dominicans to await patiently the decision of the papacy on the issue of middle knowledge.[66]

With middle knowledge on the proverbial back burner for the time being, Molina turned with vigor to an exposition of his practical theology, which centered on the law and carried significant implications for personal spirituality. Transcending local concerns, Molina also broadened his study of social justice to assess national and international concerns, including the prospect of a free market economy, the relationship between church and state, and the moral problems posed by the African slave trade.[67] Molina's analysis of these practical and juridical topics resulted in the 1596 publication of the five-volume work *De justitia et jure* (*On Justice and Law*). This work was first conceived as a commentary on questions 57 to 79 in Aquinas's Second Part of the Second Part (*Secunda Secundae*) of the *Summa Theologiae*, questions that were not covered in Molina's 1573 commentary on the *Summa*. Thus while, as we have seen, Molina disagreed with Aquinas on a number of important theological points, he continued to use the *Summa* as a springboard for his own thinking, sometimes as a negative pole against which his own distinctive ideas emerged. As a result, *De justitia et jure* ended up as far more than a commentary on Aquinas. As Alonso-Lasheras observes, it "dealt with justice and law in a more detailed way than Aquinas did, and discussed topics Thomas did not explore."[68] To this monumental work we shall turn in the next two chapters.

---

66. Pohle, "Luis de Molina," 10:437.

67. Paolo Broggio, *La teologia e la politica: Controversie dottrinali, Curia romana e Monarchia spagnola tra Cinque e Seicento* (Firenze, Italy: Leo S. Olschki, 2009), 74–76.

68. Diego Alonso-Lasheras, *Luis de Molina's De Iustitia et Iure: Justice as Virtue in an Economic Context*, Studies in the History of Christian Traditions 152 (Leiden: Brill, 2011), 8.

CHAPTER 7

Molina's Practical
Theology

⚎ ⚎ ⚎

DISPLAYING A BLEND OF PERSONAL SENSITIVITY and moral conviction, Molina's
practical theology profoundly shaped the lives of his parishioners at Cuenca
and formed the backbone of his five-volume *De justitia et jure* (*On Justice and
Law*), published in 1596. For Molina every human action must be directed
toward a proper end. Resembling the affirmation of the 1647 *Westminster
Shorter Catechism* that the chief end of humanity is "to glorify God, and to
enjoy him forever,"[1] Molina held that the proper end of every human action
is to praise, reverence, and serve Christ the Lord.[2] Everything else in creation
is oriented to aid humanity in reaching that supreme end. Notably, Molina
believed that the law designated the sum total of ways that the theocentric
end may be reached, rather than referring to particular moral rules that must
be followed to achieve merit from God or find salvation. Hence the main
emphasis of Molina's practical theology was the law. Within this theological
category, Molina included the use of Scripture in moral reasoning, natural
law, and the ecclesiastical context of Christian ethical decision making.[3] One
principal application of Molina's treatment of the law was the importance of
a simple life, a virtue that Molina impressed on his congregation. The simple
life could be characterized as a modified form of evangelical poverty that
permitted ownership of private property. Accordingly, this chapter will explore
the foundations and central themes of Molina's practical theology.

---

1. *The Westminster Shorter Catechism*, in *The Book of Confessions* (Louisville: Geneva, 2004), 175.
2. Diego Alonso-Lasheras, *Luis de Molina's De Iustitia et Iure: Justice as Virtue in an Economic
Context*, Studies in the History of Christian Traditions 152 (Leiden: Brill, 2011), 85.
3. Ibid., 62.

THE SPIRITUAL FOUNDATIONS OF MOLINA'S PRACTICAL THEOLOGY

Molina's practical theology was based on a spirituality of directing every human action to the glory and service of God. This spirituality engenders a degree of relativity in the relationship of humans to created things. Following Ignatius of Loyola,[4] Molina held that the essential rule in this relationship is to employ created things insofar as they help us to achieve our theocentric end, and to shun created things insofar as they hinder us from achieving our end.[5] This essential rule furnishes a limit as to what is permitted to the choice of human free will. While certain things are entirely forbidden, for the rest it is necessary to decide which most probably will aid us toward our supreme end and which most probably will impede us from attaining our end. Moreover, things that are not forbidden may be beneficial for us in some circumstances and not in others. Thus Molina insisted that each Christian must continually revise how her or his actions in relationship to things are aiding or impeding the accomplishment of the supreme end.[6] The determining factor in many cases amounts to the circumstances surrounding the actions. As Alonso-Lasheras observes, "This is an important working principle in Molina's fundamental moral theology ... how important circumstances are for him in determining ... the right thing to do. The norms do not change, but the circumstances of particular cases do alter the way a discerning observer will apply these norms in order to determine the right thing to do ... so as best to serve our ultimate end."[7] One could therefore denominate Molina's spirituality as a form of teleological act utilitarianism, whereby an act is right or moral to the degree that it is useful in glorifying or serving Christ. Although well intentioned, this outlook appears to be a weakness in Molina's thought, as it is inconsistent with his affirmation that God's nature constitutes the foundation of objective moral values (an affirmation that typically implies some form of nonconsequentialism). For example, most of Molina's coreligionists believed that the ongoing French Wars of Religion (1562–98) were justified because they glorified and served Christ, insofar as

---

4. Ignatius Loyola, *The Spiritual Exercises*, trans. Louis J. Puhl (New York: Vintage, 2000), §23.

5. Ludovici Molina, *De justitia et jure*, 5 vols. (Cologne: Marci-Michaelis Bousquet, 1733), 5.69.1; 5.73–74.

6. Ibid., 2.139.1, 5–7.

7. Alonso-Lasheras, *Luis de Molina's De Iustitia et Iure*, 86.

they promoted Roman Catholic "true religion" and suppressed the Huguenot "heresy." Accordingly, Molina's spirituality could be misused to support violence or other acts committed ostensibly in the name of Christ but which in fact stand opposed to the divine nature (Matt. 5:38–48).[8]

Molina endeavored to shape the spiritual sensitivity of his parishioners so that they would be able to choose which action to perform in any given situation — looking not to some exceptionless rule (as often occurred in Roman Catholic canon law) but to the God revealed in Jesus Christ. In the words of Loyola's *Spiritual Exercises*, Molina wanted each of his parishioners "to consider how God works and labours on my behalf in all created things on the face of the earth, i.e., 'He behaves in the same way as a person at work'" and then to act in the same way.[9] As his parishioners grew more discerning in action, Molina believed they would become increasingly conformed to the image of Christ. A crucial part of this discernment was picturing God at work in his creation. By finding and then joining God in his labor, Molina contended that we become collaborators with God in the task of redemption. Because of our libertarian freedom and God's providential use of our free choices to bring about the world, we stand, in the divided sense, alongside God as cocreators of the world. Hence our work in the world constitutes the prime meeting place for an encounter with God, a proposal similar to Luther's doctrine of *sola sacerdos* (the priesthood of all believers). In view of the social circumstances of the time, Molina's proposal proved quite significant. For in early modern Spain, there existed scarce cultural or religious affirmation of the positive role of work in human life. On the cultural side, the ideal comprised being a gentleman of the court. On the religious side, the ideal comprised being the monk who escaped from the world's labors in order to devote himself to contemplation. But Molina's ideal comprised a person of whatever vocation whose work in the world is vitally significant in the economy of salvation, whose earthly labors not only serve as collaboration in the task of redemption but also serve as a venue for an encounter with God.[10]

---

8. Historically, it has been all too easy for utilitarian spiritualities to degenerate into ends-justifies-the-means thinking. Loyola's own spirituality was used to legitimate Jesuit violence in seventeenth-century England and Continental Europe. For a similar critique, see John D. Woodbridge and Frank A. James III, *Church History, Volume Two: From Pre-Reformation to Present Day* (Grand Rapids: Zondervan, 2013), 208.

9. Loyola, *Spiritual Exercises*, §236.

10. Alonso-Lasheras, *Luis de Molina's De Iustitia et Iure*, 86–87.

Molina drew together the threads of this ideal from Luther as well as from patristic and medieval theologians whom the Spanish Catholic mystics and the Protestant Reformers favored, including Augustine, Jerome, Cyprian, Ambrose, Fulgence, and Bernard of Clairvaux.[11]

This ideal was embodied in Molina's pastoral career. Repeating the slogan of Jesuit leader and missionary Jerónimo Nadal, Molina frequently told his congregation, "We are not monks; the world is our house."[12] Such an observation rendered theology a practical affair to be carried out by each member of the church. For Molina the theological enterprise consisted of each Christian, lay or ordained, possessing an honest intention in all things, locating God in all things, and loving God in all things.[13] Experience in earthly affairs was indispensable for doing all three. Without experience in earthly affairs, a person would not be able to identify honest intentions in these affairs, to see God's hand at work in them, or to embrace God in them. Realizing his lack of firsthand knowledge in economic affairs, for example, Molina argued that in economic cases where justice is not obvious but where a custom or a trade practice was followed by merchants known to be righteous people, it is probably a practice rooted in an honest intention, as "merchants understand these things better than the doctors."[14] Thus Alonso-Lasheras emphasizes Molina's conviction that experience "exerted normative force" and formed "a new set" of principles that led Christians to the goals they pursued.[15] Underscoring the particular circumstances in which any action is performed as the place of encounter with God, Molina's practical theology insisted on obtaining knowledge, firsthand or secondhand, about any worldly affairs with which one has contact so as to be able to make sound ethical judgments about them.[16]

---

11. Molina, *De justitia*, 5.62, 64–65, 69.

12. John W. O'Malley, *The First Jesuits* (Cambridge: Harvard University Press, 2002), 68.

13. Alonso-Lasheras, *Luis de Molina's De Iustitia et Iure*, 88.

14. Frank Bartholomew Costello, *The Political Philosophy of Luis de Molina, S.J. (1535–1600)* (Spokane: Gonzaga University Press, 1974), 21.

15. Alonso-Lasheras, *Luis de Molina's De Iustitia et Iure*, 88.

16. Gustav Gundlach, *Zur Soziologie der Katholischen Ideenwelt und des Jesuitenordens* (Berlin: E. Ebering, 1927), 103.

THE USE OF SCRIPTURE IN MORAL REASONING

Molina concurred with the judgment of Erasmus that too much of scholastic theology was impenetrable, disconnected from the Bible, and of little use for practical Christian living. But rather than dispense with scholastic theology, Molina endeavored to reform and redeem it by freshly grounding it on Scripture and making its applicability transparent to lay believers. Molina's *De justitia et jure* exemplifies his solid reliance on Scripture, as the high density of biblical quotations throughout the work is seen in the extensive biblical index at the end of each volume.[17] Not surprisingly, the fifth volume, devoted to law, possesses the longest biblical index because of Molina's conception of law as an umbrella covering all the ways that any given human action could worship, honor, or serve God. As a result of this umbrella conception, for Molina the law was equivalent to the entirety of valid applications of the Bible to contemporary life. The law therefore shows how the Bible is relevant to living in the world, in both its public and private sectors.

Attempting to combat the excesses of allegorical interpretation of the Bible prevalent in late medieval and early modern Catholicism, in his preaching Molina stressed the literal sense and insisted that the literal sense was the basis of any other sense that could be validly derived from Scripture. Molina believed the Bible conveyed a moral (or tropological) sense that could only be tapped by taking its narratives literally and using the imagination to enter into the circumstances of its characters, putting oneself in their proverbial sandals. Here the Bible functioned not as a code of rules but as an arena for identification with the great heroes of the faith.[18] When delineating the relationship between the Old and New Testaments, Molina made use of patristic theology that unearthed in the Old Testament types of the realities that reach fulfillment in Christ. Thus Molina explained the salvation-historical link between Abraham and Jesus: "When humans had descended from God to idolatry throughout time with increasing sins, just as they displayed ignorance with regard to the natural and divine law, God himself began to deliver a people in Abraham, through whose seed he provided the Messiah and redeemer of the world."[19]

---

17. Molina, *De justitia*, 1. pp. 594–96; 2. p. 866; 3. p. 606; 4. pp. 509–12; 5. pp. 257–67.

18. Ibid., 5.46.15; 5.50.5.

19. "Discendentibus vero temporis progressu hominibus a Deo per idolatria, creccentibusque peccatis, ac ignorantia circa naturalem ac divinam legem, coepit Deus deligeresibi populum in Abrahamo, cui iterum Messiam mundi redemptorem de semine illius providit" (Molina, *De justitia*, 5.46.13).

Molina summarized the ultimacy and necessity of Christ's work, foreshadowed by the types and prophets of the Old Testament, as follows: "Although the figures and prophecies are able to provide a kind of fitness, as they are less than perfect, they point to the coming of the one who is perfect, the one who provides full understanding of all the experience of the ages and conquers the present world. How necessary is the grace of Christ for a person, that through grace he would receive such great benefits, so that in the advent of the Messiah he would take up more grace than all the previous figures and prophets in the world were able to dispense."[20]

But while the person and work of Christ were necessary for any person to receive salvation (John 14:6; Acts 4:12), Molina stressed that explicit knowledge of the facts concerning Christ's life, death, and resurrection was not necessary for a person to obtain salvation. Based on Romans 2:7 ("To those who by persistence in doing good seek glory, honor and immortality, he will give eternal life"), Molina affirmed that persons with no conscious knowledge of Christ, living at any time and in any culture, would find salvation by placing faith in God and following to the best of their ability the natural law written on their hearts. Concerning those parts of the world unreached by the gospel, Molina wrote, "However, the rest of the world lies still in the former state of the natural law, in which they are able to be saved by fulfilling the precepts of the supernatural ... insofar as they are able to understand them."[21] Thus salvation is universally accessible to all persons at all times. For Molina such salvific accessibility was not just a possibility of which no one actually availed themselves but was rather a present reality. Upon hearing reports from Spanish and Portuguese traders about the faith of indigenous Africans and Indians, Molina thought that such persons had actually received salvation via their proper response to God's general revelation in nature and conscience.[22] Since the second person of the Godhead to whom such persons had committed themselves was, in fact, Jesus, Molina reasoned that they

---

20. "Quamvis congruentiae quaedam redit possint, ut scilicet a minus perfecto ad id, quo perfectum est, deveniretur, et ut mundus experientia tot saeculorum suae misseriae melius intelligeret, quam necessaria illi esset gratia Christi, gratantiusque tanta beneficia acciperet, ut ad adventum Messiae legemque gratiae melius suscipenda, variis praeviis figures ac prophetiis mundus disponetur" (Molina, *De justitia*, 5.64.2).

21. "Relicto adhuc reliquo orbis in priori illo statu legis naturae, in quo salvari poterant, adimplendo supernaturalis praecepta ... status ille comprehendebat" (Molina, *De justitia*, 5.46.13).

22. Alonso-Lasheras, *Luis de Molina's De Iustitia et Iure*, 71.

had placed implicit faith in Jesus and so found salvation in precisely the same manner as did believers in the Old Testament, such as the patriarchs, the prophets, and the righteous Gentiles Melchizedek and Job. As a result, Molina declared, "Undoubtedly we can affirm that the righteous in the Old Testament and the righteous through natural law have truly and properly been adopted as children of God."[23] In modern terms, Molina was a salvific accessibilist (i.e., holding that salvation is universally available) and inclusivist (i.e., holding that, through Christ, some persons who lack explicit faith in Christ actually receive salvation).[24]

MOLINA'S ANALYSIS OF NATURAL LAW

While the concept of natural law seems to moderns primarily philosophical and rationalistic, this was not the case for Molina. Rather, Molina took natural law as primarily theological (specifically as a matter of practical theology) for two major reasons. First, Molina deemed the existence of natural law to be explicitly affirmed in the Bible. His chief proof text for natural law was Romans 2:14–15: "Indeed, when Gentiles, who do not have the law, do by nature things required by the law, they are a law for themselves, even though they do not have the law. They show that the requirements of the law are written on their hearts, their consciences also bearing witness, and their thoughts sometimes accusing them and at other times even defending them." Thus Alonso-Lasheras affirms that in Molina's treatment of natural law, "Saint Paul's letter to the Romans was the text most widely cited, and Romans was, after Luther, a text every good theologian was eager to address."[25] But Molina also found biblical support for natural law in Psalm 4:6 and Job 38:36. He observed: "Natural law, which is naturally implanted in the minds of us and of angels, is spoken of in Psalm 4 where the royal prophet reported after many investigations: 'Who will show us what is good?' and answered: 'The light of your countenance, O Lord, is made up of signs (that is, implanted and

---

23. "Est tanem proculdubio affirmandum, iustos veteris testamentis ac legis naturae vere ac proprie fuisse filios Dei adoptivos" (Molina, *De justitia*, 5.65.3).

24. For a full discussion of these terms, see William Lane Craig, "Politically Incorrect Salvation," in *Christian Apologetics in the Postmodern World*, ed. Timothy R. Phillips and Dennis Okholm (Downers Grove, IL: InterVarsity, 1995), 83–84.

25. Alonso-Lasheras, *Luis de Molina's De Iustitia et Iure*, 69.

impressed) upon us,' that which we naturally recognize.... And according to Job 38: 'Who has put wisdom in the inmost human parts?' The parts called inmost are those which enable our moral speculation."[26] Hence Molina perceived the testimony of both the Old and New Testaments, and not the Greek and Roman philosophical traditions, as the authoritative guarantor of natural law.

Second, natural law proved a theological issue because of its pivotal role in effectuating justification for those who have never heard the gospel. Recall from chapter 2 that Molina defined justification as the act of God whereby persons who have committed their lives to God and surrendered their possessions and desires to his will are declared to be in the right before God and are regenerated by God. For persons with no conscious knowledge of Christ, attempting to follow natural law as best they can while relying on God's grace to make up for their shortcomings is the proper response to God's general revelation. In other words, observing natural law is the way these persons commit their lives to God and surrender their possessions and desires to his will. As such, observing natural law is the human act to which God responds by declaring persons lacking the new law of Christ to be in the right before him. For this conclusion, Molina appealed to Romans 2:13: "For it is not those who hear the law who are righteous in God's sight, but it is those who obey the law who will be declared righteous."[27] According to Molina, then, natural law constituted the sole means of justification for humanity before the coming of Christ and remains the sole means of justification for the unevangelized today. To summarize the role of natural law in salvation history, Molina explained, "The New Law was not immediately transmitted from the beginning of the world ... but he sent so many years ahead of that

---

26. "Eadem lex naturalis dicitur, quoniam naturaliter est indita mentibus nostris et angelorum, iuxta illud Psali 4 ubi cum Regius propheta illam multorum interrogationnem retulisset: *Qui ostendi nobis bona?* ipse respondet: *Signarum* (hoc est, inditum ac impressum) *est super nos lumen vultus tui Domine,* quo scilicet naturaliter illud agnoscimus.... Atque iuxta illud Job 38: *Quis posuit in visceribus hominis sapientiam?* Illi nempe inditam, tam quoad speculabilia quoad moralia" (Molina, *De justitia*, 5.47.2).

27. Molina, *De justitia*, 5.64.1. Taking the law to refer to natural law, Molina cited Romans 2:25–26 as evidence that Jews and Gentiles were equally reliant on natural law for justification before the time of Jesus: "Circumcision has value if you observe the law, but if you break the law, you have become as though you had not been circumcised. So then, if those who are not circumcised keep the law's requirements, will they not be regarded as though they were circumcised?" Basing his teaching on Romans 3:28; Galatians 3:19–25; and their parallels, Molina argued that the Jews could not be justified through the written law, which was given as a pedagogue to restrain sin until the coming of Christ.

the natural law ... through which the mercy of God still follows to those who have not yet attained the law of grace."[28] Alonso-Lasheras reveals the tremendous practical importance of Molina's analysis of natural law to missiological questions emanating from the Spanish encounter with the New World:

> This ... was more than a mere discussion of some primal time or of what was the order of things before the coming of Christ. The issue became a highly topical question with the Spanish arrival in America. The salvation of the people in the Indies was a hot topic. Clearly enough, before the preaching of the Gospel, they could have not been saved by baptism.... This meant that they could only be held accountable for natural law, not for the law of Christ.[29]

But Molina's analysis raised a key question: should missionaries evangelize persons who have never heard the gospel but, as evidenced by their lifestyle, may have already received justification through natural law? For perhaps, upon receiving special revelation, they might reject Christ and so lose the salvation they once possessed. In this case, it would seem that missionaries should only evangelize persons who are obviously disobedient to natural law, a result that stands in contradiction to the Great Commission.

Molina insisted that missionaries need not concern themselves with this dilemma, as the worry on which it is based constitutes an absurdity. For, Molina held, it is logically impossible for anyone who has committed his life to God through natural law (and so has placed implicit faith in Christ) to reject Christ when presented explicitly to him.[30] Molina drew this conclusion as a straightforward corollary of Jesus' words in John 3:21 and 8:42: "But whoever lives by the truth comes into the light [i.e., Jesus], so that it may be seen plainly that what they have done has been done in the sight of God.... If God were your Father, you would love me, for I have come here from God."[31] Hence those who have appropriated salvation through natural law will accept

---

28. "Legem novam non fuisse tradendam statim a principio mundi ... sed tot saeculis praecedere debuisse ... ad tempuus legis gratiae attinentia, Dei misericordia fuisse sequenda" (Molina, *De justitia*, 5.64.2).

29. Alonso-Lasheras, *Luis de Molina's De Iustitia et Iure*, 71.

30. This, of course, assumes that Christ is truly presented to the person; someone justified via natural law may well reject a caricature of Christ (such as a Christ of European imperialism) when presented to him. Having never actually rejected Christ, such a person would stand in no danger of losing his or her salvation.

31. Molina, *De justitia*, 5.65.2–3.

special revelation if presented to them; Molina cited Cornelius and his family as a case in point (Acts 10:2–5, 15, 27–48).[32] Consequently, Molina directed missionaries to proclaim the gospel fearlessly to all the unevangelized in every nation, as only tremendous good could come through it and no harm could come from it. Molina substantiated this exhortation through the following trilemma. First, if an unevangelized person were already saved via natural law, then evangelism would cause his relationship with God to expand and his love of God to deepen as he learned that God was a Trinity and that his redemption was accomplished through the incarnation, death, and resurrection of the second person of that Trinity. Such a person would rejoice over this increased knowledge of God, just as two people in love rejoice and draw nearer together as they learn new things about each other. Second, if an unevangelized person were not previously saved, then evangelism would serve as the means to his salvation. Third, if an unevangelized and unsaved person failed to respond to the gospel, then this person would simply remain unsaved, such that evangelism would do him neither help nor harm.[33]

THE ECCLESIASTICAL CONTEXT OF ETHICAL DECISION MAKING

Molina observed the standard distinction of his time between the church militant, comprised of all who were pilgrims on earth, and the church triumphant, comprised of all the righteous who were already in heaven and the angels. Molina devoted the bulk of his attention to the church militant, which is made up of three estates: the church of the natural law, the church of the Mosaic law or synagogue, and the church of the law of grace.[34] For Molina the righteous of the church of the natural law and the church of the synagogue were truly children of God and received saving grace.[35] They obtained saving grace on the same ground, namely, by attempting to follow natural law as best they could while relying on God's grace to make up for

32. Ludovici Molina, *Liberi Arbitrii cum Gratiae Donis, Divina Praescientia, Providentia, Praedestinatione et Reprobatione Concordia*, ed. Johannes Rabeneck (Madrid: Sumptibus Societatis Editorialis "Sapientia," 1953), 7.23.4/5.1.5.

33. Molina, *De justitia*, 5.65.3.

34. Joaquín Salaverri, "La noción de Iglesia del Padre Luis de Molina," *Revista española de teología* 20 (1960): 206–7, 210.

35. Molina, *De justitia*, 2.5.1–4.

their shortcomings. On Molina's lights, the church of the synagogue was an enhanced version of the church of the natural law, since the Mosaic law was a pedagogical supplement to natural law that aided virtue and restrained vice. Molina subdivided the Mosaic law into moral, ceremonial, and judicial precepts. The Mosaic law presupposes its hearers' innate knowledge of natural law, such that many of its requirements the Mosaic law does not repeat. Nevertheless, sometimes the Mosaic law reiterates matters of natural law, as occurs in its moral precepts. Foremost among these precepts are the Decalogue and the two great commandments (maximal love of God and love of neighbor as oneself). The moral precepts serve to remind sinful people of these matters of natural law, pricking their consciences and thereby bringing these matters to a higher perfection.[36] But even if God had never given the Ten Commandments, the two great commandments, or any other moral precepts, they would still be binding on humanity via natural law.[37] When not reiterating matters of natural law, the commands of the Mosaic law served as teaching tools to bring people closer to natural law. Among these tools were the ceremonial and judicial precepts. According to Molina, these precepts are analogous to a parent who commands a child to do something or to avoid doing something not because that thing is objectively right or wrong but in order to instill in the child an objective moral principle, an illustration that fits well with the old law's function as a pedagogue (Gal. 3:24).[38] Such can be seen in the dietary commands. Based on Mark 7:8–23, Molina thought God gave the Israelites the dietary commands in order that they would internalize the conceptual difference between the clean and the unclean in the moral realm, not because certain foods were unethical to eat in and of themselves.[39]

In the church of the law of grace, believers can tap into the storehouse of infinite power created by Christ's immaculate life of perfect obedience to natural law.[40] This storehouse of infinite power was Molina's reinterpretation

---

36. In the words of Alonso-Lasheras, Molina therefore held that "if a natural law precept was binding in conscience in itself, through divine command it reached its fullness" (*Luis de Molina's De Iustitia et Iure*, 208).

37. José María Díez-Alegría, *El desarrollo de la doctrina de la ley natural en Luis de Molina y en los Maestros de la Universidad de Evora de 1565 a 1591: Estudio histórico y textos inéditos* (Barcelona: Instituto Luis Vives de Filosofía, 1951), 193–94.

38. Molina, *De justitia*, 2.5.65.1.

39. Ibid., 5.47.4.

40. For Molina, this tapping occurred through the vehicle of Jesus' atonement for our sins in his suffering and death.

of the treasury of merit, which in Catholic thought designated a vast reservoir of merit overseen by the Roman Church and earned by the "super-abundant" works and prayers of Christ, his mother Mary, and the saints of all ages.[41] That Molina's conception of the treasury of merit used the term *meritus* metaphorically to denote power and made no reference to Rome's oversight suggests influence from Luther, who thought of the treasury of merit in a similar vein.[42] For Molina, not only does Jesus absolutely embody the natural law, taking it out of the realm of the abstract and making it concrete, but Jesus also gives believers the supernatural power to follow natural law if they whole-heartedly ask for such power. The right to use this power cannot be earned, but Jesus gives it to believers as a free gift, sheerly the result of grace or God's unmerited favor. To sum up Molina's view of the position in which believers morally find themselves, believers can look for their example to Jesus' earthly life as the concrete manifestation of natural law, and believers can draw upon the infinite power created by Jesus' earthly life in order to follow that example. Here we can see why the whole of Jesus' earthly life, not simply his death, was of pivotal importance to Molina. Without Jesus' active obedience in each and every respect, natural law could not have been fully concretized or exemplified; parts of it would have forever remained an abstract ideal. Moreover, there is a direct proportionality between Jesus' performance of any facet of natural law and the creation of the infinite power we need to perform that facet. Had any portion of Jesus' perfect life not occurred such that Jesus never fulfilled some facet of the law, then no power would exist for us to fulfill that facet. Only by fulfilling each particular facet of natural law could Jesus have laid aside infinite power for us to draw upon in our observance of that facet.[43] Thus Molina entirely avoided the charge levied against the Protestant Reformers by N. T. Wright of focusing "not on the Jesus of history for his own sake" but almost exclusively on Jesus' death as the means of atonement for our sins, thereby displaying "uncertainty about the value of the history of Jesus' life in relation to the theological and hermeneutical task."[44]

---

41. Kirk R. MacGregor, *A Comparative Study of Adjustments to Social Catastrophes in Christianity and Buddhism* (Lewiston, NY: Mellen, 2011), 117.

42. Ibid., 175.

43. Ibid., 5.47.4.

44. N. T. Wright, *Jesus and the Victory of God*, Christian Origins and the Question of God, vol. 2 (Minneapolis: Fortress, 1996), 15–16.

Molina therefore held that, through Christ, there existed a natural progression between natural law and grace, as Christ exemplified the natural law and by grace gave us the power to enact it. Moreover, through Christ there existed a natural progression between justice and love, as true justice was restorative, not retributive, and found completion in the two great commandments to love God completely and to love neighbor as oneself. The latter commandment naturally found expression in civic life, particularly in the political and economic spheres. By propounding these views, Molina was fighting an intellectual battle on two fronts. On the one front, he was trying to ward off the excesses of Wycliffe, Hus, and Luther, who had so emphasized the invisibility of the church that they had nearly relinquished the church's involvement with any secular institutions in political and economic matters. Hence acceptance of this proto-Protestant and mainstream Protestant position in various European areas led to the subjugation of the church by the state in those areas. On the other front, Molina was trying to avoid the excesses of the Council of Trent, which taught, in the words of Robert Bellarmine, that "the one and true Church is the community of men brought together by the profession of the same Christian faith and participation in the same sacraments under the authority of legitimate pastors and especially of the one Vicar of Christ on earth, the Roman pontiff. . . . The one true Church is as visible and palpable as the Kingdom of France or the Republic of Venice."[45]

Molina's *media via* between mainstream Protestant and Catholic thought attempted to propose a view of Christian social ethics that brought together grace and charity through the vehicle of ecclesiology.[46] One might go so far as to say that Molina equated social ethics with ecclesiology, given his conception of the three estates of the church. Molina's ecclesiology thus sought to expand the kingdom of God over all human affairs, thereby reclaiming the church's prophetic voice in the sociopolitical arena. Hence the character of the church in the world represents a paramount instantiation of the free creaturely collaboration with divine providence made possible by the framework of Molina's philosophical theology.

Molina's ecclesiology had the effect of increasing the number of cases of

45. Robert Bellarmine, *De Controversiis*, II, 3.2, trans. in Avery Dulles, *Models of the Church* (Garden City, NY: Doubleday, 1974), 14.
46. Alonso-Lasheras, *Luis de Molina's De Iustitia et Iure*, 208–9.

conscience, or matters on which his parishioners needed moral guidance, among his congregation at Cuenca. The question for Molina's parishioners was vast: how does one live as a citizen of the kingdom of God while being a businessman, an artisan, a politician, and so forth? Recognizing that God was king over these and all other human affairs forced Molina to wrestle with this question and to supply weekly answers in lectures set aside for this purpose. Patterned after the two-year course in Jesuit universities on cases of conscience, which he knew well from his professorial days at Coimbra and Évora, Molina spent the years 1596 to 1598 furnishing Saturday lectures on the ways the Ten Commandments should be applied in "the different states of lives and their duties." These lectures were overtly practical and antispeculative in nature, as evident in Molina's statement of purpose to "refrain entirely from treating of theological questions that have no essential connections with cases of conscience."[47] Due to wide interest in its topics and the success of the lectures, the lectures attracted an average weekly audience of 120 people. Molina's lectures bore immediate fruit among the members of the merchant class, who consulted with Molina when new kinds of contracts or trade emerged. Several merchants donated sizable amounts of money to charitable works, visited those in prison, enabled prostitutes to redeem themselves, and supported the confraternity of the Mother of God, which cared for the poor.[48]

THE SIMPLE LIFE: EVANGELICAL POVERTY AND PRIVATE PROPERTY

In Cuenca particularly and in sixteenth-century Spain generally, the problem of poverty grew exceptionally severe, as socioeconomic developments pushed people from the countryside into the cities. Moreover, the riches arriving in Spanish cities from the Americas drew people from all over Europe,

---

47. As later quoted by *The Jesuit Ratio Studiorum of 1599*, trans. and ed. Allan P. Farrell (Washington, DC: Conference of Major Superior of Jesuits, 1970), 37–38.

48. Julio Caro Baroja, *Las formas complejas de la vida religiosa: religión, sociedad y carácter en la España de los siglos XVI y XVII* (Madrid: Akal, 1978), 415–30. Molina may well have instructed these merchants to follow the example of Gonzalo de la Palma, a merchant of Toledo and the father of prominent Jesuit spiritual writer Luis de la Palma (1559–1641). Gonzalo de la Palma was well known for precisely the same actions as those the Cuencan merchants undertook (Alonso-Lasheras, *Luis de Molina's De Iustitia et Iure*, 21).

seeking what they hoped would be a life of leisure.[49] In the words of Jesuit priest, politician, and economist Pedro Fernandez Navarrete (1564–1632), "all the scum of Europe has come to Spain, so that you can hardly find a deaf, a mute, a lame or a blind person from France, Germany, Italy or Flanders who has not been in Spain."[50] The situation presented Spanish theologians with two problems. First, one needed to separate the truly poor from those who only pretended to be poor. Second, one needed to provide for the truly poor. Molina left the first problem aside, entrusting its solution to his theological contemporaries, and occupied himself with the second. Molina believed that the truly poor's deficiency of goods did nothing to deprive them of the natural right to use the goods of creation that God bestowed upon humanity as a whole, a right that Molina found in Genesis 1:29–30; Psalm 8:6–8; and Psalm 113:7–8.[51] In order for the truly poor to access these goods, Molina's Jesuit theological contemporaries proposed the two typical solutions of alms and work. They also entertained the idea that in cases of emergency, the nonpoor's right of private property—their right to use various goods exclusively—no longer applied.[52] As Molina saw, implementing such a radical idea might well spark anarchy. Given the situation confronting his flock and his countrymen, Molina set out to reconcile the realities of poverty and private property.

Molina commenced by arguing on philosophical and theological grounds that private property did not exist at the beginning of creation; rather, there existed a community of goods. Philosophically, Molina followed Aristotle's assertion that nature offers indistinguishably to both animals and humans that which is necessary to biological life and offers indistinguishably to humans that which is necessary to domestic and political life.[53] Theologically, Molina grounded the community of goods in the doctrine of creation. God is the Creator and therefore the Lord (*dominus*) of created things. By virtue of their bearing the image and likeness of God, every human possesses domin-ion (*dominium*) over created things.[54] In particular, the facet of the divine image and likeness that bestows dominion upon humans and makes them

49. Alonso-Lasheras, *Luis de Molina's De Iustitia et Iure*, 99–100.
50. Translated by Alonso-Lasheras, *Luis de Molina's De Iustitia et Iure*, 100.
51. Molina, *De justitia*, 2.18.
52. Francisco Gómez Camacho, *Economía y filosofía moral: La formación del pensamiento económico europeo en la escolástica española* (Madrid: Síntesis, 1998), 109–13.
53. Molina, *De justitia*, 2.20.4–5.
54. Ibid., 2.18.2.

capable of justice is their libertarian free will, possessed at creation, lost in the fall, and restored by God's universally given prevenient grace. As Molina wrote concerning humans, "For if they are not endowed with freedom so that they are not capable of wrongdoing, they are neither capable of justice nor indeed of dominion."[55] In so arguing, Molina was claiming that animals cannot possess dominion nor experience injustice. Cognizant that he could be asked whether the same reasoning applies to children and mentally incompetent persons, Molina replied that they—as divine image-bearers—could both experience injustice and serve as lords (*domini*), but that in view of their circumstances their dominion should be exercised by legal guardians.[56]

Human dominion is therefore the result of creation. Because the divine likeness is common to all humans, so dominion is also common to all humans. This means that property over goods was common in the beginning, as was political authority. Hence Molina explained:

> When the author of nature as well as all other material things created according to the human race, at the very foundation of things he ensured that they would not be kept proper to certain humans but that they would be made for the advantage and benefit of all humans without distinction. We may conclude that, if we first look at the constitution of things by natural justice alone, dominion over all material things was common to all humans, such that dominion over things was not divided among humans.[57]

In sum, it is the fact that the Lord God has created the world and made humanity in his likeness, which, on Molina's view, has made all humans common owners of all material things. Via this ownership, all humans participate in God's dominion over the world.[58] Notice that, for Molina, property is linked to creation and libertarian freedom, not to salvation. This is vitally

---

55. "Quae namque arbitrio praedita non sunt, ut iniuriae non sunt capacia, ita neque iutis, atque adeo nec dominii" (Molina, *De justitia*, 2.18.1).

56. Alonso-Lasheras, *Luis de Molina's De Iustitia et Iure*, 106.

57. "Quod cum naturae auctor ita res omnes alias corporeas condiderit propter genus humanum, ut nihil, constitutione ipsa rerum, ciquam hominum proprium effecerit, sed omnes indistincte in hominum commodum et utilitatem condiderit; efficitur, ut, si solum ius naturale, primamque rerum constitutionem spectemus, dominium aliarum omnium rerum corporearum omnibus hominibus sit commune, nullaque rerum dominia sint inter homines divisa" (Molina, *De justitia*, 2.18.17).

58. Wilhelm Weber, *Wirschaftsethik am Vorabend des Liberalismus: Höhepunkt und Abschluss der Scholastischen Wirtschaftsbetrachtung durch Ludwig Molina, S.J. (1535–1600)* (Münster: Aschendorffsche Verlagsbuchhandlung, 1959), 70.

important because it ensures that all persons, irrespective of their salvific status, possess equal access to the goods of creation on the basis of their equal status as creatures. It also serves for Molina as a refutation of any doctrine that identifies possession of material goods as the blessing of God.[59]

Unique to Molina among the theologians of his age was the way he conceived the original human community.[60] The original community was not a negative community, in which no one owned anything but where things waited for people to take ownership of them. Neither was the original community a positive community, in which all humans collectively own all material things in the fashion of a corporation owning property. Rather, the idea of the original community was for Molina a middle community, located between a negative and a positive community.[61] Molina maintained that everything was once held by everyone in the sense that God gave all material things to humanity as a congregation without any distinctions (*congregationis indistincte*), not as separate groups or as individuals.[62] Thus there exists a right to all things by every member of the human congregation, as delineated by Alonso-Lasheras: "It is not a case in which a member of the community has some right over a part of what the community owns in common, but rather each member has a full right over all the things in creation, because of the very nature of those things."[63] This distinctive way of imagining the original community enabled Molina to defend the shift toward the division of goods after the fall.

According to Molina, private property, like concentrated political power, proved a necessity in a postfall world. Molina deemed the institution of civil government indispensable for maintaining peace and tranquility after the fall, though unnecessary before the fall.[64] Likewise, despite that common

59. Alonso-Lasheras, *Luis de Molina's De Iustitia et Iure*, 106.

60. José Caycedo, *Ideas jurídicas de Luis de Molina sobre la propiedad privada*, excerpta ex disertatione in Pontificia Universitas Gregoriana (Rome: Pontificia Universitas Gregoriana, 1957), 20.

61. Johann Kleinhappl, "Die Eignentumslehre Ludwig Molinas," *Zeitschrift für katholische Theologie* 56 (1932): 54.

62. Molina, *De justitia*, 2.20.6–7. One here senses the influence of James 2:1–8 on Molina, especially the admonition of verse 4 for church members not to make distinctions among themselves, that is, between rich and poor.

63. Alonso-Lasheras, *Luis de Molina's De Iustitia et Iure*, 108; cf. Jaroslaw Skarvad, "De Iure Proprietatis Privatae Apud Ludovicum Molinam," diss. (Pontificia Universitatis Lateranensi, 1950), 33–34.

64. Molina, *De justitia*, 2.120.1.

property was proper in an age of human innocence, after the fall private property became beneficial and indispensable.[65] Molina offered three lines of support for this conclusion:

> For when, on the one hand, the earth after the sin [of Adam and Eve] cultivated thorns and thistles and so made it necessary for us humans to supply our needs by too much toil and sweat, as experience testifies, we point to Genesis 3. On the other hand, although men were made to work, after the sin they became sluggish and weaker by depraved affections and desires. Of course, if the whole of the human community in this situation had all things in common, every single person would take control of the best temporal and material things as he or she wished, because there would be no administration of temporal things and because of the labor and annoyance by which circumstances forced each person to earn temporal things. On this account, a shortage of things would follow, leading to extreme poverty. Thus struggle between humans with regard to the use and consumption of temporal things would occur, where the stronger oppress the weaker.[66]

For Molina private property served as a prudentially necessary means to an end, namely, the end of all humans enjoying the goods of creation in a world after the fall. In the world before the fall, the earth, with virtually no human effort, abundantly provided all things necessary for human survival. Further, humans possessed no disorderly passions for things and consequently had no desire to hoard things to the deprivation of others. Thus, having all things in common proved most prudent in a prefall world. In the world after the fall, the earth proved far less generous, and tremendous effort was required to force the earth to yield the materials necessary for human survival. Likewise, the fall adversely impacted human nature, making it

---

65. This indispensability was not logical but rather "historical and existential" (Alonso-Lasheras, *Luis de Molina's De Iustitia et Iure*, 109).

66. "Quoniam cum ex una parte post peccatum terra, ut hominibus necessaria suppeditet, nimio eorum labore et sudore indigeat, ut experientia testatur, spinasque et tribulos, etiam culta, germinet, ut Genesis 3 habetur: ex alia vero parte homines post peccatum segnes ac debiliores ad laborandum effecti sint, abundentque pravis affectibus et cupiditatibus, sane si toti hominum communitati essent omnia communia, nullus culturam et administrationem temporalium rerum propter laborem et molestiam, quam adiunctam habet, curaret: cum tamen singuli optimis quibusque rebus potiri vellent. Unde necessario sequeretur penuria et rerum egestas, orietuntur rixae et seditiones inter homines circa rerum temporalium usum, ac consumptionem, robustiores opprimerent debiliores" (Molina, *De justitia*, 2.20.5).

weaker, lazier, and a generator of disorderly passions. If all things were held in common in a postfall world, poverty, need, and oppression would inevitably result.[67] Consequently, private property now ensures everyone greater access to the goods of creation than would be possible if fallen humans continued in the original prefall arrangement.

As a result, humans have either explicitly or implicitly reached an essential consensus to divide the resources of creation. As a representative illustration, Molina cited the decision of Abram and Lot when it became impossible for both to tend their livestock on the same fields: "So Abram said to Lot, 'Let's not have any quarreling between you and me, or between your herders and mine.... Is not the whole land before you? Let's part company. If you go to the left, I'll go to the right; if you go to the right, I'll go to the left.' ... So Lot chose for himself the whole plain of the Jordan and set out toward the east. The two men parted company" (Gen. 13:8 – 11).[68] Molina found this human consensus to divide goods ratified by God throughout the Old Testament. By giving (*tradere*) the Promised Land to the Israelites and giving (*tradere*) the kingdom of Israel to David, God put his stamp of approval on the right to private property.[69] Moreover, the commandment against stealing presupposes the right to private property, for stealing is impossible where all things are held in common.

Because the right to private property was a prudential necessity in the circumstances of a postfall world, the right was not for Molina absolute.[70] Molina therefore exhorted his congregation at Cuenca to adopt a modified form of evangelical poverty[71] in which they lived on precisely what they needed — no more, no less — and made all remaining goods available to the poor and needy. He instructed his parishioners that property should be held privately but could never be absolutely private. This is because property represents a trust from God. Molina repeatedly insisted that excess property

---

67. Francisco Gómez Camacho, "En torno a unos textos de Luis de Molina sobre la propiedad privada," *Revista española de teología*, 1977, 163–66.

68. Molina, *De justitia*, 2.20.8.

69. With the verb *tradere* (Molina, *De justitia*, 2.2; 2.13), Molina introduced a technical term to convey the transfer of ownership.

70. Alonso-Lasheras, *Luis de Molina's De Iustitia et Iure*, 102.

71. Evangelical poverty is best understood as the spending of all one's energies in the service of the kingdom of God and not in the pursuit or accumulation of material wealth. It requires living simply and having a spirit of detachment from material goods, a willingness to share material goods with others.

always be available to brothers and sisters in need. It is highly significant that, for Molina, the refusal to live such a simple life and to share with those in extreme or nearly extreme necessity constituted mortal sin.[72] Every person must have regard for his neighbor so that the hungry are fed, the thirsty refreshed, and the naked clothed.[73] Molina perceived that human lordship over created things includes the responsibility of being good stewards and dispensers of those things. He maintained that no one could accuse him of teaching that the poor should steal from the rich and make it common property; rather, it was the responsibility of the rich to give their surplus to the needy. Quoting John Chrysostom, Molina claimed that "refusing to enable the poor to share in our goods is to steal from them and deprive them of life."[74] Concerning the poor of Cuenca, Molina declared that the citizens of the city were obligated to meet their needs fully, such that the poor would not have to go from city to city begging alms. In this way, the Cuencan populace would adhere to the message of 1 John 3:17–18: "If anyone has material possessions and sees a brother or sister in need but has no pity on them, how can the love of God be in that person? Dear children, let us not love with words or speech but with actions and in truth."[75]

As a result of Molina's preaching, many wealthy people sold excess acres of crops, vineyards, and other property and legally bequeathed it to the Cuencan poor. Under Molina's instruction, the civil authorities dispensed this property to each person as she or he had need. Molina believed that his poor relief program best implemented the standard set forth by the apostle Paul: "Our desire is not that others might be relieved while you are hard pressed, but that there might be equality.... The goal is equality, as it is written: 'The one who gathered much did not have too much, and the one who gathered little did not have too little'" (2 Cor. 8:13–15).[76]

Molina's social program represented a compromise between the views of Juan de Medina (1490–1547) and Domingo de Soto (1494–1560). Medina argued that every poor person's city of origin must furnish their needed aid

---

72. Molina, *De justitia*, 2.20.14.

73. These acts rank among the "corporal acts of mercy" recognized by the Council of Trent.

74. Molina, *De justitia*, 2.21.1; the quotation comes from John Chrysostom, *De Lazaro Concio*, in *Patrologia Graeco-Latina*, 161 vols, ed. Jacques-Paul Migne (Paris: Garnier Frères, 1857–64), 2:5.

75. Molina, *De justitia*, 2.21.2. Molina also cites James 2:14–17 to the same effect.

76. Molina, *De justitia*, 2.20.14.

and that the poor must be barred from leaving the city to beg alms elsewhere. Soto argued that the poor must be allowed and encouraged to leave their home cities and beg alms elsewhere, thus protecting their freedom to travel. With Medina, Molina agreed that poor people's home cities must provide their vital necessities; with Soto, Molina agreed that poor people's freedom to travel could not be squelched by government.[77] Here Molina sharply distinguished between acts of justice and acts of charity. For citizens of each city to carry out their responsibility to give their excess goods to meet the needs of the native poor was an act of justice, since the poor had a natural, God-given right to these goods. The poor were simply receiving what was owed them as their natural due. In support of this notion, Molina appealed to Gregory the Great's observation that "when we attend to the needs of those in want, we give them what is theirs, not ours; far from performing works of mercy, we are paying a debt of justice."[78] If the poor, after having their needs met, traveled to another city and received alms, so much the better; persons who gave them alms would then be performing acts of charity. Acts of charity denoted instances of giving to the poor beyond necessity, thus raising the poor nearer to the status of the middle-class. According to Molina, giving more to the poor than simply what they require to survive is a principal manifestation of brotherly love. Molina derived this idea from Luke 11:41, where Jesus directed his disciples to give not just what is necessary but to "be generous to the poor," such that "everything will be clean for you."

THE VERTICAL AND HORIZONTAL RELATIONSHIPS IN HARMONY

To draw together the threads of his practical theology, Molina stressed in his preaching the symbiotic relationship between the sovereignty of God (the vertical dimension) and the proper human response of sincere humility and prompt obedience (the horizontal dimension). As implied by his middle-knowledge analysis of providence and predestination, Molina defined divine sovereignty as God's governance over his creation. God's sovereignty means

---

77. Gómez Camacho, *Economía y filosofía moral: La formación del pensamiento económico europeo en la escolástica española* (Madrid: Síntesis, 1998), 111, 129–33.

78. Molina, *De justitia*, 2.18.4.51; the reference comes from Gregory the Great, *Regula Pastoralis*, in *Patrologia Latina*, 221 vols., ed. Jacques-Paul Migne (Paris: Garnier Frères, 1841–80), 3.21.

that God is the ultimate ruler or lord—the *summum dominum*—because all of his decisions both logically prior and logically subsequent to creation were not affected by anyone or anything outside himself. By Molina's lights, God's decision to create anything and to create in the fashion he did, as well as God's plans regarding creation, are purely his choices. But as an instrument to carry out his plans, God employs the cooperation of libertarian free creatures, crafted in his image. Hence God gives humans not merely existence but also the *dominium* to act causally on their own and thereby participate in the fulfillment of his plans.[79] Our libertarian freedom, bestowed in creation and regained by prevenient grace, is a means of participation in God's intelligence and purpose, namely, in God's lordship over things. In this way, Molina disclosed the "theological link between being human and being *dominus*."[80]

For Molina this link must never lead to pride, for the human is not *dominus* in and of oneself but in God's working through all one's actions. Through his providence, God weakly causes or actualizes all good deeds, such that God is the first cause who indeterministically works through the secondary causes of human beings. Without God's primary causation (and his middle-knowledge guided placement of humans in various circumstances), humans can do nothing. Molina appealed to the Pauline epistles to justify this inference: "Scripture says in Philippians 2:13 that it is God who works in you both to will and to work for his good pleasure. And in Romans 9:16 it states that it is not of him who wills nor of him who runs but of God who shows mercy."[81] Accordingly, apart from God's providence a person "is neither able to believe, to hope, to love ... nor to attain to the prize of the high calling of God."[82] This fact ought to cultivate humility on the part of believers. Molina's preaching insisted that humility should be the primary attitude of believers before God, as they acknowledge their contingency and their utter dependence on God to place faith in Christ and to do the good they perform. In view of the fact that God has given them the privilege to participate in his sovereignty, believers should be spurred to obey Jesus' teachings in every

---

79. Molina, *De justitia*, 2.18.4.51.

80. Alonso-Lasheras, *Luis de Molina's De Iustitia et Iure*, 116.

81. "Dicentem [Phil. 2, 13]: Deus est enim qui operatur in vobis et velle et operari pro bona voluntate. Et alio loco [Rom. 9, 16]: Igitur non volentis neque currentis, sed miserentis est Dei" (Molina, *Concordia*, 3.14.13.42.7).

82. "Non possit credere, sperare, diligere ... nec pervenire ad palmam supernae vocationis Dei" (Molina, *Concordia*, 3.14.13.42.7).

area of life.[83] This means that Jesus' teachings, as the exemplification of the natural law, stand as the ultimate "ought" that prescriptively dictates what the "is" of the believer's life and what the life of the church must arrive to be.[84] Such an "ought" was immanent, imperative on Christians to actualize now rather than at some future date. That fact was implied by Jesus' warning in the Sermon on the Mount: "A good tree cannot bear bad fruit, and a bad tree cannot bear good fruit. Every tree that does not bear good fruit is cut down and thrown into the fire" (Matt. 7:18–19).[85] Given our discussion of the theoretical underpinnings of Molina's preaching, the next chapter will display in more detail how Molina cashed out this Jesus-shaped "ought" in relation to the specific economic and political affairs of his day.

---

83. Molina, De justitia, 2.22.9.
84. Alonso-Lasheras, Luis de Molina's De Iustitia et Iure, 225.
85. Molina, Concordia, 2.14.13.31.4.

CHAPTER 8

Molina's Theology
of Social Justice

✠   ✠   ✠

ACUTELY AWARE OF THE ECONOMIC and political difficulties plaguing Spain
at the local and national levels, Molina turned his scholarly attention to
issues of social justice in the remainder of *De justitia et jure*. For Molina
social justice was total justice, namely, the virtue that directs all human
actions to the common good.[1] He likened his definition of social justice to
Aristotle's concept of political prudence. In contrast to Aristotle's "monastic
prudence" that guided the private acts of an individual, political prudence
stipulated what each person ought to do as part of the total community.[2]
Political prudence impacted both the subjects and the prince. The prince
needed to show hierarchical prudence in determining the laws that fairly
established the rights and duties of each person within the community. The
subjects then needed to use their rights and carry out their duties in such
a way as to positively contribute to the commonweal. Molina also compared his definition of social justice with the idea of justice bequeathed
by the Roman legal tradition. The Roman jurist Ulpian (c. 170–223) had
characterized justice as the unswerving and perpetual will of each person
to give each other person his or her due, which represented a commutative
notion of justice. This not only entailed the individual duty to pay others
what was owed them and fairness in the distribution of social goods, but
it also presupposed the prince's duty actively to cultivate the morality of

---

1. Ludovici Molina, *De justitia et jure*, 5 vols. (Cologne: Marci-Michaelis Bousquet, 1733), 1.1.1.
2. Diego Alonso-Lasheras, *Luis de Molina's De Iustitia et Iure: Justice as Virtue in an Economic Context*, Studies in the History of Christian Traditions 152 (Leiden: Brill, 2011), 187.

his citizens. Piecing together these Greek and Roman influences, Molina contended that social justice required from the prince not just the formulation of fair laws but the nurturing in subjects of the virtues that the common good demanded.[3] Moreover, Molina contended that social justice meant that subjects should embrace the habit of a moderation that refused to seek more public or private goods for themselves than "was appropriate for geometrical proportion" (*Geometricam proportionem appropriandam*).[4] Molina proceeded to apply his definition of social justice to the moral feasibility of money lending as a profession, the prospect of a free market economy, the relationship between church and state, and the African slave trade, arguably the four most significant governmental and ethical problems confronting the Iberian Peninsula.

THE APPROPRIATENESS OF MONEY LENDING

Molina was conscious of the fact that the Roman Catholic Church had defined lending money for profit as usury and therefore condemned the practice for more than the past seven hundred years. While he upheld the biblical prohibitions of usury and declared its immorality, Molina departed significantly from his tradition in claiming that not all money lending for profit constituted usury. As John T. Noonan points out, Molina was the first theologian to recognize an honest profession of money lending in which the return exceeded the principal.[5] This is not because Molina accommodated himself to the practices of his time. On the contrary, Alonso-Lasheras has demonstrated that Molina's views resulted from his sincere effort to discern the just thing to do in view of the Scriptures and the complex nature of the

---

3. Molina, *De justitia*, 1.1.6.

4. Ibid., 1.12.5.

5. John T. Noonan, *The Scholastic Analysis of Usury* (Cambridge: Harvard University Press, 1957), 309. On this score, Molina was foreshadowed by Calvin, who did not go so far as Molina as to declare money lending an honest profession nor write any extensive treatise on the matter. However, in his commentary on Psalm 15:5, Calvin stated that "the end for which" the prohibition of usury "was framed was that men should not cruelly oppress the poor, who ought rather to receive sympathy and compassion." He went on to assert that, hypothetically speaking, if injury were not done to the borrower, a lender could receive interest without practicing usury: "Whence it follows that the gain which he who lends his money upon interest acquires, without doing injury to anyone, is not to be included under the head of unlawful usury" (*Commentary upon the Book of Psalms*, 5 vols., trans. James Anderson [Grand Rapids: Baker, 1984], 1:213–14). Whether there existed any literary dependence of Molina on Calvin regarding the subject of money lending is impossible to detect.

situation before him.[6] To give just one illustration, was there a moral duty on the borrower to compensate the damage that came from any idleness that a lender suffered in the absence of his money? For Molina it was obvious in this case that it was legitimate to charge interest. Moreover, earning interest was directly endorsed by Jesus himself in the parable of the talents. As the master said to the lazy slave, "Well then, you *should have* put my money on deposit with the bankers, so that when I returned I would have *received it back with interest*" (Matt. 25:27, emphasis added; cf. Luke 19:23). If the master, representing Jesus, should have received back his money with interest, then the charging of interest was in this case morally justified.[7] To overturn the established ecclesiastical contention that lending money for profit *ipso facto* comprised usury, Molina investigated the meaning of usury and the conditions that would allow a return beyond the capital in a loan.

Molina began by defining usury as any burden imposed on a borrower because of a loan, including a burden unrelated to the loan itself.[8] Molina then presented the following deductive argument against usury:

> It is illicit by the nature of the case, and against commutative justice, to demand or accept back in an exchange more than the value of the thing which is given, unless something else intervenes by reason of which it is more just to take it. But to accept back something more than what one gave for a loan, on account of the exchange of the thing given, is receiving more than what the thing is worth, unless something else intervenes by reason of which it may be justly taken. Therefore, by force solely of the loan (i.e., assuming no other factors than the loan), it is wrong because of the nature of the exchange and contrary to commutative justice to accept back more than what one gave for a loan. As a result, usury is illicit, contrary to commutative justice, and subject to restitution.[9]

6. Alonso-Lasheras, *Luis de Molina's De Iustitia et Iure*, 126.

7. Molina, *De justitia*, 2.315.11.

8. Alonso-Lasheras, *Luis de Molina's De Iustitia et Iure*, 137–38.

9. "Ex natura rei est illicitum, et contra iustitiam commutativam, in rei unius commutatione pro alia plus exigere, aut accipere, quam valeat res quae datur, nisi aliquid aliud interveniat, ratione cuius illud amplius juste accipiatur: sed accipere aliquid ultra sortem pro mutuo, est pro commutationte rei mutuo datae, accipere plus quam valeat, nisi interveniat aliud ratione cuius illud iuste accipiatur: ergo, vi solius mutui, nefas ex natura rei, et contra iustitiam commutativam est, aliquid ultra sortem accipere, ac proinde usura illicita est contra commutativam iustitiam, restitutione obnoxia" (Molina, *De justitia*, 2.304.4).

Accordingly, one could not ethically receive in an exchange more than the value of the amount given apart from some intervening, or justifying, reason. Sans any intervening reason, receiving back from a borrower more than the amount loaned is clearly a burden imposed on the borrower and hence constitutes usury. As a clear inequality, usury defied commutative justice. On this score, Molina condemned as usurious the vast majority of the public money lenders of his day, who typically charged rates no lower than 35 percent per year.[10] In Molina's deductive argument, we should note that a matter of principle and a matter of fact rendered usury immoral. The matter of principle was the refusal to observe the equality of exchange. But to discern when this occurred, one needed to heed a matter of fact, the value of the exchanged goods. Usury occurred when unequal values were exchanged.[11]

By appealing to value theory, Molina made the case that a lender could licitly receive back more quantitatively, but not more qualitatively, than what was given. In other words, the key to preventing usury was to compare the economic value of the goods exchanged instead of their quantity or their legal value. Usuriously receiving repayment beyond the capital, Molina insisted, meant nothing other than a lender receiving more than the value of the goods loaned. However, it is always lawful for a lender to receive the full value of the goods loaned, even if that entailed receiving a larger quantity of the goods loaned, and such would not amount to usury. The crucial presupposition of Molina's case is the observation that values assigned to goods may change over time. Furnishing an example, Molina alleged it was not usury if someone, after lending a number of measures of wheat when the cost of wheat was high, asked the borrower to return a greater number of measures of wheat when the cost of wheat was low. Despite that the lender was receiving back a higher quantity of the goods than he had loaned, there was no usury since the change in the cost of wheat preserved the equality of the value of the exchange.[12] What is noteworthy about this example is that Molina intentionally devised it to stand in direct contradiction to Aquinas's doctrine of usury, as Aquinas had employed the identical scenario to claim it was usury for the lender to get back more measures of wheat than what he loaned

10. Noonan, *Scholastic Analysis of Usury*, 294.
11. Alonso-Lasheras, *Luis de Molina's De Iustitia et Iure*, 132.
12. Molina, *De justitia*, 2.304.4.

even after the price of wheat had lessened.[13] With his intention to overturn the traditional view of usury now explicitly declared, Molina immediately proceeded to refute the three standard medieval arguments—the first two from Aquinas and the last from John Duns Scotus—that money lending for profit necessarily constituted usury.[14]

The first argument maintained that consumption and use were identical when dealing with consumable goods, and money is a consumable good. Aquinas defined a consumable good as one that was consumed or destroyed in its use, such as grain or wine. Conversely, he defined a nonconsumable good as one in which use could be distinguished from consumption or destruction, such as a building or a horse which were not destroyed by their use.[15] Aquinas held that it was unjust to charge for both the use and the consumption of a consumable good, since this represented charging twice for the same thing. Hence "charging for a loan was unjust in itself, for one party sold the other something non-existent, namely the use of money that could not be separated from its consumption."[16] The second argument maintained that money possessed a fixed legal value, namely, the value given by the lawmaker. According to Aquinas, commutative justice demanded that the same amount of money be received back as what was loaned. The third argument maintained that money bore no fruit. Scotus claimed that money had been created through law on behalf of society to play only three roles: a measure to value things, a means of payment, and a guarantee of future necessities.[17] Because money plays only these roles, money lending for profit would constitute an unnatural generation of money by money.[18]

Molina replied to all three of these arguments simultaneously. He asserted that it was indeed possible to distinguish use from consumption in money, such that money proved disanalogous to grain or wine. For Aquinas had failed to take into account the variable purchasing power of money, and both Aquinas and Scotus had failed to take into account the concept of money as capital, a productive good that can be used to bear the fruits of wealth.

13. Thomas Aquinas, *Summa Theologiae*, trans. Fathers of the English Dominican Province (New York: Benziger Brothers, 1947), 2.2.78.1.

14. Noonan, *Scholastic Analysis of Usury*, 81.

15. Aquinas, *Summa Theologiae*, 2.2.78.1.

16. Alonso-Lasheras, *Luis de Molina's De Iustitia et Iure*, 133.

17. Ibid., 135.

18. Noonan, *Scholastic Analysis of Usury*, 45–47.

206 *Luis de Molina*

Regarding variable purchasing power, the identical quantity of money could buy different amounts of goods depending on variation in the prices. Regarding money as capital, the value of money itself could vary depending on factors such as location, inflation, and deflation; thus money's value was not necessarily fixed by its legal value.[19]

To support his insight, Molina offered a general analysis of lending, which he would then particularly apply to the case of lending money. Upon the lending of various goods, those goods could be utilized in two different ways. First, they could be utilized "for trade and profit, this profit made by selling, exchanging, or taking them to another place."[20] Second, the goods could simply be consumed by the purchase of "necessary or curious and superfluous things," by virtuously "donating them," or by wasting them to "indulge with prostitutes."[21] According to the first case, money could be employed for trading, which rendered money, contra Scotus, more than a barren measure to value things, a means of payment, and a guarantee of future necessities. In the merchant's hands, money was an instrument (*instrumenta*) for creating wealth.[22] Because it could be considered as capital, money constituted an indispensable tool for the merchant. So if it was ethical, as was admitted on all hands, to demand an additional monetary return when a craftsman loaned his tools since he would be incapable of performing his craft during that time, Molina concluded that it must also be ethical to charge money for the labor and the trade that a merchant could not accomplish with the money he had loaned.[23] In these ways, Molina dispatched with the three standard medieval arguments that money lending for profit automatically equaled usury, thus opening an ethical door for business money lending.

To review Molina's case thus far, although usury was immoral by its very nature, there existed accidents, or extrinsic reasons to the act of lending, that permitted a return above the principal in a loan. By the late medieval period, some of these accidents had become known as titles of interest, where "interest"

---

19. Molina, *De justitia*, 2.304.6. On this score, Molina argued that when currency had lost its value between the beginning and the end of a loan, the borrower was morally obligated to repay the equivalent of the old value rather than simply the face value of the loan (ibid., 2.312.10).

20. "Ad negotiationem et lucrum, illam lucri causa vendendo, permutando, vel transferencdo in alium locum" (Molina, *De justitia*, 2.304.6).

21. "Necessaria, aut etiam curiosa, et superflua ... donando illam, aut vane cum meretricibus" (ibid.).

22. Ibid., 2.315.11.

23. Ibid.; Alonso-Lasheras, *Luis de Molina's De Iustitia et Iure*, 136.

referred in the Roman legal sense to the payment a negligent party owed to an injured party to compensate for the damage caused. Titles of interest were especially recognized in the event of forced borrowing on the part of the state. When short on money, the Italian and other city-states would forcefully borrow cash from rich citizens, typically merchants. Without the borrowed money, merchants lost opportunities to trade and gain profit. Hence forced lending warranted some kind of compensation; otherwise city-states would surely abuse their power to forcefully borrow money and inflict frequent injustice on the lenders.[24] Molina attempted to expand the recognized titles of interest from forced lending to commercial lending through consideration of three categories that characterized the money lender's occupation: *damnum emergens* (emerging damage), *lucrum cessans* (ceasing profit), and *periculum sortis* (the risk of much).[25]

Molina defined *damnum emergens* as "the loss in the lender's own goods — whether it be in present goods or in possible future goods — , the expenses which he incurred, the inferior return on his capital or the destruction of his goods as a result of the loan."[26] Accordingly, Molina's conception of *damnum emergens* was quite broad. It did not need to be an actual loss, but it could be a possible future loss that necessitated the paying of interest.[27] Molina provided two examples of *damnum emergens*.

> If you have any money to repair a house but grant the money as a loan, and the house suffers destruction or other houses suffer damage as a result, these houses would suffer what is called *damnum emergens*. Suppose one has the money to buy wheat at the time of the harvest to support one's family and then gives the money to another. But after receiving the money back, the wheat is far more expensive to buy due to a price increment, and in buying the wheat one loses many good things to which one was devoted. This is also called *damnum emergens* from the loan.[28]

---

24. Noonan, *Scholastic Analysis of Usury*, 120–23.
25. Ibid., 309; Alonso-Lasheras, *Luis de Molina's De Iustitia et Iure*, 141.
26. Alonso-Lasheras, *Luis de Molina's De Iustitia et Iure*, 142; cf. Molina, *De justitia*, 2.314.1.
27. Francisco Belda, "Ética de la creación de créditos según la doctrina de Molina, Lesio y Lugo," *Pensamiento* 1 (1963): 58.
28. "Si quis pecunias habeas ad reficiendas domos et quo mutuo illas det, passurus est ruinam, aut detrimentum aliud domorum, factura haec domorum emergens damnus in bonis ipsius nuncupatur. Si item pecunias habeat ad triticum messis tempore in familia sustentationem emendum, et, quod illas mutuo det, empturus est illud postea longe maiori pretio incrementum illud, quod postea de bonis suis insumet, damnum ex mutuo emergens appellatur" (Molina, *De justitia*, 2.314.3).

In both these cases, Molina asserted that it was just to demand some compensation, namely interest, for the loan. Molina then conceived of *lucrum cessans* as the cost resulting from the absence of an acquisition. If a person ceased from an acquisition in order to confer a loan, that person incurred a *lucrum cessans*. Here Molina gave an example more general than the one he furnished for *damnum emergens*. A merchant who had money ready for trade and loaned the money to someone else was thereby precluded from profiting with that money. Although the merchant never incurred a direct loss, there existed a profit he never acquired because of the loan.[29]

Molina proceeded to quote selectively from Aquinas and the Dominican theologian Domingo de Soto (1494–1560) in defense of *damnum emergens* as a title of interest. While it is likely that neither Aquinas nor Soto would have agreed that *damnum emergens* constituted a title of interest, there certainly existed material in both theologians that one could exploit—and Molina did exploit—to support this position.[30] In view of this apparent medieval and early modern backing, Molina suggested that the *damnum emergens* could be estimated by the lender and approved by the borrower prior to the loan. Molina then took the innovative step of equating *lucrum cessans* with *damnum emergens*, so as to extend both the reasoning and, more importantly, the support of significant authorities for *damnum emergens* to *lucrum cessans*. Hence Molina wrote, "At this point I observe that *lucrum cessans* is also able to be called *damnum emergens*, as we may borrow the term for damage (*damni*) to the extent that not acquiring the income which one could lawfully gain and from which one desists is equivalent to the losses in goods which otherwise one could legally optimize."[31] From Molina's discussion of these categories, Alonso-Lasheras remarks that Molina "had a concept of money more refined, at least from an economic point of view, than previous theologians."[32] Money, on Molina's reckoning, had the power to create wealth in the same manner as other assets. Because Molina knew both that no material

---

29. Noonan, *Scholastic Analysis of Usury*, 261–62; Karl Pribram, *A History of Economic Reasoning* (Baltimore: Johns Hopkins University Press, 1983), 28–30.

30. Molina, *De justitia*, 2.314.5; Aquinas, *Summa Theologiae*, 2.2.78.2; Domingo de Soto, *Libri Decem De Iustitia et Iure* (Lugduni: Apud heredes Iacobi Iuntae, 1569), 1.3.

31. "Quo loco observa, lucrum cessans posse etiam dici damnum emergens, late sumpto vocabulo damni, prout, non comparare lucrum, quod quis licite poterat, et a quo desistit, damnum in bonis, quae alioquin habiturus erat, iure optimo dici potest" (Molina, *De justitia*, 2.314.5).

32. Alonso-Lasheras, *Luis de Molina's De Iustitia et Iure*, 143.

in the recognized authorities could be used to support *lucrum cessans* and that Pope Innocent IV, Aquinas, and Soto explicitly denounced *lucrum cessans*, Molina felt obliged to formulate five arguments in favor of *lucrum cessans* as a title of interest.

First, it was possible to estimate both ceasing profit and the incidence of a loss. According to Molina, a discreet merchant could consistently estimate the *lucrum cessans* of a particular amount of money. Second, if in the case of a forced loan—such as when a king went to war and seized a certain merchant's money—the king should pay the merchant compensation for the loss, any loan that was made voluntarily but with an agreement of compensation for the trade the merchant sacrificed on account of the loan ought also to be considered ethical. This reasoning displays how Molina felt the acceptance of *damnum emergens* leads inescapably to the acceptance of *lucrum cessans*.[33] Third, when a thief robs a merchant of goods, he not only takes something away from the merchant, but he also deprives him of the ability to implement his purposed activity and hence from making a profit. Restitution in this instance entails more than simply returning the stolen goods; it demands some form of additional compensation. Applying this kind of reasoning to a loan, Molina claimed that a merchant could morally make a profit out of lending money due to the profit he had failed to obtain with the money he loaned.[34] Fourth, money constituted the tools of a merchant, which, when he rented them via loan, he was unable to carry out his trade. By rights, the merchant ought to be compensated for both the tools and the incapacity to work. Fifth, it was universally recognized that persons in other trades could sell something unpredictable that would happen in the future. Thus it was moral for a fisherman to sell the catch of that day before setting out to sea. On the same score, it was moral for a merchant to sell the use of his money for what he anticipated gaining as a return from it.[35]

With this final argument in mind, Molina turned to a defense of *periculum sortis*, or risk, as a title of interest. Even if, for the sake of argument, it were true that nothing could validly be charged by reason of the loan itself, something could still validly be charged for the risk of nonrepayment. For only God

33. Albert R. Jonsen and Stephen Edelston Toulmin, *The Abuse of Casuistry: A History of Moral Reasoning* (Berkeley: University of California Press, 1988), 191–94.

34. Alonso-Lasheras, *Luis de Molina's De Iustitia et Iure*, 144–45.

35. Molina, *De justitia*, 2.315.11.

knew the contingents of creaturely freedom whose cognizance would alone remove the prospect of risk. Furthermore, risk diminished the value of money, such that a return greater than the principal was not usury but a fair return for the toil and troubles of the lender.[36] However, Molina sternly reproached any unequal sharing of risk, which he believed did constitute usury. While risk justified a reasonable interest, where more or less interest should be charged proportional to a higher or lower amount of risk, an excessive interest proved usurious. By discussing the issue with merchants in his role as a parish priest, Molina judged charging any interest rate higher than 12 percent to be usury.[37] This was consistent with the precedent of Roman law, which allowed interest rates from 6 percent to 12 percent per year.[38]

By establishing *damnum emergens, lucrum cessans*, and *periculum sortis* as valid titles of interest, Molina was able to legitimate the occupation of the commercial money lender who charged a maximum interest rate of 12 percent.

MOLINA'S ENDORSEMENT OF A FREE MARKET ECONOMY

The topic of just prices proved controversial in the early modern period. For the sixteenth century was a period of heavy inflation due to the so-called curse of gold. One significant consequence in Europe of the Spanish conquest of vast areas of the Americas was the arrival of overwhelming quantities of gold and silver. Likewise, the Portuguese exploration of the African coast brought vast amounts of gold and silver to the Iberian economy.[39] By the middle of the sixteenth century, the quantity of gold and silver grew to be more than what the Spanish and Portuguese economies could handle. As a result, waves of inflation, which started in the Iberian Peninsula, swept across Europe, a situation economist Earl J. Hamilton dubs a "price revolution."[40] Since their capacity to adjust to price increases was limited, inflation began to affect people who lived on fixed incomes, causing a redistribution of wealth.

---

36. Ibid., 2.304.8.
37. Ibid., 2.311.5.
38. Alonso-Lasheras, *Luis de Molina's De Iustitia et Iure*, 130.
39. Pierre Vilar, *Oro y moneda en la historia, 1450–1920* (Barcelona: Ariel, 1969), 199.
40. Earl J. Hamilton, *American Treasure and the Price Revolution in Spain, 1501–1650*, Harvard Economic Studies 5 (New York: Octagon, 1965), 43.

While redistribution of wealth was by no means a new economic phenomenon, the lightning-fast rapidity with which this occurred was a new phenomenon. Moreover, the inflationary problem affected Spanish manufacturers, as Spanish goods lost their competitive advantage. Goods imported from other European nations began filling the ships crossing the Atlantic Ocean, bringing increased participation of English, French, and Dutch merchants in trade with the New World.[41] Hence Spanish manufacturers surrendered ground to foreign merchants. By the end of the sixteenth century, Iberian theological moralists regularly spoke about the curse of gold ruining the realm. Between 1586 and 1593, the Spanish Parliament, or Cortes, lamented that Spain functioned as a mere fence for the gold and silver arriving from America, which was leaving the nation impoverished.[42] This situation made the question of just price all the more pressing.

Any answer to the question of how to determine a just price presupposed a certain economic structure. To answer that the just price vacillated according to time, place, and circumstances presupposed a free market economy, where the forces of the market determined the just price.[43] By contrast, to answer that the just price was determined by magistrates presupposed a government-regulated market in which the government was engaged in price-fixing.[44] For Molina the forces of a free market were the primary factors to be taken into account in arriving at a just price, but his notion of the just price was theologically broader than the classic economic notion of the market price.[45] Following the Aristotelian-Thomistic tradition on this score, Molina conceived of the creation of money as a result of the defects of the barter system. When trying to trade various goods, people had found how difficult it was to locate someone who both had exactly what one needed and needed the goods one could offer; the result was the creation of money. However, money brought inequality into the exchange.[46] Whereas under the barter system each person held an equal position in the transaction, now money distinguished

41. Alonso-Lasheras, *Luis de Molina's De Iustitia et Iure*, 15–17.

42. Vilar, *Oro y moneda en la historia*, 230–31.

43. Noonan, *Scholastic Analysis of Usury*, 85.

44. Raymond Adrien de Roover, *La pensè èconomique des scolastiques: doctrines et mèthodes* (Montreal: Institute d'Études Mèdiévales, 1971), 52.

45. Alonso-Lasheras, *Luis de Molina's De Iustitia et Iure*, 149.

46. Here Molina anticipated the perspective of John Locke, *Two Treatises of Government*, Everyman's Library (London: Dent, 1975), 141.

buyer from seller, the buyer paying money for a product and the seller offering a product in exchange for money. In the barter system, the equivalence
of the goods exchanged was determined by the mutual concurrence of the
two people bartering. But the utilization of money put the element of the
legal value of money into the exchange. Alonso-Lasheras insightfully depicts
Molina's view as follows: "The equality of the exchange ceased to be a matter
between the two people bartering, but now involved the community, which
had created money and guaranteed its value. A wider circle suddenly became
part of the transaction. Money had thoroughly transformed the question
about justice in trade, now giving a new role to the community."[47]

For Molina parity in the exchange between buyer and seller proved
necessary so that commutative justice would not be violated. Hence in any
exchange involving money, the equality of the value of the money and the
value of the exchanged goods must be upheld. Molina stipulated that the
value of a good and hence its price should, as far as possible, be based on
the preference of the buyers. Of this point, Molina provided two examples.
First, the Japanese were ready to pay high prices for rusted things precisely
on account of their antiquity. Second, the Ethiopians desired cheap jewelry
and were willing to pay a higher price for it than for gold.[48] But the issue of
a just price also had a profound moral relevance, as the price of goods in fact
controlled the access of each person to the goods of creation. An unjust price
would deprive some persons of their divinely given rights to creation's goods.
In his discussion of pricing, Molina distinguished between natural prices and
just prices. The natural price represented the price of a good determined by
the usefulness of the good itself, apart from the intervention of any human
law or decree. A just price designated a price no lower than the natural price
that ensured the access of each person to that good. According to this distinction, the natural price did not obviate the conditions in which that good
was priced. For many of the new goods coming into Europe from the West
and East Indies, Molina admitted the problematic nature of arriving at a
just price and delineated the numerous variables to be taken into account
in determining their price. These included the costs and risks incurred in
obtaining the goods, their quantity, their usefulness, their scarcity, and their

---

47. Alonso-Lasheras, *Luis de Molina's De Iustitia et Iure*, 150.
48. Molina, *De justitia*, 2.348.3.

distinctiveness. In such cases, buyers and sellers should together determine the price through *communis estimatio* (common valuation).[49]

Molina held that *communis estimatio* must occur among a concrete group of merchants, buyers, or sellers who assembled together in a particular place, such as Cuenca, Seville, Lisbon, or Medina. This group needed to contain prudent persons who would assess difficult matters and factor in the numerous variables of the market. On Molina's view, this assessment was not merely a mathematical calculation; more importantly, it was a moral act that gave due place to the community dimension of the market and the social nature of trade.[50] Molina maintained that a just price for goods commonly traded in a region revolved around the price at which those goods were typically sold, although the actual price changed according to various conditions. Lack raised the price of a good, while abundance lowered its price. Also impacting the price of a good was the number of buyers as well as their desire for it. The necessities of a given time raised the price of certain goods, as occurred with horses and weapons at the time of war. These variables represented the demand side of pricing. Further, the money supply comprised a factor of the just price: the scarcity of money lowered prices, just as abundance of money raised prices.[51] The manner in which a good was sold also impacted its price, where retail trade validly prompted a higher price for a good.[52] The multiplicity of diverse factors generated a range in the just price. In the words of Alonso-Lasheras, "the just price was not to be found in a specific figure, but within a range, as there was a maximum and a minimum just price. A sale would be just if the price was within the range of the just price."[53] The median between the maximum and minimum just price would be the average sale price of the good in a region. A good's minimum just price would be its natural price, while the good's maximum just price would be the highest price consistent with the aforementioned economic factors that still allowed each person regardless of class access to the good.[54]

This understanding of the just price range allowed Molina to differentiate between economics and chrematistics. Economics denoted the natural

49. Ibid., 2.348.9.
50. Alonso-Lasheras, *Luis de Molina's De Iustitia et Iure*, 151–53.
51. Molina, *De justitia*, 2.348.4.
52. Ibid., 2.348.7.
53. Alonso-Lasheras, *Luis de Molina's De Iustitia et Iure*, 152.
54. Molina, *De justitia*, 2.347.3.

attainment of wealth, while chrematistics denoted the obtaining of unlimited wealth or hoarding. The constant element in all legitimate forms of buying and selling was the satisfaction of a social need. Hence the goal of economics was meeting social needs, not making money for its own sake, which in the Christian tradition amounted to the cardinal sin of greed.[55] Accordingly, Molina warned severely against gaining exorbitant profits, a rebuke specifically directed at business practices with which he was familiar. These practices transpired as part of the Genovese-controlled wool trade in Cuenca. Molina dealt with the Genovese wool trade in Disputation 345 of *De justitia et jure*, titled "Concerning monopolies, to what degree they render the sale unjust, and concerning concealing and holding back goods in time of need."[56] Here Molina defined a monopoly as "the situation in which a person or a group of persons was able to impose and force an unjust price in the sale of a certain kind of goods, thereby doing wrong to the commonwealth."[57] This situation included the agreement among merchants not to sell under a certain price or not to buy over a certain price. Consequently, a monopoly prevented the workings of a free market. Ironically, since a monopoly comprised a crime against the commonwealth, its magistrates could tolerate a monopoly for the sake of the common advantage. For instance, if a good was required in a certain place, the magistrates could set up a monopoly to supply it. The opposite situation could also happen when the magistrates desired to exclusively sanction the export of a good produced in the nation.[58]

Although purchasing below the minimum just price or selling above the maximum just price was unethical and demanded restitution, Molina declared that not every instance of price fixing on the part of the merchants demanded restitution. So long as the price remained within the just price range, no punishable damage was done, despite that collusion (which satisfied Molina's broad definition of monopoly) was a sin. However, collusion

---

55. To illustrate the evils of greed, Molina quoted 1 Timothy 6:9–10: "Those who want to get rich fall into temptation and a trap and into many foolish and harmful desires that plunge people into ruin and destruction. For the love of money is a root of all kinds of evil. Some people, eager for money, have wandered from the faith and pierced themselves with many griefs" (*De justitia*, 2.339.5).

56. "Monopoliis quousque emptio et venditio illicita, aut iniusta, reddatur: et de recondentibus ac asservantibus merces in tempus caritatis" (Molina, *De justitia*, 2.345).

57. Alonso-Lasheras, *Luis de Molina's De Iustitia et Iure*, 157.

58. Molina, *De justitia*, 2.345.3.

was a sin against charity, not against justice. While it harmed the commonwealth, then, any instance of price-fixing in times of lack would be a sin against charity and not against justice if the price remained within the just price range.[59] On this score, Molina furnished a detailed account of the practice of projected wool sale that occurred at Cuenca and at several other places in Castille. This account formed a case study in which Molina carried out field research in order to make an educated moral judgment on the issue.[60] Castille was the biggest wool exporter in Europe, and wool constituted a chief raw material in early modern trade. The significance of the wool trade had prompted the formation of the Burgos Consulate, to which in 1501 Ferdinand and Isabella granted a monopoly of wool trade in the Cantabric Sea ports, all of which traded with Flanders.[61] By the end of the sixteenth century, in Cuenca the Genovese had effectively attained a monopoly on the wool trade. Leading Genovese merchants sent to the city representatives who purchased wool; due to their low number and their tremendous buying power, these commodity brokers dominated the demand side of the market. A select group of brokers readily concurred on a ceiling price over which they would not purchase wool, constraining the producers to sell at that fixed price. The domination of the Genovese over the market prompted Molina to assert that "much of the price of wool depends on the will of the Genovese in this city."[62]

The low bargaining power of the wool producers compelled them to sell at the price fixed by the brokers, which meant selling at a loss. To guarantee that they filled the orders coming in from Genoa, the brokers traded in wool futures, making the producers sell in advance the wool not yet shorn. In so doing, the brokers exploited the monetary shortage of the flocks' owners.[63] The exchange of wool futures typically began on the Feast of Saint Michael (29 September), immediately before flocks retired to their winter pastures. This situation spelled loss for the flock owners. The wool would not be delivered until July, when the sheep shearing occurred.[64] For Molina

59. Ibid., 2.345.6.
60. Ibid., 2.359.1.
61. Alonso-Lasheras, *Luis de Molina's De Iustitia et Iure*, 158–59.
62. "Ex eodem capite proficiscitur, ut lanarum pretium multum in hac civitate pendeat a Genuensium voluntate" (Molina, *De justitia*, 2.359.9).
63. Ibid., 2.359.10.
64. Ibid., 2.359.14.

here the danger of monopoly overlapped with the sin of usury, as the credit sale performed was nothing less than thinly veiled usury. That was because the resulting difference in prices could not be accounted for by the range of the just price or the risk assumed, but wholly constituted the advance of money to the brokers.[65] Hence Molina condemned monopolistic practices that enabled a select number of economic agents to fix prices. While he did not favor governmental price regulation, Molina opposed practices by which, in modern parlance, big business dominated the market.[66]

At this juncture, one may wonder why Molina did not endorse Spain's price regulation of wool, which would seem the obvious answer to the problems of the wool market. The reason was not economic but theological in nature, as Molina believed that governmental price regulation would be harmful to people's eternal salvation. For any law imposing a legally fixed price for wool would be violated by many people.[67] Since a civil positive law bound the conscience, anyone breaking it was committing sin. Thus any fixed price law would lead people to commit sin and actually obstruct their salvation. Such a scenario violated the purpose of the law, which was to instruct rather than to condemn.[68] This reasoning led Molina to formulate a general principle which he felt should be applied across the board to any civil positive law. If the result of a positive law was to jeopardize people's salvation instead of enabling them to lead better lives, the law should be repealed because it was clearly not accomplishing its goal.[69]

CHURCH AND STATE: DISTINCT YET MUTUALLY COMPLEMENTARY

In concert with most other sixteenth-century reformers, Molina believed that church and state were mutually complementary rather than contradictory. However, Molina separated in significant ways the spiritual role of the church from the physical role of the state. He did so to defend both the service of

---

65. Ibid., 2.360.2.
66. Alonso-Lasheras, *Luis de Molina's De Iustitia et Iure*, 160–61.
67. Here the issue was, quite pragmatically, the bare consideration of whether people would obey the law, rather than the reasonableness of the law per se.
68. Molina, *De justitia*, 2.365.13.
69. Alonso-Lasheras, *Luis de Molina's De Iustitia et Iure*, 163.

Christians in government (against the protestations of Anabaptist writers) and the principle of religious tolerance (an idea with Renaissance roots enshrined in Cuenca's city Code but associated primarily with the Anabaptists).[70] Here Molina maintained a precarious balance. On the one hand, Molina held that obedience to Christ entailed civic involvement, such as wielding the sword as magistrates and soldiers. On the other hand, Molina decried any exertion of force to compel dissenters into the Roman Catholic Church or to preserve doctrinal conformity among the faithful. Hence Molina, himself under the provisional denunciation of the Spanish Inquisition and facing the threat of capture if he risked leaving Cuenca, responded in kind by denouncing the raison d'être of the Inquisition.[71]

Disagreeing with the Protestant Reformers' doctrine of the invisible church, Molina conceived of the true church as visible and existing in the visible world. As the divinely ordained "pillar and foundation of the truth" (1 Tim. 3:15), the church reconciles individuals to God and nurtures them to righteousness through preaching, administration of the sacraments, apologetics, and acts of charity.[72] But agreeing with the Protestant Reformers' doctrine of the state, Molina viewed the state as God's ordained instrument of social justice. On the basis of Romans 13:1–7, Molina asserted that God had invested the state with the sword in order to safeguard the good and defenseless from the depravity of the world.[73] Unlike the Anabaptist notion that the state was identical to the world, or the antithesis of the church, Molina differentiated between these three entities. For Molina the world is the kingdom of the devil made up of everything contrary to the will of Christ that aims to harm good and evil people indiscriminately. In the quest for salvation, the church and the world are opposing forces, such that the church is not essentially of, and would only be ruined by integration with, the world. But because the church still finds itself in the world, God has instituted the state as his servant to protect the church from the evils incited by the world.

70. William R. Estep, *The Anabaptist Story: An Introduction to Sixteenth-Century Anabaptism*, 3rd rev. ed. (Grand Rapids: Eerdmans, 1996), 257–61; *The Code of Cuenca*, trans. James F. Powers (Philadelphia: University of Pennsylvania Press, 2000), 29.

71. Molina, *De justitia*, 2.5.65.

72. Lewis W. Spitz, *The Protestant Reformation, 1517–1559* (St. Louis: Concordia, 1985), 94, 209; Molina, *De justitia*, 1.2.27.

73. Spitz, *Reformation*, 94, 210; Molina, *De justitia*, 1.2.19.

The world and the state can be differentiated by their motives for inflicting harm. Unlike the world, the state, at least ideally, punishes only criminals in order to protect the commonweal against evildoers. Therefore, while the church reconciles fallen humanity to God through the gospel, Molina argued that the state furnished the church with the security necessary to bring its divinely ordained charge to completion.[74]

In Molina's theology, the state is not seen as a necessary evil but as a friend and protector of the church. Based on the Pauline language of the authorities as "God's servants" (Rom. 13:4, 6; cf. 1 Peter 2:14), Molina deduced that the state could legitimately endorse the Christian faith. Moreover, the state could financially support the church, as surmised from the fact that Joanna, affiliated with the household of King Herod Antipas, was one of the prominent women who financed Jesus' ministry from her own resources (Luke 8:3).[75] The church, in exchange for public safety and private funding, is obliged to pray for the state and to support and assist it in the execution of its sacred duties. For this reason, Christians must pay taxes and serve the government as magistrates and soldiers if they are called or chosen for these positions. Moreover, Christian activity in civic affairs increases the probability that society will be ruled by Christians, who will in turn govern according to God's will. Molina claimed that the best magistrates and soldiers are Christians, as they would wield the sword according to their passions but would wield the sword with extreme restraint and only when demanded by justice.[76] Molina tried to furnish scriptural backing for this claim through an exegesis of Matthew 26:52–54, where Jesus instructed Peter to put his sword back into its sheath at Gethsemane. Since Jesus told Peter to put away his sword rather than throw it away, Molina contended that the text is not an admonition to discard the sword but is a warning against vigilantism, or wielding the sword on one's own authority. By allowing Peter to return the sword to its sheath, Jesus distinguished between the proper and improper use of the sword based on whether or not one has been given divine sanction to wield it. Far from forbidding the

---

74. Molina, *De justitia*, 2.5.66.

75. Ibid., 1.1.19; 1.2.31.

76. To me this claim seems incredibly naive, failing to take sufficient account of the sinful nature against which Christians wrestle and the corrupting temptations of political and military power.

sword, Molina asserted that Jesus implied that the sword can be properly kept at the Christian's side and drawn on the divine authority exercised through the state.[77]

Nevertheless, it is imperative, Molina asserted, that neither the church nor the state impinge on the authority of the other by transgressing the functional boundaries that God has established between them. Hence the church has no right to engage in civic administration or municipal jurisprudence, including corporal punishment, and the state has no right to engage in church discipline.[78] This judgment yields two provocative corollaries, one concerning the church and the other concerning the state. First, Molina precluded any concept of "holy violence," like the one used by the Spanish Inquisition, whereby the church had the right to oppose or coerce unbelievers (such as Jews and Muslims) by force.[79] More than that, God has not ordained the use of the sword by the church under any circumstances, even to defend itself. Second, Molina declared that the state had no right to persecute people who dissented from the official religion, to compel dissenters to attend endorsed religious services, or to prevent dissenters from practicing their own religious beliefs or refraining from religious activities altogether. As a result, Molina insisted that magistrates leave free from punishment and

---

77. Molina, *De justitia*, 1.2.99. One could legitimately object to this interpretation by arguing that it reads far too much into the text and stands at odds with the text's face-value meaning. Molina's interpretation here is extremely close to that of Anabaptist theologian Balthasar Hubmaier, who departed from his fellow Anabaptists in sanctioning the legitimacy of Christians' serving in government and wielding the sword. For further discussion see Kirk R. MacGregor, *A Central European Synthesis of Radical and Magisterial Reform: The Sacramental Theology of Balthasar Hubmaier* (Lanham, MD: University Press of America, 2006), 232–33. Despite this similarity, any speculation about Molina's use of Hubmaier would be extremely tenuous at best.

78. Molina, *De justitia*, 1.2.32–33.

79. During the sixteenth century on the Iberian Peninsula, an estimated 150,000 Jews were forcibly converted to Christianity by the Spanish Inquisition. Many of these persons secretly continued to practice Judaism; the Inquisition labeled them with the extremely pejorative title *marranos* (lit., "pig") as well as the title *conversos* (carrying the implication of "pretended converts"). Monitoring which homes lacked smoke coming from their chimneys on Saturdays (indicating the inhabitants' refraining from work on the Sabbath), the Inquisition would often arrest secret Jews and have them burned at the stake for heresy. For further analysis, see Cecil Roth, *A History of the Marranos*, 5th ed. (New York: Intellectbooks, 1974), 168–94. Likewise, the Spanish Inquisition converted an estimated 300,000 Muslims to Christianity by force. Many of them likewise secretly continued to practice Islam and were given the label *moriscos* (lit., "Moorish"). In Molina's own region of Castille, specific villages including Arévalo, Cinco Villas, and Hornachos contained a majority (or even a totality) of *moriscos*. These *moriscos* were virtually indistinguishable from the larger Catholic population, and they did not speak Arabic. Spain would eventually expel them from its borders between 1609 and 1614. For further discussion see L. P. Harvey, *Muslims in Spain, 1500 to 1614* (Chicago: University of Chicago Press, 2005), 102–378.

banishment everyone unwilling to embrace the state religion.[80] Addressing both church and state, Molina declared on the basis of the Sermon on the Mount and the Johannine discourses that Jesus himself advocated religious tolerance, since Jesus did not murder, execute, or burn but charged his followers to love their enemies and accept abuse at their hands without retaliation.[81] Here Molina seems to be suggesting a theological basis for religious freedom that is quite profound: to persecute a person for heresy amounts to an implicit denial of the incarnation, since the God revealed in Jesus is the God of the invitation, not of coercion. The accuracy of this inference is corroborated by Molina's analysis of the relationship between God's character and libertarian human freedom. For Molina God created humans with the faculty to choose either spiritual good or evil, such that God would not himself violate that very faculty. If not even God compels people into the church but extends to them an invitation that they can freely accept or deny, it follows that humans have no right to compel people into the church either.[82]

Without separating church and state, Molina proceeded to explicate in more detail the limitations on ecclesiastical and civil authorities in the treatment of dissenters. As one of the outstanding dialecticians of his day, Molina instructed priests and deacons to employ apologetics in an attempt to win people who rejected the state church. Moreover, he forbade these clerics from handing dissenters over to the civil government. This logic is based on Molina's doctrines of divine omniscience and sovereignty, whereby God alone knows the difference between the wheat and tares and has exclusive authority to judge the tares (Matt. 13:24–30).[83] Consequently, God has not placed in human hands the right to burn heretics, be they truly heretics or not. From this it follows that the Inquisitors were themselves the greatest heretics of all in burning alleged heretics contrary to the teaching and example of Jesus, thereby uprooting the wheat with the tares before the harvest at Jesus' return. In Molina's assessment, God has clearly prescribed nonviolent methods of

80. Molina, *De justitia*, 1.2.19.

81. Ibid., 1.2.28; 2.5.1–10.

82. Ludovici Molina, *Liberi Arbitrii cum Gratiae Donis, Divina Praescientia, Providentia, Praedestinatione et Reprobatione Concordia*, ed. Johannes Rabeneck (Madrid: Sumptibus Societatis Editorialis "Sapientia," 1953), 1.14.13.23.2; Joaquín Salaverri, "La noción de Iglesia del Padre Luis de Molina," *Revista española de teología* 20 (1960): 204–15.

83. Molina, *De justitia*, 2.5.11.

evangelism for Christians, any transgression of which constitutes mortal sin. As for the state, Molina ran contrary to the widespread early modern Catholic and Protestant notion that heretics amounted to spiritual murderers who must, even more than physical murderers, be executed by the state for the common good. Rather, Molina convicted of spiritual murder any government official who executed potential heretics. This is because such officials condemned those who really were heretics to hell before the end of their natural lives, which God granted precisely to furnish them further opportunities to receive his prevenient grace and be saved.[84]

Molina then furnished a refutation of Aquinas's idea that the godless comprised a spiritual cancer ravaging society that must be cut out of the *corpus christianum* (lit. "body of Christ," here understood as Christendom) by whatever means necessary.[85] For Molina the power of God is manifested more abundantly when a notorious opponent of the faith is freely converted, thereby possibly drawing other outsiders into the church. To obviate the magistrates' desire to Christianize society, Molina utilized the same argument employed by Luther and Zwingli to quell the Anabaptists' desire to purify the earthly church from carnal Christians. This argument was an exposition of Jesus' parable of the net that held both good and bad fish until judgment day (Matt. 13:47–50). Following Augustine, Luther and Zwingli maintained that the net referred to the church, in which spiritual Christians (good fish) and carnal Christians (bad fish) must be allowed to coexist until Christ's return.[86] By contrast, Molina posited that the net referred to earthly society, in which Christians (good fish) and non-Christians (bad fish) must live together peacefully until Christ's return. As we have already seen, Molina interpreted the parable of the wheat and tares in the same manner. Thus appealing to both parables, Molina pronounced that religious differences between citizens must not undermine social tranquility.[87] Arguably a century

84. Ibid., 2.5.13–8.

85. Ibid., 1.2.28; Aquinas, *Summa Theologiae*, 2.2.11.3.

86. Augustine, *De Civitate Dei* (*The City of God*), in Nicene and Post-Nicene Fathers, vol. 2, First Series, trans. Marcus Dods and J. F. Shaw, ed. Philip Schaff (repr. ed., Peabody, MA: Hendrickson, 2004), 18.49; Martin Luther, *Ad Librum Eximii Magistri Nostri, Magistri am Brosii Catharini, Defensoris Silvestri Prieratis Acerrimi*, in *D. Martin Luthers Werke* (Weimar: Böhlau, 1888), 8:715; idem, *Against the Antinomians*, in *Luther's Works*, American ed., 47:117; Huldrych Zwingli, *Auslegung und Begründung der Thesen oder Artikel*, in *Huldreich Zwingli Sämtliche Werke*, ed. Emil Egli and Georg Finsler (Leipzig: M. Heinius Nachfolger, 1908), 2:58.

87. Molina, *De justitia*, 2.5.20–22.

or two ahead of his time, Molina announced a groundbreaking transformation in the vocation of magistrates from enforcers of ecclesiastical decrees to those who, through righteous governance, would create an environment amenable to the free spread of the gospel.

OPPOSITION TO THE AFRICAN SLAVE TRADE

Molina viewed the coming of Europeans to the New World as a missiological problem, wondering how the Christian faith could best be spread.[88] Through his discussions with Spanish and Portuguese merchants, Molina acquired a detailed knowledge of the African slave trade, in which slaves would be captured on the African coasts and sent to Portugal and Brazil. Molina was also cognizant of non-European slave trading practices in India, China, Cambodia, and Japan through the writings of Jesuits who evangelized all these places.[89] Molina decisively rejected the widespread pro-slavery argument that Christian ownership of slaves would likely bring about the conversion of those slaves.[90] Conversely, Molina held that such an arrangement would put undue pressure on slaves to ostensibly convert to Christianity while never making a personal commitment to follow Christ. In fact, such forced pseudo-conversion would incite slaves to harden their hearts against Christ, thus vastly heightening the probability of their eventual damnation. As entailed by his doctrine of libertarian free will, Molina insisted that true conversion could never be coerced. The only way missionaries could procure the genuine conversion of unbelievers in pagan lands is to oppose their enslavement and to work for the emancipation of any unbeliever who was already enslaved.[91] Moreover, social justice itself demanded that the cause of freedom from slavery be championed by all Christians. Hence Molina spoke out forcefully in favor of the liberation of the slaves, as it would prove tremendously beneficial to the cause of evangelization and promote the just cause of liberty:

---

88. Louis Vereecke, *Da Guglielmo d'Ockham a sant'Alfonso de Liguori: Saggi di storia della teologia morale moderna, 1300–1787* (Cisinello Balsamo: Edizioni Paoline, 1990), 597–613.

89. Molina, *De justitia*, 2.33.

90. Matthias Kaufmann, "Slavery between Law, Morality, and Economy," in *A Companion to Luis de Molina*, ed. idem and Alexander Aichele (Leiden: Brill, 2014), 214.

91. Alonso-Lasheras, *Luis de Molina's De Iustitia et Iure*, 94.

But if foreign ministers of the gospel are sent to those barbarous nations, and if these ministers are to be capable of converting unbelievers to the faith in the countries of their families and friends, then, of course, to provide for everyone the godly ought rather to favor the liberation of these wretched people and to provide service to each one of them, despite what the interests of the secular authorities wrongfully lead them to deem just. Moreover, on account of the cause of freedom itself, the liberation of the slaves must itself be supported, as it is shown to be the most gracious course of action. It is also necessary to liberate the slaves in order that our Christian faith and morals can be propagated in those places.[92]

While financial motives seduced the state to promote the cause of injustice by enslaving those in foreign lands, the church must do the opposite, taking a stand against the powers that be and serving those in foreign lands. For Molina the example set by God in giving spiritual liberty to all persons, regardless of his middle knowledge of whether or not they would use it properly, must be followed by believers in extending physical liberty to all persons regardless of their religious persuasions.[93]

Molina did believe there were rare conditions under which the institution of slavery was licit. For instance, someone could become another person's slave to pay off a debt to that person, as occurred in biblical times. An individual convicted of a capital crime could have the death penalty commuted to the loss of physical freedom and serve the rest of his life as a slave. Likewise, the losers of a just war could be taken as slaves by the victors instead of given the death penalty.[94] But the African slave trade met none of these conditions. Rather, it was nothing but the cruel and iniquitous treatment of one's fellow human being, the diametric opposite of the second great commandment to love one's neighbor as oneself. Slaves were maltreated, whipped, chained, threatened with death, and stored day and night in very

92. "Quod si ministri Evangelii ad nationes illas barbaras idonei mitterentur, in suisque regionibus ad fidem converterentur, tunc sane omnes pii consulere potius deberent ac favere miserorum hominum libertari neque aliter servitus cuiusque illorum est permittenda, quam si luce cularius eam iustam esse constet. Tum quod libertatis causae, quippe quae piissima est, per se sit suffragandum. Tum etiam quod id magno esset adiumaneto, ut fides nostra, moresque Christiani in illis locis propagaretur" (Molina, *De justitia*, 2.35.17).

93. Ibid., 2.35.17. This is clearly an argument from the greater to the lesser.

94. Ibid., 2.32.1–3; 2.33.1; Alonso-Lasheras, *Luis de Molina's De Iustitia et Iure*, 75.

narrow, dungeon-like spaces to optimize the profits of the traders. Hence slave traders were guilty of mortal sin.[95] As Molina explained:

> To me, it is very likely dictated that such trading is to buy slaves from the unbelievers in the region and afterwards to snatch the slaves away, brand them, and treat them inhumanely.... One hears confessions of all these things.... All those who do these things commit mortal sin and are in a state of eternal damnation, unless a person is excused by invincible ignorance, which I dare say none of them is.[96]

For Molina, not merely slave traders but all others involved in the African slave trade were guilty of mortal sin, including the king of Portugal, his heads of state, and the priests and bishops who readily absolved slave traders of their sins without restitution.

On this score, Molina rejected all of the pseudo-religious racial justifications of slavery, which had been circulating on the Iberian Peninsula since the mid-fifteenth century.[97] These racist justifications alleged that a non-European people group was inherently guilty of some moral or spiritual defect that necessitated a just war against them; upon Christian victory in this war the members of the people group could rightfully be captured as slaves. Matthias Kaufmann summarizes these arguments and Molina's evaluation of them: "That a particular group of people happens to be crude and barbaric, and thus might be better off being ruled by others—Molina mentions the Brasilienses and Aethiopienses (i.e., black African people)—cannot be sufficient reason for a war to enslave its members. Molina also ... [says] that idolatry cannot be a reason for just war and enslavement either."[98] By virtue of their creation in the *imago Dei*, all people groups were equally valuable. And by virtue of God's general revelation in nature and conscience, all people groups had access to salvation. Hence no argument could be validly

---

95. Kaufmann, "Slavery between Law, Morality, and Economy," 213; Frank Bartholomew Costello, *The Political Philosophy of Luis de Molina, S.J. (1535–1600)* (Spokane: Gonzaga University Press, 1974), 198–201.

96. "Mihi longe verosimilius est, negotiationem hanc emerium eiusmodi mancipia ab infidelibus illis in locis, eaque inde asportantium, inustam, iniquam esse.... qui horum omnium confessiones audiunt.... omnesque qui illam exercet, lethalither peccare, esseque in statu damnationis aeternae, nisi quem invincibilis ignorantia excuset, in quam neminem eorum esse affirmare auderem" (Molina, *De justitia*, 2.35.16).

97. Ibid., 2.105.1–3, 8.

98. Kaufmann, "Slavery between Law, Morality, and Economy," 193.

made from the vulgarity or religious ignorance of any people group to their enslavement. In this way, Molina proved a forerunner of the abolitionist cause of later centuries.

IMPLEMENTING THE VIRTUE OF SOCIAL JUSTICE

In his *De justitia et jure*, Molina strove to furnish his theological contemporaries with a comprehensive treatise that surveyed each major problem impinging on the governance of the church and the Christian commonweal. The ultimate, yet abstract, answer to these problems was the virtue of social justice, summarized for Molina by Zechariah 7:9–10, "Show mercy and compassion to one another. Do not oppress the widow or the fatherless, the foreigner or the poor. Do not plot evil against each other."[99] In other words, this virtue ordered all actions to the common good.[100] Nevertheless, how to concretely apply this virtue to particular situations often proved a difficult task. To carry out this task, Molina utilized a blend of Scripture, philosophy, and experience.

Regarding economics and ethics, Molina was the first theologian to authorize a morally legitimate career devoted to money lending. Scriptures such as Matthew 25:27, the philosophical analysis of what did and did not constitute usury, and Molina's discussions with Spanish and Portuguese merchants led to this authorization. It is worth emphasizing that Molina was never attacked for his position by fellow theologians, either Catholic or Protestant. As Alonso-Lasheras rightly infers, "We cannot think that this happened because no one paid any attention to what he wrote. We know that ... Molina's works were not just being read, but scrutinized. If he was able to make such a move, we should think that this can only be attributed to the solidity—the internal probability as a scholastic doctor would say—of his case."[101] But Molina was careful to insist on the absolute proscription of usury, which he considered any interest rate over 12 percent or any monopolistic business practices.

Accordingly, Molina defended the principles of a free market economy, which he believed would profit local farmers and artisans, over against papal

99. Molina, *De justitia*, 5.46.29–30.
100. Alonso-Lasheras, *Luis de Molina's De Iustitia et Iure*, 231.
101. Ibid., 221–22.

and ecclesiastical intrusion into the economy.[102] Based on a series of relevant factors surrounding a good, including the costs and risks incurred in obtaining it, its amount, its usefulness, its scarcity, and its uniqueness, Molina believed a just price range could be arrived for that good through *communis estimatio*, the estimation reached by consensus of merchants, buyers, or sellers in a particular place. That prices of goods should not be fixed but rightfully varied under particular circumstances was biblically proven for Molina by Genesis 41, in which Joseph charged a fair but steep price for grain during a seven-year famine. If a range of just prices was unethical, then Joseph would have acted unethically. To the contrary, the Bible lauded Joseph for his wisdom in the sale.[103]

Regarding church and state, Molina advocated a greater degree of distance between them than was commonly accepted in the sixteenth century. Without separating the two institutions, Molina maintained that church and state were distinct yet mutually complementary. The church works for the salvation of souls while the state works for the protection of physical lives. Contrary to the early modern actions of the papacy and the Spanish Inquisition, the church never has the right to take up the sword on its own authority. The power of the sword belongs exclusively to the state, which must wield it only to protect those innocent of material crimes and to punish those guilty of material crimes. In doing so, the state serves as a buffer between the church and the evils of the world. In exchange, the church ought to gladly render to the state all types of support necessary to execute the virtue of social justice. This will increase the probability that society will be ruled by Christians, who will govern according to the divine will. As disclosed in the incarnation, the divine will includes giving all persons the opportunity to freely respond to prevenient grace and thenceforth freely live in obedience to Jesus. Jesus' universal invitation precludes the use of coercion in spiritual matters. For Molina the idea of a spiritual crime punishable by church or state was a contradiction in terms. Therefore the only sword that either church or state may use against unbelievers or heretics is the Word of God (Eph. 6:17; Heb. 4:12).[104]

---

102. Molina, *De justitia*, 2.365.8–13.
103. Ibid., 2.354.3.
104. Ibid., 1.2.29–31.

Despite the racism already prevalent in his day, Molina was one of the first Western thinkers to oppose the African slave trade. As David Brion Davis points out, Molina "delivered scathing attacks on the ways in which Africans were being enslaved," although the early modern world "was hardly ready for an abolitionist movement."[105] According to Molina, the slave trade in Africa promoted every kind of violence, duplicity, and fraud. Slave traders were thus almost certainly guilty of mortal sin. On the issue of slavery, Molina claimed that the church must prophetically oppose the state, on the grounds of such general principles as liberty and on the grounds of the grave threat to a person's salvation if that person is enslaved by so-called Christians. For slavery not only deprives individuals of their divinely given freedom, but slavery at Christian hands typically causes individuals to harden their hearts against Christ, notwithstanding any forced external conversion.

On each issue with which he dealt, Molina regarded the socially just course of action as a course of action that he felt manifested love. This is because of the symbiotic relationship he perceived between the virtues of love and justice. Only if society is held together by the bonds of love can society give to its members and all others whom it encounters what, in the sight of God, is properly owed them as divine image-bearers.[106]

---

105. David Brion Davis, *Inhuman Bondage: The Rise and Fall of Slavery in the New World* (Oxford: Oxford University Press, 2008), 96.

106. Alonso-Lasheras, *Luis de Molina's De Iustitia et Iure*, 231.

CHAPTER 9

The *Congregatio de auxiliis gratiae*

⬛　⬛　⬛

WE RECALL THAT IN 1596 Pope Clement VIII ordered that Molina's writings and the writings of his interlocutors be sent to the Vatican and instructed the Jesuits and Dominicans to await patiently the papal decision on the issue of middle knowledge. This admonition to patience bore little fruit, as the next year saw twelve reports sent to the pope by Spanish universities, bishops, and church leaders in favor of and in opposition to Molina's *Concordia*. In October 1597 Domingo Báñez composed a memorial in the name of the Dominican order and its general, imploring Clement to finally allow Dominicans to teach their doctrine of grace and permanently prohibit the Jesuits from teaching theirs. Clement responded by allowing both orders to teach their respective doctrines in university settings, although they were to refrain from doing so from the pulpit and in public disputations until a papal pronouncement was made. In November 1597 Clement commanded the Dominican cardinal Michele Bonelli to gather a small group of bishops and theologians for the purpose of studying Molina's positions from the *Concordia* and his commentary on Aquinas's *Summa Theologiae*. This group was to compare Molina's positions with those of ancient theologians, church councils, and papal decrees in order to determine whether Molina had in fact broken from the Catholic faith.[1] Clement then placed in charge of the group Cardinal Ludovico Madrucci and Cardinal Pompeio Arrigoni, both of

---

1. Guido Stucco, *The Catholic Doctrine of Predestination from Luther to Jansenius* (Bloomington, IN: Xlibris, 2014), 163–64.

whom were inquistors general. Clement made the entire group swear an oath before Cardinal Guilio Antonio Santorio, prefect of the Congregation of the Holy Office, that they would render their judgments with a clear conscience unprejudiced by loyalty to either the Dominican or Jesuit order and strictly on the merits of the information they would acquire. This commission consisted of twelve members, including the aforementioned cardinals Madrucci and Arrigoni, three bishops, and seven theologians.[2]

Beginning its work in January 1598, the commission adopted the name *Congregatio de auxiliis gratiae* (Congregation on the Help of Divine Grace), in light of its assignment to investigate what kind of gracious help God gives to human beings to perform acts leading to salvation. The *Congregatio* first inquired about the purpose of the *Concordia* and, more particularly, what prompted Molina to compose it, since the commission regarded it simpler to reach an opinion about the *Concordia* upon comprehending its motives. This chapter recounts how, in its early stages, the *Congregatio* displayed a stern opposition to middle knowledge. It also exposes the consequences of this hostility on Molina's physical health, which steadily declined until his death on October 12, 1600.

INITIAL DENUNCIATION OF MIDDLE KNOWLEDGE

The *Congregatio* devoted its opening three sessions to the analysis of books 1 through 4 of the *Concordia*. It took severe exception to Molina's charge that, prior to his tome, insufficient effort had been expended throughout church history to reconcile in a biblically faithful way the doctrines of grace, foreknowledge, predestination, and human freedom.[3] Not only did they find this insulting to Catholic tradition, especially the labors of Augustine and Aquinas, but they viewed it as a tacit admission that middle knowledge was indeed a doctrinal innovation and therefore foreign to the received wisdom of the church.

---

2. Gregorio Coronel, *Brevis enarratio actorum omnium, ad compendium redactorum, quae circa controversiam de Auxiliis Divinae Gratiae sub Clemente PP. octavo & coram ipso celebrata sunt* (Frankfurt: Arnaud, 1687), 13.

3. Stucco, *Catholic Doctrine of Predestination*, 164; interestingly, this charge was made in book 7 (Ludovici Molina, *Liberi Arbitrii cum Gratiae Donis, Divina Praescientia, Providentia, Praedestinatione et Reprobatione Concordia*, ed. Johannes Rabeneck [Madrid: Sumptibus Societatis Editorialis "Sapientia," 1953], 7.23.4/5.1.14.6) but was apparently too inflammatory not to color the *Congregatio*'s reading of the earlier chapters.

According to the *Congregatio*, middle knowledge was not a theological discovery of something objectively true about God independently of human consciousness that had been previously unrealized by human beings. Rather, middle knowledge was a theological invention of Molina, namely, a human contrivance that did not objectively exist as a logical moment within the structure of God's omniscience. With these conclusions in mind, the *Congregatio* spent the next eight sessions aiming to show that the theological difficulties about human freedom, divine grace, good works, faith, hope, perseverance, and avoiding temptation that the *Concordia* solved through middle knowledge could be solved in ways that did not require middle knowledge. On demonstrating this thesis to its satisfaction, the *Congregatio* recommended that the debate over middle knowledge must not extend beyond Spain. Thus after eleven sessions, on March 13, 1598, the *Congregatio* censured Molina's theology as "very foreign to the views of the ancient Fathers, especially Augustine and Aquinas, church councils and past papal decrees," pronounced that the *Concordia* "should be forbidden," and declared that all of Molina's writings be suspended "until purged of new and foreign ideas by censors appointed by the Apostolic See."[4]

However, this denunciation did not fully satisfy Clement VIII, who was troubled at the speed at which the *Congregatio* had reviewed the material he had set before it. This material included a large box of writings totaling about fifteen hundred pages that could be split into three groups: Dominican anti-Molinist polemics; Jesuit explanations and defenses of Molinism; and the opinions of prominent scholars, bishops, and universities on Molinism, both pro and con. Báñez himself had commented that it would take two full years to master this intellectually taxing material.[5] Hence Clement reconvened the *Congregatio* for the purpose of studying this material, which it did for the next eight months. Obviously, neither did this denunciation satisfy Molina, who on September 22, 1598, sent a letter to Clement VIII. In this letter, Molina pled his case, denounced his accusers Báñez and Zumel, and conveyed his outrage at being the center of a papal commission's investigation.[6] Guido Stucco summarizes this outrage: "Molina went on to complain he was

4. Stucco, *Catholic Doctrine of Predestination*, 165–66; Coronel, *Brevis enarratio actorum omnium*, 19; Stefano Possanzini, *Giovanni Antonio Bovio carmelitano, teologo e vescovo di Molfetta*, Textus et studia historica carmelitana 10 (Rome: Insititutum carmelitanum, 1970), 41.

5. Antonio Astrain, *Historia de la Compania de Jesus en la asistencia de Espana*, 7 vols. (Madrid: Razón y Fé, 1912–25), 4:228–44.

6. Ibid., 4:257–62.

being unjustly persecuted, claiming he fiercely upheld the Council of Trent's definitions and canons; that numerous Spanish and non-Spanish universities approved of his *Concordia*; and accusing his detractors of following Luther's and Calvin's views."[7] But this letter proved to be of no avail. On November 22, 1598, the *Congregatio* upheld and reinforced its original ruling. It first pronounced the Dominicans' views to be "sound and Catholic" and protested that the Jesuit arguments on behalf of Molina failed to make any impression because these arguments were new and unknown to the church fathers. It then renewed its condemnation of the *Concordia* in over two hundred pages written on behalf of the assembly by Gregorio Coronel, Augustinian theologian and secretary of the *Congregatio*. This condemnation delineated sixty-one objectionable propositions made by Molina. It was signed by all members of the *Congegatio* with one exception, the Carmelite Enrico Silvio, who would soon be replaced by his anti-Molinist coreligionist Giovanni Antonio Bovio.[8] With this second condemnation, it now seemed apparent that an official papal anathematization of Molina was sure to follow.

THE FOUR CONFERENCES OF 1599

Attempting to rescue Molina from a seemingly impending papal anathema, the Jesuits requested an audience with Clement VIII to discuss the efficacy and nature of God's grace. For they speculated that perhaps the tenor in which Molina presented his views was the actual problem, such that a diplomatic, conciliatory conversation without theological censors and Dominican polemicists would dissolve any hostility toward middle knowledge. But Clement felt that such an audience would give the appearance of papal bias toward the Jesuit order. Hence Clement proposed a compromise solution, summoning Claudio Acquaviva and Ippolito Beccaria, the respective superiors of the Jesuit and Dominican orders, to appear before the Jesuit cardinal Robert Bellarmine and the Dominican cardinal Bernerio Madrucci in order to delineate further their positions and work out their differences.[9]

7. Stucco, *Catholic Doctrine of Predestination*, 167.

8. Ibid., 167–68; Pierre S. Gourlin, *Tractatus theologicus de Gratia Christi Salvatore ac de praedestinatione sanctorum*, 6 vols. (Paris: Bon François Rivière, 1781), 2:281.

9. Gerhard Schneemann, *Controversiarum de Divinae Gratiae liberique arbitrii concordia initia et progressus* (Freiburg: Herder, 1881), 254.

This group would form a new, specialized branch of the *Congregatio*, with the original members ready at any time to resume their service.

The first conference commenced on February 22, 1599. Here Beccaria asserted that he had no squabble with the Jesuit order but only with the *Concordia* and some of its propositions. Seeking to take advantage of this statement, Acquaviva responded that the controversies over the efficacy of grace and predestination should be settled at the outset. He quickly distinguished between two strands of Molina's teaching. First was Molina's analysis of the efficacy of grace and his claim that predestination logically followed God's knowledge of conditionally future contingents. Acquaviva stated that this strand, ultimately concerning the nature of God, was universally accepted by Jesuits. Because divine prepredestinary knowledge of conditional future contingents logically amounted to God's possession of middle knowledge, Acquaviva averred, middle knowledge was nothing more than new terminology for a fundamental Jesuit tenet. And since Beccaria already professed that he had no squabble with the Jesuit order, the efficacy of grace and middle knowledge should not be on the table for debate. Second was Molina's doctrine of the natural powers of the human will, including its ability to repent, believe, love God, and resist temptation. Acquaviva stated that this strand, ultimately concerning the nature of humanity, was not universally accepted by Jesuits. Therefore only Molina's doctrine of humanity should be open for discussion.[10] However, Cardinal Madrucci viewed Acquaviva's maneuverings as theological sleight of hand and an attempt to dodge the real issue, which concerned the structure of divine omniscience. This was because Madrucci denied that prepredestinary knowledge of conditional future contingents was the same as middle knowledge. Madrucci contended that God, in the logical order of things, first issued his creative decree, from which followed his knowledge of actual future contingents. Then God freely chose which conditional future contingents were true and which were false. Finally, God predestined actual persons to salvation or condemnation by decreeing to save all who will believe and to condemn all who will refuse to believe.[11] Therefore Madrucci demanded that both Beccaria and Acquaviva produce

---

10. Juan Martinez de Ripalda, *De ente supernaturali disputationes in universam theologiam tomus posterior* (Lyons, 1645), 527–31.

11. Astrain, *Historia de la Compania de Jesus*, 267–69.

three documents respectively delineating their views on divine omniscience, what they opposed in the other order's view, and reasons why the other order's view was less probable and plausible than their own.[12]

The second conference occurred six days later on February 28, 1599. Beccaria produced only one of the three documents demanded by Madrucci, containing various propositions of Molina with which the Dominicans dissented. Madrucci briefly examined this document and turned it over to Acquaviva. Anticipating and trying to block one of Acquaviva's principal objections to the Dominican view, Beccaria then insisted that Aquinas's doctrine of efficacious concurrence by which God premoves humans to bring about effects infallibly was inadmissible as a topic of debate, since it was Molina and not Aquinas who stood on trial. On the other hand, Acquaviva produced all three of the documents Madrucci demanded. Using his compliance to play a game of legal chess, Acquaviva motioned for Madrucci to turn over to Beccaria only the document corresponding to the document Beccaria had provided him, withholding the other two documents until Beccaria produced their counterparts. Madrucci agreed with this arrangement, supplying Beccaria with simply the one document and then adjourning the conference.[13]

The third conference was the lengthiest and lasted from March 11 to March 28, 1599. Taking advantage of the fact that Clement was in attendance with Bellarmine and Madrucci, Acquaviva stood up to speak first. Acquaviva appealed to the letter Clement had received from Molina (dated September 22, 1598), which included a short, concise defense of his theological system. Aware that Molina was furious about not being personally summoned to Rome but instead being holed up in Cuenca on pain of capture by the Inquisition, Acquaviva requested that Clement read to the conference the defense Molina provided with his letter. Since Beccaria had no knowledge of the contents or even the existence of the letter, Clement denied the request.[14] Angry at being taken by surprise in what he perceived as a game of one-upmanship, Beccaria slammed the two documents he failed to provide

---

12. Stucco, *Catholic Doctrine of Predestination*, 168.

13. Ibid., 169; Astrain, *Historia de la Compania de Jesus*, 269.

14. Until this disclosure, very few people knew about the existence of the letter and the attached defense. Besides Molina himself, this select group included Clement, Bellarmine, Madrucci, Acquaviva (to whom Molina had sent a copy), and a handful of high-ranking Jesuit officials with whom Acquaviva shared the document.

in the second conference down on the table before Madrucci. Beccaria then demanded that Acquaviva immediately answer his eight questions concerning Molinist predestination raised in the document turned over to Acquaviva at the previous conference, as Acquaviva clearly had ample time to prepare. These questions read as follows:

> (1) Are predestination and foreknowledge found in God *before* the good use of human free will which man will make, out of his innate freedom, in order to dispose himself to justification and attain eternal life? (2) If such predestination and foreknowledge are indeed found in God, is any freedom left in the human free will, as displayed in the actions with which a man disposes himself to justification or to eternal life? (3) Are divine predestination and predetermination efficacious in and of themselves; and are the human deeds which are necessary for salvation coming from God? (4) Are some aids efficacious in and of themselves, thus ensuring that free will is going to consent to them? Or do these divine aids receive their efficacy or inefficacy from free will itself, stemming from its own innate freedom? (5) Is divine predestination frustrated in the effects or means that are necessary unto salvation? (6) Does predestination apply itself efficaciously, as it were, to that good use of free will which a predestined person displays, while he applies himself the aids of prevenient grace, by making good use of them? (7) Or is good use of free will merely foreknown by God, but not predestined or predetermined? (8) Is this foreknown good use of free will the reason for predestination?[15]

When Clement then ordered Acquaviva to respond, Acquaviva pleaded that he needed ten days to formalize his answers to these questions. Clement granted Acquaviva his requested continuance.

On March 21, 1599, Acquaviva presented his formal answers to the conference, aiming to represent faithfully Molina's sentiments on each question. Regarding (1), Acquaviva insisted that, yes, predestination and foreknowledge are indeed found in God before the good use of human free will. Regarding (2), Acquaviva declared that even though predestination and foreknowledge precede the existence of the human will, its total freedom of choice remains

---

15. Stucco, *Catholic Doctrine of Predestination*, 212; emphasis his. The original Latin translated by Stucco is found in Jacques Hyacinthe Serry, *Historiae congregationis de auxiliis divinae gratiae* (Padua, 1700), 174.

intact, such that any person may choose whether to dispose oneself toward salvation. Regarding (3), Acquaviva maintained that predestination, though not predetermination, is the efficient cause of those free human acts carried out with the assistance of God's grace that are necessary for receiving justification. Predestination and the helps of God's grace are efficacious in and of themselves, but not at the expense of their relationship with human free choice. Regarding (4), Acquaviva averred that some helps are efficacious because they bring about the consent of free choice. But free choice could make these helps ineffective. So when considered in and of themselves and apart from any relation to free choice, the helps of God's grace are not efficacious. However, this does not mean that the efficacy of these helps springs from human free choice alone. Rather, their efficacy springs from God and human free choice acting in unison.[16] Regarding (5), Acquaviva claimed that, no, predestination is not frustrated but instead stands faultless. Regarding (6), Acquaviva replied affirmatively that predestination applies itself efficaciously to that good use of free choice that an elect person displays. Regarding (7), Acquaviva held that the good use of human free choice was both foreknown and predestined by God, though not determined by God. Regarding (8), Acquaviva asserted that God's foreknowledge of an individual's good use of free choice is not the cause of that person's predestination.[17] After Acquaviva had finished, Clement, Bellarmine, and Madrucci agreed to take his answers into consideration and to let both parties know in one week's time how the three of them wanted to proceed. When the conference reassembled on March 28, 1599, Clement, Bellarmine, and Madrucci declared that, having now heard the negative side (i.e., Dominican objections to Molina and Jesuit responses), they wanted to hear the positive side, namely, what the Dominicans and Jesuits agreed on concerning divine omniscience. Hoping to build a bridge of reconciliation between the two orders, the papal party announced this positive side as the subject of the fourth and final conference.

This fourth conference commenced on May 16, 1599, and continued to meet intermittently until November 30, 1599. Beccaria and Acquaviva began by listing seven propositions on which they concurred. These propositions rendered it immediately obvious that Acquaviva had shifted significant

---

16. Ripalda, *De ente supernaturali disputationes,* 524.
17. Stucco, *Catholic Doctrine of Predestination,* 212.

ground since the third conference from Molina's actual views to a variant on Molina's views dubbed Congruism. Newly formulated by the Jesuit theologian Francisco Suárez (1548–1617), Congruism maintained that standing logically between God's middle knowledge and creative decree was God's act of predestination, in which he freely chose particular individuals to receive salvation. (We recall that, according to Molina, predestination was logically simultaneous with the divine creative decree.) Through his middle knowledge, God knew which helps of grace would be efficacious in obtaining the free, affirmative response of these individuals. Hence, in his creative decree, God chooses a world in which these elect individuals exist and in which God gives them precisely the helps of grace they need. In other words, while God gives all persons a completely sufficient grace for salvation, God gives the elect a grace that is so perfectly adapted to their unique characters, temperaments, and situations that they infallibly yet freely respond affirmatively to its influence. Like Thomistic grace, this grace is extrinsically efficacious (not, per Molina, intrinsically efficacious). For even though the wills of the elect are free to reject this grace, the particular gifts making up this grace are selected according to God's middle knowledge to be congruent with the elect's wills, such that the grace is infallibly embraced.[18]

In accordance with Acquaviva's new Congruist convictions, the seven propositions on which Beccaria and Acquaviva professed their agreement ran as follows:

(1) Man is given the help of prevenient efficacious grace, through which God brings about that man does what is good. (2) This help is a peculiar gift of God, distinct from sufficient grace. (3) This help is intrinsic to both man's intellect and will, consisting in the stimulation of both, which is to say, in the illumination of the intellect and in the motion of the will. (4) This help is supernatural and sent by God. (5) This help does not only exist on the part of the object, but also on the part of the power. (6) The motion of the will is real and precedes the application of the will to a specific action. (7) Once this efficacious help is put in place, it infallibly converts man.[19]

---

18. William Lane Craig, "'Lest Anyone Should Fall': A Middle Knowledge Perspective on Perseverance and Apostolic Warnings," *International Journal for Philosophy of Religion* 29 (1991): 69–70.
19. Stucco, *Catholic Doctrine of Predestination*, 169.

We observe how prevenient grace, which Molina took as synonymous with sufficient grace and therefore as neither efficacious nor inefficacious in and of itself, is here differentiated from sufficient grace and defined as intrinsically efficacious. This shift in Acquaviva's thinking was perceived by Cardinals Bellarmine and Madrucci, who stated that if these seven points were a faithful representation of Molina's thought, then no theological quarrel would have arisen.[20] Both cardinals smelled a proverbial rat in that they felt Acquaviva was trying to sneak Molina's views into acceptance by the conference under the revisionary guise of Congruism. Whether or not this was indeed Acquaviva's strategy, it made Molina look guiltier of heresy than ever, as even Molina's own superior in the Jesuit order would no longer defend his true positions. When Acquaviva informed Molina of his actions by letter in June 1599, Molina felt disappointment in what he regarded as Acquaviva's cowardice amid pressure by the other members of the conference, and Molina felt betrayal in that he believed Acquaviva was no longer representing his best interests. Furthermore, Molina grew increasingly terrified that a papal anathema was sure to come down the pike, after which he would be forcibly taken from Cuenca by the Spanish Inquisition and burned at the stake as a heretic. All of this took a tremendous psychological and physical toll on Molina's health.[21]

After the opening of the fourth conference, an extended correspondence—sometimes face-to-face and sometimes via letter—took place between Clement, Beccaria, Acquaviva, and other theologians through the mediation of Madrucci. At this point, both Beccaria and Acquaviva were permitted to assemble a small team of theological advisers who could participate in the discussion. However, these advisers could not include any of the principals in the debate. Thus Beccaria could not invite Báñez or Zumel to serve on the Dominican side, and Acquaviva could not invite Molina or Suárez to serve on the Jesuit side. The tone of this correspondence reached a fever pitch on June 8, 1599, when the Dominican team accused the Jesuit team before the pope of "scheming, manipulating, and resorting to various gimmicks in order to evade the main question, namely to establish whether Molina's doctrine was heretical or not."[22] Interestingly, this charge provoked the Jesuit theologians,

---

20. Ripalda, *De ente supernaturali disputationes*, 525.
21. Astrain, *Historia de la Compania de Jesus*, 270–74.
22. Stucco, *Catholic Doctrine of Predestination*, 170.

with the exception of Acquaviva, to take up the defense of Molina's doctrine of grace over against that of Suárez.[23] The Jesuit team responded in kind on June 24, 1599, accusing the Dominican team before the pope of stealthily bringing certain Lutheran and Calvinist doctrines into the Roman Catholic Church. As Antonio Astrain remarks, these twin accusations "echoed in Rome like two explosions of dynamite."[24] Following this exchange, the two sides argued until November 1599 about the Thomistic doctrine of premotion, whether the efficacy of divine grace stems from the one cause of God or the two causes of God and human free choice, and whether it is up to free choice to make prevenient grace efficacious or inefficacious. By November 30, 1599, the two sides had reached a stalemate, and Madrucci declared the conferences to be unfortunately concluded without bringing the controversy over grace any closer to a mutually agreeable resolution.[25]

THE UNBEARABLE TURMOIL OF 1600

In light of the conferences' failure, Clement VIII summoned the original members of the *Congregatio* to resume their analysis of Molina's works on April 20, 1600. This review lasted from the end of April to the end of August. On receiving word of this third meeting, Molina figured the *Congregatio* would condemn him more thoroughly than it had in its second meeting, just as it condemned him more thoroughly in its second meeting (a denunciation

---

23. Apart from any possible political motives, Acquaviva had become sincerely convinced of the truth of Congruism. In 1613 Acquaviva famously directed Jesuit theologians to teach Congruism instead of strict Molinism, as Congruism stood more in agreement with the thought of Augustine and Aquinas. He exhorted: "Henceforth let our Fathers always teach that efficacious and sufficient graces do not differ merely in completed act (*actu secundo*), because the one obtains its effect by the cooperation of the free will and not the other. But they differ also in their first movement (*actu primo*), in this sense that, presupposing *scientia media*, God Himself, with the fixed intention of producing good, designedly chooses those determinate means and employs them in the manner and at the moment which He knows infallibly will insure that the effect will be produced. Consequently, if He had foreseen the inefficacy of these means, God would have made use of other means. That is why, morally speaking and considering it as a favor, there is something more in efficacious grace than in sufficient grace even in its first movement (*actu primo*). In this way God brings it about that we actually do something, and not merely gives us the grace to be able to do it. The same may be said of perseverance, which is undoubtedly a gift of God" (John Hardon, *History and Theology of Grace: The Catholic Teaching on Divine Grace* [Washington, DC: Catholic University of America Press, 2006], 352; the original Latin translated by Hardon is found in Schneemann, *Controversiarum*, 203). However, the directive was never incorporated into the Jesuit Institute and thus never became binding on the Society of Jesus.

24. Astrain, *Historia de la Compania de Jesus*, 4:282.

25. Coronel, *Brevis enarratio*, 22; Schneemann, *Controversiarum*, 258–64.

of sixty-one objectionable propositions made by Molina) than in its first meeting (a simple denunciation). By contrast, Molina was deeply gratified when the Society of Jesus offered him the newly founded chair of moral theology at the University of Madrid, which he took up in April 1600. Now in Madrid and encouraged by the support of his fellow Jesuits, Molina made one last effort to sway Clement VIII with a May 1600 letter articulating the following three points. First, the way in which the sixty-one propositions were interpreted by the *Congregatio* was completely foreign to Molina's intent. Second, Molina's intended meaning resonated with the views of the ante-Nicene Fathers and many of the medieval Scholastics. Third, in 1590 the positions in Molina's *Concordia* had been judged "probable" and "Catholic" after a long and detailed examination by Bartolomeu Ferreira, the chief censor of the Inquisition, who gave the work a glowing imprimatur. Molina pointed out that Ferreira's decision had not been reached on his own but with the assistance of both Portuguese and Spanish censors. In addition, Molina's positions had been endorsed by other professors of theology from various European universities and religious orders, including the Benedictines, Franciscans, Carmelites, and Augustinians.[26]

By October 1600 the *Congregatio* indeed submitted to Clement a third censure, as Molina had anticipated. Moreover, Clement had made no overtures to acknowledge Molina's letter. These developments placed increased psychological pressure on Molina, which caused his already deteriorating health to reach the breaking point. Tormented by dysentery, Molina suffered under no delusions about his physical decline, taking to what he knew would be his deathbed on October 10, 1600. When asked by a fellow priest what he wished done with his writings, Molina answered with an air of humility yet resignation, "The Society of Jesus may do with them what it wishes."[27] However, Molina remained resolute until the end that nothing he had professed was in error, but that his writings only presented the biblical data and their philosophically necessary implications on the topics of omniscience, freedom, grace, providence, and predestination. Accordingly, Molina showed no signs of despairing of his own salvation, but trusted that he would be

26. Ripalda, *De ente supernaturali disputationes*, 524.

27. Joseph Pohle, "Luis de Molina," *The Catholic Encyclopedia*, 15 vols., ed. Charles G. Herbermann (New York: Robert Appleton, 1907–12), 10:438.

240 Luis de Molina

received into Christ's presence. On October 12, 1600, in Madrid, Molina died of dysentery at the age of sixty-five, taking to the grave the impression that he would be posthumously yet wrongfully anathematized.[28] Thus ended the life of one of the greatest philosophical and moral theologians in the history of Christianity.

MOLINA'S POSTHUMOUS VINDICATION

Molina would certainly have suffered a posthumous papal anathema in late October 1600 were it not for the last-minute intervention at the papal court of theologian Benedetto Giustiniani, former rector of the Jesuit Roman College. Despite the three censures of the *Congregatio*, Giustiniani pleaded with Clement VIII not to condemn Molina.[29] Using a document recently drawn up by Acquaviva (who did not want strict Molinism condemned but felt Congruism was true), Giustiniani compared thirteen points of the most recent censure with thirteen passages from Molina, illustrating how badly Molina had been taken out of context in each point. This demonstration verified in Clement's mind the truth of Molina's previous allegation that the way the *Congregatio* interpreted the sixty-one denounced propositions stood diametrically opposed to his intended meaning. As a result, Clement added two new members to the *Congregatio* who had a reputation for academic honesty, the Franciscan procurator General Juan de Rada and the Franciscan theologian and Padua professor Girolamo Pallantieri.[30] These additions would obviate any further anticontextual readings of Molina by the *Congregatio*. Moreover, Clement decided to change the question that occupied the *Congregatio*. No longer asked to investigate whether Molinism was an innovation, Clement now asked the group to establish to what degree Molinism agreed with Pelagianism and Semi-Pelagianism, which were respectively deemed heresy by the Third Ecumenical Council at Ephesus (431) and the Synod of Orange (529).

From February 8, 1601, to January 22, 1605, the *Congregatio* met an astonishing 142 times for either sessions or debates on this new question, with

---

28. Schneemann, *Controversiarum*, 273.

29. Stucco, *Catholic Doctrine of Predestination*, 172.

30. Coronel, *Brevis enarratio*, 24.

no ultimate headway made by the group.[31] Clement VIII died on March 3, 1605, to be succeeded by Pope Leo XI (the so-called *Papa Lampo* or "lightning pope" whose reign lasted less than a month from April 1 to April 27, 1605) and then by Pope Paul V (who would reign until 1621). A few months after his May 16, 1605, appointment, Paul resumed the *Congregatio's* sessions on September 14, 1605. Paul expanded the *Congregatio* from two to fourteen cardinal inquisitors general and from three to five bishops, thus doubling the group's total membership from fourteen to twenty-eight. From this time until August 28, 1607, the *Congregatio* met twenty-seven times for either discussion or debate, never bringing up any new ground or producing any definitive evidence linking Molinism to Pelagianism or Semi-Pelagianism.[32] The fact that the *Congregatio* could meet a total of 169 times from 1601 to 1607 without finding Molinism guilty of Pelagianism or Semi-Pelagianism proved to Paul V that Molinism was neither of these heresies, a position shared by ten of the fourteen cardinal inquisitors. However, Paul remained personally unsure whether Molinism, Thomism, or some other view was true.

Therefore, on August 28, 1607, Pope Paul V officially pronounced Molina's system to be acceptable Catholic doctrine, without taking sides on whether or not it was true. He stated that Molinism was permissible for Catholics to believe, and that the *Concordia* and Molina's other works could be read and studied without any fear of spiritual harm. According to Paul, Molina markedly differed "from the Pelagians, who made salvation begin from ourselves, the former maintaining the very opposite."[33] Likewise, the doctrine of the Dominicans was permissible for Catholics to believe, and any works presenting it could be safely read and studied. Paul then sternly charged that neither Molinism nor Thomism could be qualified or censored by anyone, and that "severe punishment would be meted out to transgressors (*ut severa castigatione plecteretur*)."[34] Paul thus allowed wide options within the Roman Catholic Church on the matters of divine omniscience, human freedom, grace, providence, and predestination. He then permanently

---

31. For a detailed history of the contours of these sessions and debates, see Stucco, *Catholic Doctrine of Predestination*, 173–84.

32. For a detailed history of the contours of these sessions and debates, see Stucco, *Catholic Doctrine of Predestination*, 184–89.

33. Paul V, "Edict of 28 August 1607"; translated in *The Month and Catholic Review* 41 (1881): 298.

34. Stucco, *Catholic Doctrine of Predestination*, 192.

disbanded the *Congregatio de auxiliis gratiae*, imposing silence on its members regarding any talk that either the Jesuit or Dominican positions represented heresy. In this way, seven years after Molina's death, Molina's life work had been finally vindicated.

Our next and final chapter will trace Molina's legacy on Christian thought from the seventeenth century to today. We will focus predominantly on the renaissance of Molinism in contemporary philosophy of religion and theology and on the tremendous relevance of Molinism for twenty-first-century evangelicalism and the theological and missiological challenges it faces.

CHAPTER 10

Molina's Legacy

⠿   ⠿   ⠿

THE LAST FOUR DECADES have witnessed a tremendous revival of interest in Molinism from philosophers of religion and theologians, especially among evangelicals. Historically speaking, this resurgence is quite noteworthy, since Molinism has largely been limited to the confines of the Jesuit order from the seventeenth century until recently. From the Synod of Dort (1618–19) up to the 1970s, Molinism was essentially lost to the Protestant world. For, as we recall from this book's introduction, Arminius borrowed from Molina the doctrine of middle knowledge and then significantly revised it. A national synod of the Dutch Reformed Church, Dort, explicitly rejected Arminianism and, on the faulty assumption that Arminianism faithfully represented Molinism, implicitly rejected Molinism as well. Henceforth, Calvinists shunned Molinism as a Catholic form of Arminianism, and Arminians neglected Molinism on the misguided grounds that they had already captured its true essence. Ironically, neither side actually knew what Molinism was.

This situation changed in 1974, when the Dutch Reformed philosopher of religion Alvin Plantinga unwittingly reformulated the central tenets of Molinism in his free will defense against the logical version of the problem of evil.[1] That Plantinga's insights were not original to him but harked back to Molina was pointed out by the philosopher Robert Adams, a critic of Molinism, in 1977.[2] Afterward, Plantinga openly expressed his agreement with Molina and has since emerged as one of the leading defenders of middle

---

1. Alvin Plantinga, *God, Freedom, and Evil* (New York: Harper & Row, 1974), 41–64.
2. Robert M. Adams, "Middle Knowledge and the Problem of Evil," *American Philosophical Quarterly* 14 (1977): 107–12.

knowledge.[3] As evident in Plantinga's work, the perceived success of Molinism both in dismantling the logical version of the problem of evil and in reconciling divine sovereignty with libertarian human freedom drew several leading philosophers of religion to embrace Molinism in the 1980s. These philosophers included Thomas Flint, Jonathan Kvanvig, Richard Otte, William Lane Craig, and Alfred Freddoso.[4] Since that time, Craig has established himself as arguably the world's leading defender of Molinism. With Craig's voluminous scholarship, Molinism exploded onto the evangelical scene in the 1990s. From that decade until the present, middle knowledge has received some of its most fruitful and innovative applications among evangelical philosophers and theologians. Thus evangelicals have been largely responsible for carrying on and enhancing Molina's legacy, now gaining an appreciation well deserved and long overdue. Today many prominent evangelical thinkers laud Molinism as the long-awaited rapprochement between Calvinism and Arminianism and the antidote to open theism.

Accordingly, this chapter begins by briefly surveying the seventeenth-century developments that led to modern Protestant ignorance of Molinism, so as to clear away any lingering misunderstandings that Molinism and Protestantism are incompatible. The bulk of the chapter proceeds to examine the significant place Molinism now occupies at the table of philosophy of religion in general and of evangelical theology in particular. Turning to recent developments, we shall see the fresh application of Molinism to topics as wide-ranging as biblical inerrancy, the relationship between Christianity and other world religions, the problem of evil, and creation, evolution, and quantum indeterminacy.

---

3. Alvin Plantinga, "Self-Profile," in *Alvin Plantinga*, ed. James Tomberlin and Peter van Inwagen, Profiles 5 (Dordrecht: Reidel, 1985), 50; idem, "Reply to Robert Adams," in *Alvin Plantinga*, ed. Tomberlin and van Inwagen, 372–82.

4. Thomas P. Flint, "The Problem of Divine Freedom," *American Philosophical Quarterly* 20, no. 3 (1983): 225–64; Jonathan L. Kvanvig, *The Possibility of an All-Knowing God* (New York: St. Martin's Press, 1986), 121–77; Richard Otte, "A Defense of Middle Knowledge," *Philosophy of Religion* 21 (1987): 161–69; William Lane Craig, *The Only Wise God: The Compatibility of Divine Foreknowledge and Human Freedom* (Grand Rapids: Baker, 1987), 127–52; idem, *Divine Foreknowledge and Human Freedom: The Coherence of Theism: Omniscience*, Studies in Intellectual History 19 (Leiden: Brill, 1990), 237–78; Alfred J. Freddoso, "Introduction," in Luis de Molina, *On Divine Foreknowledge*, trans. Alfred J. Freddoso (Ithaca, NY: Cornell University Press, 1988), 1–81.

ARMINIUS'S VARIANT ACCOUNT OF MIDDLE KNOWLEDGE AND ITS USES

Acquainted with the controversy surrounding middle knowledge from 1598 to 1607, Jacob Arminius saw that middle knowledge was being used by Jesuits as a weapon against Calvin's doctrine of predestination, specifically Calvin's conviction that God's predestinary decree occurred logically prior to and therefore independent of God's knowledge of who would place their faith in Christ. Given his own disquietude about Calvinist predestination, Arminius, on rare occasions (i.e., twice),[5] appealed to this new weapon in his disputations without investigating what it actually meant. Hence there is not a shred of evidence that Arminius ever read Molina's *Concordia*. Rather, all his understanding of middle knowledge self-confessedly came from "the schoolmen," namely, the Jesuit scholastics he had encountered in the course of his theological education (part of which occurred at the University of Padua, a Roman Catholic institution) and his professorial duties at the University of Leiden.[6] Unfortunately, Arminius profoundly misunderstood Molina's doctrine of middle knowledge by denying its central tenet—that it belongs to God's prevolitional knowledge and not to God's postvolitional knowledge.

Both for Molina and for contemporary philosophers of religion, Arminius's concept of middle knowledge reduces to simple foreknowledge. Arminius wrongfully thought that whether divine knowledge comes before or after the *actual creation* of the world—not whether it comes before or after God's *decision to create* the world—makes a difference in whether it is middle knowledge or foreknowledge. But, philosophically speaking, it is the latter criterion that differentiates middle knowledge from foreknowledge; the former criterion is irrelevant. Because of divine immutability, upon God's decision to create a particular world, it is certain (though not necessary) that all events making up that world *will* happen, rendering knowledge of all these events as foreknowledge. It is no longer the case that these events merely *would* happen on the unactualized condition that God chooses to create that world;

---

5. Jacob Arminius, *Public Disputations*, in Jacob Arminius, *The Writings of Arminius*, 3 vols., trans. James Nichols and W. R. Bagnall (Grand Rapids: Baker, 1956), 1:448–49; idem, *Private Disputations*, in Arminius, *Writings of Arminius*, 2:38–39.

6. Richard A. Muller, *God, Creation, and Providence in the Thought of Jacob Arminius* (Grand Rapids: Baker, 1991), 161.

knowledge at this earlier logical juncture is properly denominated as middle knowledge. Hence what Arminius called middle knowledge is not truly middle at all, as everything God knows at this point, including who will and will not freely receive Christ, is certainly going to occur in the future. God cannot change it, as he has already immutably settled on making the actual world. This knowledge is just as much foreknowledge as it is at the moment of the world's creation. Arminius implicitly conceded this point in his statement that God's "decree to save and damn particular persons ... has its foundation in God's foreknowledge,"[7] not in God's middle knowledge. Accordingly, what Arminius termed free knowledge is simply a terminological redundancy that represents no logical change in the status of God's knowledge. Once the decision to create the world is made, then any divine knowledge about what will happen in the world is foreknowledge, regardless of whether God has yet made the world. In short, the temporal moment of the world's actual creation makes no difference in the epistemic status of divine knowledge.

By contrast, what Molina recognized as the distinction of middle versus free knowledge represents a profound difference in the epistemic status of God's knowledge. Middle knowledge is God's knowledge of what *would* happen under the conditions that God were to create various agents and circumstances that do not yet exist. God does not know what *will* happen in the future at this logical moment, as he has not yet chosen which world he will create. Only after apprehending his middle knowledge does God choose one particular world composed of various logically compatible (i.e., compossible) agents and circumstances to be the actual world. It should be emphasized that Molina did not say God creates the actual world at this point, but rather that God decides or decrees which feasible world will be actual. In fact, Molina did not believe that God brought the actual world into being simultaneous with his divine creative decree.[8] For the divine creative decree was issued from eternity past (and God's free knowledge was held from eternity past), whereas the actual world came into being at the first moment of time. In contemporary scientific terms, the Big Bang did not occur when God issued

7. Jacob Arminius, *Declaration of Sentiments*, in Jacob Arminius, *The Writings of Arminius*, 3 vols., trans. James Nichols and W. R. Bagnall (Grand Rapids: Baker, 1956), 1:248.

8. This conclusion is necessitated by Luis de Molina, *On Divine Foreknowledge*, trans. Alfred J. Freddoso (Ithaca, NY: Cornell University Press, 1988), 4.14.13.52.8.

his creative decree. Rather than the temporal moment of creation, Molina was solely concerned with the fact that God's creative decision has now been made, as this act of God's will alone brings with it a logical change in the status of divine knowledge about the actual world. Consequently, free knowledge is God's knowledge of what *will* happen in the actual world given God's logically prior decision to create it and is synonymous with foreknowledge.[9] So, contra Arminius, Molina believed that God brought the world into being logically after the apprehension of his free knowledge.

Unfortunately, the crucial differences between Molina's version of middle knowledge and Arminius's version of middle knowledge went unperceived by the Synod of Dort. Broadly representative of the Reformed Church, the Synod included official delegates from Geneva, Bremen, Basel, Bern, Zurich, and England (i.e., the bishops of Chichester and Salisbury). In a classic case of guilt by association, Dort seized upon Arminius's two references to middle knowledge to argue that his view of conditional election had Molinist middle knowledge at its basis. Hence Dort polemicized against Arminius's system as being founded on a doctrine invented by a Jesuit.[10] When Dort proceeded to condemn Arminianism, it effectively yet unfairly condemned Molinism with it as a live option for the Reformed faith. This situation has only changed in the last four decades, as prominent Reformed thinkers such as Plantinga, Terrence Tiessen, Bruce Ware, John Feinberg, and Luke Van Horn have attempted to incorporate Molinist middle knowledge into Calvinism.

Moreover, the Remonstrants, or followers of Arminius, did no better than the Reformed in preserving Molinism as a live option for Arminianism. Since Arminius's version of middle knowledge was in fact simple foreknowledge, Arminians have historically held to simple foreknowledge and grounded God's predestination upon it.[11] Thus a person is part of the elect community

9. Technically speaking, once God creates the world and various foreknown events happen in it, then those events shift from God's foreknowledge to God's knowledge of the present and then of the past.

10. Henri A. Krop, "Philosophy and the Synod of Dordt: Aristotelianism, Humanism, and the Case against Arminianism," in *Revisiting the Synod of Dordt (1618–1619)*, ed. Aza Goudriaan and Fred van Lieburg, Brill's Series in Church History 49 (Leiden: Brill, 2011), 75.

11. As Roger Olson has meticulously demonstrated in Roger E. Olson, *Arminian Theology: Myths and Realities* (Downers Grove, IL: IVP Academic, 2006), 185–94. Leading Arminian thinkers who have grounded predestination on simple foreknowledge include Simon Episcopius and Philip Limborch (seventeenth century); John Wesley (eighteenth century); Richard Watson, William Burton Pope, and John Miley (nineteenth century); Henry Thiessen and H. Orton Wiley (twentieth century); and Thomas Oden, Jack Cottrell, Leroy Forlines, I. Howard Marshall, Robert Shank, and William Klein (present day).

because God foreknows that one will freely receive Christ in the world already chosen by God, and a person is part of the reprobate community because God foreknows that one will not freely receive Christ in the world already chosen by God. We recall from this book's introduction that Molina found this view of election a violation of divine sovereignty, as certain individuals could put an obligation on God to save them. God would have no choice in the matter as to whether to save them, condemn them, or refrain from creating them.[12] But Molina insisted that election and reprobation were sovereign choices of God. Accordingly, a person is individually elected because God chooses to actualize a world in which he freely receives Christ instead of a world in which he freely rejects Christ. And a person is individually reprobated in exactly the same manner. During the past four decades, thinkers in the Arminian tradition, most prominently William Lane Craig, have embraced Molinist middle knowledge.[13]

In sum, since what the Reformed tradition historically denounced as middle knowledge was not Molina's doctrine of middle knowledge, and since the Arminian tradition has never disclaimed Molina's doctrine of middle knowledge, there is no reason why members of both traditions cannot draw on it as a rapprochement.[14]

THE CONTEMPORARY PROMINENCE OF MOLINISM AND ITS APPLICATIONS

The prominence of Molinism in contemporary philosophy of religion stems principally from two factors. First, Molinism is the only theological

---

12. Ludovici Molina, *Liberi Arbitrii cum Gratiae Donis, Divina Praescientia, Providentia, Praedestinatione et Reprobatione Concordia*, ed. Johannes Rabeneck (Madrid: Sumptibus Societatis Editorialis "Sapientia," 1953), 7.23.1/2.1.1–8.

13. Note that William Lane Craig does not fully endorse Molina's view of election and reprobation, suggesting instead (but not committing himself to the view) that God may have graciously chosen a world where all reprobate individuals are those who suffer from transworld damnation and where anyone who would be freely saved under any circumstances are, in fact, elect in the actual world (William Lane Craig, "'No Other Name': A Middle Knowledge Perspective on the Exclusivity of Salvation through Christ," *Faith and Philosophy* 6 [1989]: 183–87). By contrast, Molina felt that no person suffered from transworld damnation and that some persons who are reprobate in the actual world would have been elect in other feasible worlds.

14. This conclusion was famously proffered by William Lane Craig, "Middle Knowledge: A Calvinist-Arminian Rapprochement?" in *The Grace of God, The Will of Man*, ed. Clark H. Pinnock (Grand Rapids: Zondervan, 1989), 141–64.

stance that consistently maintains both God's all-encompassing providence (i.e., the strong traditional sense of providence that includes his sovereignty over and prescience of each and every event that occurs) and libertarian human freedom. Thomas Flint contends that since Bible-believing Christians have strong prima facie reasons for embracing both of these truths, they have strong prima facie reasons for accepting Molinism.[15] Second, Molinism possesses tremendous explanatory power and scope to make sense of a wide range of pressing theological issues that are often deemed intractable. The theological promise of Molinism is captured well by William Lane Craig: "Once one grasps the concept of middle knowledge, one will find it astonishing in its subtlety and power. Indeed, I would venture to say that it is the single most fruitful theological concept I have ever encountered."[16] We shall now examine each of these factors in turn.

The first factor could be summarized by saying that Molinism gives the Christian the "best of both worlds" of Calvinism and Arminianism and, in the process, removes the motivation and the appeal of open theism. Per Calvinism, one retains God's sovereignty over every detail of the world, good and evil. One also retains unconditional, individual election, where God chooses (but in no way determines or is morally responsible for) who is saved and who is lost. For any possible person, God can choose to actualize a world in which he is freely saved or a world in which he is freely lost. God could also choose not to create that person at all. The decision is entirely the result of God's sovereign good pleasure. Per Arminianism, one retains God's genuine desire to save all persons and the libertarian freedom of all persons. If there existed a feasible world where all the lost people in this world were freely saved and all the saved people in this world remained freely saved, God would have created it. However, God middle-knows that such a world is impossible given libertarian human freedom, thus necessitating God's choice

---

15. Thomas P. Flint, "'A Death He Freely Accepted': Molinist Reflections on the Incarnation," *Faith and Philosophy* 18 (2001): 4. In view of this situation, Flint goes on to argue, I think rightly, that the burden of proof lies on the shoulders of the anti-Molinist to find lethal objections to Molinism and that this burden of proof has not come anywhere close to being met. Since "the arguments against middle knowledge are a far cry from offering the compelling reasons that a Christian should demand from those asking that she renounce the Molinist position … the most reasonable position for a Christian is to embrace the picture of providence that middle knowledge makes possible."

16. William Lane Craig, "The Middle-Knowledge View," in James K. Beilby and Paul R. Eddy, *Divine Foreknowledge: Four Views* (Downers Grove, IL: InterVarsity, 2001), 125.

of who is saved and who is lost.[17] But this choice, based as it is on middle knowledge, exerts no causal power over anyone's salvation or damnation, as knowledge is not causally determinative. God gives everyone sufficient grace for salvation, such that each person has an equal chance to be saved. Each person then freely embraces or freely rejects that saving grace. It should be emphasized that the deck is not stacked for or against anyone, as there is nothing about the freedom-preserving circumstances in which one is created that inclines one ineluctably toward salvation or damnation. It is simply that God middle-knows, even though things could have turned out oppositely, how persons would freely choose. Hence one has only oneself to blame if one is lost; one could have just as easily, or even more easily, been saved. As Craig nicely presents the Calvinist-Arminian compromise between predestination and human freedom offered by Molinism, "It is up to God whether we find ourselves in a world in which we are predestined, but it is up to us whether we are predestined in the world in which we find ourselves."[18]

The typical motivation of open theism is to safeguard libertarian human freedom and ward off divine determinism.[19] The typical appeal of open theism is to preserve biblical fidelity, particularly to what I dub "divine relational changeability" texts, or texts portraying God as changing his mind or learning truths due to his relationship with humans.[20] Molinism evaporates the motivation of open theism because, as we saw in chapters 3 through 5, Molinism preserves libertarian freedom and obviates divine determinism without doing so at open theism's steep price of denying divine foreknowledge

---

17. As Kenneth Keathley points out, God's election and reprobation are logically posterior to his middle knowledge that humanity would fall into sin and is therefore a form of infralapsarianism. Keathley contends, correctly in my judgment, that Molinism is the only consistent form of infralapsarianism, as traditional Reformed infralapsarianism cannot adequately reconcile divine sovereignty with divine permission of humans to freely sin. See Keathley, "A Molinist View of Election, or How to Be a Consistent Infralapsarian," in *Calvinism: A Southern Baptist Dialogue*, ed. E. Ray Clendenen and Brad J. Waggoner (Nashville: Broadman & Holman, 2008), 195–215.

18. Craig, *Divine Foreknowledge and Human Freedom*, 242.

19. Clark H. Pinnock, Richard Rice, John Sanders, William Hasker, and David Basinger, *The Openness of God: A Biblical Challenge to the Traditional Understanding of God* (Downers Grove, IL: InterVarsity, 1994); see especially Pinnock, "Systematic Theology," 101–25.

20. Foremost among such passages are claims that God "changes his mind" (Exod. 32:9–14; Isa. 38:1–5; Jer. 18:4–11; 26:7–19; Joel 2:12–13; Jonah 3:9–4:2), "repents of" or "regrets" decisions he himself made (Gen. 6:6; 1 Sam. 13:13; 15:10–11; 15:35; 1 Chron. 21:15), confronts situations other than or contrary to what he had expected (Isa. 5:2–5; 63:8–10; Jer. 3:3–20; 7:31; 32:35; Ezek. 22:30–31), and tests people to learn the level of their commitment to him (Gen. 22:12; Deut. 8:2–21; 13:1–3; Judg. 3:4; 2 Chron. 32:31).

of future contingents or artificially redefining divine sovereignty. Further, Molinism quashes the biblical appeal of open theism by coherently explaining the divine relational changeability texts while remaining faithful to texts that affirm God's knowledge of counterfactuals of creaturely freedom and his full-blown sovereignty, texts that open theism is impotent to explain. In short, the Molinist can consistently affirm the full scope of the biblical data, while the open theist can only consistently affirm a subset of that data and is forced to explain away or ignore the sizable remainder. Regarding the divine relational changeability texts, openness theologians reject the traditional interpretation that these texts are anthropomorphisms. They do so not on the grounds that Scripture lacks anthropomorphisms, but on the grounds that valid anthropomorphisms always point to literal truths about God and that there is no literal truth about God that divine relational changeability texts figuratively express. Hence Gregory Boyd asserts: "Expressions like 'the right hand of God' or 'the eyes of the Lord,' for example, communicate something true of God's strength and knowledge. But what does the concept of God's changing his mind communicate, for example, if indeed it is an anthropomorphism? If God in fact never changes his mind, saying he does so doesn't communicate anything truthful: it is simply inaccurate."[21]

But Molinism makes sense of the divine relational changeability texts by affirming that they are anthropomorphisms while disclosing the literal truth to which they point. This truth is that God's sovereignty does not consist of arbitrary decrees functioning irrespective of free human choices. Rather, the divine decrees take into account and are conditioned by what God middle-knows the free acts of creatures would be in all feasible worlds. Such a reality is expressed anthropomorphically from the human vantage point in terms of God's changing his mind, regretting previous actions, disappointment, frustration, learning about creatures, or relenting on planned action. In short, whereas divine relational changeability texts indeed undercut the hyper-Calvinistic conception that God determines everything, they resonate perfectly with the Molinist conception that God possesses and bases his decrees on middle knowledge.[22]

---

21. Gregory A. Boyd, "The Open-Theism View," in James K. Beilby and Paul R. Eddy, *Divine Foreknowledge: Four Views* (Downers Grove, IL: InterVarsity, 2001), 39.

22. William Lane Craig, "The Open-Theism View: A Middle-Knowledge Response," in James K. Beilby and Paul R. Eddy, *Divine Foreknowledge: Four Views* (Downers Grove, IL: InterVarsity, 2001), 59.

The exegetical superiority of Molinism to open theism is especially seen in its ability to explain texts affirming God's providence over evil events without making God the author of evil. We shall illustrate this point with two examples. Consider Saul's suicide, described in 1 Samuel 31:1–6 and 1 Chronicles 10:8–12. This was considered a sinful and dishonorable act and hence could not have been causally determined by God. Yet the Chronicler then makes the astonishing remark, "So the LORD put him to death and turned the kingdom over to David son of Jesse" (1 Chron. 10:14). While open theism can make no sense of this coalescence of human freedom and divine sovereignty, Molinism holds that Saul was directly, and so morally, responsible for his own death (i.e., responsible in the divided sense) while God was indirectly, and so not morally, responsible for it (i.e., responsible in the composite sense). In other words, Saul freely chose to kill himself despite that this was contrary to God's will, and for that act he has no one but himself to blame. But it was God who chose to create a world in which he middle-knew that Saul would freely kill himself, thereby weakly actualizing Saul's death as affirmed by the Chronicler. Likewise, consider Joseph's statement to his brothers in Egypt, "You intended to harm me, but God intended it for good to accomplish what is now being done, the saving of many lives" (Gen. 50:20). The brothers' crime could not have been caused by God, and yet it was intended by God to bring about his foreseen end. Of this situation open theism can furnish no account. By contrast, Molinism claims that Joseph's capture and sale into slavery were strongly actualized by the brothers (who freely chose to do these things against God's will) but weakly actualized by God (who freely chose to create a world where the brothers would commit these transgressions so that he could work them for good).[23]

We shall now explore the second factor that has led to the resurgence of Molinism, namely, its vast explanatory power and scope to solve a host of pressing theological conundrums. To do this, we will analyze just a few of the many significant issues on which contemporary thinkers have made great and arguably decisive strides through the application of Molinism.

---

23. Ibid., 58.

BIBLICAL INERRANCY

Molina's doctrine of middle knowledge has been utilized by Craig in providing a logically consistent and philosophically persuasive defense of biblical inerrancy.[24] Although denied by some in modern times,[25] throughout church history a doctrine of inerrancy persisted as the backbone of scriptural interpretation, as demonstrable by examining a representative sample of the primary sources.[26] This classic doctrine of inerrancy stipulates that for each pericope within every document of the scriptural canon, when we first take into consideration that pericope's original literary genre and the rules for what does and does not constitute an error in that genre, the pericope contains no errors. As a result, the Bible contains no errors in what it means to teach or affirm. Inerrancy is a logically necessary corollary of the doctrine of Scripture's plenary, verbal, and confluent inspiration by God. Plenary inspiration means that the full breadth and depth of Scripture is inspired, such that inspiration is complete in its extent. In other words, not simply the doctrinal parts or the prophetic parts of the Bible are inspired, but all parts of the Bible are inspired, including its ostensible trivialities. Verbal inspiration claims that it is not simply the concepts of Scripture or the meaning of its sentences that are inspired, but that the exact words of Scripture in the original autographs are God-breathed. This is why a single word can make a theological difference in various cases where New Testament figures are quoting passages of the Old Testament (e.g., Mark 12:26; Gal. 3:16). Confluent inspiration holds that the Bible is fully the work of its human authors and fully the work of God. Given that God cannot err, and given that Scripture is plenarily, verbally, and confluently inspired, it follows inescapably that Scripture is inerrant. So we now come to the pressing question: *How* is it that the Bible can be plenary, verbal, and confluent in its inspiration?

To maintain all three factors, one needs to hold to a supervision theory of inspiration. In other words, God superintended the composition of Scripture by sovereignly guiding its human authors so that they would write God's

---

24. William Lane Craig, "'Men Moved by the Holy Spirit Spoke from God' (2 Peter 1:21): A Middle Knowledge Perspective on Divine Inspiration," *Philosophia Christi*, new ser. 1 (1999): 68–82.

25. Jack B. Rogers and Donald K. McKim, *The Authority and Interpretation of the Bible: An Historical Approach* (San Francisco: HarperCollins, 1980), 89–176.

26. As done by John D. Woodbridge, *Biblical Authority: A Critique of the Rogers/McKim Proposal* (Grand Rapids: Zondervan, 1982), 31–140.

254 Luis de Molina

Word to us. The human authors would use their own words, languages, styles, and emotions, such that the Bible would be a genuinely human writing. However, this composition would be so superintended or supervised by the Holy Spirit that what the human authors wrote would be the words of God. On the supervision theory, it is not surprising that there would be trivialities (*levicula*), like Paul's greeting of various persons in Romans 16:3–16. For God did not dictate to Paul to greet these persons. Instead, in the supervising process, God knew that Paul would freely send these greetings, these greetings are acceptable to God, and hence these greetings are part of God's Word. But the question still remains of *how* the Holy Spirit can supervise the composition of Scripture so that the human authors freely write what God wants them to write. This question is one to which many Catholic, Lutheran, and Reformed theologians alike have confessed they have no answer; one must simply affirm and live with the mystery of the supervision theory.[27]

Craig observes that if God has middle knowledge, then God knows which persons would freely write certain compositions if they were in various sets of circumstances. This is all God needs to know in order to produce a plenarily, verbally, and confluently inspired Bible. For God middle-knows which feasible worlds are made up of persons and circumstances that would freely result in the human production of God's own Word. So by opting to create this world with those persons and those circumstances, God guarantees that they will write what God wants them to write without in any way impinging on their free choice. Thus, if God wanted to produce the Pauline epistles, all God needs to do is create the world in which Paul of Tarsus, along with all the pertinent circumstances, freely writes his epistles. These circumstances included not only Paul's background, personality, environment, idiosyncrasies, and the like, but also any promptings or gifts of the Holy Spirit to which God middle-knew Paul would freely respond. The Pauline epistles are genuinely the work of Paul, who freely chose their words and crafted their styles. Their arguments and reasoning represent the reflections of Paul's own mind, as God did not dictate the premises to him. Nor did God dictate *levicula* like the interjection of Paul's amanuensis Tertius (Rom. 16:22). Paul's complete

---

27. For representative examples from these three traditions, see John Henry Newman, *Lectures on the Scripture Proofs of the Doctrines of the Church*, Tracts for the Times 85 (London: Rivington, 1838), 30; Robert D. Preuss, *The Theology of Post-Reformation Lutheranism*, 2 vols. (St. Louis: Concordia, 1970), 1:290–91; Benjamin B. Warfield, *Calvin and Calvinism* (Oxford: Oxford University Press, 1931), 62.

range of emotions (Gal. 5:12), memory lapses (1 Cor. 1:14–16), and personal asides (Gal. 6:11) are genuine results of human consciousness. Perhaps some elements of Paul's epistles are matters of indifference to God, such that maybe it would not have mattered to God whether Paul told Timothy to bring the cloak that he left with Carpus at Troas (2 Tim. 4:13). Maybe God would have been just as pleased if Paul had worded some things differently. Regardless, we do know that the Pauline epistles as they stand are God-breathed and therefore inerrant.[28] What goes for the Pauline epistles also goes for all the other books of the Bible, such that the Bible is confluent in the truest sense. Middle knowledge therefore explains how the Bible can be the inerrant word of God and the freely chosen word of human beings.[29]

THE RELATIONSHIP BETWEEN CHRISTIANITY AND OTHER WORLD RELIGIONS

Arguably the most burning issue facing Christianity today is the challenge of religious pluralism. At its most basic level, the challenge may be posed by the following series of questions. Can persons in non-Christian religious traditions find salvation? If so, how can their salvation be compatible with the New Testament teaching that salvation is to be found in Christ alone (John 14:6; Acts 4:12)? If not, how can their damnation be compatible with the fairness, love, and universal salvific will of God, also attested in Scripture (Ezek. 18:23, 30–32; 33:11; Acts 10:34; Rom. 2:11; 1 Tim. 2:4; 2 Peter 3:9; 1 John 4:8, 16)? From chapter 7 we recall that Molina believed that explicit knowledge of the facts concerning Jesus' life, death, and resurrection were not necessary for a person to attain salvation. However, the person and work of Christ were necessary for a person to attain salvation. Molina held, based on Romans 2:7, that persons living at any time, in any culture, and—by clear implication— in any religion could be saved by placing faith in the one God witnessed in creation and following the natural law written on their hearts. By so committing their lives to God, such persons would implicitly commit their lives to Christ, the second person of that Godhead and find salvation in exactly the

---

28. Craig, "'Men Moved by the Holy Spirit,'" 70–72.
29. Without awareness of the doctrine of middle knowledge, Warfield practically endorses a middle knowledge perspective on biblical inerrancy in "The Biblical Idea of Inspiration," in *The Inspiration and Authority of the Bible*, ed. Samuel G. Craig (Philadelphia: Presbyterian & Reformed, 1970), 154–55.

same manner as did believers in the Old Testament, both inside and outside Israel. Although not spelled out in any detail, it may safely be gleaned from Molina's statements on the issue that such implicit Christians would need to reject whatever teachings in their religions were contrary to monotheism and the natural law. Hence Molina asserted that contemporaneous indigenous Africans and Indians who, despite their polytheistic or animistic religious backgrounds, believed in the one true God and refused to indulge the moral dissipation of their cultures were fellow sisters and brothers in Christ.[30] We may summarize Molina's answer to the basic problem of pluralism by stating that persons can be saved *in* other world religions but not *through* other world religions; they may be saved only *through* Christ. For instance, a sixteenth-century Nigerian who practiced Yoruba religion cannot be saved by following Yoruba religion. But, within the context of Yoruba religion, he could be saved by properly responding to God's general revelation in nature and conscience, thus implicitly coming to Christ. This response would entail his rejecting Yoruba tenets inconsistent with monotheism and the natural law, although he may well keep Yoruba tenets consistent with monotheism and the natural law.

Keeping with this Molinist backdrop, Craig has significantly advanced the conversation by applying the doctrine of middle knowledge to the deepest level of the pluralistic challenge. For the contemporary pluralist may grant Molina's accessibilism-inclusivism and still find wanting the prospect of Christianity's unique truth, on the grounds that simply supplying all persons with the authentic possibility of salvation through general revelation is not enough for a maximally great being to do. This is because there may be some people in the actual world who do not respond to God's general revelation and so are lost but who would have responded to God's special revelation (i.e., the Christian gospel) if only they had heard it. In that case, the damnation of such persons seems to be the result of bad luck; they just happened to be born at a time and place where the gospel was unavailable to them. But it seems incompatible with the existence of an all-loving and all-just God that people's salvation or damnation would be the result of historical and geographical accident. To this objection, Craig replies that God, through his

---

30. Ludovici Molina, *De justitia et jure*, 5 vols. (Cologne: Marci-Michaelis Bousquet, 1733), 5.65.3; Diego Alonso-Lasheras, *Luis de Molina's De Iustitia et Iure: Justice as Virtue in an Economic Context*, Studies in the History of Christian Traditions 152 (Leiden: Brill, 2011), 71.

middle knowledge, has so providentially ordered the world that all persons in the actual world who never hear the gospel and are lost would not have received salvation even if they had heard the gospel.[31] God is simply too good to allow anyone to be in the situation imagined by the religious pluralist; God chooses to actualize a world where he ensures that everyone whom he middle-knows would not respond to general revelation but would respond to special revelation does in fact receive special revelation. Thus no one is lost as a result of historical or geographical accident.[32]

At this point, the pluralist may counter by posing two further queries. First, why would God create the actual world when, given the truth of Christian theism, he knew that so many people would freely reject him and be lost? Second, why didn't God create a different world in which every person is freely saved? This wouldn't be a world of puppets or marionettes, but one where all persons voluntarily avail themselves of the possibility to embrace God's saving grace. Regarding the first query, Craig observes that God, out of sheer kindness, wanted to share his love and fellowship with created persons. As an all-loving being, God desires the salvation of all persons and furnishes each one with sufficient grace for salvation. Although God middle-knew that many would freely reject his grace and be lost, God also middle-knew that many others would freely embrace his grace and be saved. Indeed, many of the lost may receive far greater gifts of prevenient grace than many of the saved, but the former freely choose to reject it. The happiness and blessedness of those who freely receive God's love should not be obviated by persons who would freely spurn God, rebuffing his every effort to save them. Such persons should not be allowed to hold a veto power, as it were, over which worlds God is free to create. However, God does want to maximize the number of people who are saved and minimize the number of people who are lost. Thus Craig proposes that God has actualized a world with an optimal balance between belief and unbelief, creating no more of the lost than is necessary to achieve the maximum number of the saved.[33] This solution does not imply that only

---

31. William Lane Craig, "Politically Incorrect Salvation," in *Christian Apologetics in the Postmodern World,* ed. Timothy R. Phillips and Dennis Okholm (Downers Grove, IL: InterVarsity, 1995), 82–84; idem, "'No Other Name,'" 184–85.

32. This does not stand at odds with Molina's rejection of transworld damnation. It simply countenances a question that Molina never raised, namely, "What about persons who fail to respond to general revelation but who would have responded to special revelation if presented to them?"

258 *Luis de Molina*

one feasible world obtains to the optimal balance, as there is likely an infinite spectrum of feasible worlds obtaining to this balance.[34]

Regarding the second query, Craig argues that while worlds in which every person is freely saved are indeed logically possible worlds and so known to God in his natural knowledge, God may well know in his middle knowledge that such worlds are not feasible worlds and hence not available for him to create in view of human freedom. Given God's universal salvific will, if a world of universal salvation were feasible, God would have created it, barring any overriding deficiencies that might make such a world less preferable than worlds like the actual world. In other words, suppose there existed feasible worlds containing universal salvation but that all such worlds were extraordinarily underpopulated, containing only a handful of people. Clearly God's omnibenevolence does not compel him to choose one of these worlds over a world where the maximum number of persons finds salvation but where, in view of that maximum, a minimum of intransigent persons spurn God's every effort to save them.[35] In sum, God middle-knows that worlds of universal salvation are either infeasible worlds or feasible worlds containing other, overriding deficiencies that are therefore less preferable than worlds obtaining to the optimal balance of saved versus lost.

Accordingly, the foregoing application of Molinism shows that no logical contradiction exists between the statements "God is all-powerful and

---

33. Craig, "'No Other Name,'" 178–84.

34. I have argued elsewhere that this proposal is compatible with God sovereignly choosing, for each person P in the actual world, for P to be saved or for P to be lost. God carries out his individual predestination by narrowing down our infinite spectrum of feasible worlds to a lower-order infinite spectrum in which every person A meets one of two conditions. First, if A is lost in any world where A only receives general revelation, then A is also lost in every world where A receives special revelation without first appropriating salvation through general revelation; hence the only world or worlds in which A is saved entail A appropriating salvation through general revelation either without or before hearing the gospel in the future. Second, if A is saved in any world only after receiving special revelation, then A is also saved in every world where A only receives general revelation; hence the only world or worlds in which A is lost entail A rejecting salvation through both general and special revelation. Thus for any A, A's election or reprobation can only occur in what we may denominate "salvifically comparable worlds," where each A potentially freely saved only after hearing the gospel would only be freely lost in other worlds where A heard the gospel, and each A potentially freely lost upon never hearing the gospel would only be freely saved in other worlds where, at the moment of regeneration, A would not have heard the gospel. By selecting one of these worlds to be actual, such that P is a subset of A, God decides whether each actual person is freely saved or freely lost while ensuring that no one who is freely lost would have been freely saved if only that person had heard the gospel. For a full account, see Kirk R. MacGregor, *A Molinist-Anabaptist Systematic Theology* (Lanham, MD: University Press of America, 2007), 79–84.

35. Craig, "'No Other Name,'" 186–88.

all-loving" and "Some people never hear the Christian gospel and are lost." On top of that, it shows exactly how these two statements are simultaneously true: God has used his middle knowledge to craft a world containing an optimal balance between saved and lost, where those who fail to accept general revelation and do not hear the gospel (thus being lost) would not have accepted the gospel even if they had heard it.

Here the pluralist could try one last strategy, arguing that this scenario, though possible, is highly improbable. For people, by and large, appear to adopt the religion of the culture in which they were raised. But in that case, the pluralist could claim that if many of those who never hear the gospel had been raised in a Christian culture, they would have believed the gospel and, by Christian lights, been saved. Craig points out that the Molinist can respond by conceding that it would indeed be fantastically improbable that by chance alone it simply turns out that all who never hear the gospel and are lost would not have believed the gospel even if they had heard it. But that is not the Molinist scenario. The scenario is that a God endowed with middle knowledge has providentially ordered the world in the manner described. Such a world would not outwardly appear any different from a world in which the circumstances of a person's birth are a matter of chance. The Molinist can agree that persons generally embrace the religion of their cultures and that if many of those born into non-Christian cultures had been born in a Christian society instead, they would have become nominally or culturally Christian. However, that says nothing about whether they would have been saved, which depends on personally committing one's life to Jesus as Lord and Savior. It is a simple empirical fact that many nominal or cultural Christians have never committed their lives to Jesus, as evidenced by their contrary beliefs and actions (Matt. 7:21 – 23). So there is no way for us to predict accurately by examining a person whether and under what circumstances that person would commit one's life to Jesus. Because a world providentially ordered by God would appear externally identical to a world where one's birth is a matter of historical and geographical accident, the pluralist cannot justifiably deem the Molinist scenario improbable.[36] Therefore the presence of other world religions does not undercut the Christian message of salvation through Jesus alone.

---

36. William Lane Craig, *On Guard: Defending Your Faith with Reason and Precision* (Colorado Springs: Cook, 2010), 281 – 82.

THE PROBLEM OF EVIL

The problem of evil may be viewed as a generalization of the same problem arising from persons' implicitly or explicitly rejecting Christ, namely, the soteriological problem of evil. As a result, Molinism has been brought to bear on the problem of evil in similar ways as it has on the problem of those who reject Christ. In contemporary philosophy of religion, the evidential or probabilistic argument from evil remains the most potent argument against the existence of God. This argument deals specifically with gratuitous evil (i.e., pointless or morally unnecessary evil), positing the improbability of its coexistence with God. The argument runs as follows:

1. Probably, if God exists, then gratuitous evil does not exist.
2. Probably, gratuitous evil exists.
3. Therefore, probably, God does not exist.

In 1974 Plantinga, in his rediscovery of middle knowledge, essentially argued that a world with less gratuitous evil than the actual world is not feasible for God to create. God, via his middle knowledge, knows there is no feasible world of libertarian creatures who freely commit less gratuitous evil than the actual world. Libertarian freedom entails that its holders possess not only the unconstrained ability to choose anything on the moral spectrum from the greatest goods to the worst evils but also the unimpeded power to actualize their choices.[37] By choosing to create creatures with libertarian freedom, God voluntarily places himself under the logical constraint of being unable to stop those creatures either from choosing anything on the moral spectrum or from carrying out those choices. Hence not even an omnipotent being can create a world of libertarian creatures with less gratuitous evil than a world with the same amount of gratuitous evil as the actual world. This observation does not detract from divine sovereignty, as there is every reason to believe that such equally good feasible worlds form an infinite spectrum from which an all-good God chooses. Accordingly, Plantinga dubbed this

---

37. In Plantinga's words, "If a person is free with respect to a given action, then he is free to perform that action and free to refrain from performing it; no antecedent conditions and/or causal laws determine that he will perform the action, or that he won't. It is within his power ... to take or perform the action and within his power to refrain from it" (*God, Freedom, and Evil*, 29).

solution the "free will defense."[38] Given this defense, premise 1 in the evidential argument from evil is false, making the argument unsound.

The free will defense depends for its success on the reduction of all gratuitous evil in the world to moral evil, namely, evil caused by libertarian creatures. However, it has historically been recognized that much of the evil in the world is natural evil, brought by earthquakes, tornadoes, sickness, disease, and so forth. To account for natural evil, Plantinga suggested that natural evil may be caused by Satan or lesser demons, all of whom are fallen angels with libertarian freedom who rebelled against God before the creation of humanity and have been wreaking havoc ever since.[39] But since this possibility strikes most theists and nontheists alike as extraordinarily implausible, it appears that premise 1 in the evidential argument from evil still stands with respect to gratuitous natural evil. However, it seems that Plantinga has indeed dissolved the problem of gratuitous moral evil.

In 2012 I offered a new Molinist line of defense that aims to demonstrate the coexistence of God and gratuitous natural evil.[40] If successful, this line of defense, in conjunction with Plantinga's free will defense, completely demolishes premise 1 in the evidential argument from evil and so defeats the problem of evil in its strongest form. My work also bolsters the plausibility of the free will defense by explaining why God rarely intervenes immediately after creaturely (and natural) evils are committed so as to blunt their force.

My proposed demonstration of the coexistence of God and gratuitous natural evil begins by defining perfection as completeness or wholeness in each and every respect. It then argues that perfection is an essential attribute of God that may only reside intrinsically in God as Necessary Being. In each and every respect, contingent being depends on Necessary Being for its existence and therefore lacks intrinsic completeness and wholeness. Thus in each and every respect, contingent being is finite and limited. Hence it is logically impossible for God to create anything that is intrinsically perfect, for the simple reason that it constitutes contingent being that is in every respect ontologically dependent on Necessary Being. Since Augustine, Christian theologians have overwhelmingly held that evil is not an independently

38. Ibid., 29, 44–57.
39. Ibid., 57–59.
40. Kirk R. MacGregor, "The Existence and Irrelevance of Gratuitous Evil," *Philosophia Christi* 14, no. 1 (2012): 165–80.

existing thing but rather a lack, limitation, or incompleteness in something that is good, namely, an absence of the complete limitless fulfillment that equals perfection. It then follows deductively that evil is necessary to the creation, both to the natural order and to the human constitution, as God obviously cannot create anything with an intrinsic attribute exclusively proper to the divine nature. So it is logically impossible for God to create a world without natural evil; if God chose to create anything at all, natural evil would necessarily come into existence, not because God created or caused it, but because whatever God created would not be God. Notice that all such evils are, in and of themselves, gratuitous; their only reason for existence is the logically unavoidable lack of ontological necessity exhibited by created entities. The only way that any created entity could display perfection is nonessentially, that is, God supernaturally acting to overwhelm or "make up for" its resident imperfections; it could not display perfection in and of itself.[41] Therefore gratuitous natural evil is ontologically inescapable for contingent being every bit as much as perfection is essential to Necessary Being. Gratuitous natural evil is therefore logically necessary to the universe, and God simply has to put up with it if he chooses to create a universe at all.[42]

The skeptic of God's existence could retort that although gratuitous natural evil is logically necessary to the universe considered in and of itself, an all-good God would always supernaturally prevent that gratuitous natural evil from actually occurring. In other words, an omnibenevolent God would always overwhelm the resident imperfections in the created order in general and the human constitution in particular so that all things operated perfectly. Such constant overwhelming of resident imperfections would entail that God be definitively present in the universe (that is, exhibiting the qualitatively highest mode of his presence where he fully displays his glory) rather than repletively present in the universe (that is, exhibiting a qualitatively lower mode of presence where he is causally active and knows what is happening

---

41. Some may find my account incompatible with the Genesis creation narrative, while I do not perceive any incompatibility. While I will not here argue for either a metaphorical or historicist interpretation of the narrative, I believe it is fundamentally an instance of theological poetry that accurately recounts historical truths. So I think it would be pushing the Genesis creation narrative too far to say that it, contra modern scientific recountings of earth history, precludes any natural evil before the fall. Genesis 1:31 tells us that the world was "very good," not that it contained zero instances of natural evil or was perfect.

42. MacGregor, "Existence and Irrelevance of Gratuitous Evil," 173–74.

at, but does not fully display his glory at, each time-space location). If God were now definitively present in the universe, this immediate presence would make up for the universe's existent defects and cause the universe to reflect his perfection, just as the sun makes up for the nonluminous nature of the various objects on which it shines and causes them to reflect its light.

We observe that the skeptic's retort is based on the presupposition that God's overriding desire (that is, what an all-good God would want most) is to prevent gratuitous natural evil in the world. But if God had some other overriding desire, then the skeptic's retort would be evacuated of any substance. Indeed, it seems that God has such an overriding desire, namely, people's coming freely to commit their lives to him. At this juncture I argue, in concert with Molina, that libertarian human freedom is only possible if God creates the universe at a metaphysical and epistemic distance, or at arm's length, such that God is not definitively present but repletively present in it.[43] For if, currently, God were definitively present in the universe, overwhelming all its resident imperfections, the loveliness and majesty of God's immediate presence would also infallibly prevent people from sinning and infallibly draw them to live out the desires of the Holy Spirit. This state of affairs believers will experience in the new heaven and new earth.[44] But in order to guarantee that the communion of saints will be comprised of those who, without compulsion, embrace him, God is not present in the universe to such a degree that libertarian freedom is obviated. Rather, only after people make uncoerced premortem decisions to accept or reject his love does God permanently seal persons in those decisions at the general resurrection. Hence God is now repletively present in the universe, which presence allows the existence of libertarian freedom but does not preclude gratuitous natural evil. Consequently, gratuitous natural evil can only be eliminated at the expense of libertarian human freedom.[45]

---

43. Ludovici Molina, *Commentaria in primam divi Thomae partem* (Venice, 1602), 52.1.1.2.

44. This account works equally well on a metaphorical or a historicist interpretation of Genesis 2–3. On a metaphorical reading, the fall is symbolic for the inherent moral and natural defects in contingent being over against Necessary Being (Paul Tillich, *Systematic Theology*, 3 vols. [Chicago: University of Chicago Press, 1963]: 1:252–54). On a historicist reading, God miraculously prevented the display of the inherent defects in the natural order but without going so far as to definitively reveal himself until the primal human couple freely chose that they did not even want God to exhibit that much involvement in the world. When God respected their decision by allowing the natural order to run its course, "the creation was subjected to frustration ... its bondage to decay ... by the will of the one [Adam] who subjected it" (Rom. 8:20–21).

45. MacGregor, "Existence and Irrelevance of Gratuitous Evil," 176–77.

Given the impossibility of God's consistently preventing gratuitous natural and moral evils, one could ask why God sometimes though rarely intervenes thereafter to remedy them. Here a word about Christian eschatology is in order. The biblical worldview stipulates that at the end of the age, there will come the "Day of Yahweh" in which the souls of all those in Paradise will be reinfused into their resurrected bodies (John 5:24–30) to live forever with God in the transfigured physical universe or new heaven and new earth (Rev. 21:1–22:6). Although the new heaven and new earth will not be intrinsically perfect, God's definitive presence will overwhelm its existent limitations and so automatically prevent the display of its defects. In the new heaven and new earth, moreover, the physical bodies of the resurrected saints, although inherently defective, will have those defects overridden by virtue of God's definitive presence. However, we know that often God graciously provides "foretastes" of the new heaven and new earth by responding to evils before the Day of Yahweh, though not via such an overwhelming display of his glory that human free will is abnegated. Examples would include all miraculous and nonmiraculous answers to prayer, all biblical miracles, and all other strongly actualized divine events.

So the real question is not, "*Will* God respond to each evil"—the answer is an unambiguous yes—but rather, "*When* will God respond to each evil?" Will he respond at the end of the age, as with most evils, or will he give a "foretaste" of the transfigured universe by responding immediately after the evil transpires or at some later point in human history? In addition, one could ask why God responds when he does; for example, why did God choose to heal the Johannine paralytic thirty-eight years after he became an invalid (John 5:1–15) rather than healing him when he first came to the pool of Bethesda or waiting until the general resurrection to restore his body? Why did God prevent the lions from eating Daniel (Dan. 6:16–24) but not liberate John the Baptist from prison before his beheading (Mark 6:17–28)? In view of God's middle knowledge, the answer to all such queries is simple: God chooses to respond to each evil at the point when it would best contribute to achieving an optimal balance between saved and lost, that is, to producing a world containing no more of the lost than necessary to achieve the maximal number of the saved. Our solution is implied by the healing of the paralytic, as it seems apparent that Jesus' specifically healing the man in Jerusalem led many people to place their trust in him who would not have done so had the miracle been performed elsewhere.[46] Moreover, our solution is directly identified by Jesus himself as the reason he did not attend to Lazarus immediately upon the latter's death but waited four days before revivifying him: "Lazarus is dead, and for your sake I am glad I was not there, so that you may believe. But let us go to him" (John 11:14–15; cf. 11:41–46).[47] By furnishing a reasonable model of why God responds to evil when he does (i.e., in order to bring about the greatest good of maximal human salvation), we buttress the free will defense from those who object that God, although unable to stop gratuitous moral evil from occurring, ought to intervene immediately after it happens to undo its effects.

CREATION, EVOLUTION, AND QUANTUM INDETERMINACY

The hypothesis that God created the world is often indicted for the problem of creaturely flaws, or undesirable features in creatures that were allegedly designed. The biologist Kenneth Miller articulates the problem quite forcefully:

> Almost by definition, an intelligent designer would have to be a pretty sharp fellow.... Biologists can have great fun with that notion. Living organisms, ourselves included, are loaded with what Stephen Jay Gould once called "the senseless signs of history." ... To adopt the explanation of design, we are forced to attribute a host of flaws and imperfections to the designer. Our appendix, for example, seems to serve only to make us sick; our feet are poorly constructed to take the full force of walking and running; and even our eyes are prone to optical errors and lose their ability for close focus as we age.... We would also have to attribute every plague, pestilence, and parasite to the intentional actions of our master designer.... Finally, whatever one's views of such a designer's motivation, there is one conclusion that drops cleanly out of the data. He was incompetent.[48]

John Laing points out that in order to answer the problem, the believer in divine creation must show the possibility that the intelligent designer could not have developed creatures with the complexity they possess without the

---

46. This observation is reinforced by the miracle's identification as a *sēmeion*, or special faith-engendering sign, by the evangelist.

47. MacGregor, "Existence and Irrelevance of Gratuitous Evil," 177–78.

48. Kenneth R. Miller, *Finding Darwin's God* (New York: Perennial, 1999), 100–102.

flaws they possess. Middle knowledge may be used to establish this possibility. We recall at this juncture that middle knowledge comprises God's knowledge of all things that would happen in every possible set of circumstances. Hence middle knowledge includes what Laing dubs counterfactuals of genetic mutation, namely, propositions of the form "If situation S were to prevail, then random genetic mutation M would occur" and "If situation S were not to prevail, then random genetic mutation M would not occur."[49] The believer in divine creation—whether a young earth creationist, a progressive creationist, or an evolutionary creationist—can give an account of creation using, in varying degrees, the same mechanisms that the naturalist does, namely, random genetic mutation. Young earth and progressive creationists will appeal to random genetic mutation only within species (i.e., microevolution), while evolutionary creationists will also appeal to random genetic mutation between species (i.e., macroevolution). But the believer in divine creation will insist that these mutations fall under the purview of an intelligent designer.

As we saw in our discussion of natural evil, we may hold that various defects are ontologically necessary to the creation, as perfection is an incommunicable attribute of God. So suppose God middle-knows that S is necessary for M to occur. In other words, God knows that both of the following counterfactuals of genetic mutations are true: if S were to prevail, then M would occur; and if S were not to prevail, then M would not occur. Moreover, suppose S entails undesirable mutations or the existence of useless organs for some creature C but that M instantiates a level of complexity that is beneficial to C. In this case, if God wants M to occur, God would have to actualize S, either strongly or weakly. Therefore the flaws in any creature C prove in no way incommensurate with God's direct or indirect creation of C, such that the problem of creaturely flaws is dissolved.[50]

In diametric contrast to the popular dichotomy between creation and macroevolution, Del Ratzsch has employed middle knowledge to illustrate how God can sovereignly create all things through the macroevolutionary process, with all its randomness. This randomness is of two types: teleological and nomic. Teleological randomness means that macroevolution is comprised of

---

49. John D. Laing, "Intelligent Design, Middle Knowledge, and the Problem of Creaturely Flaws," paper presented at the Middle Knowledge/Molinism Consultation of the 64th Annual Meeting of the Evangelical Theological Society, November 14, 2012, 16–17.

50. Ibid., 18–19.

events that are not determined by any future state, aim, or goal. Thus whether or not an absolutely essential variation occurs in an organism is completely independent of the needs, desires, or prospects of that organism. Nomic randomness stems from the governance of every macroevolutionary process by laws that are purely and ultimately stochastic, or "driven fundamentally by utterly random, chance events."[51] Combining these two sorts of randomness, macroevolutionary events are random not merely in the sense that they occur irrespective of the good or harm of the respective organisms on which they operate but also in the sense that they are sparked by indeterminate and spontaneous quantum phenomena. Now if God chose to create simply any universe where a teleologically and nomically random evolutionary process would take place, it is vastly more probable that a life-prohibiting sequence of events rather than a life-permitting sequence of events would naturally ensue. For example, the physicists John Barrow and Frank Tipler have highlighted ten steps necessary to the course of human evolution.[52] Each of these, they have calculated, is so improbable that before it could have occurred by chance alone, the sun would have ceased to be a main sequence star and would have incinerated the earth. Consequently, the odds for the evolution of the human genome are on the order of 1 chance out of 4 to the power of 360 times 110,000, a number which is incomprehensibly low.[53] Thus Barrow and Tipler tellingly remark that "there has developed a general consensus among evolutionists that the evolution of intelligent life ... is so improbable that is unlikely to have occurred on any other planet in the entire visible universe."[54]

But since God, in his middle knowledge, knows all counterfactuals concerning nature, God knows what would randomly ensue in a world if he were to set up any given primordial initial conditions and laws. Assuming the standard indeterministic interpretation of quantum mechanics (known as the Copenhagen interpretation), the fabric of the world contains small

---

51. Del Ratzsch, "Design, Chance and Theistic Evolution," in *Mere Creation*, ed. William Dembski (Downers Grove, IL: InterVarsity, 1998), 303.

52. These steps are the development of the DNA-based genetic code, the development of aerobic respiration, the development of glucose fermentation, the origin of photosynthesis, the origin of mitochondria in the cells, the formation of the centriole/kinetosome/undulipodia complex necessary to eukaryotic reproduction and nerve cells, the development of the eye, the development of the inner skeleton, the development of chordates, and the evolution of *Homo sapiens* in the chordate lineage (John D. Barrow and Frank J. Tipler, *The Anthropic Cosmological Principle* [Oxford: Clarendon, 1986], 561–64).

53. Ibid., 565.

54. Ibid., 133.

quantum gaps, in which energy quanta randomly assume only one of their possible values. Thus God knows what we may style counterfactuals of quantum indeterminacy. Such counterfactuals, I have argued, include but are not limited to the following five categories:

1. What spontaneous quantum phenomenon would indeterminately occur under any possible set of circumstances;

2. For each quantum phenomenon, what macroevolutionary event (*e.g.*, random genetic mutation), if any, that phenomenon would cause;

3. How each macroevolutionary event would affect the organism on which it operates;

4. How each macroevolutionary event would randomly cluster with other quantumly generated macroevolutionary events;

5. How each cluster of macroevolutionary events would affect the organism(s) on which it operates.[55]

With this in mind, suppose that God were to create a world by setting up some set of primordial initial conditions and establishing a set of laws to govern developments springing from those conditions. As Ratzsch observes, "If some of those laws involve irreducible randomness, then there will be no one inevitable and law-driven outcome. But it may still be true that given the way that all the purely random, uncaused quantum events would just happen to go, an evolutionary process resulting in human beings would in fact (and completely depending on those random events) occur."[56] Thus the following counterfactual may well be true: "If God were to set up the requisite primordial initial conditions and laws, the evolution of human beings by a path essentially incorporating teleologically and nomically random events would indeterministically ensue." Given God's knowledge of the aforementioned five categories of counterfactuals of quantum indeterminacy, God would discern precisely what initial conditions and laws would, against all the odds, randomly inaugurate an extraordinarily lengthy chain of further indeterministic, random events producing life in all its complexity and culminating in the

55. Kirk R. MacGregor, "The Impossibility of Evolution apart from a God with Middle Knowledge," paper presented at the Middle Knowledge/Molinism Consultation of the 64th Annual Meeting of the Evangelical Theological Society, 14 November 2012, 4.

56. Ratzsch, "Design, Chance and Theistic Evolution," 304.

biological evolution of humans. By directly creating these initial conditions and laws, God would indirectly accomplish the desired ends of fashioning the various kinds of organisms up to and including human beings, incorporating the middle-known results of utterly indeterminate, random processes. This accomplishment would be deliberate and intentional and yet entail no direct supernatural intervention at any point throughout the evolutionary chain.[57] In this way, middle knowledge serves to reconcile God's creation of the world with the biological evolution of all life forms.[58]

CONCLUDING REFLECTIONS

Debates over the truth of Molinism and the validity of Molinism's applications rage in the philosophical and theological community today more than at any time in the past four centuries. In the judgment of Molinism's many defenders (including myself), Molina formulated a logically consistent and highly compelling account of divine omniscience that successfully reconciles full-blown divine sovereignty and full-blown human freedom. To date, it is the only account proposed that enjoys this significant theological benefit. Molinism also enjoys an advantage from the perspective of scriptural fidelity, for it enables one to embrace the grammatico-historical exegesis of all the biblical texts regarding the matters on which it touches. Hence on Molinism (1) passages teaching God's predestination of individuals, (2) passages teaching God's all-encompassing providence, (3) passages teaching genuine human freedom, and (4) passages teaching God's universal salvific will may all be simultaneously taken at face value. Such cannot be said for Calvinists or Arminians who deny middle knowledge. Apart from a belief in middle knowledge, the Calvinist can accept 1 and 2 at face value but will be forced to deny the plain meaning of 3 and 4, resorting instead to theologically driven yet grammatico-historically implausible alternative readings of 3 and 4. Matters are exactly flipped when it comes to the Arminian sans middle knowledge, who can accept 3 and 4 at face value but will be forced to deny the plain

---

57. Ibid., 304, 307.

58. Of course, whether one avails oneself of this reconciliation will depend on one's theory of biological origins. A theistic evolutionist would appropriate this reconciliation, while a young earth or progressive creationist could only go so far as admitting that while this reconciliation is logically possible, it does not represent what actually happened in the history of biology.

meaning of 1 and 2. Like the non-middle-knowledge Calvinist with 3 and 4, the non-middle-knowledge Arminian must resort to theologically driven yet grammatico-historically implausible alternative readings of 1 and 2. To put it baldly, if a person wants to accept simultaneously the face value reading of Deuteronomy 30:11–20; Romans 9:11–24; Ephesians 1:11; and 1 Timothy 2:3–4, it appears that person must subscribe to middle knowledge.

Christian philosophers and theologians, especially evangelicals who place great stock in faithfulness to the inerrant Word of God, have fruitfully applied Molinism to a panoply of current philosophical, theological, and scientific issues.[59] Besides those discussed in this chapter, these issues include Christology,[60] the perseverance of the saints,[61] missionary evangelism,[62] nonmiraculous special providence,[63] prophecy,[64] petitionary prayer,[65] original sin,[66] and the demographics of theistic belief.[67] Due to the boundless potential of Molinism successfully to handle future issues (especially vexing ones) in philosophically cogent, theologically enriching, and biblically consistent ways, it is safe to assign Molinism permanent and prominent seats at the tables of philosophy and theology. Hence, in the philosophical and theological academies, the legacy of Molina is now being carried out and will continue to be carried out in far greater ways than Molina ever could have imagined. It seems that Molina has finally assumed his rightful place among the greatest philosophical theologians and ethicists in the history of Christianity. Accordingly, no future history of the Christian tradition, history of Christian thought, history of the Reformation, philosophical theology, or systematic theology can legitimately afford to ignore Molina and his influence.

---

59. Ken Perszyk, "Introduction," in *Molinism: The Contemporary Debate*, ed. Ken Perszyk (Oxford: Oxford University Press, 2011), 12.

60. Flint, "'A Death He Freely Accepted,'" 3–20.

61. William Lane Craig, "'Lest Anyone Should Fall': A Middle Knowledge Perspective on Perseverance and Apostolic Warnings," *International Journal for Philosophy of Religion* 29 (1991): 65–74.

62. William Lane Craig, "Should Peter Go to the Mission Field?" *Faith and Philosophy* 10 (1993): 261–65; idem, "Should Peter Get a New Philosophical Advisor?" *Philosophia Christi* 6 (2004): 273–78.

63. William Lane Craig, "Creation, Providence, and Miracles," in *Philosophy of Religion*, ed. Brian Davies (Washington, DC: Georgetown University Press, 1998), 136–62.

64. Thomas P. Flint, *Divine Providence: The Molinist Account* (Ithaca, NY: Cornell University Press, 1998), 197–211.

65. Ibid., 212–50.

66. Michael C. Rea, "The Metaphysics of Original Sin," in *Persons: Human and Divine*, ed. Peter van Inwagen and Dean Zimmerman (Oxford: Clarendon, 2007), 345–53.

67. Jason Marsh, "Do the Demographics of Theistic Belief Disconfirm Theism? A Reply to Maitzen," *Religious Studies* 44 (2008): 465–71.

Bibliography

PRIMARY SOURCES

Andrade, Alonso de. *Varones illustres de la Compañia de Jesús*. Madrid, 1666.

Aquinas, Thomas. *Summa contra Gentiles*. 4 vols. Trans. Anton C. Pegis. Notre Dame, IN: University of Notre Dame Press, 1933.

_____. *Summa Theologiae*. Trans. Fathers of the English Dominican Province. New York: Benziger Brothers, 1947.

Aristotle. *Categories and De interpretatione*. Trans. J. L. Ackrill. Clarendon Aristotle Series. Oxford: Oxford University Press, 1975.

_____. *De animina*. Trans. D. W. Hamlyn. Clarendon Aristotle Series. Oxford: Oxford University Press, 1993.

_____. *De generatione et corruptione*. Trans. C. J. F. Williams. Clarendon Aristotle Series. Oxford: Oxford University Press, 1982.

_____. *The Nicomachean Ethics*. Trans. Roger Crisp. Cambridge Texts in the History of Philosophy. Cambridge: Cambridge University Press, 2000.

Arminius, Jacob. *The Writings of Arminius*. 3 vols. Trans. James Nichols and W. R. Bagnall. Grand Rapids: Baker, 1956.

Augustine. *De Civitate Dei (The City of God)*. In *Nicene and Post-Nicene Fathers*, vol. 2, First Series. Trans. Marcus Dods and J. F. Shaw. Ed. Philip Schaff. Repr. ed., Peabody, MA: Hendrickson, 2004, 1–511.

_____. *De Correptione et Gratia* (On Rebuke and Grace). In *Nicene and Post-Nicene Fathers*, vol. 5, First Series. Trans. Peter Holmes, Robert Ernest Wallis, and Benjamin B. Warfield. Ed. Philip Schaff. Repr. ed., Peabody, MA: Hendrickson, 2004, 468–91.

_____. *De Gestis Pelagii* (On the Proceedings of Pelagius). *In Nicene and Post-Nicene Fathers*, vol. 5, First Series. Trans. Peter Holmes, Robert Ernest Wallis, and Benjamin B. Warfield. Ed. Philip Schaff. Repr. ed., Peabody, MA: Hendrickson, 2004, 178–212.

_____. *De Spiritu et Littera* (On the Spirit and the Letter). *In Nicene and Post-Nicene Fathers*, vol. 5, First Series. Trans. Peter Holmes, Robert Ernest Wallis, and Benjamin B. Warfield. Ed. Philip Schaff. Repr. ed., Peabody, MA: Hendrickson, 2004, 80–114.

Báñez, Domingo, Pedro Herrera, and Didacus Alvarez. *Apologetica fratrum prædicatorum in provinciâ Hispaniæ sacræ theologiæ professorum, adversus novas quasdam assertiones cujusdam doctoris Ludovici Molinæ nuncupati.* Madrid, 1595.

Bernard of Clairvaux. *De gradibus humilitatis et superbiae.* In *Sämtliche Werke* II. Innsbruck: Tyrolia-Verlag, 1990, 29–136.

_____. *De gratia et libero arbitrio.* In *Sämtliche Werke* I. Innsbruck: Tyrolia-Verlag, 1990, 153–256.

_____. *Sermones super Cantica Conticorum.* In *Sämtliche Werke* V–VI. Innsbruck: Tyrolia-Verlag, 1995.

Calvin, John. *Institutes of the Christian Religion.* Ed. John T. McNeill. Trans. Ford Lewis Battles. Philadelphia: Westminster, 1960.

The Canons and Decrees of the Council of Trent. Trans. H. J. Schroeder. Rockford, IL: TAN Books and Publishers, 1978.

Chrysostom, John. *De Lazaro Concio.* In *Patrologia Graeco-Latina.* 161 vols. Ed. Jacques-Paul Migne. Paris: Garnier Frères, 1857–64, 48:975–1050.

Cicero. *On Duties (De officiis).* Trans. Walter Miller. Loeb Classical Library 30. Cambridge: Harvard University Press, 1913.

The Code of Cuenca. Trans. James F. Powers. Philadelphia: University of Pennsylvania Press, 2000.

Coronel, Gregorio. *Brevis enarratio actorum omnium, ad compendium redactorum, quae circa controversiam de Auxiliis Divinae Gratiae sub Clemente PP. octavo & coram ipso celebrata sunt.* Frankfurt: Arnaud, 1687.

Descartes, René. *Philosophical Letters.* Trans. Anthony Kenny. Oxford: Clarendon, 1970.

Franco, Antonio. *Imagem da virtude em o Noviciado de Coimbra I.* Évora, 1719.

Gourlin, Pierre S. *Tractatus theologicus de Gratia Christi Salvatore ac de praedestinatione sanctorum.* 6 vols. Paris: Bon François Rivière, 1781.

Gregory the Great. *Regula Pastoralis.* In *Patrologia Latina.* 221 vols. Ed. Jacques-Paul Migne. Paris: Garnier Frères, 1841–80, 77:1–159.

Henriquez, Enrique. *Theologiæ Moralis Summa.* Salamanca, Spain, 1593.

Hubmaier, Balthasar. *Summa of the Entire Christian Life.* In *Balthasar Hubmaier: Theologian of Anabaptism.* Trans. and ed. H. Wayne Pipkin and John H. Yoder. Scottdale, PA: Herald, 1989, 81–89.

The Jesuit Ratio Studiorum of 1599. Trans. and ed. Allan P. Farrell. Washington, DC: Conference of Major Superior of Jesuits, 1970.

Kautz, Jacob. *The Seven Articles.* In *Anabaptism in Outline: Selected Primary Sources.* Ed. Walter Klaassen. Scottdale, PA: Herald, 1981, 48.

Lemos, Tomas de. *Acta omnia Congregatioum et disputationum, quae coram SS. Clemente VIII et Panlo V Summis Pontificibus sunt celebratae in causa et controversia illa magna de auxiliis divinae gratiae.* Louvain, 1702.

Lessius, Leonardus. *De perfectionibus moribusque divinis.* Amberes, Belgium, 1620.

Locke, John. *Two Treatises of Government.* Everyman's Library. London: Dent, 1975.

Loyola, Ignatius. "Rules for Thinking with the Church." In *Documents of the Christian Church*, 4th ed. Ed. Henry Bettenson and Chris Maunder. Oxford: Oxford University Press, 2001, 261–64.

———. *The Spiritual Exercises.* Trans. Louis J. Puhl. New York: Vintage, 2000.

Luther, Martin. *Ad Librum Eximii Magistri Nostri, Magistri am Brosii Catharini, Defensoris Silvestri Prieratis Acerrimi.* In *D. Martin Luthers Werke.* Weimar: Böhlau, 1888, 8:705–19.

———. *Against the Antinomians.* In *Luther's Works*, American ed., 55 vols. Ed. Jaroslav Pelikan. St. Louis: Concordia, 1955–86, 47:107–19.

———. *The Bondage of the Will.* Trans. James I. Packer and O. R. Johnston. Grand Rapids: Revell, 1957.

———. *Commentary on Romans.* Trans. J. Theodore Mueller. Grand Rapids: Kregel, 1976.

———. *The Freedom of a Christian.* In *Luther's Works*, American ed., 31:327–79.

Mariana, Juan de. *Tractatus VII. Theologici et historici.* Cologne, 1609.

Meyer, Livinus de. *Historia Controversiarum de Divinae Gratiae Auxiliis.* Antwerp, Belgium, 1705.

Molina (Molinæ), Ludovici (Luis de). *Apologia Concordiae.* Cuenca, Spain, 1594.

———. *Appendix ad Concordiam, continens responsiones ad tres objectiones et satisfactiones ad 17 animadversiones.* Lisbon, 1589.

———. *Commentaria in primam divi Thomae partem.* Venice, 1602.

———. *De justitia et jure.* 5 vols. Cologne: Marci-Michaelis Bousquet, 1733.

———. *Liberi Arbitrii cum Gratiae Donis, Divina Praescientia, Providentia, Praedestinatione et Reprobatione Concordia.* Ed. Johannes Rabeneck. Madrid: Sumptibus Societatis Editorialis "Sapientia," 1953.

———. *On Divine Foreknowledge.* Trans. Alfred J. Freddoso. Ithaca, NY: Cornell University Press, 1988.

Nadal, Jerónimo. *Instructiones Conimbricae de Cursu Artium Datae* (1561). In *Monumenta paedagogica Societatis Iesu*, 5 vols. Ed. Ladislaus Lukács. Rome: Institutum Historicum Societatis Iesu, 1965, 2:59.

Paul V. "Edict of 28 August 1607." Translated in *The Month and Catholic Review* 41 (1881): 298.

Porreño, Baltasar. *Mapa del obispado de Cuenca.* In *Biblioteca Nacional, Madrid.* Ms. 12961.7 (1622).

Ribadeneira, Pedro de. *Illustrium Scriptorum Religionis Societatis Iesu Catalogus.* Lyons, 1609.

Ripalda, Juan Martinez de. *De ente supernaturali disputationes in universam theologiam tomus posterior.* Lyons, 1645.

Serry, Jacques Hyacinthe. *Historiae congregationis de auxiliis divinae gratiae.* Padua, 1700.

Soto, Domingo de. *Libri Decem De Iustitia et Iure. Lugduni: Apud heredes Iacobi Iuntae,* 1569.

Stegmüller, Friedrich, ed. and trans. *Geschichte des Molinismus: Neue Molinaschriften 1. Beiträge zur Geschichte der Philosophie und Theologie des Mittelalters* 32. Münster: Aschendorffschen, 1935.

Telles, Balthazar. *Crónica de Companhia de Jesus da Província de Portugal.* Lisbon, 1647.

Thomas à Kempis. *The Imitation of Christ.* Ed. and trans. Joseph N. Tylenda. New York: Vintage, 1998.

Villaescusa, Ramírez de. *Constituciones sinodales del obispado de Cuenca.* Cuenca, Spain, 1545.

The Westminster Shorter Catechism. In T*he Book of Confessions.* Louisville: Geneva, 2004, 173–91.

Zwingli, Huldrych. *Auslegung und Begründung der Thesen oder Artikel.* In *Huldreich Zwingli Sämtliche Werke.* Ed. Emil Egli and Georg Finsler. Leipzig: M. Heinius Nachfolger, 1908, 2:1–457.

SECONDARY SOURCES

Adams, Robert M. "Middle Knowledge and the Problem of Evil." *American Philosophical Quarterly* 14 (1977): 109–17.

Almedo, Felix G. *Diego Ramírez de Villaescusa.* Madrid: Editora Nacional, 1944.

Alonso-Lasheras, Diego. *Luis de Molina's De Iustitia et Iure: Justice as Virtue in an Economic Context.* Studies in the History of Christian Traditions 152. Leiden: Brill, 2011.

Althaus, Paul. *The Theology of Martin Luther.* Trans. Robert C. Schultz. Minneapolis: Fortress, 1966.

Alves, André A., and José M. Moreira. *The Salamanca School.* Major Conservative and Libertarian Thinkers 9. New York: Continuum, 2010.

Andrés Martín, Melquíades. *La teología española en el siglo XVI.* Madrid: Biblioteca de Autores Cristianos, 1977.

Araújo, Jorge. "Luís de Molina regressa a Évora. Alocução de abertura das Jornadas." In *Luís de Molina: regressa a Évora: actas das jornadas, Evora,* 13, 14 de junho 1997. Évora: Fundação Luís Molina, 1998, 13–6.

Astrain, Antonio. *Historia de la Compania de Jesus en la asistencia de Espana.* 7 vols. Madrid: Razón y Fé, 1912–25.

Bac, J. Martin. *Perfect Will Theology: Divine Agency in Reformed Scholasticism as Against Suárez, Episcopius, Descartes, and Spinoza.* Church History 42. Leiden: Brill, 2010.

Backer, Augustin de and Carlos Sommervogel. *Bibliographie des éscrevains de la compagnie de Jésus.* 7 vols. Liège: Grandmont-Donders, 1853–97.

Baroja, Julio Caro. *Las formas complejas de la vida religiosa: religión, sociedad y carácter en la España de los siglos XVI y XVII.* Madrid: Akal, 1978.

Barrow, John D., and Frank J. Tipler. *The Anthropic Cosmological Principle.* Oxford: Clarendon, 1986.

Basinger, David. "Divine Omniscience and Human Freedom: A 'Middle Knowledge' Perspective." *Faith and Philosophy* 1, no. 3 (1984): 291–302.

Beilby, James K., and Paul R. Eddy. *Divine Foreknowledge: Four Views.* Downers Grove, IL: InterVarsity, 2001.

Belda, Francisco. "Ética de la creación de créditos según la doctrina de Molina, Lesio y Lugo." *Pensamiento* 1 (1963): 53–92.

Boyd, Gregory A. "The Open-Theism View." In Beilby and Eddy, *Divine Foreknowledge*, 13–47.

———. "Neo-Molinism and the Infinite Intelligence of God." *Philosophia Christi* 5, no. 1 (2003): 187–204.

Broggio, Paolo. *La teologia e la politica: Controversie dottrinali, Curia romana e Monarchia spagnola tra Cinque e Seicento.* Firenze, Italy: Leo S. Olschki, 2009.

Cairns, Earle E. *Christianity through the Centuries: A History of the Christian Church.* 3rd rev. ed. Grand Rapids: Zondervan, 1996.

Carson, D. A. "Matthew." In *The Expositor's Bible Commentary*, 12 vols. Gen. ed. Frank E. Gaebelein. Grand Rapids: Zondervan, 1984, 8:3–599.

Caycedo, José. *Ideas jurídicas de Luis de Molina sobre la propiedad privada.* Excerpta Ex Disertatione in Pontificia Universitas Gregoriana. Rome: Pontificia Universitas Gregoriana, 1957.

Coors, Michael. *Scriptura efficax.* Göttingen: Vandenhoeck & Ruprecht, 2009.

Copan, Paul. *"True for You, but Not for Me": Overcoming Objections to Christian Faith.* Rev. ed. Bloomington, MN: Bethany House, 2009.

Costello, Frank Bartholomew. *The Political Philosophy of Luis de Molina, S.J. (1535–1600).* Spokane: Gonzaga University Press, 1974.

Coxito, Amândio A., and Maria L. C. Soares. "Pedro da Fonseca." In *História do Pensamento Filosófico Português* v. II, *Renascimento e Contra-Reforma.* Ed. Pedro Calafate. Lisbon: Caminho, 2001, 455–502.

Craig, William Lane. "Creation, Providence, and Miracles." In *Philosophy of Religion.* Ed. Brian Davies. Washington, DC: Georgetown University Press, 1998, 136–62.

———. *Divine Foreknowledge and Human Freedom: The Coherence of Theism: Omniscience.* Studies in Intellectual History 19. Leiden: Brill, 1990.

———. " 'Lest Anyone Should Fall': A Middle Knowledge Perspective on Perseverance and Apostolic Warnings." *International Journal for Philosophy of Religion* 29 (1991): 65–74.

_____. "'Men Moved by the Holy Spirit Spoke from God' (2 Peter 1:21): A Middle Knowledge Perspective on Divine Inspiration." *Philosophia Christi*, new ser. 1 (1999): 45–82.

_____. "Middle Knowledge: A Calvinist-Arminian Rapprochement?" In *The Grace of God, the Will of Man*. Ed. Clark H. Pinnock. Grand Rapids: Zondervan, 1989, 141–64.

_____. "Middle Knowledge, Truth-Makers, and the Grounding Objection." *Faith and Philosophy* 18 (2001): 337–52.

_____. "The Middle-Knowledge View." In Beilby and Eddy, *Divine Foreknowledge*, 119–43.

_____. "'No Other Name': A Middle Knowledge Perspective on the Exclusivity of Salvation through Christ." *Faith and Philosophy* 6 (1989): 172–88.

_____. *On Guard: Defending Your Faith with Reason and Precision*. Colorado Springs: Cook, 2010.

_____. *The Only Wise God: The Compatibility of Divine Foreknowledge and Human Freedom*. Grand Rapids: Baker, 1987.

_____. "The Open-Theism View: A Middle-Knowledge Response." In Beilby and Eddy, *Divine Foreknowledge*, 55–60.

_____. "Politically Incorrect Salvation." In *Christian Apologetics in the Postmodern World*. Ed. Timothy R. Phillips and Dennis Okholm. Downers Grove, IL: InterVarsity, 1995, 75–97.

_____. *The Problem of Divine Foreknowledge and Future Contingents from Aristotle to Suarez*. Studies in Intellectual History 7. Leiden: Brill, 1988.

_____. "Should Peter Get a New Philosophical Advisor?" *Philosophia Christi* 6 (2004): 273–78.

_____. "Should Peter Go to the Mission Field?" *Faith and Philosophy* 10 (1993): 261–65.

_____. *The Tensed Theory of Time: A Critical Examination*. Synthese Library 293. Dordrecht: Kluwer Academic, 2000.

_____. *The Tenseless Theory of Time: A Critical Examination*. Synthese Library 294. Dordrecht: Kluwer Academic, 2000.

_____. *Time and Eternity: Exploring God's Relationship to Time*. Wheaton, IL: Crossway, 2001.

Daurignac, J. M. S. *History of the Society of Jesus from Its Foundation to the Present Time*. 2 vols. Trans. James Clements. Cincinnati: Walsh, 1865.

Davis, David Brion. *Inhuman Bondage: The Rise and Fall of Slavery in the New World*. Oxford: Oxford University Press, 2008.

Davis, John Jefferson. *Frontiers of Science and Faith: Examining Questions from the Big Bang to the End of the Universe*. Downers Grove, IL: InterVarsity, 2002.

Dekker, Eef. *Middle Knowledge*. Peeters: Leuven, 2000.

_____. "Was Arminius a Molinist?" *The Sixteenth Century Journal* 27, no. 2 (1996): 337–52.

Díez-Alegría, José María. *El desarrollo de la doctrina de la ley natural en Luis de Molina y en los Maestros de la Universidad de Evora de 1565 a 1591: Estudio histórico y textos inéditos.* Barcelona: Instituto Luis Vives de Filosofía, 1951.

Dulles, Avery. *Models of the Church.* Garden City, NY: Doubleday, 1974.

Erickson, Millard J. *God the Father Almighty: A Contemporary Exploration of the Divine Attributes.* Grand Rapids: Baker, 1998.

Estep, William R. *The Anabaptist Story: An Introduction to Sixteenth-Century Anabaptism.* 3rd rev. ed. Grand Rapids: Eerdmans, 1996.

Feinberg, John S. *No One Like Him: The Doctrine of God.* Wheaton, IL: Crossway, 2001.

Ferguson, Everett. *Church History, Volume One: From Christ to Pre-Reformation.* Grand Rapids: Zondervan, 2005.

Flint, Thomas P. "'A Death He Freely Accepted': Molinist Reflections on the Incarnation." *Faith and Philosophy* 18 (2001): 3–20.

_____. *Divine Providence: The Molinist Account.* Ithaca, NY: Cornell University Press, 1998.

_____. "The Problem of Divine Freedom." *American Philosophical Quarterly* 20, no. 3 (1983): 225–64.

Freddoso, Alfred J. "Accidental Necessity and Logical Determinism." *Journal of Philosophy* 80 (1983): 257–78.

_____. "Introduction." In Molina, *On Divine Foreknowledge*, 1–81.

Garcia, Marcelino Ocaña. *Luis de Molina (1535–1600).* Biblioteca Filosífica Colección Filósofos y Textos. Madrid: Ediciones del Orto, 1995.

Garrigou-Lagrange, Réginald. *The One God.* Trans. Bede Rose. St. Louis: Herder, 1943.

Geisler, Norman L. *Baker Encyclopedia of Christian Apologetics.* Grand Rapids: Baker, 1999.

Gingerich, Owen. "Sacrobosco Illustrated." In *Between Demonstration and Imagination: Essays in the History of Science and Philosophy Presented to John D. North.* Ed. Lodi Nauta and Arjo Vanderjagt. Studies in Intellectual History 96. Leiden: Brill, 1999, 211–24.

Gómez Camacho, Francisco. "En torno a unos textos de Luis de Molina sobre la propiedad privada." *Revista española de teología*, 1977, 159–68.

_____. *Economía y filosofía moral: La formación del pensamiento económico europeo en la escolástica española.* Madrid: Síntesis, 1998.

Goris, Harm J. M. J. *Free Creatures of an Eternal God: Thomas Aquinas on God's Infallible Foreknowledge and Irresistible Will.* Thomas Instituut te Utrecht 4. Leuven: Peeters, 1996.

Gundlach, Gustav. *Zur Soziologie der Katholischen Ideenwelt und des Jesuitenordens.* Berlin: E. Ebering, 1927.

Gundry, Robert H. *Matthew: A Commentary on His Handbook for a Mixed Church under Persecution.* 2nd ed. Grand Rapids: Eerdmans, 1994.

Hamilton, Earl J. *American Treasure and the Price Revolution in Spain, 1501–1650.* Harvard Economic Studies 5. New York: Octagon, 1965.

Hammerstein, Notker. "Relations with Authority." In *A History of the University in Europe, Volume II: Universities in Early Modern Europe (1500–1800).* Ed. Hilde de Ridder-Symeons. Gen. ed. Walter Rüegg. Cambridge: Cambridge University Press, 1996, 113–53.

Hardon, John. *History and Theology of Grace: The Catholic Teaching on Divine Grace.* Washington, DC: Catholic University of America Press, 2006.

Harvey, L. P. *Muslims in Spain, 1500 to 1614.* Chicago: University of Chicago Press, 2005.

Hasker, William. *God, Time, and Knowledge.* Ithaca, NY: Cornell University Press, 1989.

_____. "Response to Thomas Flint." *Philosophical Studies* 60, no. 1/2 (1990): 117–26.

Hasker, William, David Basinger, and Eef Dekker, eds. *Middle Knowledge: Theory and Applications.* Contributions to Philosophical Theology 4. Frankfurt am Main: Peter Lang, 2000.

Hughes, Philip. *A History of the Church.* 3 vols. London: Sheed & Ward, 1947.

Hunt, David Paul. "Middle Knowledge: The 'Foreknowledge Defense.'" *International Journal for Philosophy of Religion* 28, no. 1 (1990): 1–24.

Jensen, Jennifer. "The Grounding Objection to Molinism." PhD diss., University of Notre Dame, 2008.

Jonsen, Albert R., and Stephen Edelston Toulmin. *The Abuse of Casuistry: A History of Moral Reasoning.* Berkeley: University of California Press, 1988.

Kaufmann, Matthias, and Alexander Aichele, eds. *A Companion to Luis de Molina.* Leiden: Brill, 2014.

Keathley, Kenneth. "A Molinist View of Election, or How to Be a Consistent Infralapsarian." In *Calvinism: A Southern Baptist Dialogue.* Ed. E. Ray Clendenen and Brad J. Waggoner. Nashville: Broadman & Holman, 2008, 195–215.

_____. *Salvation and Sovereignty: A Molinist Approach.* Nashville: Broadman & Holman Academic, 2010.

Kleinhappl, Johann. "Die Eigentumslehre Ludwig Molinas." *Zeitschrift für katholische Theologie* 56 (1932): 46–66.

Koester, Robert. "Grace as Taught by Augustine and Luther." *Lutheran Synod Quarterly* 35/36 (1995): 80–119.

Kreeft, Peter J. *Catholic Christianity.* San Francisco: Ignatius, 2001.

Krop, Henri A. "Philosophy and the Synod of Dordt: Aristotelianism, Humanism, and the Case against Arminianism." In *Revisiting the Synod of Dordt (1618–1619)*. Ed. Aza Goudriaan and Fred van Lieburg. Brill's *Series in* Church History 49. Leiden: Brill, 2011, 49–79.

Kvanvig, Jonathan L. *The Possibility of an All-Knowing God.* New York: St. Martin's Press, 1986.

Laing, John D. "Intelligent Design, Middle Knowledge, and the Problem of Creaturely Flaws." Paper presented at the Middle Knowledge/Molinism Consultation of the 64th Annual Meeting of the Evangelical Theological Society, November 14, 2012.

Latourette, Kenneth Scott. *A History of Christianity.* Rev. ed. 2 vols. New York: Harper & Row, 1975.

Lewis, David. *Counterfactuals.* Cambridge: Harvard University Press, 1973.

Lincoln, Andrew T. *Ephesians.* Word Biblical Commentary 42. Dallas: Word, 1990.

Lines, David A. "Moral Philosophy in the Universities: Medieval and Renaissance Europe." In *History of Universities*, Volume XX/I. Ed. Mordechai Feingold. Oxford: Oxford University Press, 2005, 38–80.

Little, Bruce A. *A Creation-Order Theodicy: God and Gratuitous Evil.* Lanham, MD: University Press of America, 2005.

MacGregor, Kirk R. *A Central European Synthesis of Radical and Magisterial Reform: The Sacramental Theology of Balthasar Hubmaier.* Lanham, MD: University Press of America, 2006.

_____. *A Comparative Study of Adjustments to Social Catastrophes in Christianity and Buddhism.* Lewiston, NY: Mellen, 2011.

_____. *A Molinist-Anabaptist Systematic Theology.* Lanham, MD: University Press of America, 2007.

_____. "The Existence and Irrelevance of Gratuitous Evil." *Philosophia Christi* 14, no. 1 (2012): 165–80.

_____. "The Impossibility of Evolution Apart from a God with Middle Knowledge." Paper presented at the Middle Knowledge/Molinism Consultation of the 64th Annual Meeting of the Evangelical Theological Society, November 14, 2012.

Mackenzie, Ann L. "Further Studies of the Spanish Mystics: Allison Peers on Miguel de Molinos' Spiritual Guide." In *Spain and Its Literature: Essays in Memory of E. Allison Peers*, ed. idem. Hispanic Studies Textual Research and Criticism 15. Liverpool: Liverpool University Press, 1997, 109–40.

Madeira, João. "Pedro da Fonseca's Isagoge Philosophica and the Predicables from Boethius to the Lovanienses." PhD diss., Katholike Universiteit Leuven, 2006.

Marsh, Jason. "Do the Demographics of Theistic Belief Disconfirm Theism? A Reply to Maitzen." *Religious Studies* 44 (2008): 465–71.

Matava, Robert Joseph. "Divine Causality and Human Free Choice: Domingo Báñez and the Controversy de Auxiliis." PhD diss., University of St. Andrews, 2010.

McTaggart, John M. E. *The Nature of Existence.* Ed. C. D. Broad. Cambridge: Cambridge University Press, 1927.

Miller, Kenneth R. *Finding Darwin's God.* New York: Perennial, 1999.

Monfasani, John. *George of Trezibond: A Biography and a Study of His Rhetoric and Logic.* Leiden: Brill, 1976.

Moreland, J. P., and William Lane Craig. *Philosophical Foundations for a Christian Worldview.* Downers Grove, IL: InterVarsity, 2003.

Muller, Richard A. *Dictionary of Latin and Greek Theological Terms.* Grand Rapids: Baker, 1985.

_____. *God, Creation, and Providence in the Thought of Jacob Arminius.* Grand Rapids: Baker, 1991.

_____. "Grace, Election, and Contingent Choice: Arminius's Gambit and the Reformed Response." In *The Grace of God, The Bondage of the Will: Historical and Theological Perspectives on Calvinism,* 2 vols. Ed. Thomas R. Schreiner and Bruce A. Ware. Grand Rapids: Baker, 1995, 2:251–78.

Murugarren, Paulino Iradiel. *Evolución de la industria textil castellana en los siglos XIII–XVI.* Salamanca, Spain: Ediciones Universidad Salamanca, 1974.

Nalle, Sara T. *God in La Mancha: Religious Reform and the People of Cuenca, 1500–1650.* Baltimore: Johns Hopkins University Press, 1992.

Newman, John Henry. *Lectures on the Scripture Proofs of the Doctrines of the Church.* Tracts for the Times 85. London: Rivington, 1838.

Nicholls, Jason A. "Openness and Inerrancy: Can They Be Compatible?" *Journal of the Evangelical Theological Society* 45, no. 4 (2002): 629–49.

Noonan, John T. *The Scholastic Analysis of Usury.* Cambridge: Harvard University Press, 1957.

O'Connor, Timothy. "The Impossibility of Middle Knowledge." *Philosophical Studies* 66, no. 2 (1992): 139–66.

O'Malley, John W. *The First Jesuits.* Cambridge: Harvard University Press, 2002.

Olson, Roger E. *Arminian Theology: Myths and Realities.* Downers Grove, IL: IVP Academic, 2006.

Otte, Richard. "A Defense of Middle Knowledge." *Philosophy of Religion* 21 (1987): 161–69.

Partee, Charles. *The Theology of John Calvin.* Louisville: Westminster John Knox, 2008.

Perszyk, Ken, ed. *Molinism: The Contemporary Debate.* Oxford: Oxford University Press, 2011.

Picirilli, Robert E. *Grace, Faith, Free Will.* Nashville: Randall House, 2002.

Pinelo, Gabriel. "R. P. Ludovici Molinæ, e Societate Jesu, Vitæ Morumque Brevis Adumbratio." In *Molinæ, De justitia et jure,* 1:i–vi.

Plantinga, Alvin. *God, Freedom, and Evil.* New York: Harper & Row, 1974.

———. *The Nature of Necessity.* Oxford: Clarendon, 1974.

———. "Reply to Robert Adams." In *Alvin Plantinga.* Ed. James Tomberlin and Peter van Inwagen. Profiles 5. Dordrecht: Reidel, 1985, 372–82.

———. "Self-Profile." In *Alvin Plantinga.* Ed. James Tomberlin and Peter van Inwagen. Profiles 5. Dordrecht: Reidel, 1985, 3–97.

Pohle, Joseph. "Luis de Molina." *The Catholic Encyclopedia.* 15 vols. Ed. Charles G. Herbermann. New York: Robert Appleton, 1907–12, 10:436–37.

Possanzini, Stefano. *Giovanni Antonio Bovio carmelitano, teologo e vescovo di Molfetta.* Textus et studia historica carmelitana 10. Rome: Insititutum carmelitanum, 1970.

Posset, Franz. *Pater Bernhardus: Martin Luther and Bernard of Clairvaux.* Kalamazoo, MI: Cistercian Publications, 1999.

Preuss, Robert D. *The Theology of Post-Reformation Lutheranism.* 2 vols. St. Louis: Concordia, 1970.

Pribram, Karl. *A History of Economic Reasoning.* Baltimore: Johns Hopkins University Press, 1983.

Rabeneck, Ioannes. "De vita et scriptis Ludovici Molina." *Archivium Storicum Societatis Jesu,* 1950, 75–145.

Ratzsch, Del. "Design, Chance and Theistic Evolution." In *Mere Creation.* Ed. William Dembski. Downers Grove, IL: InterVarsity, 1998, 289–312.

Rea, Michael C. "The Metaphysics of Original Sin." In *Persons: Human and Divine.* Ed. Peter van Inwagen and Dean Zimmerman. Oxford: Clarendon, 2007, 319–56.

Rogers, Jack B., and Donald K. McKim. *The Authority and Interpretation of the Bible: An Historical Approach.* San Francisco: HarperCollins, 1980.

Roover, Raymond Adrien de. *La pensè èconomique des scolastiques: doctrines et methods.* Montreal: Institute d'Ètudes Mèdiévales, 1971.

Roth, Cecil. *A History of the Marranos.* 5th ed. New York: Intellectbooks, 1974.

Roy, Steven C. *How Much Does God Foreknow? A Comprehensive Biblical Study.* Downers Grove, IL: InterVarsity, 2006.

Salaverri, Joaquín. "La noción de Iglesia del Padre Luis de Molina." *Revista española de teología* 20 (1960): 199–230.

Schneemann, Gerhard. *Controversiarum de Divinae Gratiae liberique arbitrii concordia initia et progressus.* Freiburg: Herder, 1881.

Seeberg, Reinhold. *Text-Book of the History of Doctrines.* 4 vols. Trans. Charles E. Kay. Grand Rapids: Baker, 1956.

Skarvad, Jaroslaw. "De Iure Proprietatis Privatae Apud Ludovicum Molinam." Dissertatio: Pontificia Universitatis Lateranensi, 1950.

Spitz, Lewis W. *The Protestant Reformation, 1517–1559.* St. Louis: Concordia, 1985.

Stucco, Guido. *The Catholic Doctrine of Predestination from Luther to Jansenius.* Bloomington, IN: Xlibris, 2014.

282 Luis de Molina

Tamburello, Dennis E. *Union with Christ: John Calvin and the Mysticism of St. Bernard.* Louisville: Westminster John Knox, 1994.

Tiessen, Terrence. *Providence and Prayer: How Does God Work in the World?* Downers Grove, IL: InterVarsity, 2000, 289–362.

_____. "Why Calvinists Should Believe in Divine Middle Knowledge, Although They Reject Molinism." *Westminster Theological Journal* 69, no. 2 (2007): 345–66.

Tillich, Paul. *Systematic Theology.* 3 vols. Chicago: University of Chicago Press, 1963.

Van Horn, Luke. "On Incorporating Middle Knowledge into Calvinism: A Theological/ Metaphysical Muddle?" *Journal of the Evangelical Theological Society* 55, no. 4 (2012): 807–27.

Vansteenberghe, Edmond. "Molinisme." In *Dictionnaire de théologie catholique*, ed. Alfred Vacant, Eugène Mangenot, and Émile Amann. Paris: Letouzey et Ané, 1929, 10.2.2094–2187.

Venema, Cornelis P. *Accepted and Renewed in Christ: The Twofold Grace of God and the Interpretation of Calvin's Theology.* Göttingen: Vandenhoeck & Ruprecht, 2007.

Vereecke, Louis. *Da Guglielmo d'Ockham a sant'Alfonso de Liguori: Saggi di storia della teologia morale moderna, 1300–1787.* Cisinello Balsamo: Edizioni Paoline, 1990.

Vilar, Pierre. *Oro y moneda en la historia, 1450–1920.* Barcelona: Ariel, 1969.

Ware, Bruce A. *God's Greater Glory: The Exalted God of Scripture and the Christian Faith.* Wheaton, IL: Crossway, 2006.

Warfield, Benjamin B. *Calvin and Calvinism.* Oxford: Oxford University Press, 1931.

Warfield, Benjamin B., and Samuel G. Craig, eds. *The Inspiration and Authority of the Bible.* Philadelphia: Presbyterian & Reformed, 1970.

Weber, Wilhelm. *Wirschaftsethik am Vorabend des Liberalismus: Höhepunkt und Abschluss der Scholastischen Wirtschaftsbetrachtung durch Ludwig Molina, S.J. (1535–1600).* Münster: Aschendorffsche Verlagsbuchhandlung, 1959.

Williams, J. Rodman. *Renewal Theology: Systematic Theology from a Charismatic Perspective.* 3 vols. in 1. Grand Rapids: Zondervan, 1996.

Witt, William G. "Creation, Redemption and Grace in the Theology of Jacob Arminius." PhD diss., University of Notre Dame, 1993.

Woodbridge, John D. *Biblical Authority: A Critique of the Rogers/McKim Proposal.* Grand Rapids: Zondervan, 1982.

Woodbridge, John D., and Frank A. James III. *Church History, Volume Two: From Pre-Reformation to the Present Day.* Grand Rapids: Zondervan, 2013.

Wright, N. T. *Jesus and the Victory of God.* Vol. 2 of *Christian Origins and the Question of God.* Minneapolis: Fortress, 1996.

Index

affirmation of, 75–77, 170
belief in, 57–59, 72
Christianity and, 106
divine sovereignty and, 157, 199, 244
enabling, 127
need for, 104
obtaining, 220, 229, 263
possessing, 55–59, 88–89
predestination and, 133, 150–52
safeguarding, 249–50
loans, 202–10, 225
Loyola, Ignatius of, 14, 33, 37–38, 40, 43, 167, 170, 179, 180
lucrum cessans, 207–10
Luther, Martin, 15, 18, 29–30, 32, 35–37, 50, 61–62, 65–72, 85–90, 176, 180–81, 221
Lutheranism, 151, 170

M

macroevolutionary events, 266–68
Madeira, João, 60
Madrucci, Bernerio, 231–35, 237–38
Madrucci, Ludovico, 228–29
Mariana, Juan de, 14, 166–72, 174, 177
Medina, Juan de, 198
merchants, 181, 191, 206–15, 222, 225–26
middle knowledge
   Arminianism and, 243–49, 269
   conception of, 11–12, 79–105
   counterfactual knowledge and, 79–91, 96–98
   denunciation of, 229–31
   development of, 80–105
   for divine providence, 106–32
   doctrine of, 11–13, 19–23, 29, 79–105
   explanation of, 11–12
   of God, 11–12, 19–23, 29, 79–105, 232, 243–69
   opposition to, 158–63, 166, 174–77
   predestination and, 135, 140–41, 145–57
Miller, Kenneth, 265
Molina, Ana García de, 31
Molina, Luis de
   background of, 11–13
   birth of, 31
   conferences of, 231–38
   death of, 240
   early years of, 31–32, 43–44
   education of, 33, 45–60
   legacy of, 29, 243–70
   life of, 14–30
   misconceptions about, 16–28
   posthumous vindication of, 240–41
   as professor, 73–78
   religious conversion of, 31–44
   spiritual journey of, 33–41
   theological system of, 11–13, 18–19
Molinism
   application of, 248–69
   Arminianism and, 18–24, 243–49, 269
   defenders of, 243–44, 269
   evangelicalism and, 12–13, 29, 242
   prominence of, 244, 248–69
   revival of, 243–44
   theological system of, 12
money lending, 202–10, 225
money matters, 74, 202–11, 218, 223–25
moral reasoning, 178, 182–84
moral theology, 179, 239–40
Mosaic law, 187–88, 191

N

Nadal, Jerónimo, 181
Nalle, Sara, 40
natural knowledge, 20, 92–95, 117, 140–41, 258
natural law, 184–87
natural powers, 102–3, 232
"necessary being," 56–57, 261–63
New Testament, 63, 182, 185, 253, 255
Nicene Creed, 119
nominalism, 46–47
Noonan, John T., 202
Nuño, Diego, 175

O

Old Testament, 63, 182–85, 196, 253, 256
omniscience
   divine omniscience, 79, 85, 92, 101, 220, 232–35, 241–42, 269
   doctrine of, 92, 101, 220, 241, 269
   structure of, 85, 91–105, 232
open theism, 13, 29, 244, 249–52
Orejón, Diego de, 31
Origen, 26, 138
Otte, Richard, 244

P

Padilla, Antonio de, 175, 176
Pallantieri, Girolamo, 240
pastoral sensitivity, 41, 44
Paul IV, Pope, 76
Paul V, Pope, 29, 241
Pauline epistles, 61, 138, 199, 218, 254–56
Pelagianism, 240–41
Pelagius, 26, 134, 138
periculum sortis, 207, 209, 210